SOCCER

in a Football World

This book is dedicated to Anne, whose tolerance,
encouragement and support have been more than even
the most patient soul should be asked to provide.

SOCCER
in a Football World

David Wangerin

First published in 2006 by WSC Books Ltd
17a Perseverance Works, 38 Kingsland Road, London E2 8DD
www.wsc.co.uk
info@wsc.co.uk

ISBN 0 9540134 7 6
All pictures have been credited where their origin is known
Would any unacknowledged copyright holders please get in contact
Cover design by Doug Cheeseman
Printed and bound by Biddles Ltd, Kings Lynn, UK

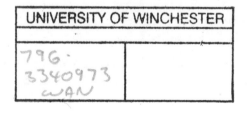

Contents

Acknowledgments

My work towards this book owes an enormous amount of gratitude to my father, Ronald, who three decades after I moved out of the family house invited me back home and let me stay as long as I needed to put the manuscript together. Thanks as well to my brother and sister and their respective families for their help during my time in the States.

I spent many productive hours in the archives of the US Soccer Hall of Fame in Oneonta, New York, and for this I am grateful to Jack Huckel and his staff. A special thank-you to George and Peggy Brown for their kindness, patience and generosity, and to Colin Jose, whose meticulous research and long-standing contribution to North American soccer history – and tolerance of my barrage of emails – was an enormous help.

I'm also obliged to Grant Millar for his research assistance in Scotland, and to Gunnar Persson in Sweden, Ulrich Körner in Germany, Richard Perry in England and Roger Allaway and Dan Morrison in Pennsylvania. For their advice on the manuscript thanks are due to Jonathan Davies, Evan Garcia, Simon Jenkins, David Litterer and Ian Plenderleith. I would also like to acknowledge Alan and Eleanor Kreider for providing inspiration at a time when it was badly needed.

Thanks as well to the staff at the city libraries of Birmingham and Liverpool and the National Library of Scotland in Edinburgh, and to Richard McBrearty and his colleagues at the Scottish Football Museum in Glasgow. In the United States, I am particularly indebted to Steve Kerber and his assistants at the Lovejoy Library at Southern Illinois University-Edwardsville, and the microforms team at the Wisconsin State Historical Society Library in Madison, in whose company I spent countless happy hours.

Most importantly of all, though, I would like to thank everyone at *When Saturday Comes* – Andy Lyons, Doug Cheeseman, Richard Guy, Ed Upright and especially Mike Ticher – for their interest in American soccer history, and for allowing me to write about it.

About the author
David Wangerin has been a contributor to *When Saturday Comes* since 1988, a year after he came to England to help Aston Villa win promotion from the Second Division, and two years after coaching his high school's soccer team to a debut season of unbroken defeats. He now lives in Scotland, where he has developed an affection for Raith Rovers. There's more at www.davidwangerin.net.

The 'S' word
The challenge of charting soccer's peculiar course through American sport is compounded by the challenge of describing it in a language those on both sides of the Atlantic will understand and approve of. This is a British book written by an American expatriate, so it leans towards British usage, but those who have divided their lives between different English-speaking countries will appreciate how easy it is to be played offside by our common language. Soccer has become football to me, in spite of whatever interest I take in the padded game. In America, though, it's soccer, and it probably always will be, however much that grates on British ears. In the hope of appeasing those who recoil at the 's' word – unavoidable here, given that 'association football' is far too cumbersome and 'American football' means something else entirely – I have slipped in the occasional 'f' word where its meaning will be unambiguous.

For reasons which I trust are just as obvious, the word 'coach' has been generally used where Americans would more commonly use 'head coach' and where Britons might expect to see 'manager'. On the other hand, 'squads' have often remained as 'rosters'. I have also retained the American penchant for switching between 'college' and 'university' (and colloquially referring to either as 'schools'), and denoting American sports as 'athletics' on occasion.

Cover photo
Pelé takes to the field for the last time in the US, as a guest for the New York Cosmos against an NASL select side, in a farewell match for Franz Beckenbauer at Giants Stadium on September 24, 1980. Despite a goal from the Brazilian, the Cosmos lost 3-2.
Peter Robinson/Empics

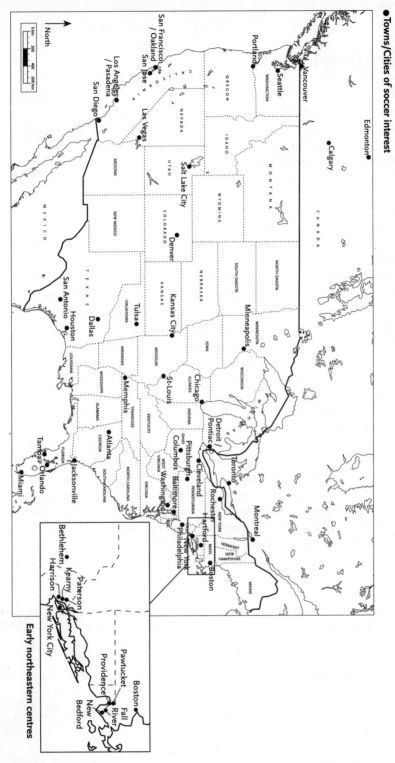

The United States

● Towns/Cities of soccer interest

Early northeastern centres

Careless Hands

Introduction

Wisconsin in October can be a sight to behold, bathed in dazzling autumn colour under crisp, azure-blue skies. This, though, was one of its less memorable afternoons: grey and raw, barren and bleak. All the same, it was a remarkable enough day for me. For the first time in 22 years I was returning to the familiar plot of land behind the big football stadium, the bumpy pitch where I had spent many an afternoon keeping goal for the college soccer team.

It wasn't something to look back on too fondly. We were one of the worst teams in the midwest, and I was only ever a reserve. Once or twice we won, but usually we lost. Sometimes we got slaughtered. I can't remember many of the scorelines, but I won't easily forget the 14 goals we conceded to a university from central Illinois. I got to play for much of the second half – to the intense relief of our besieged first choice – and for the last few minutes my opposite number was a young man with only one leg.

Trouncings were only to be expected. The other defeats may have been less emphatic, but they didn't disguise our inexperience. Most of us hadn't played soccer for very long, and only a few had been coached to any standard. I'd joined from a high school that didn't even have a team, and all I knew about goalkeeping had come from books and TV. Like the rest of the squad, though, I was spared from too much embarrassment by rank anonymity. Soccer was hardly a campus attraction. When the weather was fair, passers-by might linger, more out of curiosity than interest. But once the temperature began its descent toward winter, when November skies masked the sun and the north winds started whipping across the exposed field, we were virtually on our own.

The wind was just as biting 22 years on. But a lot of other things had changed. Certainly the players had. They could shoot with either foot now, and flick on an in-swinging corner, and bring the ball under control with a single deft touch. Some of us had been able to do those things, but not many could do them all, and very few would have been given a run-out in this team. Far from being one of the worst in the midwest, it had become one of the best. It had also been granted many of the accoutrements of American sports events: pre-match music, player introductions, standing for the national anthem. Ball-boys chased down errant shots, substitutions were announced over the public address, a huge electric scoreboard counted down the time. Twenty-odd years ago, we just got changed and went out to play. Sometimes we needed the referee to remind us what the score was.

What struck me more, though, was what hadn't changed. The team still played on the same patch of grass behind the football stadium and, for all its prowess and promotion, still attracted only a scattering of fans. Perhaps there were a few more than there used to be, but most of the aluminium on the portable stand along the touchline was bare, and many of those in attendance seemed more interested in talking to each other than in encouraging their team.

An entire generation of soccer had passed since I'd last come this way. I was one of the millions who had been introduced to the sport by the North American Soccer League. Pelé arrived in New York when I was 13, and I don't remember seeing a soccer ball until he did. Was there even a place in town to buy one? I'd never heard of a penalty kick, the World Cup – or for that matter the NASL, whose nearest team the season before was 400 miles away.

How quickly it all changed. By the time I entered college, the shops were selling all manner of balls and boots and shin guards and even I ❤ SOCCER T-shirts. I'd been to my first professional match, in Chicago – 21,000 to watch the Cosmos – and seen my first FA Cup final on US television. My home town had spawned two teams, and I played for one of them.

All of this had happened before any of these players were born. For them, soccer was a familiar activity, not some exotic arrival or the 'phenomenon' it had been in my youth. Events such as the World Cup were not the obscure, esoteric affairs of decades earlier. The United States had hosted the competition three times – twice for women and once for men – and, to considerable fanfare, it had even won one of them. Yet soccer's impact on the average Wisconsinite, like the average American, was still terribly limited. For many the game was still the same 'pussy sport' it had been when I was a teenager. This, after all, was a part of the country that adored the Green Bay Packers and other he-men in suits of armour, where autumn weekends were spent in the stadium or in front of the TV listening to how one player or another 'really loves to hit people'.

In 1987 I emigrated to Britain, worn down by repeated attempts at justifying an 'unnatural' and/or 'un-American' activity. Defending a sport which prohibited the use of the hands and produced very little scoring was as close to 'discussing' soccer as I had usually come, while sitting among thousands of impassioned, knowledgeable supporters had been an impossibility in a country whose teams and leagues appeared and disappeared without anyone taking much notice. As I wallowed in my new life as a fan in Britain, I began to think that the US did not deserve soccer, that it might be best for everyone if the Yanks stuck to their own hand-friendly, high-scoring games and left the rest of the world alone.

Since then some attitudes have changed, including my own. But many have not. In spite of its staggering popularity as a recreational activity, in spite of the country's international success, and in spite of the stubborn perseverance of MLS, soccer in the United States remains a minority sport. Consequently, as with other minority sports, its history is deemed to be of little significance, or is even dismissed out of hand. We still hear claims that Pelé's time with the Cosmos represents the 'true birth' of the American game – a spurious assertion, but hardly surprising in an age when colour television has eroded the significance of eras preserved only in grainy black-and-white. Yet it is a great pity that names such as Thomas Cahill, Archie Stark and Billy Gonsalves – or, for that matter, John Harkes and Kasey Keller – count for so little in such a sports-happy country. Even today the most obsessive fan, the sports anorak who has committed to memory the hallowed numbers of Pete Rose's 4,256 base hits and Dan Marino's 420 touchdown passes, struggles to name 11 American soccer players of any repute. Historians have not treated the game with much sympathy, either. Even the most comprehensive accounts of the birth and growth of the country's sporting pursuits make virtually no reference to soccer. It's almost as if it didn't exist.

Admittedly, for much of the 20th century the game in the US was almost unremitting in its anonymity, moribund even after the famous 1950 World Cup victory over England, by which time even the most sympathetic newspapers saw little reason to treat soccer with any more reverence than the municipal dog show. Only when professional sport discovered the power of television did it receive any sort of resuscitation, but sadly it was left largely in the hands of the wrong people: those whose love of money eclipsed whatever interest they had in the game. One by one, they disappeared.

There are far too many people who think American soccer didn't amount to anything before Brazil's most famous No 10 turned up in New York, or who might agree with the assertion made by one *New York Times* correspondent in 1994 that 'the history of the World Cup in the United States begins and ends with a game in the Brazilian mining town of

Belo Horizonte on June 29, 1950'. In truth these are merely convenient signposts, events any fan of the game easily recognises. The rest takes a little more unravelling.

Though not as steeped in legend as baseball or college gridiron, or the football of other lands, soccer has existed in America for much longer than many give it credit for. The United States joined FIFA not in 1994 or 1975, but 1913. The National Challenge Cup, which, warts and all, produced the country's first official national champion in 1914, survives to this day as the US Open Cup. One need only examine the early 20th-century sports pages of newspapers the size of the *Boston Globe* or *Chicago Tribune* – replete with photos, match reports and line-ups – to realise that soccer once mattered. The country's first serious professional venture, the original American Soccer League, came to fruition before its gridiron equivalent, playing to thousands of devoted fans who often defied the most miserable of conditions. For a time the ASL, which lured dozens of top professionals from Europe and was a significant factor in America's success at the first World Cup, threatened to secure a permanent place on the country's sporting landscape. Its hopes, though, rapidly disappeared through a toxic combination of factors: many economic, some self-inflicted and a few propagated by the media.

By the time Pelé arrived, the roots had been forgotten. In 1980 the veteran sportswriter Zander Hollander edited an ambitious 544-page book titled *The American Encyclopedia of Soccer* which, for all its meticulous record-keeping of the college game and the NASL, failed in the rather more significant task of chronicling what most regard as the country's first professional league. The 'encyclopedia' mentions that 'several old-timers interviewed in 1978 recalled a "soccer war of 1931" and an "old American Soccer League" in the 1920s', but goes no further. Reference to the National Challenge Cup is limited to a single paragraph. America's dismal World Cup qualification efforts of the Fifties and Sixties are entirely ignored.

One can't really blame Hollander for some of his omissions. The historian Colin Jose, in a preface to his book on the ASL published in 1998, recalls:

> Back in 1969 I received from the American Soccer League of that time a list of the winners of the ASL championship. The list began with the winners of the 1933-34 season, the Kearny Irish-Americans. At the time I thought nothing about it, but imagine my surprise when, many years later, in searching

through microfilm of the *New York Times* of 1925 for details of the United States versus Canada international of that year, I found details of the American Soccer League. How could this be, I wondered, when according to the American Soccer League, the league began operating in 1933?

American soccer has been careless with its fragile history. Even official statistics for the country's first coast-to-coast professional leagues of 1967 have disappeared, while the US's early international record seems to have been worked out largely after the fact. In a 1994 book, Jose noted:

> In 1972 I wrote to Mr Kurt Lamm, then Secretary of the United States Soccer Federation, asking for a list of all the internationals played by the United States down through the years. Mr Lamm replied that, to the best of his knowledge, no such list existed.

If all this seems rather peculiar for a game with such universal appeal, then the plight of British sports with North American roots is worth bearing in mind. Ice hockey has a longer history there than its marginalised status would suggest, and basketball is still treated largely as a curiosity by the press. Both face the same struggles that have plagued American soccer: under-investment, a shortage of suitable venues and overwhelming media indifference.

I have never believed something needs to be achingly popular for it to be interesting, and to a soccer fan born in the wrong country at nearly the wrong time, few things are more fascinating than the peculiar rollercoaster the game in America has ridden across the decades. As far as I can tell, its story has never really been told – not from start to finish, and certainly not in the context of American sport in general – and that's something I hope to have achieved here. It has not been my intention to chronicle every famous player, team or match, or to use history for some sort of evangelical purpose. All I have set out to do is to tell the story as I understand it, from what I have read and heard, as well as what I have witnessed first-hand, occasionally in packed stadiums but much more often on windswept college fields and other modest arenas where the heart of American soccer kept beating – faintly, but persistently.

1. A Game of its Own

America's path to football isolation

I believe in outdoor games, and I do not mind in the least that they are rough games, or that those who take part in them are occasionally injured. I have no sympathy whatsoever with the over-wrought sentimentality which would keep a young man in cotton wool, and I have a hearty contempt for him if he counts a broken arm or collarbone as of serious consequence when balanced against the chance of showing that he possesses hardihood, physical address and courage.

Theodore Roosevelt

To many Americans the United States is the greatest sports nation on earth. To many elsewhere it is merely the most insular. Few would deny, though, that its array of leagues, circuits and tournaments has become an indelible part of modern American culture. The zeal with which its television networks have harnessed the country's fiercely competitive psyche has transformed popular games into powerful brands and star players into potent commodities, while reinforcing their place in the heart of the average fan.

On less glittering stages, the fascination with sport is deep-seated and pervasive. Competitions such as Little League baseball and high school gridiron are precious community institutions, as valued as good teachers and paved streets. However faintly, nearly every life seems to be touched by one sporting endeavour or another: the basketball team's trip to the state tournament, the company softball game, the hefty wager on the outcome of the Super Bowl.

It's tempting to mock the American pretension to sporting superiority when so little of the country takes any interest in contests staged in other corners of the world. It should hardly be surprising that the winners of the Super Bowl are designated 'world champions' and baseball's showcase is known as the World Series (the popular assertion that the *New York World* newspaper once sponsored the event, and thus gave it its name, is completely spurious). Even basketball, whose recent surge in global popularity has helped to devalue America's Olympic currency from the unconquerable 'dream team' of 1992 to the bronze medallists of 2004, must still contend with the NBA's claims of world dominance.

All this seems to suggest that Americans have built their formidable sporting pride on little more than ignorance and conceit. But other, more charitable, traits have also played a part: the country's obsession with progress and improvement, its independence of thought and spirit, and a deep-seated collective sense of identity. The onset of the television age and its accompanying juggernaut of bluster and hype may have intensified America's notorious self-obsession, but it scarcely created it. Virtually from the time of the first organised games, the United States has been much more concerned with establishing its own existence and playing by its own rules than in joining any international fraternity. And there is probably no better example of this than the attitude it has adopted towards its most cherished pastime, baseball.

Until the mid-19th century, the most popular team sport in the United States was cricket. In 1860 the country could lay claim to about 400 clubs with perhaps 10,000 participants – sizeable numbers in an age when few sports had even agreed on their rules. Contests with Canada often attracted large crowds (10,000 were said to have attended a match in 1856) and an All-England XI drew 25,000 to a private estate in Hoboken, New Jersey, for a two-day match in 1859.

But by the end of the Civil War in 1865 cricket had fallen into decline, and by the 1920s it hardly existed at all. During the 1840s, the juvenile diversion of baseball had been adopted by a haughty, genteel New York City social group known as the Knickerbocker Club, the first organised team about which anything is known. In a matter of years, the game took the country by storm. Livelier, easier to understand and requiring hours rather than days to complete, it was also perceived as more American, even if it did bear more than a passing resemblance to the English game of rounders. As America's time and tolerance for sport grew, so did baseball. By 1856, one New York publication claimed that every patch of green land within ten miles of the city had given way to enthusiasts.

From the outset, the press waved a star-spangled wand over the new game. Baseball, it maintained, had triumphed over cricket because it was more suited to the American temperament and a better representation of its national character. It was surely intolerable that such claims could be made of an activity with roots in the old world. Yet well into the new century, historians continued to ascribe the origins of what was now firmly embedded as the 'national game' to rounders. By 1907 this had become a severe enough irritation to the baseball patriarchs for them to form a commission to settle the matter. The version they proceeded to treat as gospel – the hazy, 68-year-old recollections of a solitary elderly gentleman that General Abner Doubleday of the US Army had invented the sport in Cooperstown, New York, in 1839 – even the most myopic historian now accepts as absurd. Yet it proved startlingly enduring. Elaborate centennial celebrations were duly held in 1939, including the opening of a Hall of Fame in Cooperstown. As late as 1952 a US congressional report decreed baseball to be 'a game of American origin'.

Cricket had not disappeared from the American sporting landscape because it was inherently foreign, dull or confusing, or even because its matches couldn't be completed in an afternoon. It disappeared largely because it had remained the domain of middle-class Anglophiles who were determined to keep it that way. Baseball proved more open-minded. Its appeal rapidly spread from the gentlemanly haunts of the Knickerbocker Club to working-class neighbourhoods, rural homesteads and everything in between. The penchant for developing and embracing 'American' games was not confined to baseball, and by the end of the 19th century the seeds of another indigenous sporting institution – gridiron football – had been sown by men equally determined to clear their own path.

Charting the peculiar course of soccer in America will require more than a passing reference to its distant and violent cousin. The fact that gridiron has come to be known as 'football' when so little of its play has anything to do with the feet illustrates better than anything how closely intertwined the histories of the two games are, even if they no longer bear even a passing resemblance to each other. For most of the 19th century the lines were too blurred to separate one from the other – or from other, less enduring versions of football.

If America, like any other part of the world, claimed to be playing 'football' during the early 19th century, it was a game only marginally related to its descendants. Unbounded by much in the way of rules, most of which weren't written down and varied according to occasion, ball games of various descriptions had been played in America long before someone thought to brand them with a name. Often they were discouraged by a populace still largely governed by attitudes that had sailed into Massachusetts with the Pilgrim Fathers. Sport, especially in places like New England, was associated with gambling, drinking and other sinful pleasures. In the south, where a less morally exacting Protestantism held sway, the presence of a landed gentry helped to advance a more indulgent culture, but one that favoured other pastimes, particularly horse racing.

Nevertheless, as early as 1685 an English traveller claimed to have witnessed a 'great game of football' between young men on a Massachusetts beach and there is evidence to suggest that George Washington encouraged his troops to take part in 'games of exercise for amusement', a form of football among them. But it was only during the industrial revolution that such activities emerged as a truly popular form of leisure in the teeming new cities.

It was the universities that led the way in encouraging sport and – as with the English public schools – organising it. As far back as 1734, freshmen at Harvard were requested to provide 'the rest of the scholars with bats, balls and foot-balls' as part of their campus initiation duties. Life at most American colleges in the 18th century was tediously rigid and dull: endless Greek and Latin recitations, twice-daily visits to the chapel and bans on frivolities such as dancing and playing cards. Eventually, rebelling – or just letting off steam, with a ball or otherwise – came to be tolerated. In the words of one scholar: 'Even a rigidly religious faculty could likely see that it was less harmful, and maybe even beneficial, to allow a certain degree of indecorous physical mayhem on campus than try to subdue it completely.' Initially, this mayhem consisted of 'rushes' between classes, with beleaguered freshmen in particular being ritualistically wrestled, punched, kicked, trampled, submerged and otherwise manhandled in the name of scholarly high jinks.

Fortunately for future applicants, the student body would come to feel the need for a more collective form of thrills. In England, Oxford and Cambridge had given birth to university sport in 1827 by playing cricket at Lord's. In 1852, 23 years after the first Boat Race, Harvard and Yale rowed across Lake Winnipesaukee in New Hampshire in what is generally regarded as America's first intercollegiate sporting event. A thousand spectators saw Harvard win, even though its crew had practised only a few times for fear of developing blisters on their hands.

Attitudes changed after the Civil War. In 1869 Harvard sailed to England to race Oxford University's crew on the Thames, having trained for an entire month (they still lost). Rowing emerged as the most popular of the early college sports, though by the 1870s there were plenty of other pursuits in which a young collegian could test his mettle. The first intercollegiate baseball game took place in 1859, the first cricket match five years later. Three colleges contested a two-mile foot race in 1873, and before the turn of the century universities would face each other in tennis, polo, lacrosse, cycling, cross-country, fencing, ice hockey, basketball, golf, swimming, gymnastics and water polo. Baseball remained the most widely played sport on campus, regattas the showcase event.

But another sport – one far more bruising and complex, and unequivocally American – would soon overtake them all. It claimed the name football and could trace its origins to a variety of unruly kicking activities periodically outlawed by campus officials. One such variant had taken place between freshmen and sophomores at Harvard in the 1820s, where, according to some sources, the contests did not always involve the use of a ball. The introduction of an object to kick – alongside all the shins – seems to have had little effect on the game's brutality. Harvard's infamous 'Bloody Monday', an initiation ritual held on the first day of the autumn term, seemed to include a ball as something of an afterthought. By 1860 the practice had been banned. Similar activities elsewhere met with similar fates.

Many historians claim that American football was conceived during the era of Muscular Christianity, a doctrine which espoused vigorous exercise and bravery among young men in Britain and the US alike. For much of America, 'sport' still carried connotations of idleness and sin, but fears that its men were becoming effeminate and unhealthy began to alter this thinking. Muscular Christianity gained acceptance through the promotion of clean, arduous outdoor activity. Its most visible champion was President Theodore Roosevelt, a well-known advocate of 'the strenuous life'. Roosevelt and other disciples considered ball sports to be part of wholesome, masculine living, promoting teamwork, fair play and character – not to mention empires. In 1896 Henry Cabot Lodge, the Massachusetts congressman who would help to shape the country's early 20th-century foreign policy, told a Harvard commencement dinner that 'the time given to athletic contests and the injuries incurred on the playing field are part of the price which the English-speaking race has paid for being world conquerors'.

Muscular Christianity helped make rugged, combative games accepted in higher education, where the 'extracurriculum' was emerging as a feature of campus life and where 'character' needed to be 'instilled'. Sport was establishing strong links with American colleges and universities, which were far more egalitarian than those across the Atlantic and whose leaders did not restrict the educational experience to purely academic pursuits. As Roosevelt, Lodge and a number of other influential statesmen were studying at Harvard, the university was building impressive gymnasiums and even assigning an academic status to physical education. This was in stark contrast to its European counterparts. Even universities such as Oxford and Cambridge, which embraced competitive sport, did so under the auspices of gentlemanly avocation.

By the 1860s football had worked its way back onto campuses in a more organised and regulated guise, but rules still varied wildly. Princeton played a game with 25 players, while others awarded victory to the first team to score a set number of goals. One variation, known as the Boston Game, seems a hybrid of rugby and soccer. Players could run with the ball, but only if they were chased; if the pursuer gave up the chase he would shout, and the person with the ball was obliged to stop. The Boston Game gave rise in 1862 to the first organised 'football' team in America, and one of the first anywhere outside England: the Oneida Football Club, which drew its players from the elite secondary schools of greater Boston. Facing makeshift opposition drawn from gentlemanly society – and benefiting enormously from the fact that only its own participants had any experience of playing together – the Oneidas did not concede a single goal between 1862 and 1865.

In the midst of this dynasty came the pivotal meeting in October 1863, when the London Football Association made the first attempt to lay down a set of rules that would satisfy a number of competing clubs. Among other things these outlawed running with the ball (though not catching it) and deliberate hacking, decisions which led dissenting clubs down the path of the game that quickly developed into rugby. Three years later, Beadle and Co of New York published a set of rules for both 'Association Foot Ball' and the 'Handling Game'. Until this point, few American schools played 'foot ball' under the same rules, but these events helped to homogenise it enough for intercollegiate competition to be considered.

Although November 6, 1869 is widely cited as the day of the first American football game, it is more akin to the birthday of American soccer. Indeed, the ball used in this match is on display not at the College Football Hall of Fame in South Bend, Indiana, but at the US Soccer Hall of Fame in Oneonta, New York. On that day, teams of 25 from the universities of Princeton and Rutgers met and, after removing their hats and coats, contested a variation of the 1863 London FA rules. The ball could only be kicked or butted with the head, though it could also be caught. If this happened in the air or on the first bounce, the recipient was entitled to a free kick. Points were scored through posts set 25 feet apart, with the first team doing so six times declared the winner. Rutgers won 6-4, but a rematch the following week saw Princeton win 8-0 under rules with which it was more familiar. A deciding game never came about, perhaps because the two schools could not agree how it should be played, or perhaps because of faculty opposition.

Within two years, Columbia University and the University of

Pennsylvania had formed teams. By 1872 a codified form of football existed at Harvard, Yale and Princeton, three pivotal members of the American sporting fraternity. The precise rules still varied from school to school, but crucially by 1871 Harvard had adopted the Boston Game, deviating from the general preference for the association code (some evidence suggests Harvard did not find the kicking game rugged enough). Two years later the university rejected an early attempt to create a common set of rules when it failed to attend a convention on the matter.

Desperate for another school to play its handling game, Harvard turned its attentions towards McGill University in Canada, which favoured rugby. In May 1874 the two agreed to contest a match under each code. Not surprisingly, Harvard won at the Boston Game, but they then held McGill to a scoreless draw in rugby. This proved a pivotal moment in American sport, for not only was Harvard immensely satisfied with its achievement, it also found rugby more to its liking. In October of that year it played McGill again at rugby and won. The days of the Boston Game were numbered; so smitten were the Americans with the Canadian code they declined the rematch, leaving the editor of Harvard's campus newspaper to concede that 'the Rugby game is in much better favour than the somewhat sleepy game played by our men'.

Harvard then turned its attention to finding another American school to play. In particular, it was keen to sway its arch-rival Yale from the kicking game. By 1875 the two schools had arranged an exhibition match, drafting concessionary rules which allowed the ball to be handled and thrown. On November 13 Harvard beat Yale by four goals and four touchdowns to nil in what is much closer to America's first gridiron game than the Princeton-Rutgers encounter of 1869.

From that moment on, American football never looked back. Despite an emphatic defeat (hardly surprising, given that its team scarcely knew the rules), Yale agreed that the handling game was much more hardy and scientific and, unable to resist the allure of a regular encounter with its nemesis, soon gave up on soccer. With two of the nation's most influential institutions converted, it was only a matter of time before others followed. This left Princeton, with its fondness for the kicking game, to arrange matches with less prestigious schools, a situation it found intolerable. In 1876 it invited Harvard, Yale and Columbia to a conference in Springfield, Massachusetts, with a view towards 'adopting a uniform system of rules and considering the advisability of forming an Intercollegiate Football Association'. This meeting would leave soccer out in the cold for decades to come. The association was duly formed in November of that year, settled on rugby as its game – and 28 years passed before another intercollegiate soccer match took place.

Can American soccer's tiny footprint be attributed solely to the predilections of Harvard University? It is tempting to claim that had Yale and Princeton been less acquiescent, the game Americans call football might never have developed, and that the association game would have risen to heights similar to those it has attained elsewhere. But America's strong desire to assert its cultural independence by developing games of its own would almost certainly have prevented this. In the years that followed, the rugby code agreed to by the Intercollegiate Association was subjected to countless modifications, to the point where the colleges had created their own game, one that looked very little like its antecedent. Soccer would surely have got off no less lightly.

It took less than a decade for Harvard's rugby evangelism to bear fruit, but rather longer for their game to approach the popularity of baseball, which had already captured the attention of the working classes and a number of promoters. In 1869 the first openly professional baseball team brought notoriety to the city of Cincinnati and by 1876 the professional game had evolved into a fully-fledged league, the National Association (the first of the two major leagues that survive to this day). By the mid-1880s, though, gridiron contests had begun to capture the imagination of New York newspapers embroiled in a circulation war. After buying the struggling *New York World* in 1893, the famed Joseph Pulitzer created a sports page in an effort to boost circulation, a practice which was quickly copied by rivals and soon gave rise to weekend sports sections, rich in textual and pictorial accounts of the big games. This naturally fuelled spectator interest, and even forced some of the bigger collegiate contests to be played in New York because campuses had no grounds large enough to stage them. As a result, gridiron acquired a significance well beyond the competing schools and their localities, and attracted fans keen to attach themselves to the social elite of the top colleges.

At the same time, soccer was beginning its proliferation across Europe and into Latin America, spread by the railwaymen, traders, mill owners, engineers and sailors dispatched far and wide on behalf of British commerce. By the end of the 1890s it had put down firm foundations in almost all the countries that would play influential roles in 20th century football and clubs such as Peñarol, AC Milan and Barcelona had taken their first steps. All this mattered not one jot to the US. It knew how to build its own railways, was not particularly beholden to the British

Empire and was certainly disinclined to accommodate a sport merely on the basis of its popularity elsewhere. In fact, though Americans seemed to have fallen for rugby, hardly any time passed before they began reworking its rules. A Yale graduate and Muscular Christianity disciple named Walter Camp claimed responsibility for much of the change, quickly coming to be regarded as 'the father of American football'. Camp had participated in the first intercollegiate season of 1876 and went to work for a clock company. Just as men like Frederick Taylor were revolutionising the industrial workplace through the application of science and mathematics, Camp's disapproval of the randomness of the rugby scrum and his desire to more systematically regulate possession of the ball did the same for sport.

Camp's development swept across the nation and by 1894 had left the *Manchester Guardian* bemoaning how the Americans had 'spoiled and brutalised' dear old rugby. By the turn of the century gridiron legends were being written in every corner of the country, but objections to the staggeringly popular sport continued to surface. Ironically, one of its most outspoken opponents was the Harvard president, Charles Eliot. Concerns were persistently raised that the drive to produce winning teams and star players had led universities to take liberties with the amateur code, or encourage players to neglect their studies. More grave was the brutality still inherent in the game. In 1904 the *New York Times* reported that 21 deaths and about 200 injuries had occurred from football that season.

Such carnage and corruption attracted the attention of journalists as well as university officials and politicians, and in 1905 President Roosevelt – whose son had recently joined the freshman team at Harvard – felt compelled to take action. Summoning representatives from Harvard, Yale and Princeton to the White House, he urged them to redraft football's rules to encourage safer and fairer play, and to better uphold the ideals of amateurism and university life. But the intervention of America's Muscular Christian *nonpareil* came to little. Football remained dangerously violent and for the next few years proponents, abolitionists and reformers debated what role, if any, such a popular yet flawed game should play on the nation's campuses. Some institutions, such as Columbia, dropped the sport entirely, while on the west coast the universities of Stanford and California substituted it with rugby, having apparently been swayed by an exhibition between New Zealand and Australia.

That soccer was not put forward as a substitute suggests that attitudes towards the kicking game were already entrenched. Neither players nor spectators appeared to favour its emphasis on individual skill and elusiveness over the fierce physical contact and pseudo-military science of the Americanised game. The *Washington Post* maintained in 1906 that 'association football, whatever its merits, seems to appeal to persons quite different from those who like the other [football]'. Americans believed they were inherently unable to adhere to its more genteel code, particularly after years of trampling, slugging and gouging each other on the gridiron. After watching a soccer exhibition between English and American teams at Harvard in 1905, Eliot noted that 'there is plenty of opportunity for brutality in the socker ... our American college boys would spoil it in five minutes'.

All the same, 'the socker' did make a slow return to campuses.* One of its earliest appearances was at Haverford College in Philadelphia. An enthusiastic student newspaper editor, Richard Gummere, who had played the game as a schoolboy in England and then in Switzerland, is credited with forming a college team in 1902. Later, as a graduate student at Harvard, Gummere helped to restore the game there. A two-match series with Haverford staged in 1904 – with Haverford winning both games 'in close and exciting fashion' according to the school newspaper – marked a return to intercollegiate play.

Within a few years Columbia, Cornell and Pennsylvania joined an Intercollegiate Association Football League with Haverford and Harvard. Even at this stage, though, the prominence of foreign players was evident. According to one account, when Haverford – the league's first champions – travelled to Cornell, its players spent part of the train journey attempting to learn how to pronounce the names of opposing players. By this time, though, whatever hope soccer had of supplanting the other football was purely illusory. 'As far as soccer is concerned,' an official at Princeton declared in 1909, 'this game is now classed among the minor sports, and it is very unlikely that it will ever take the place of football at Princeton.'

This was an accurate prophecy, but it didn't stop Gummere and other enthusiasts with old-world links from working to put the game on a

---

* After the turn of the century, many newspapers began substituting the phrase 'association football' with the word 'socker' out of deference to the gridiron game (the *Washington Post* asserted that 'the new term is much easier to pronounce and altogether more euphonious than the correct appellation'). By 1906 the *New York Times* had changed its spelling to 'soccer', though some provincial papers persisted with 'socker' well into the 1920s.

firmer footing. One such group was a collection of public school-educated Englishmen who toured North America in 1905 as the Pilgrim Football Club. Though amateurs, several in their ranks were with Football League clubs, including the captain, Fred Milnes of Sheffield United. Backed by Sir Alfred Harmsworth, the future Lord Northcliffe of newspaper publishing fame, the Pilgrims were not short of ambition: they were said to be prepared to offer universities the services of top English coaches in an effort to re-establish the sport on campus.

Stretching from Canada to St Louis – a surprisingly westward trail – the Pilgrims' two-month tour included only one match against a team representing a university. Nevertheless, their presence helped to revive interest in the game and generated huge crowds. Milnes later asserted that 28,000 turned out to watch the team's second match in St Louis, an almost unfathomable figure for the era – a local newspaper later cited the official gate as 15,986 but claimed that several thousand others had gate-crashed. Interest was heightened by one paper brashly billing the contest as the 'Championship of the World'. 'Such a bold title made us wonder what we were up against,' reflected Milnes, though his team strolled to a ten-goal victory.

The gulf in ability between the English and their foes was plain. The Pilgrims scored 72 goals and conceded only seven in their 12 matches. Their only defeat came at the hands of an all-Chicago team in front of a small crowd ('the Chicago goal seemed charmed ... we retired beaten by a team of triers, who possess a splendid defence,' noted Milnes). Such superiority was only to be expected, but to many American observers, having never seen an association game played to any standard, the scoreline was not nearly as revealing as the level of entertainment a good team could produce.

Four years later, the Pilgrims returned for another tour, in which they scored 123 times in 24 matches. A more famous group of English amateurs, the Corinthians, made three tours beginning in 1907, and demonstrated similar superiority and flair. Without such visits, turn-of-the-century American soccer would almost certainly have fallen into an even deeper hole than the one football had already dug for it.

Gridiron's survival was safeguarded by a series of dramatic rule changes and better policing under the auspices of the National Collegiate Athletic Association, founded in 1905. Eventually, and to the relief of their students, Stanford and California dropped rugby and returned to football; Columbia resumed play in 1915. With Walter Camp at the helm, gridiron soon evolved into something recognisable to the modern fan, with the legalisation of such tactics as throwing the ball forward and the abolition of the flying wedge and other hazards. By the start of the First World War its pride of place on American campuses was assured, and whatever tiny hope soccer had of rivalling it had vanished. In the *New York Times*, the Athletic Director at Northwestern University of Illinois declared:

> We do not believe in its success in the ordinary college community. It takes a leaven of good Scotch, English, and Scandinavian players to make the game a success. It looks tame to boys after American football and baseball.

A representative of Ohio's Wesleyan University added:

> Its only desirable feature with us is that it can be played out of doors after the tennis courts and ball fields can no longer be used because of the weather. It is not a game that appeals to those of our students who are engaged in other forms of athletics. It is not scientific enough. Others do not care to take it up because it requires too much running.

In the decades to come soccer would be introduced to increasing numbers of universities. Yet it never won over the student body in the way that later inventions, particularly basketball, did. Well into the 1960s, long after a national collegiate championship had been organised, many colleges regarded the soccer team as little more than a training fillip for other, more important, sports such as football or even wrestling. The formation of a team on campus often had more to do with the presence of a soccer-disposed member of the faculty than any groundswell of interest. In 1922 the University of Florida became one of the earliest colleges in the deep south to form a team. But when its coach, Harry Metcalf, died in 1925, the team disbanded – and did not reform until the 1950s. As late as 1918 only 12 colleges played soccer against each other, all in the east and all to little public attention. Training began in December – after the end of the football season – and the fixtures often not until January, continuing as best they could through the brunt of the winter. Although this often resulted in wretched playing conditions, there was little hope of beginning any earlier and interfering with gridiron, in some cases because soccer teams depended on football players to make up their numbers.

Soccer in the colleges may have struggled for air, but among the country's burgeoning immigrant communities there was greater cause for optimism. The 1890 census established that nearly 15 per cent of the nation's population was foreign-born – as high as it has been before or since. One out of seven of them had come from England or Scotland, where association football had taken a firm hold. Although the majority of English and Scottish emigrants followed their kinfolk into the rural south, enough gravitated towards the northern conurbations to keep the country's flickering soccer torch alight.

In a select few communities, the fire burned very brightly, owing to a peculiar combination of circumstances. Nowhere was this more true than in unassuming Kearny, New Jersey, a town less than eight miles from Ellis Island and the Statue of Liberty. Separated from the city of Newark by the Passaic River to its south and west, and from Jersey City by the Hackensack River to the east, Kearny had become a Scottish enclave, largely because of its principal employers. Michael Nairn & Co, whose headquarters were in Kirkcaldy, opened a substantial linoleum mill in 1886. More importantly, six years earlier the Clark Thread Company of Paisley had built the second of its New Jersey factories in Kearny. In November 1883 the firm established an athletic association for its workforce, proudly naming it after its groundbreaking product, ONT: Our New Thread, a filament which was the first suitable for use in sewing machines and which would soon revolutionise the industry. Since the athletic association was headed by two employees who had arrived from England only a few months earlier, it was little wonder soccer was given such attention.

Other places near Kearny – in fact much of the West Hudson area – displayed a similar Britishness and affection for the game. The hamlet of Harrison immediately to the south and the 'Silk City' of Paterson 15 miles to the north proudly fielded teams of their own. Paterson's links with silk-producing Macclesfield in Cheshire were strong enough for one historian to claim that 'in Macclesfield, men spoke of Paterson as familiarly as if it were only a run of half an hour by train'. For generations to come, the area's enduring ethnic make-up would keep the game alive long after it had virtually died elsewhere, producing an impressive array of semi-professional and amateur teams well into the middle of the 20th century. Even after this influence waned, the area remained a soccer stronghold, producing players such as Tony Meola, Tab Ramos and John Harkes.

The West Hudson communities were well represented in one of the earliest efforts to organise a top-class league in the United States, the National Association Foot Ball League, which began in 1895. In spite of its name, its imprint was confined to greater New York, northern New Jersey and, by 1917, eastern Pennsylvania, and its composition fluctuated wildly from season to season. From 1898 to 1906 it did not even operate. Yet over its three decades of existence, the National League established itself as probably the strongest in the country. As late as 1912 five of its eight clubs were based in or near Kearny, underlining the area's intense level of interest. One club, Kearny Scots – an enduring name in ethnic soccer – was a rare ever-present until the First World War, and claimed two of the first three championships.

Another foothold was established in New England, along the Massachusetts-Rhode Island border. Its heart was the town of Fall River, Massachusetts, about 50 miles south of Boston. In the 1870s Fall River experienced a period of frenetic economic growth, driven by the demand for linen (southeastern New England was the birthplace of the American textile industry), and came to be known as 'Spindle City'. By 1876 the city was home to 43 factories, more than 30,000 looms and more than one million spindles. Keeping them all turning required more labour than the nation could supply, and while some arrivals were French-Canadian and Irish, many others came from two of the earliest strongholds of British football, Lancashire and the Clyde.

Nearby New Bedford, Massachusetts, and the cities of Providence, Tiverton and Pawtucket in Rhode Island, also relied heavily on immigrant workers. This area, much wider than the river-locked West Hudson, produced its own slew of clubs and, by 1886, a Bristol County League. The creation of a Southern New England League in 1914 placed teams such as Fall River Rovers and the Pawtucket-based works club of Howard & Bullough – a cotton machinery firm established in Lancashire – among the country's elite.

American soccer's other early epicentre was in the more unlikely location of St Louis, Missouri, the fourth-largest city in the country, but at that time still a decidedly western outpost. Here the reasons for the sport's popularity were remarkably different: the immigrant population was predominantly Irish and it was the involvement of the Catholic Church in community affairs, rather than immigration, that offered an impetus. A St Louis Athletic Club is recorded as having played the game in 1881, but it wasn't until the church introduced soccer into its recreational programme that the sport began to thrive – and with home-grown teams. Kensington, winners of the 1890 city championship, featured a line-up consisting almost entirely of players born in the city. This unwittingly removed the 'un-American' stigma attached to the sport elsewhere and with it, fan resistance – one match in April 1897 was said to have been witnessed by 6,000 people. (A newspaper account refers to this contest as being refereed by a man named Rogers who 'wore a big Texas cowboy hat, suspenders, civilian shoes and a big moustache' and notes that 'in the grandstand were dudes wearing big stove-pipe hats'.)

St Louis shows how the game might have developed across the country under different circumstances. Almost from the formation of the city's first league in 1886, organisers showed little respect for the laws of mother England. For much of its history, St Louis teams played halves of 30 minutes instead of 45; as early as 1919, the St Louis League allowed injured players to be substituted. Experiments with goal judges, two referees and other manifestations of 'Americanisation' were made before the Second World War. And its relative isolation even helped to foster an indigenous playing style, one predicated on speed, stamina and muscle, with players needing to work as hard as the ball. The Scottish passing game came to be looked down upon – enough for the *St Louis Globe-Democrat* to insist: 'Any neutral observer who has an opportunity to compare the two systems, must admit that there is more pep, punch, and thrill in the American style of play.'

No US city embraced soccer more unreservedly than St Louis, which operated all manner of junior, amateur and semi-professional leagues, most stocked with red-blooded Americans equally at home on the baseball diamond. Before the turn of the century, at least one ambitious team had lured players from Chicago and Canada in an effort to regain the league championship it had unexpectedly lost. Able to attract gates of a few thousand and with no travelling expenses to speak of, soccer in St Louis was, if not a money-spinning proposition, at least one which paid its own way. For decades to come the St Louis Soccer League, founded in 1903, would produce some of the strongest teams in the country, and many of the top American-born players.

One of the city's newspapers even offered a charming example of soccer poetry around the time of the First World War. Attributed to a WH James, *Arabella's Favorite Game* may not have scaled any artistic heights, but it illustrated soccer's ambition, in St Louis at least:

Miss Arabella Simpkins Brown would leave her book and rocker
And travel half across the town to see a game of soccer.
For there's a sport that's full of thrills, excitement, 'pep' and action,

Of snap and ginger, bumps and spills to lend it rare attraction.
A baseball game is lame and tame, or so it seems in winter,
Compared with this quick-moving game where every man's a sprinter.
There's something doing all the time, no weary waits or stalling,
For laziness is here a crime and speed a noble calling.
O, see the agile forward go a speeding fast as thunder;
The ball he carries on his toe, though how is good for wonder,
And then somebody else cuts in and gets that sphere and boots it,
Or juggles it upon his chin, or through the goal he shoots it,
Or neatly bumps it with his head and sends it off a kiting,
O, sure when all is done or said there's nothing more exciting.
Now Tyrus Cobb is quite a star when on the diamond posing
But where the soccer speed boys are he'd seem to be a-dozing,
And Honus Wagner at the bat, his mighty stick out-sticking,
Would seem a puny little gnat where Billy Quinn is kicking.
And that's why Arabella Brown would leave her book and rocker
To travel half across the town and see a game of soccer.

Outside the bastions of St Louis, Kearny and Fall River, small groups of exiled devotees nurtured soccer in the cities. There were, of course, plenty of British immigrants in New York – although those who founded the game there were generally drawn from the more affluent social positions. Chicago's roots can be traced to 1893, when the game was featured at the city's influential Columbian Exposition. By 1904 a Chicago Association Football League had been formed, and by 1909 a cup competition which was soon regarded as the city (and later the state) championship. Philadelphia also established soccer strongholds, in particular its Kensington district, where an organisation known as the Lighthouse Boys Club provided countless youngsters with an opportunity to learn and play the game. Detroit, Cincinnati and Cleveland were other important early midwestern centres. Further west, a Greater Los Angeles League had been formed by 1902, with San Francisco and Denver instigating their own equivalents.

It was all very fragmented, of course, especially in an era when travelling 100 miles was more unusual than travelling 1,000 today. A first attempt at unifying the game was made in 1884 when a group of British expatriates, led by the Clark brothers of New Jersey, formed the American Football Association, the first supposedly 'national' governing body outside the British Isles. This, though, was more of a loose collective, driven by the northeastern states and the West Hudson area in particular. Its domain was only an area roughly from Boston to Philadelphia, and even then it failed to enlist the majority of teams from the latter or from New York City. Decidedly Anglocentric, it even established an informal working relationship with the Scottish and English Football Associations, a source of concern to those preoccupied with American autonomy.

The association's most notable achievement was the creation in 1884 of a prototype national championship, a virtual facsimile of the FA Cup which it christened the American Cup. Though scarcely a national competition (it initially attracted 13 entries from four states) the winners of the first three titles, the ONT club of Kearny, were perhaps as strong as any team in the country. They were also one of the pioneers of name-changing that would come to beleaguer American soccer. By the time of their fourth American Cup win in 1907, they had become the less cryptic Clark Athletic Association. Clark and other Kearny teams featured regularly in American Cup finals, but the Fall River area produced the next seven winners. By 1894, though, economic depression and labour unrest in New England were starting to cripple the industrial towns and their budding teams, while the association's authority was undermined by the continual poaching of players. It suspended operations in 1899.

Another thorn in the AFA's side had manifested itself in October 1894 as the first attempt at a professional league outside Britain. It lasted all of 17 days – setting a precedent of failure pro soccer would unwittingly follow for decades to come – and represented the first of many attempts by baseball owners to expand their sporting empires through the game. The spectacularly ill-fated venture, known as the American League of Professional Foot Ball, was conceived by the owners of six major league clubs, not out of an interest in soccer so much as a means of keeping their ballparks occupied during the winter. Their motives aroused the suspicions of the AFA, which passed a resolution barring anyone who signed a contract with the league from playing in AFA-sanctioned events – an ultimatum unlikely to have given the deep-pocketed baseball men much cause for concern. In an effort to capitalise on the appeal of their baseball teams, the owners insisted that each club take the name of its baseball counterpart, and many hired their baseball managers as 'coaches'. Some even teased the public with promises that their favourite baseball players would feature in matches (which in Philadelphia they actually did).

With the baseball moguls possessing more money and better facilities, assembling talented teams proved relatively straightforward, in spite of the AFA's threats. The Philadelphia and New York entries played friendlies against local sides and won them easily. But the best club, and the best-supported, was Baltimore. Baseball champions in 1894, the Orioles had taken the trouble of hiring a bona fide soccer coach, AW Stewart, who doubled as the team's goalkeeper. Stewart in turn imported a number of professionals from Manchester City and Sheffield United, many of whom had broken their contracts and were working in the US illegally. The Orioles had little trouble winning every game they played, but made few friends in doing so. After trouncing Washington 10-1, the losing manager complained bitterly of the opposition's use of foreign professionals. Baltimore are alleged to have defended themselves ingeniously by maintaining that the players with unusual accents came from Detroit.

The league practically died at birth. Although the admission price (25 cents) was not beyond the reach of working-class fans, many matches were held on weekday afternoons when they could not attend. The Orioles drew a total of 12,000 to their two weekend home fixtures, but just 500 turned up for a weekday afternoon game, which proved to be their last. Reports surfaced of fewer than 100 fans attending a match in New York, and with rumours of a rival professional baseball league distracting the owners, they soon baled out.

In 1901 another group of baseball owners proposed a new league, this one in the midwest, with teams in Chicago, Detroit, St Louis and Milwaukee. Their motives were much the same, but their efforts proved even more ephemeral. Detroit withdrew before a ball had been kicked and the Milwaukee entry did likewise after its owners, according to the *Milwaukee Daily News*, 'found that the railroad rate between here and St Louis was too strong'. Initially, the venture was merely put on hold and the players retained, but it collapsed soon after the Chicago team travelled to Milwaukee for a friendly and drew just 300 to the local baseball park.

Economic conditions were not especially favourable for such bold projects, and it was not until the resurrection of the college game and the first Pilgrims tour of 1905 that soccer started to recover from its gridiron-induced body-blow. By 1906 it had recuperated enough for the AFA to stumble back into life, though the association was now chiefly concerned with the semi-professional clubs from areas such as Kearny and Fall River. The American Cup was relaunched in 1906, and for the next four years it became the property of teams from the Kearny area.

In 1911 the amateur game created an umbrella organisation of its own. Members of the Southern New York State Association formed an American Amateur Football Association and elected an English-born,

German-educated doctor, 'Guss' Randolph Manning, as president. As a medical student in Freiburg, Manning had been instrumental in the formation of the German FA in 1900. Five years later he emigrated to New York and became active in the game there. Now he set out to gain the AAFA recognition from a fledgling FIFA as the nation's governing body. In 1912 he sent the association secretary Thomas Cahill – soon to become one of the dominant figures of the American game – to a FIFA congress in Stockholm. The AFA was also represented but, curiously, by the secretary of the English FA, Sir Frederick Wall. FIFA, perhaps at Wall's instigation, instructed the two associations to come back when they could speak with one voice.

It took another year for them to do so, and the voice was that of the upstart AAFA, which quickly abandoned its devotion to amateurism and in April 1913 rechristened itself the United States Football Association. The occasional name change notwithstanding, it remains the country's governing body. Federations from states as far west as Utah quickly lined up behind it, but some areas – most notably St Louis – did not. The bruised AFA managed to stagger on for a few more months, but after the USFA's application for FIFA membership was provisionally accepted in August 1913, its forlorn struggle reached an end, leaving behind a cluster of embittered officials.

Brimming with optimism, Manning declared in the *New York Times* of December 28, 1913, that the USFA 'aims to make soccer the national pastime of the winter in this country'. But it faced all manner of obstacles. It lacked the financial clout to promote and organise the game effectively, and by leaving the high schools and colleges effectively to run themselves, it ignored its most promising area for growth. Perhaps most crucially, it failed to distance itself adequately from the ethnic foundations on which the game still tottered. In the memorable words of soccer writer Paul Gardner, the USFA quickly became 'a gathering place for immigrants whose devotion to soccer was a pretty good measure of their reluctance to become Americans, and for people who were amateurs mainly in the pejorative sense of the word'.

Not until 1928 did it elect an American-born president, and well into the latter part of the century its chieftains were largely men who spoke with conspicuously foreign accents (mostly British and Irish at first). In a country whose national motto, *e pluribus unum* (out of many, one), articulated a desire for assimilation, leaving soccer in the hands of what Roosevelt, Lodge and their ilk disparagingly referred to as 'hyphenated-Americans' was tantamount to marginalising it for good. The migrants may have helped to keep soccer alive during its bleakest decades, but the establishment of ethnic clubs and leagues was poison to the game's chances of breaking through into the mainstream of American sports.

Perhaps the best hope for the game's broader development was the St Louis-born Cahill, whose appointment as USFA secretary placed him in a pivotal role. Cahill earned his living as a representative of a sports equipment manufacturer, the famous AG Spalding Company, and in his twenties had helped to organise a semi-professional baseball circuit of some standing, the Illinois-Missouri 'Trolley' League. Such an enthusiasm for the 'national game' doubtless furthered his standing as a 'real' American (he was even on friendly terms with the owner of one of the city's two major league teams). Though his forthright, confrontational style led some St Louis newspapers to refer to him occasionally as 'Bullets' – and certainly left him with no shortage of enemies – over the next two decades he energetically attempted to make Manning's lofty declaration a reality.

Behind the assiduous secretary, whose day-job had taken him to Manhattan, the USFA was not long in asserting its powers. Not everyone cheerfully fell into line, and some even accused Cahill of taking up his position chiefly so that he could sell more sports equipment (though he stridently claimed 'never to have sold or solicited soccer paraphernalia to anyone connected with the game'). Antipathy towards the new body festered in many AFA strongholds, an attitude which must have hardened once the USFA announced the formation of its own cup competition and declared that its fixtures would take priority over all others, including those of the American Cup. The National League responded by turning its back; only one of its 12 teams entered the new competition. But though the American Cup retained a high profile for some years, it was fated to become an inferior prize, limited to eastern teams and trading largely on its history.

The new National Challenge Cup attracted amateur and professional teams from as far west as Chicago and as far north as Niagara Falls, though reasonably strong soccer centres such as Cincinnati remained absent for some time and the first west coast entry did not appear until 1951. Much of this was attributable to the cost of travel, though some was rooted in an aversion to the new association. Like the American Cup, the Challenge Cup drew its inspiration from Britain: it was a knockout competition, a strange concept to a nation which staged a best-of-seven-games final to determine its national baseball champions. Forty clubs entered the draw in October 1913, with play beginning the following month and continuing through the winter. Liberally sprinkled with teams named Rangers and Celtic, the draw also featured such entries as the Cowboy Club of New Jersey and Presbyterian FC of Connecticut. (The following season they were joined by Our Boys FC of Brooklyn, Viscose FC of Philadelphia and the Young Men's Catholic Total Abstinence Society FC of Massachusetts.)

But attempting to play soccer during the most inhospitable months of the year was still a dire proposition, leaving the Challenge Cup to run hot and cold in more than just a figurative sense. It achieved some early successes, including in Pittsburgh, where the nearby town of Braddock played its second-round tie in the city's major league baseball park and drew a crowd of almost 3,000. Just as often, though, the weather turned prospective fans away, while rendering playing surfaces all but unusable. The lone National League entrant, the Brooklyn Field Club, contested its quarter-final tie on a pitch 'which would have been more suitable for ice hockey than it was for football', according to one account. 'Scattered all over the field were little ponds. Just when a player would get going he would strike an icy spot, which would either send him sprawling or he would slip around until he lost possession of the ball.' Elsewhere, a tie between Yonkers FC and Fulton FC saw the teams 'floundering around in a sea of mud'; Brooklyn Celtic beat the Babcock & Wilcox club of New Jersey 'on a field partly covered with ice'; and in Chicago, the Hyde Park Blues and Clan MacDuff FC endured 'arctic conditions' at the city's Aviation Field, 'not one of the coziest spots on earth when the north wind is in its best winter form'.

Gate receipts were thus left at the mercy of the elements. An attendance of just 200 was reported for a quarter-final tie in New York, played in steady rain, while the Detroit derby between Packard FC and Roses FC attracted only about 500, a great pity in the light of the *Detroit Free Press*'s assertion that 'those who witnessed the game ... were unanimous in the opinion that there was never a game staged in Detroit fraught with more brilliant play'. One could sympathise with the manager of the Niagara Falls Rangers, when asked whether his team would journey to Detroit in snowy January and honour its third-round tie with the Roses, certain to be a loss-making proposition. 'Yes, we'll go all right,' he replied. 'I don't know whether we'll ever get back, though.'

The Rangers and the other survivors slogged towards the spring, but the bad weather persisted, reducing the gate for one of the semi-finals – staged on neutral territory as in England – to about 1,000. Nearly 5,000 saw the other, with the Brooklyn Field Club edging New Bedford

2-1 on a more amenable April afternoon in Pawtucket. The Field Club returned to the same venue a month later for the grand final, defeating the amateurs of Brooklyn Celtic in front of more than 6,000 patient fans. The *Providence Sunday Journal* claimed that spectators 'began to arrive at the field shortly after 2.30 o'clock [for the 3.45 kick-off] and by 3.15 the fans filled the grandstand and the bleachers and were lined 12-deep around the field'.

The *Journal* rated the match a 'smashing one from start to finish', which it may have been in more ways than one. Five minutes from the end James Ford, the Field Club's outside-right, headed in the winner, but by this time plenty of private battles had been waged – and, in the eyes of some, had gone scandalously unpunished. The sports editor of the *New Bedford Times* offered this view:

> The game was a success from every standpoint. The crowds were well handled, there was no disorder, the grounds were policed properly and everything possible to make the contest a good one was provided for ... To my mind the only real flaw was the referee work of [Charles] Creighton. Perhaps it is his style of handling a game to let the players go to the limit, but there was enough of the rough stuff in the contest to have barred several of the men on the field but Creighton let them finish with 11 on each team. It also seemed as though Creighton overlooked some very open violations of the rules but he was undoubtedly doing his best.

The USFA appropriated a trophy which had been donated for an earlier competition by Sir Thomas Dewar, the Scottish whisky distiller and sporting enthusiast, and hailed the Field Club as national champions. It had grossed more than $1,000 from the competition, aided by an insistence that clubs charge a minimum admission of 25 cents. But not even the sight of a baseball park brimming with soccer fans was enough to convince everyone in the host city that the game's time had come. 'Association football is still a game for English folk,' sniffed the *Pawtucket Times*, 'and Pawtucket, on account of its peculiar manufacturing interests, is the home of many who followed the game closely across the water.'

The next season, the number of cup entries swelled to 82, including virtually all the clubs in the National League. Entries from Ohio appeared for the first time and the number from Illinois and Michigan grew significantly. St Louis remained the most conspicuous absentee, operating with resolute independence. In fact, the city had never even bothered to establish any sort of governing body of its own, a foible which had produced some chaotic side-effects. In 1913 a second St Louis League sprang up and, having affiliated to the USFA, attempted to suffocate its rival. The damage proved to be mutual and the two leagues – identically named – wandered down a perilous path before finally amalgamating in 1915. But the city's ambivalence toward the USFA lingered, and it would be another four years before any of its teams entered the Challenge Cup. This was a pity, particularly given the boasts made by many St Louis fans that their home-grown, hard-working teams were the equal of any in the country. The periodic western tours made by top clubs from the east – which often pulled in large crowds during the holiday season – were regarded as litmus tests, and while victories by eastern powerhouses over clubs from Cleveland, Detroit or Chicago were generally predictable, outcomes became less certain once they reached Missouri.

Yet the top team of the era, and probably the first in America that could be considered genuinely professional, originated not in St Louis, or Fall River, or Kearny, or even New York. It came instead from the steel mills of eastern Pennsylvania, bearing the name of an industrial colossus. Sixty miles north of Philadelphia, the town of Bethlehem and the mammoth Bethlehem Steel Corporation created what many still consider to be the most successful of America's soccer clubs. The firm had been founded in 1904 by Charles Schwab, a notorious union-buster and a businessman of questionable ethics, who later circumvented American wartime neutrality laws by sneaking his steel into Britain via Canada. Like many of his kind, though, he was also a philanthropist, erecting a top-class hotel for the town and underwriting various artistic endeavours. Such munificence found its way to the workforce in 1915, when Schwab donated an enormous $25,000 for them to spend on sport however they wished. The high proportion of immigrant labour at the firm ensured that soccer would be provided for, though few could imagine just how well.

The success of Bethlehem's team is largely attributable to another company executive, Horace Edgar Lewis. Born in south Wales in 1882, Lewis emigrated to Pennsylvania when he was 14 and at 17 was employed in the steel industry. In 1906 he came to work for Bethlehem, where soccer seems to have first caught his eye. Enamoured of the locals' adroit ball skills, he was said to have become determined to learn the game himself, and a year later captained the city's first team. As a member of the Bethlehem FC which entered the first Challenge Cup, he conceded a penalty against the Brooklyn Field Club which led to his team's third-round exit.

The rise of Lewis to company vice-president in 1916 mirrored that of the soccer club. Although the steel firm had formed a team as early as 1909, it was designed principally to promote the virtues of exercise and teamwork. But by 1915 Bethlehem FC had officially become Bethlehem Steel Company FC; a strong soccer team, it seems, was good for business. With corporate resources at his disposal, Lewis could make frequent trips to Britain for fresh talent, tempting candidates with the offer of a job as well as a place in the team.

No club in the country recruited players quite as effectively, and as a result Bethlehem rapidly outgrew whatever league they joined. In 1913 they finished first in the Eastern Pennsylvania League. The following year they won every match they played in the Allied League of Philadelphia – often by embarrassing scores – and took the American Cup as well, the first of its many 'doubles' of varying magnitude.

Lewis's fatal handball had kept Bethlehem out of the Challenge Cup final that season, but five years passed before they missed out again. In 1915 Bethlehem won their first and second round ties by a combined score of 23-1 on the way to a semi-final with the Homestead Steel club of Pittsburgh (a duel ostensibly pitting Schwab against another industrial tycoon, Andrew Carnegie). Bethlehem won 4-1 in a match it was curiously allowed to hold in its own city. The USFA designated the football stadium on the campus of Lehigh University in Bethlehem a neutral site, since it was not the home ground of either participant. In the first soccer match of any significance to be staged at a college gridiron facility, a crowd of around 3,000 saw Bethlehem reach the final.

Lewis had offered the USFA a sizeable financial guarantee to play at Lehigh and his offer of another to stage the final there was gratefully received. The opposition were the beaten finalists of the previous year, Brooklyn Celtic, who two months earlier had knocked Bethlehem out of the American Cup (their only defeat of the season). In front of nearly 7,000 fans, the Bethlehem Steel Corporation brass band and one of the earliest film crews at an American soccer match, the home side claimed a 3-1 victory, one apparently less feisty than the previous year's final. 'Soccer experts from all over the country were in the Bethlehems on Saturday,' claimed the *Bethlehem Globe*, 'and all agree that Saturday's contest was one of the cleanest games played in recent years.'

This was the last time the Steel played at home in such a showpiece game, though most of its famous team were rather a long way from home to begin with. The origins and career of Jock Ferguson, one of its stars, were typical. Born in Dundee, the full-back had played there as well as for Arbroath, St Johnstone and Leeds City before arriving in Pennsylvania, where he played until the age of 41. It may have been this decided Britishness which, in spite of all the success and national acclaim, prevented the team from becoming more popular in its home town. Year after year, local support for the Steel remained pitifully small. The relatively large crowds at Lehigh's stadium were an aberration, and much more akin to what the club could expect away from home, where they sold tickets far more easily. No matter how hard officials tried to fill the company's state-of-the art, multipurpose ground for soccer, they could rarely attract more than a few hundred. Attributing such apathy solely to the team's ethnicity may be too simplistic, but there is little doubt soccer would have been seen by many as un-American – particularly in a town with a college football team.

The mood was entirely different in Fall River, whose Rovers consisted largely of American-born players and were busy staking their own claims to national superiority. Indeed, the next three Challenge Cup finals were contested by Bethlehem and Fall River, fuelling the greatest of the game's early inter-regional rivalries. Rovers carried the flag not just for New England, but also – at least for a time – the home-grown philosophy of the St Louis clubs. Bethlehem, the pride of Pennsylvania, were their British foils.

Neither was immune from the damaging trait of fan violence which the game had acquired. The 1916 final, held in Pawtucket, attracted a frenzied crowd of 10,000, almost all backing Rovers. Ten minutes from time came a penalty for a push on a Bethlehem player, triggering animated protests from Fall River and howls of outrage from the stands. Bethlehem converted the kick, further enraging the crowd and sending Rovers into a desperate flurry of attacks. When, with only seconds to play, a deflected ball was seen to strike a Bethlehem arm, opposing players and fans screamed for a spot-kick of their own. The *Pawtucket Evening Times* describes what happened:

> Referee Whyte awarded Bethlehem a penalty kick on a foul by Burns. From then on until the finish the Rover rooters, distinguished by the yellow cards in their hats, kept up a fearful din of disapproval. Suddenly, just as Referee Whyte was about to blow his whistle and end the game, a short, thick-set man was seen running out toward the centre of the field. That was all

there was needed to precipitate a riot. In an instant the field was black with people, and Referee Whyte disappeared in a vortex of struggling humanity. The players formed a cordon about the official, and, aided by the police, who used their clubs freely, Whyte was dragged to the J & P Coats clubhouse, his shirt torn from his back and his body black and blue from the pummelling he received. During the riot the police arrested Arthur Brodeur of Fall River, Mass., who is alleged to have been one of the ringleaders, and other Rover sympathizers left the field with unwelcome souvenirs of their encounters with the police.

Such behaviour was already carving out an unfortunate reputation for soccer. Baseball had taken emphatic steps to curb violence towards its arbiters, with the celebrated cry of 'Kill the Umpire!' long since reduced to rhetoric. Headlines such as **Fists Fly at Soccer Contest** or **Soccer Game Halted After Riot** soon became grist for the sports editor's mill, with the game's authorities seemingly unable to control the hostilities. Part of this could be attributed to politicking and administrative spinelessness, but in the cramped, primitive arenas common to the sport, restraining unruly fans was quite a challenge.

Even less manageable was the weather. The 1916-17 season saw Bethlehem's cup ties pushed back on five occasions while the Southern New England League, weighed down by winter postponements, never completed its season. Establishing soccer as a winter game might have been practical in Britain, but in the northern part of America sub-zero temperatures and copious snow cover could last for months. Baseball was untouchable as the ritual of summer and the country had yet to establish any winter equivalent. However impractical the season proved, the USFA seemed entrenched in its old-world views.

It rained steadily during the 1917 Challenge Cup final, one which the referee survived without the loss of his shirt, and which attracted a crowd of 5,000 to Pawtucket (one account claimed 'some of the spectators stood over two hours in the rain waiting for play to start') to see Fall River avenge their 1916 loss to Bethlehem with a goal in the first minute. The following season Rovers took their rivals to a replay before losing 3-0 in New Jersey, the last of their famous Challenge Cup confrontations. Their claim to American soccer supremacy may have been quashed, but Fall River's halcyon days were far from over. Bethlehem continued to search for a league worthy of their team. In 1916 they chose not to play in one at all, but even with the freedom to choose their opposition won their first 18 games with little difficulty.

St Louis still gave a wide berth to the Challenge Cup, but its tradition of exhibitions against eastern powers reached new heights in 1916 with the arrival of Bethlehem for a two-match tour. On Christmas Eve 7,500 turned out to watch the national champions play an all-St Louis XI, winning 3-1. The next day Bethlehem took on the winners of the St Louis League and, in front of 6,000, drew 2-2– enough for the *Bethlehem Globe* to concede that 'St Louis now has a legitimate claim to premier ranking in soccer'.

That the sport was not as tarred with the ethnic brush in St Louis as it was elsewhere certainly helped to sell tickets, but it created problems of its own. Clubs in other parts of the country were often either works teams or outcrops of ethnic organisations, but St Louis came to rely on local businesses, whose primary attraction was not the sport so much as an opportunity to promote the company name. One of the city's earliest sponsors was the Ben W Miller Hat Company (catchphrase: 'Ben Miller wants your head'), which first attached its name to soccer in 1913 and continued to do so for two decades. The Ben Millers, as they were frequently known, won league championships in 1916, 1917, 1918 and 1920. Few other sponsors in the city proved as loyal, and in years to come the life of a single St Louis club would typically encompass several name changes: Minit-Rubs, Correnti Cleaners, National Slug Rejectors.

The Millers undertook an eastern tour at the end of the 1917 season (losing 2-0 in Bethlehem) as the St Louis League continued to pursue national bragging rights in its own way. But America's entry into the war in 1917 curtailed the game there and elsewhere. By 1918 entries for the Challenge Cup had dwindled to 48. The Southern New England League was suspended for two seasons, taking Fall River with it. The Rovers would return; other clubs would not.

Bethlehem, as might be expected of a team sponsored by a steel company in wartime, carried on without too much hardship. As perhaps the one soccer club in the country with true name recognition, they continued to pull in crowds virtually everywhere but at their own ground. More than 9,000 witnessed their fifth straight Challenge Cup final appearance – in Fall River – though the opponents from New Jersey attracted most of cheers. 'The Fall River followers of the sport showed clearly from the start of the game that they wanted the Paterson club to win,' observed the *Fall River Evening Herald*, illustrating that feelings between the two areas remained high. But the patronage proved of little help to Paterson FC, a National League team which featured players born in England, Scotland, Germany, Belgium and Switzerland as well as a few from the United States. In a victory which perhaps marked the peak of their existence, Bethlehem won 2-0. The scoreline was repeated the following week when the same two teams contested the American Cup final before a decidedly smaller crowd in Philadelphia.

Inter-regional rivalries acquired an extra dimension the following year when St Louis finally entered the Challenge Cup and intensified arguments over the importation of foreign talent. The Ben Miller club, American-born to a man, emerged from the western half of the draw as one of the finalists; the eastern winners were the Fore River club of greater Boston, composed entirely of British players. By now the USFA had changed its mind over the use of neutral venues, and both the semi-final – which the Millers won convincingly over Packard FC of Detroit – and the championship match were to be played in St Louis. Keen to spread interest in the competition, as well as its own influence, the governing body had decided that the final would now be held in eastern and western cities in alternating years. The decision must have delighted the *St Louis Globe-Democrat*, which had earlier declared:

> St Louis really deserves to be honored with the contest, if for no other reason than because of the fact that the Ben Miller club is composed of players born and bred within the environs of the city, whereas the Fore River eleven, the other finalist, as well as the more prominent teams of the East, is made up of players of foreign birth.

More than 12,000 turned up in one of the city's baseball parks for the final, a figure which if nothing else vindicated the financial propriety of the decision. The Millers won 2-1, taking the trophy west for the first time, a remarkable triumph considering the club was more accustomed to playing in 60-minute matches.

As champions, Bethlehem Steel had accepted an invitation from Tom Cahill to spend the summer of 1919 touring Scandinavia. Their touring team included several players from other clubs, including 21-year-old Archie Stark, who would go on to greater things than anyone else in the squad. Bethlehem's own front line had been strengthened by the arrival of Harry Ratican, arguably the best American-born forward of his day, though the St Louis native would soon join the formidable Robins Dry Dock team of Brooklyn, and then a string of other clubs in the northeast.

Bethlehem lost only two of their 14 tour games – nearly a match every three days – and staged a number of baseball contests against whatever local opposition it could find. Cahill, acting as the team's manager, found himself elevated to a level of esteem rather different from what he was used to at home. Both King Gustav V of Sweden and King Christian of Denmark granted him audiences amid the secretary's busy schedule. 'To attend the different banquets and dinners you have to change clothes about three times a day,' he noted, 'and be prepared to make a talk on any subject that may be under discussion.'

Cahill returned to Scandinavia the following season, ostensibly with the new national champions, but because many in the Ben Miller team spent their summers playing baseball, a mythical 'St Louis Football Club'– which included several eastern players – went instead. They too lost just twice in 14 games. Bethlehem almost broke further new ground with a tour of South America, only for organisers to withdraw the invitation at the last minute.

In spite of the rampant political in-fighting, the violent behaviour of fans and players, the miserable weather and the inexorable rise of gridiron, this was still a promising time for American soccer. And it owed a considerable debt to Cahill, who, in the words of one St Louis sportswriter, had 'fought his way into the cliques and inner circles of the old countrymen who handled the game for themselves'. He had made a good fist of the Challenge Cup – by 1921, entries were back up to 118, helping to put the USFA on more solid ground. The older American Cup yielded to its increasing irrelevance, and with the advent of a National Amateur Cup in 1923 it was contested only twice more. (The trophy is now said to be in the possession of a Texas man who keeps it in a bank vault and wants the US Soccer Hall of Fame to pay him $100,000 for it.)

Of course, in other parts of the world the game was positively flourishing – particularly in Europe, where it had transformed itself from a largely middle-class amateur undertaking to a professional enterprise with working-class appeal. Indirectly, this evolution would leave its mark on the US, where immigration patterns were changing markedly. American teams began to take a more central European turn, with clubs named Thistle, Rangers and Sons of St George giving way to others called Sparta, Schwaben and Magyar. In Chicago, the new wave of arrivals precipitated the start of an International Soccer Football League, which survives to this day as the only slightly less grandiloquent National Soccer League, the oldest in the country. By 1920 the *New York Evening Telegram* reported that Cleveland, with its large Hungarian community, was primed for a two-division, professional league 'with the first decidedly stronger than the second'. In western Pennsylvania, coal-mining towns near Pittsburgh were starting to produce gritty teams of locally born players whose impact on national amateur competitions in particular would be considerable.

Soccer had established a toe-hold on America's sporting landscape, albeit some distance behind baseball and college football and the two other most popular endeavours of the day, horse racing and boxing. Yet its subservience to hyphenated-Americans continued to worry Cahill. 'If this game is ever to take its place as a first rank sport in this country,' he warned, 'it will have to get away from its present moorings.' But his and others' efforts to popularise the sport seemed to be bearing fruit. Few could have guessed how high it would climb – nor how far it would fall – in the next two decades.

2. Tangled Roots
The first American Soccer League

*Of course I'm sorry in a way to leave the Old Country. But I'm an optimist –
always was – and I feel certain there's a good time awaiting me in America.
My guarantees are all right – the minimum I shall earn is double what I had
last season from Celtic, and the maximum is double the highest salary I have
ever earned in any one year. Then the prospects! If what I have been told is
true – and I have no reason to doubt my informant – I'll be in clover within a
year or two.*

Charlie Shaw, goalkeeper, New Bedford Whalers (1925)

Few decades in American sport have proved as pivotal as the 1920s.
Emerging from the First World War, the country's prosperity
combined with an unprecedented amount of leisure time to create what
many still regard as the Golden Age of Sport. As with most golden ages
the myth often outstripped a more prosaic reality, in no small part
because of the fawning descriptions of sportswriters bent on creating
mystique and the increasing savvy of promoters and publicists. But
the heroes of the era are still well known to even the most casual
American fan: the Sultan of Swat knocking out home runs for the New
York Yankees; the Galloping Ghost racing across the gridiron for the
University of Illinois; the Manassa Mauler sending another pugilistic
foe to the canvas. In an age when a sizeable minority of readers began to
buy newspapers for their sports coverage, Babe Ruth, Red Grange and
Jack Dempsey – and to a lesser extent golfer Bobby Jones, tennis star Bill
Tilden and the racehorse Man-o-War – became national icons, attracting
interest even from those who had remained impervious to sport. That
soccer could find a place among such hero-worship might seem implau-
sible, but by the middle of the decade the fledgling American Soccer
League had become popular and powerful enough to deprive European
teams of genuine talent and produce a standard of play which many
claim was among the highest in the world at the time.

This is not to say that the ASL is at all associated with the Golden
Age. For many years after its demise, its existence was scarcely recognised. Famous sportswriters rarely attended soccer matches or saw fit
to chronicle such an un-American game. As a result, while the ASL did

provide a showcase for some of the finest footballers the country had seen, none of them became a Ruth, Grange or Dempsey. The league's fleeting existence helped see to that. Although at the beginning of the decade professional soccer's footprint was no smaller than professional gridiron's, the ASL's success flickered only briefly before succumbing to the Depression and to administrative feuds which culminated in what is known as the 'soccer war'.

The years leading up to the First World War had seen a steady growth in professional sport. Baseball was unchallenged as its king, particularly among the working classes, with the World Series established as a highlight of the sporting calendar. Professional gridiron teams had first appeared in the 1890s and by the mid-1910s occasionally drew crowds approaching 10,000. The infant game of basketball, developed in 1891 by James Naismith, a young Canadian minister and part-time PE instructor, gave rise to an openly professional team in Trenton, New Jersey, as early as 1896. Two years later a pro league formed in the area, and soon appreciable numbers of young men were playing for pay. (The game's real strength, though, remained at an amateur level. By 1910 no fewer than 200 colleges and universities fielded basketball teams, about eight times as many as played intercollegiate soccer.)

By the early 1920s, then, a number of sports could be considered ripe for a big-time professional league, and it was scarcely a foregone conclusion as to which would succeed. It's easy to forget how fluid the sporting landscape was in the interwar years. In Britain, too, new sports such as greyhound racing and speedway, and the imported game of ice hockey, enjoyed periods of considerable popularity. In the US, fads such as roller polo, a sort of ice hockey on roller skates, had found an audience earlier in the century, but three sports – baseball, college gridiron and boxing – now stood proud of the others by virtue of their mass appeal. Everything else was still up for grabs.

The ASL represented soccer's first serious attempt at a top-flight professional circuit. The success of major league baseball had established professional sport as a profitable and socially acceptable venture and helped cultivate a new breed of entrepreneur, the club owner. Soccer was outgrowing its aggregation of regional leagues, with clubs of varying levels of financial resources, aspirations and organisational acumen.

The legacy of the war had been the creation of a number of teams with an ambition to match Bethlehem Steel's. In line with other sports at the time, these were clubs backed either by prosperous individuals or 'works' teams, such as Bethlehem, keen to advance their company's name. Such deep pockets had helped to escalate substantially the outlay required for a top-class team. In 1919 the *New York Tribune* reported that 'salaries of professional soccer football players – and of some who still pose as amateurs – are approaching the level of the average major league baseball player's stipend in some sections of the country' and that annual earnings 'ranging from $3,000 to more than $6,000 are commonplace in the East'. Considering that in 1919 baseball's highest-paid player, the legendary Ty Cobb, earned about $20,000, this was good money. The *Tribune* noted that when Bethlehem's touring team had sailed back from Scandinavia that autumn, 'managers and other officials or accredited agents of a score of Eastern elevens of the first rank' were waiting at the South Brooklyn pier to introduce themselves to players not under contract. The result, its reporter observed, was 'a spectacle which reminded somewhat of auctions':

> Bonuses of $100, $200, and in one case, it is reliably reported, $500, for signing up for the 1919-20 season were offered by the bidding clubs, most of which also offered all-the-year-round jobs at simple tasks, such as shipyard timekeeper, paying from $75 up to $110 a week. Of these jobs the players are required to put in short hours and are given two or three afternoons a week 'off' for training.

Among such high rollers, frustration mounted over the slipshod manner in which their leagues often operated. Even in the best of them, it was not unusual for a visiting team to travel to a match without a full complement of players – or not to turn up at all, saddling the home team with hordes of angry fans. Kick-off times were often aspirations, competent referees were at a premium and finding a decent place to play was far harder than it ought to have been. The *Bethlehem Globe* even reported on a match in 1921 between Bethlehem Steel and the Erie club of New Jersey (admittedly only a friendly) which took place on a pitch whose goalposts 'were not at right angles to the general field layout, so that the players were continually at a handicap in their sense of direction'.

Many believed – among them Tom Cahill – that soccer had grown to the point where it should yield something more polished. The success of the Bethlehem and St Louis tours of Scandinavia suggested to Cahill that America was emerging as a soccer nation, and more than a few sportswriters warmed to the idea of a 'world's championship' with the British, as had been conceived in other, more genteel, sports such as yachting and golf. In 1921 Cahill had helped to organise a tour of Scottish professionals which travelled under the name of Third Lanark but included players from a number of different clubs. This aggregation undertook an exhausting tour of 19 matches in Canada and six in the US. They won all but the final game, a 2-2 draw against the newly formed Fall River FC – their fourth match that week.

Far from being dispirited by the results, which included an 8-1 drubbing of Bethlehem Steel, Cahill was encouraged. But he had become intolerably frustrated by the petty jealousies and politicking weighing down the fledgling USFA. The causes were numerous: the game's fragmented geography had yielded a number of rancorous factions; remnants of the old-world AFA were still groping for power; and the autonomous, no-nonsense approach of the secretary himself had produced more than a few festering grudges. One of them was with Guss Manning, who strenuously objected to the USFA's failure to side with the British associations in their desire to exclude Germany and Austria from FIFA after the war. Much to Manning's annoyance, Cahill's high regard for an international governing body held sway. While the British pulled out of FIFA in 1920 (they rejoined four years later, only to quit again in 1928 over definitions of amateurism), the US showed commendable foresight by staying put.

In February 1921 Cahill, perhaps sensing a plot to overthrow him, announced that he would not stand for re-election as USFA secretary, calling attention to what he perceived as a growing band of malcontents, of which Manning was almost certainly one. 'Their efforts to violate rules, or to skate along the thin edge of what is permissible and what is not, and to protect those of their friends who follow their example, have precipitated protests and reams of wholly unnecessary correspondence and time-consuming annoyances,' Cahill wrote. 'As long as this element can be kept innocuous by the limitation of its members, the organisation can thrive; once it gets in the saddle, its destructive habits will have full sway and the end can be looked for just around the corner.'

The remarks proved regrettably prescient, but Cahill was sadly mistaken if he thought the development of a bona fide professional league would offer the game any stronger direction. For all its popularity in the years to come, the ASL would be dogged by similar petty-mindedness and political in-fighting. It also lacked a true visionary, someone capable not only of bridging the widening gap between ethnic soccer and 'American' sports, but balancing the financial interests of the new entrepreneurial breed against the development of the game as a whole. It certainly wouldn't be for the last time.

By May 1921 Cahill's new enterprise, the first to connect the various soccer hotbeds of the northeast, was ready to test the waters. In calling itself an American 'soccer' league instead of a 'football' one, it showed itself to be more pragmatic and enlightened than its parent organisation, which still resisted all attempts to insert the word 'soccer' into its name. Eight clubs were chosen to take part, scattered across a 200-mile swathe of northeastern coastline: from New England came Fall River United and J & P Coats of Pawtucket; from New Jersey, Harrison FC and Jersey City Celtic; from New York, Todd's Shipyards of Brooklyn and New York FC of the Bronx; and from eastern Pennsylvania, Philadelphia FC and Bethlehem Steel. So close were most of the teams to the sea that travel – by player and fan alike – was often undertaken by steamship rather than train.

It was far from a national league, but it represented a significant advance on anything that had gone before it, and the states involved represented close to a quarter of the nation's population. Not surprisingly, Cahill assumed the crucial position of secretary, with Bethlehem Steel's Luther Lewis, the brother of Horace Edgar, elected president. The bonds between Cahill and the Lewises had become strong, and would remain so to the end. The 28-match fixture list – four contests against every other team – left little room for the assortment of friendlies and secondary competitions which clubs had relied on. Reasoning that the establishment of an elite league would create enough interest to make such contests unnecessary, the ASL kept its clubs occupied every weekend from late summer to late spring, often with back-to-back fixtures on Saturday and Sunday. The only exception it was prepared to make – as it might, with Cahill at the helm – was for the Challenge Cup, which retained its status as the official national championship.

Before a ball was kicked the league lost its most famous member, principally because of a dispute over the allocation of gate receipts. All but ignored at home, Bethlehem Steel relied on away matches for revenue, and consequently demanded a share of that income. But Fall River and others did not want to concede any of the proceeds from their expected large crowds – a majority view, as it turned out. While claims that Charles Schwab and the Lewis brothers were not involved in soccer for monetary gain had been treated as gospel by the Pennsylvania press, operating at a financial disadvantage didn't seem to appeal to them either, so Bethlehem Steel withdrew from the league. The Lewises, though, acquired the rights to the Philadelphia FC franchise and, having summarily discarded American soccer's most famous team, proceeded to sign up most of its players. According to the *Philadelphia Evening Public Ledger*, it was all purely in the game's best interests:

> The Lewises are not out to make money. That is one of the emphatic points they make in placing a team here. They are anxious to impress upon Philadelphia the wonders of soccer, for they hold the belief that the game, properly conducted, is the entering wedge of a movement that will soon put soccer in the forefront of American sports.

Other clubs seemed similarly convinced of such a lofty destiny. Many secured leases on baseball parks, which tended to offer amenities like dressing rooms and public toilets that were absent from many soccer venues. Others with more primitive and cramped facilities spent several thousand dollars upgrading them. But most of the attention and the money was spent on players, and here the ASL's arrival was ideally timed. The withdrawal of the four British associations from FIFA meant players could break their contracts and venture overseas without fear of international reproach.

Yet the earliest ASL rosters relied on imports who had found their way to America years earlier. One of the best-known was Paisley-born Bob Millar, a future US World Cup coach, once of St Mirren but who more recently had helped the Brooklyn Field Club to the inaugural Challenge Cup title. Bethlehem had Harold Brittan, who had spent several frustrating seasons with Chelsea, as well as Willie Porter, 'the crack Hearts forward of the Scottish League'. What native talent there was included a couple of notable goalkeepers: Bobby Geudert (who at least one newspaper thought had been imported from France) and Pete Renzulli, a New Yorker said to have discovered the game by accident – visiting the park to play baseball one afternoon, he came across a kickabout and asked to join in, but because of his baseball spikes was limited to playing in goal.

Whatever the ASL's pretensions, its start was inauspicious. Crowds fluctuated from a few hundred to a few thousand, largely depending on the weather. By December the newly formed Jersey City Celtics, who were said to have ploughed $6,000 into their start-up franchise, had folded, their brief existence terminated by a string of defeats and intransigence from their baseball park landlords. The remaining seven clubs lasted the season, but winter postponements and apathy towards meaningless end-of-season matches – particularly when visiting teams had little financial incentive to travel – meant some did not fulfil all their fixtures. This became something of a league tradition, to the extent that the ASL never completed a season with every club playing the same number of games.

Twenty-seven goals from a revitalised Brittan made him the league's top scorer – an admirable feat considering he was injured for part of the season – and propelled Philadelphia to the championship, comfortably ahead of the New York Field Club. But the ex-Bethlehemers scarcely dominated league rivals in the way to which they had been accustomed. More significantly, the move from the Steel plant had failed, for dolefully familiar reasons. The *Philadelphia Inquirer* noted from the earliest part of the season 'a feeling among certain followers of the game in this city that there is not enough home flavor attached to the Philadelphia club for it to have the unstinted support of Philadelphians'.

The cost of ferrying players to and from Bethlehem compounded the club's problems, but theirs was far from the most critical case. Fall River United, a side of whom bumper gates had been expected, finished perilously near the bottom of the table and on the verge of collapse. The entry from Holyoke, Massachusetts, called in to replace Bethlehem Steel, won only twice all season and withdrew from the league, as did Todd's Shipyards, even though they reached the Challenge Cup final that season, losing to Scullin Steel of St Louis. Most clubs were left licking financial wounds. One report claimed New York, whose owner happened to have bought his team's humble playing field, was the only club to have made any money.

None of this seemed to discourage Cahill. In fact, he spent part of the spring of 1922 energetically defending a fanciful assertion he had made in the afterglow of Scullin Steel's Cup final victory, one which handed the national championship to a team of native-born St Louis talent for the second time in three years. It prompted the plain-spoken secretary to claim he could pick a team of 11 American-born players which would defeat any all-British team, even on their own soil:

> They have stood still in England or gone back. The United States is still inferior in finesse; the Britons are past masters at trapping and controlling the ball. But a team of ten-second men breaks up this combination. In America they play the game in high for the entire contest, whereas in England they want to relax. In goal shooting, speed, aggressiveness and other factors America is equal to or better than the old country today. This opinion is shared in Sweden, Norway and

Denmark, elevens from which have met football elevens from this country and from the British Isles, too.

How much of this braggadocio might be attributed to the secretary's desire to send a US team to Britain, and how much was down to rank ignorance, is difficult to tell. Either way, Cahill's words quickly found their way across the Atlantic. Dent McSkimming, a young St Louis reporter, forwarded a copy of them to Britain's *Athletic News*, together with his own interpretation:

Naturally, it is our ambition to defeat some day an English eleven, a good English team. We have become very enthusiastic over the victory of our native born Scullin team over the largely British Todd Shipyard team. We are quite aware that the game is but in its infancy here ... Please bear in mind that if our comments on America v England seem to you a bit overdrawn, we are but young at the game and tremendously proud of our early success.

Athletic News responded with disdain:

The confidence of Mr Cahill may be taken as typical of the land which has a mission to produce world-beaters ... If Mr. Cahill has founded his opinion on the tours of Third Lanark and the views of the Scandinavians who have met some English elevens, mostly amateur, his evidence of British ability is very poor stuff ... No doubt the game is making headway in the United States, but our transatlantic cousins would do well to avoid conflict, and to remember that pride goeth before a fall.

Needless to say, England did not pick up the gauntlet. No American team of any significance would set foot on British soil until after the war, although in 1950 the best team England could muster would receive a painful reminder about pride going before a fall.

For 1922-23 the ASL conceded enough ground on gate receipts to restore Bethlehem to their natural home. New clubs were admitted (including one in Philadelphia) to replace those which had left, but it wasn't until the season had been under way for more than a month that the final entry appeared: the Brooklyn Wanderers, whose very name hinted at its old-world foundations. The club was fronted by a Sheffield-born chartered accountant, Nat Agar, soon to become a pivotal figure in the destiny of the league. After emigrating to the US Agar had, at 17, entered a team in the New York State League. Sixteen years later his boots remained laced, and for a few seasons he occasionally inserted himself into the Wanderers' line-up to become the rarest of breeds, a player/manager/owner.

Another addition to the ASL's intriguing cast of characters that season was Sam Mark, described by one local newspaper as 'Fall River's leading athletic promoter', who stepped in to rescue the city's franchise. Mark was no soccer fan, but the sizeable crowds that had occasionally infiltrated Fall River's athletic grounds certainly weren't lost on a man with such entrepreneurial leanings. Mark was willing to invest in his club, and certainly let everyone know it. Fall River United became known as the Fall River Marksmen and moved to Mark's Stadium, a 15,000-capacity ground their owner had built for them across the state line in Tiverton, Rhode Island. This enabled the team to play on Sundays, which was then illegal in Massachusetts and other states. The change of ownership would soon steer both team and town to soccer supremacy. In their first season the Marksmen climbed to third place with a squad heavily reinforced from Canada. Crucially, Mark had also succeeded in luring Harold Brittan from Bethlehem Steel. The Derby-born striker responded with 19 goals and nearly a decade of service as a player and manager.

But the 1922-23 season was memorable more for the sorry conclusion to the Challenge Cup than for anything Mark or his counterparts could produce. The date of this match – ostensibly the most important on the American soccer calendar – varied wildly from season to season, largely according to the severity of the winter. The year before it had taken place in mid-March; more typically, it was held over to May. In 1923 the clash between Scullin Steel of St Louis and the ASL's Paterson FC of New Jersey was arranged for April 1, which was still late enough to alarm four Scullins who also played baseball and were due to report for spring training. Further inconveniencing them was the fact that an eastern city had been selected as the venue. Nearly the whole of St Louis appealed to the USFA to move the match to Missouri (Cahill even received a telegram from the mayor) with the local professional league offering a tempting $12,000 inducement. But the USFA insisted that its policy of alternating between eastern and western venues – which would prove to be little more than a passing fancy – could not be revised. It scheduled the game for Harrison, New Jersey. Begrudgingly, the Scullins made the 900-mile trip, and even raised eyebrows by turning out in numbered jerseys for the big occasion.* In front of 15,000 at the Harrison baseball park they held Paterson to a 2-2 draw, but insisted they could not stay behind for a replay. When the USFA refused to change the venue, the Scullins went home, and Paterson claimed the Cup by forfeit.

But if such anti-climaxes showed how far soccer trailed behind baseball, the ASL was still a step ahead of one or two other fledgling professional enterprises. The first season of gridiron's American Professional Football Association, the precursor to today's NFL, took place in 1919. It included 14 clubs, but there was no set fixture list and no obligation to play a minimum number of contests (a team from Muncie, Indiana, played only one recognised game). With a number of clubs claiming to have finished first, and the league never having drafted any criteria to settle the matter, the champions were not declared until five months after the season had finished. The NFL learnt quickly from such experiences, though its professional brand of gridiron would still take many years to find its feet. By the middle of the 1920s it attracted the occasional crowd above 10,000, but its ability to sustain mass attention was no better than the ASL's. Some have even argued that, at least for a time, soccer was the more viable prospect.

College football was another matter, growing in leaps and bounds in the 1920s. A tiny Catholic school in Indiana, the University of Notre Dame, became a national institution entirely through the prowess of its gridiron team. Huge stadiums, many surviving to this day, were erected to accommodate ever-larger crowds, including the Rose Bowl in Pasadena (built in 1922) and Chicago's Soldier Field (1924). In 1927 the University of Michigan built a new stadium seating 72,000 but within a year increased its capacity to more than 85,000. The country's appetite for gridiron seemed insatiable, and when Red Grange famously scored six times to almost single-handedly defeat Michigan before a crowd of 70,000 at the University of Illinois in 1924 the college game became a national media event for the first time.

The new arenas had not escaped the notice of Tom Cahill. 'It is a matter of history that better stands have assisted materially in the increase of attendance at baseball,' he observed. 'We need permanent fields and stands of high grade to show our desire to care for spectators and to prove

---

* As early as 1916 the Cleveland Indians had experimented with numbers on their sleeves for a few weeks, but it was not until 1929 that baseball teams wore them on their backs. By then, numbered jerseys had appeared in English League matches for the first time (two games in 1928), but they did not become compulsory until 1939. The University of Chicago gridiron team had experimented with numbering its players in 1913.

we are a permanent sport in the United States.' The New York *Evening Telegram* agreed:

> The biggest problem of the men interested in the advancement of the sport nationally is that of the parks – of modern, enclosed playing fields where big matches may be staged. There are perhaps fewer than a hundred strictly soccer parks in the United States – enclosed fields, that is, that were laid out primarily for soccer football play. The natural tendency of American soccer managers, however, has been to acquire major, minor and semi-professional baseball parks in all localities for the long stretch of months from the end of one baseball season to the start of the next.

Cahill's words fell on deaf ears. There were no stadiums in the ASL that could hold 70,000, or even half that. Only one, Bethlehem's, could lay claim to an all-grass pitch. At some grounds match officials were forced to use the same dressing rooms as the players – an understandable source of annoyance – or change at home. Worse, there were very few places where spectators could shelter from the winter.

For the enterprising baseball magnate, the lack of venues represented a prime business opportunity. The *New Bedford Daily Sun* reported at the start of the 1923-24 season:

> Outstanding in the list of big openings was that of the American Soccer League season in the Polo Grounds, New York City. It is a new experiment staging Soccer in this great baseball stadium, but Adolph Buslik, owner of the National Giants franchise proved that he had a splendid basis for his confidence when he had a turnout of 8,000 for the game. A good percentage of this crowd, too, was made up of new followers, people who just attended out of curiosity, and before half time were standing in their places in the stands yelling. One of the most enthusiastic was Charles A Stoneham, owner of the New York National League baseball club, to whom the game was an altogether new thing when he was first approached on the subject of putting it into his park. Now Col. Jack Ruppert, owner of the Yankees, is figuring around to see if he can't put a team in his wonderful stadium in the Bronx.

Buslik, a millionaire fur dealer, had pulled his Paterson club out of New Jersey after their Challenge Cup triumph failed to galvanise local interest (only 849 paid to see what proved to be their last match there). The National Giants did not occupy the Polo Grounds for long – in fact, Buslik sold them before the season ended – but the stadium became a frequent soccer venue for big matches against touring teams.

Many regard Mark's Stadium as the first soccer-specific facility of any consequence to be built in America, even though Mark also operated a semi-professional baseball team, and his stadium's configuration – with a lone covered stand curiously L-shaped and placed behind one of the corner flags – seems decidedly baseball-friendly. But in 1923-24 it became a fortress for the Marksmen, who dropped only four points there and emerged with the league title, just ahead of Bethlehem. Harold Brittan again spearheaded the attack, but the strength of the team was its defence which, like the rest of the team, largely consisted of former Scottish league journeymen recruited from other ASL teams.

The support Fall River offered its Marksmen may have been feeble compared with the enormous gates college gridiron could produce, but it was encouraging enough to its owner. Though attendance figures appeared infrequently in newspapers, it seems even in the most rank conditions the club could count on the support of a few thousand intrepid fans. When conditions and the opposition were at their most enticing, the numbers swelled to five figures.

Considering the economic conditions the city was now suffering, this was little short of miraculous. 'Spindle City' was no more – its factories had failed to keep up with improvements in textile production technology, and as a result it lost most of its livelihood to the more modern mills of the southern states. As Roger Allaway relates in his 2005 book *Rangers, Rovers and Spindles*, the removal of machinery from two Fall River mills to Tennessee in July 1924 marked the beginning of the end, and the magazine *New Republic* soon wrote of Fall River as 'a city of misery, want, unemployment, hunger and hopelessness. The cloud that shadows her seems to have no silver lining.' That same year, though, the Marksmen claimed the first ASL-Challenge Cup double and began to eclipse Bethlehem as the game's front-runners.

The torch was passed at an epic cup semi-final between the two clubs in Brooklyn, when about 20,000 shoe-horned themselves into tiny Dexter Park to witness the Marksmen's surprise 2-0 victory. The final in St Louis attracted 14,000 to another baseball park, where Fall River beat the local Vesper-Buick club with a defence 'as strong as the proverbial rock of

Gibraltar', in the eyes of the *New York Times*. Fred Morley, a striker with Football League experience at Blackpool and Brentford, scored twice in a 4-2 win.

Mark's accomplishments represented a watershed in the league's development and, despite his city's economic despair, helped to usher in the ASL's peak years. Franchises continued to come and go, but the league seemed on the verge of establishing professional soccer as a viable entity. For 1924, membership increased to 12, bloating the fixture list to 44 matches. In Boston, the millionaire president of the Mystic Steamship Company, AG Wood, bought an expansion franchise which came to be known as the Wonder Workers, most likely in honour of one of his firm's tugboats.[*]

The Wonder Workers arrived with an almighty splash. From the Coats club, they obtained the evergreen 'Whitey' Fleming, still one of the best wingers in the country, and from elsewhere a high calibre of imports. They included Alec McNab, Morton's outside-right, who had twice played for his country; Johnny Ballantyne, Partick Thistle's promising 24-year-old striker; Mickey Hamill of Manchester City, a Northern Ireland international; and two Dunfermline Athletic exports, full-back Tommy McMillan and goalkeeper Willie Paterson. For a time the club was managed by Tommy Muirhead, who had spent the previous seven seasons with Rangers. The Cowdenbeath-born Muirhead had left Ibrox after the club refused to permit him a second income as a whisky salesman, and his arrival in Boston soon persuaded others to join him. Yet after only a few months, claiming to have been hounded by immigration authorities, Muirhead made his peace with Rangers and returned. Many Scots, though, viewed the wing-half's change of heart with suspicion: had he returned just to scout for more players to take back across the Atlantic?

The paranoia was understandable. By the start of the 1925 season the drain on talent had reached proportions perturbing enough for the

---

[*] Clubs of this era were decidedly less proprietary about their nicknames. Philadelphia teams in any sport were frequently called Phillies or Quakers; entities in Boston, colloquially known as the Hub City, were Hubmen; and in St Louis, the Mound City, Moundmen. Other nicknames were ascribed to the surname of a club official: Fall River were the Marksmen and the Wonder Workers often became the Woodsies, while the ASL franchise in Providence were sometimes the Fletchermen in deference to their manager, Sam Fletcher. Several professional teams effectively acquired 'official' nicknames through newspaper usage. Brooklyn's major league baseball club wasn't officially christened the Dodgers until 1932, long after writers had made their first (rather pejorative) references to local residents as 'Trolley Dodgers'.

Scottish FA to call a special meeting over what newspapers referred to as the 'American Menace' or 'American Tangle'. Ballantyne, it seemed, had joined Boston while still under contract to Thistle; so, according to *The Scotsman,* had McMillan and Paterson, Queen of the South's Hugh Collins (Brooklyn) and Helensburgh's Bobby Blair (Boston). What began as a trickle of disaffected peripheral players had progressed into a steady stream of top-flight professionals, men only too aware of their value in the marketplace.

The contractual set-up of British clubs was as restrictive as baseball's reserve clause and, they assumed, internationally binding now that they were again members of FIFA. But it could scarcely stop players from boarding a ship. 'The offer came suddenly, and I had to make my mind up suddenly,' Ballantyne told one reporter shortly before his departure. 'I hope to make about £12 a week in America. What chance have I of doing that here?'

Not all the top players were British, and not all were recruited on the sly. One of the more exotic arrivals was Tewfik Abdullah, a Cairo-born inside-forward who had played for Egypt in the 1920 Olympics. Abdullah, his forename somewhat predictably corrupted into Toothpick, had made fleeting appearances for Derby, Hartlepools, Bridgend Town and Cowdenbeath before ending up with the new Providence club in 1924, where he scored 15 goals. Boston acquired Norwegian-born Werner Nilsen, who had been playing in the city, acquiring the nickname Scotty along the way. Most cosmopolitan of all was the Indiana Flooring Company team, which had obtained the New York FC franchise (and kept the club in that city, despite its name). It signed a number of Scandinavian players, including one-time Gothenburg forward Caleb Schylander – known as Kairo or Skyhook – and his club and national team-mate Herbert 'Murren' Karlsson. The club's new owner, Ernest Viberg, didn't seem to have a nickname, but he had been the interpreter for the American teams that toured Scandinavia and was also a sportswriter for the New York *Evening Telegram.*

But the best player in the league that season by some distance was not a new arrival, nor anyone who had learned the game across the ocean. Admittedly, the powerful and deceptively quick Archie Stark had been born in Glasgow, but he emigrated to the United States as a child and signed his first professional contract in New Jersey. After serving in France during the war Stark made his name with the Erie club of Kearny and joined Bethlehem Steel in 1924. There he set one of the most prolific goalscoring records professional soccer has ever seen.

Stark's arrival in Bethlehem was triggered by the departure of the Jackson brothers, Alec and Walter, who had scored 27 goals between them in 1923-24. Walter, the older brother, was the more celebrated catch, given his league experience with Kilmarnock, but 18-year-old Alec had also proved his worth as a striker. In the close season the two returned to their native Scotland, ostensibly for a family visit, but they abruptly decided to resume their professional careers there. Walter returned for another season in Bethlehem years later, but Alec signed for Aberdeen and never came back. He became a star of Herbert Chapman's formidable Huddersfield Town side and won 17 caps for Scotland, including one as a member of the famous 'Wembley Wizards' that destroyed England 5-1 in 1928. Of all the exceptional players to grace the ASL, Alec Jackson, 'the Gay Cavalier', is probably the most famous – even if he spent only a single season there. And he might never have made it home after he misjudged the water depth at a swimming pool in Fall River and split his head open.

Hard as it might be to believe such a talented combination wouldn't have been missed in Bethlehem, Stark proved a worthy replacement – for them both. In his debut season with the Steel he managed no fewer than 67 goals in 44 games. The achievement was all the more remarkable in that it came in the last season before the offside rule was changed to undermine the stifling defensive tactics that had developed in Britain, a move that immediately produced a deluge of goals and led to the two historically unmatched scoring feats in a Football League season: George Camsell's 59 for Middlesbrough in 1926-27 and Dixie Dean's 60 for Everton the following year. (Dean reportedly turned down a £25-a-week offer to play for the New York Giants in 1928.)

Stark stood head and shoulders above his ASL peers: 67 was more than the second- and third-best league scorers put together, and five times as many as Bethlehem's second top scorer. He found the net in 33 of his 44 league matches, at one point scoring in 15 out of 17. 'He is a great opportunist and given the slightest chance will slip past the opposing defenders like an eel,' observed one publication, which also noted Stark's 'wonderful aggressiveness and great speed together with a natural cleverness which is dazzling'. At the height of Stark's fame, Ed Sullivan, the New York sportswriter later to become television's premier variety show host, termed Stark 'the Babe Ruth of soccer' (at a time when there was a Babe Ruth of virtually anything one could think of). Sniffy outsiders might assume that his rampant form was simply the by-product of a uncompetitive league, one where genuine talent could easily make an impression. In fact, the American Menace had raised standards to levels few other countries could match. In January 1924 the *New York Times* reported:

> There was once a time when a star from England would be met on his arrival in this country by many club officials seeking to obtain his services, but of late there have been occasions when a player from the other side of the Atlantic Ocean has come to this country only to find that the competition was stronger than he expected and has returned again without having gained a position as a player.

This certainly suggested that the ASL had come into its own, but perhaps even more telling was its growing intransigence toward the USFA. The 1924-25 season – in which the title was won again by Fall River, just in front of Bethlehem – had pushed American soccer to new heights, but it also planted the seeds of a war which proceeded to choke the life out of it.

In seeking to become a winter counterpart to professional baseball, the ASL owners naturally looked to that sport for inspiration. 'Organised baseball', as it was collectively known, was firmly controlled by the major leagues, not by any independent administrative body, and certainly not one with any international obligations. Financial considerations, rule changes and even contractual matters like the reserve clause all emanated from the 16 major league clubs. Little wonder that so many ASL owners were reluctant to submit to the authority of the USFA by paying registration fees, obtaining clearances for foreign signings and handing over a chunk of the proceeds from Challenge Cup ties. (Of the nearly $16,000 the USFA had pocketed from such ties in 1923-24, more than $13,000 was from contests involving ASL or St Louis League teams.)

Tom Cahill had abruptly returned to the USFA as secretary in 1922 after his replacement, the Oldham-born James Scholefield, had absconded with most of the entry fees for that season's Challenge Cup. With one foot firmly in each camp, Cahill was undoubtedly the man most capable of seeing off any mutiny, but he proved unable to save himself from his enemies. At the 1923 USFA convention Peter Peel, a former president, was voted back into the position by a tiny margin. Within a year he had sensationally (and quite illegitimately) dismissed Cahill on charges of 'insubordination and incompetence'. Both men were strong-willed and outspoken, but the Dublin-born Peel seems to have been more Machiavellian. He even accused Cahill of assaulting him with a knife during a heated exchange (Cahill claimed to have been cutting a plug of tobacco and maintained that Peel chose that moment to offer to 'take care of me mentally or physically'). Peel was voted out of office the following year and declared bankrupt not long after that, but remained an association figure for decades to come, and his name is still respected in American soccer circles. No competition of any note is named after Cahill, but the Peel Cup is still awarded each year to the champions of Illinois.

Cahill's banishment proved temporary, but it came at a critical moment. His replacement, Scottish-born Andrew Brown, a former Presbyterian minister and one-time president of the AFA, soon found out just how uncomfortable the secretary's seat had become. The professionals' financial demands, largely to do with the Challenge Cup, were too onerous, and in August 1924, a month after a stormy annual convention, the ASL withdrew its clubs from the competition. They immediately devised a tournament of their own, the Lewis Cup (Horace Edgar had donated the trophy), and invited the champions of the St Louis League, whose clubs had also withdrawn, to play its winners for the 'professional championship of the United States'.[*]

The paltry crowd of less than 1,000 for the Challenge Cup final, won by the Shawsheen club of Massachusetts, seemed to vindicate the ASL's intransigence. Their Lewis Cup semi-final between Fall River and New Bedford – a new entry to the league, and destined to become the Marksmen's bitterest local rivals – drew nearly 13,000 to Providence's Kinsley Park, a figure touted by the *Providence Journal* as not only 'the second largest crowd ever to "come out" for a soccer game in the United States' but also 'the biggest crowd ever present at a sporting event in Providence'. Fall River won 3-0, but went down in the final to Boston, despite persuading the ASL that Mark's Stadium was the only ground able to hold the anticipated number of fans ('the whole thing reeks of commercialism of the worst sort', sighed one Boston newspaper). The tie drew a full house of 15,000, but the visitors pulled off a 2-1 win.

Unable to attract such gates to their own uncovered, rickety park – which was outmoded enough for its major league baseball tenant to have abandoned it ten years earlier – Boston were again disadvantaged

---

* The Lewis Cup was awarded to the winner of various knockout competitions until the 1960s. The last winners were the Newark Ukrainian Stich in 1963, after which the trophy found its way to a museum in Kiev.

by box office pressures in the Professional Cup final. They and the Ben Miller club of St Louis split the first two matches of a best-of-three series, leaving the Wonder Workers to assume, not unreasonably, the deciding game would take place on a neutral site. Ben Miller, though, had drawn 10,000 to their home leg, while only 4,000 had turned up in Boston, and the ASL surrendered the final game to St Louis. Furious protests from the Bostonians were eventually quelled by giving them a greater share of the gate receipts, but there was no large crowd – less than 4,000 on an amenable April afternoon – only the poetic justice of the Wonder Workers winning a thrilling match, 3-2.

The US Professional Cup was never played again, but it had served its purpose. With the USFA's financial position weakened by the Challenge Cup boycott, the ASL was able to wring from the association enough concessions to re-enter the competition the following season. That settled the first soccer war, but a transatlantic showdown was still brewing. After Fall River raided Motherwell for full-back Tommy Martin and striker James 'Tec' White, and Third Lanark for defender Charlie McGill, one Scottish newspaper observed:

> Fall River, of course, have paid no transfer fees to Motherwell or Third Lanark. Sam Mark points out that there is no need, nor will there be for a long time. When the American clubs have got all they can get from this side, when they have nothing more to learn from us, they may consider an agreement with our football associations.

Little wonder, then, that by the end of the season FIFA were considering a proposal that would require emigrating professionals to live in their new country for a year before being allowed to play, an idea which stirred feelings of persecution in some quarters. The *Fall River Globe* was in no doubt the suggestion was 'calculated to halt the serious inroads American soccer football promoters have been making on British and Continental European First Division League teams'.

For the moment Mark and his cohorts continued to flaunt international protocol, and displayed similar attitudes towards FIFA's laws of the game, generally regarded as in need of 'Americanisation'. Nowhere was this more apparent than in the international body's austere stance on substitutions, or more precisely the absence of them. The decade-old exhortation of at least one newspaper – 'If soccer football is to be made popular in this country, this is one rule that should be doctored at once'

– remained a widespread view, largely for reasons of fair play ('for an unavoidable accident, possibly brought about by the rough tactics of an opposing player, or sudden sickness, by which a player is incapacitated, it is very unfair to the team that is handicapped'). Though St Louis probably pioneered the practice in 1919, by 1922 American universities had also agreed to a limited substitution rule, ostensibly to entice students into trying the game. It proved to be the thin end of a mighty wedge, which by the late 1950s had helped college soccer mutate into a wholly different beast. Even in the 1920s collegiate rules committees were excitedly contemplating other innovations: four 20-minute quarters, kick-ins instead of throw-ins, limiting offside to the penalty area and even moving the penalty spot back four yards.

This creative freedom, permitted by the colleges' tenuous 'associate membership' of the USFA, was exactly what the ASL sought: their 'direct membership' tied them too securely to the international mast and seemed to be the only thing keeping the USFA in the black. Requests for associate membership were thus rejected, but the veto scarcely dampened the ASL's quest for autonomy. League positions were now calculated in a more American way: not by the number of points earned, but by the percentage of possible points taken. The champions of 1925-26, Fall River, finished not with 72 points but with a 'winning percentage' of .819. This was the criterion used by both baseball and the fledgling professional gridiron circuit (the NFL did not insist on all its teams playing the same number of games until 1935).

The Marksmen lost only twice that season, nine times fewer than second-placed New Bedford, and their arrivals from Lanarkshire had satisfied expectations: White scored 33 goals, and McGill and Martin became mainstays of the league's best defence. Overseas recruiting seemed at last to have caught up with Bethlehem, who dropped to third, losing an unprecedented 12 times, but their defeat of an under-strength Ben Miller club in the Challenge Cup final brought them one last national title. In front of 18,000 at Ebbets Field, the 7-2 drubbing cemented Archie Stark's reputation as the finest centre-forward of his era. Though his sensational goalscoring the season before had been reduced to a slightly more earthly 54 (43 in the league, only second-best), he scored a hat-trick in the final – a first for the competition – and was said to have rejected overtures from Newcastle United ('I started soccer in America, and here is where I stay'). His goal output would never again reach such sensational levels, but Stark remained a fearsome ASL goalscorer for several seasons to come.

Inevitably, some newspapers claimed the attendance at Ebbets Field, home of baseball's Brooklyn Dodgers, had broken the record for a match on American soil. If that was true, it stood for less than a fortnight. A few days after Bethlehem's victory the Austrian champions of 1925, Hakoah Vienna, began a close-season tour of America which attracted unprecedented crowds – and left a legacy that helped to keep American soccer alive, however feebly, for the next 40 years. The standard of soccer in Vienna at that time was extremely high and Hakoah were one of its best teams. Two years earlier they had been the first foreign side to defeat an English club on its own soil (West Ham United, though admittedly in a low-key friendly). But it was not so much the quality of their play as their Jewish identity – Hakoah being the Hebrew word for strength – that persuaded record numbers of Americans to watch them play. Nat Agar and another Jewish ASL owner, Maurice Vandeweghe of the New York Giants, helped to underwrite the tour.

Though they finished only seventh in the Austrian League in 1926, Hakoah arrived in the US robustly promoted as the best the old country had to offer. One could be forgiven for thinking this was what brought people to see them in such huge numbers: 25,000 in Philadelphia, 15,000 in Chicago and 22,000 at Ebbets Field. Their fourth match lives most vividly in the annals of American soccer: 46,000 at the Polo Grounds for an exhibition against what was rather pretentiously billed as 'the best XI in the United States' (actually a collection of players from the ASL's Giants and Indiana Flooring, neither of whom had done much that season). By a yawning margin, this was a record gate for soccer on American soil; incredibly, it would stand for half a century. Though the 'New York Stars' won 3-0 the result was inconsequential. Hakoah had tapped into the collective consciousness of a heterogeneous ethnic group, one still seeking its place in the new world. Even Jews who had become fans of 'American' sports still lacked Jewish idols – their first baseball star, Hank Greenberg, did not join the major leagues until 1930.

Hakoah returned the following summer and so did the crowds. When 40,000 came to the Polo Grounds for a match on May Day, 1927, the New York *Evening Telegram* observed:

> It was estimated by Jewish experts that two-thirds of them had never indulged in sporting activities other than folding up the sporting sections of their dailies to be used as table covers or wrapping paper. Not that they were prejudiced against sports – but such a thing had never been brought to their attention

until the all-Jewish team from Vienna visited this country. They read it last year and many nibbled, but yesterday the climax was reached, a climax that sent thick streams of bewildered but happy Jewish people through the Polo Grounds turnstiles ... The advent of the Hakoah team served as an awakening, for blood ties called the thousands to the Polo Grounds on Sunday, blood ties that were as ignorant of sports as they were eager to witness their brothers in combat.

Strangely, the club claimed to have lost as much as $30,000 from that tour, a circumstance which forced their founder, Dr Ignatz Körner, to resign. Hakoah never returned to the US and did not regain their leading role in Austria – American clubs poaching their best players didn't help – yet they had etched themselves firmly enough on America's soccer landscape for generations of teams to adopt their famous name.

The prospect of a foreign soccer team filling big-league ball parks during the more pleasant close-season weather proved irresistible and others soon followed Hakoah, though none would attract quite such staggering interest. Sparta Prague, champions of Czechoslovakia, arrived to some fanfare in the autumn of 1926, and reportedly drew 25,000 for a match with the Ulster United club of Toronto, staged in Chicago. Sparta won seven of their 12 matches, and were said to have returned home to a heroes' welcome from 100,000 people. Teams from Britain, Hungary, Italy, Spain and Argentina also came across. Inevitably, given the ASL's ethnic composition, it was visits from Scotland that proved the most regular. Rangers toured North America in 1928 and 1930, the same year Kilmarnock made their first trip; in 1931, 30,000 were said to have seen Celtic at the Polo Grounds. Preston North End, the first Football League visitors, arrived in 1929. Overseas trips by ASL clubs were much more rare, though in 1930 a diluted Fall River squad visited Central Europe for what proved a disappointing and ill-managed venture. The club won only two of six matches and made a premature return, unhappy with arrangements over gate receipts.

Though the ASL still relied heavily on British imports, like America it was growing more cosmopolitan. The central European tourists helped to expose a new seam of talent which would be mined with similar ruthlessness. A number of Hakoah players signed for ASL clubs, including the Hungarian internationals Lajos Fischer and Jozsef Eisenhoffer. Both joined Nat Agar's Brooklyn Wanderers, as did full-back Dezso Grosz of Budapest VAC (also a Jewish club) and, near the end of the season, Franz

Sedlacek, thought to be the highest-paid player in Czechoslovakia. The New York Giants obtained another Jewish Hungarian international, Bela Guttmann, later to become one of the most successful managers in Europe (he led Benfica to two European Cups in the 1960s). In New York Guttmann played alongside Moses Häusler, capped at inside-forward for Austria, and Erno Schwarcz, who had twice played for Hungary and later became the ASL's business manager.

While the influx of continental stars seemed to be bringing America closer to the rest of the football world, it was actually doing nothing of the sort. Some ASL owners were now so aggrieved by their lack of autonomy that reports of a breakaway league – playing by whatever rules it deemed appropriate – began to surface in newspapers, many of them sympathetic to the cause. 'The game should be Americanized and must be Americanized if it is to be popular with the sporting public of the US,' insisted the *Fall River Globe*. 'True, soccer is soccer the world over, and the rules have been standardized by FIFA ... [but] what of it?' A columnist in the New York *Evening Post* agreed:

> The American sport public has definite likes and dislikes. It likes some of the things which please our British cousins and dislikes others. It is futile to bring this game of soccer here with a set of rules which are splendid for conditions in England and Scotland and say: 'Here is the game. Take it or leave it'. Many years ago the game of English rugby was brought here for our collegians. But it was not suited to the American temperament. We want more contact, more vitality. This experience is interesting in its relation to soccer. There may be little things here and there that can stand improvement.

Or even big things, like the national championship itself. In January 1926 the *Detroit News* presented the remarks of an unnamed, soccer-ambivalent 'New York sports editor', deeming them to be 'of great value to those in Michigan who have strived for years to stabilize soccer without any marked degrees of success':

> 'Soccer,' the editor said, 'is being played under a multiplicity of handicaps which makes the task of boosting it very difficult. The leaders of the game are its worst enemies because they fail to see the American viewpoint and insist on conducting soccer along British lines which are not suited to American

conditions. The present method of conducting the American championship under the worst weather and field conditions by a special hit-and-miss plan is altogether wrong. The meaning of these national games as indices of superiority is almost negligible. Yet they decide the championship. Why? Because it is done that way in England and Scotland, and American soccer must be conducted along the same lines.'

The threat of a splinter league was averted, but trouble was just around the corner, and it began in earnest with the removal of Cahill as the ASL's guiding force. Factions in New England and elsewhere helped force his resignation and ushered in a more sympathetic and pliable replacement. Bill Cunningham was a sportswriter for the *Boston Globe* with fairly tenuous links to the game, but he had been an Ivy League gridiron star and thus something of a celebrity. Duly proclaiming himself 'converted' to soccer ('the greatest athletic sport in the world today'), Cunningham presided over a more laissez-faire and independently minded operation. Cahill, who had probably done more than any other individual to get the USFA and the ASL off the ground, now found himself removed from both organisations. 'I am not through with soccer yet,' he declared, 'and time will tell the story.'

And how it would. Cunningham duly rubber-stamped the owners' rule changes – with the USFA's blessing – which included the long sought-after use of substitutes: two per team, to be used only during the first 75 minutes of play. This was an innovation which had come very late in relation to other American sports, though it was not until 1965 that the Football League allowed substitutes and another five years before they were seen at the World Cup.

The ASL also commissioned the use of judges at each end of the pitch to help the referee determine whether the ball had crossed the goal-line. And, seemingly caught up in ice hockey's sudden surge of popularity, it incorporated that sport's penalty-box (not yet known as the sin-bin) as a further disciplinary measure. Players could be sent to the box for 'ungentlemanly conduct', which included bad language, yelling or 'making other noises' (penalty: five minutes, or ten for a second offence), or 'rough play' (ten to 15 minutes). Fines were also levied for each visit, though only on registered professionals; amateurs were to be dealt with by the league 'as it deems fit'.

The penalty-box, which resurfaced briefly as a FIFA experiment 70 years later, was perhaps the most honest indictment of the disorderliness which still haunted the game, not just in the ASL, but across the country. Fist-fights, assaults on referees and pitch invasions seemed to recur almost as often as the bad weather. On March 29, 1926, the *Providence Journal* reported matter-of-factly:

> Soccer ceased to be soccer and began to be 'sock' when Referee George Lambie of Newton, Mass. penalized Fall River after Wilson had 'back-heeled' Drummond. The Coats player took Wilson's act as a personal affront and sought to relieve his feelings by swinging at the other ... A minute later the battle was resumed. The mounted police broke it up. But only for a brief space of time. This round saw about 2,000 fans rush from their seats to the scene of the combat and add to the difficulties of the police. Referee Lambie became the object of more booing ... John Harvey of the Coats team had taken up the battle with Dougal Campbell of Fall River. Several other players of the opposing teams had singled each other out for an exchange of compliments both oral and physical. Finally the mounted officers, aided by their brethren on foot, succeeded in restoring order and Referee Lambie was escorted from the field by players, his exit marked by adverse criticism from the crowd.

As it turned out, sending off players for short spells often served only to heighten perceived injustices, while the new goal judges were usually locals and thus susceptible to intimidation. After only a few weeks their role was dispensed with – and, inevitably, the ensuing matches produced a controversial scoring incident which held up play for seven minutes in Bethlehem as the beleaguered referee fended off protests from indignant Indiana Flooring players.

The season ended with Bethlehem interrupting Fall River's run, taking their only ASL title. Hampered by injury, Archie Stark made only 29 appearances but still managed 23 goals, giving him a remarkable 133 in 110 appearances. It had been another exhausting campaign: 44 league matches plus two major cup competitions, much of it staged on the usual glue-pot pitches and ersatz skating rinks. Back-to-back fixtures remained an accepted part of the workload. In one hardly remarkable instance, Bethlehem, having played ASL contests on Saturday and Sunday, boarded an overnight train to Toronto to play in a Monday afternoon friendly, collecting their share of the receipts from a healthy gate of 5,000.

By the mid-1920s the general opinion seemed to be that soccer in America was taking off, establishing itself or otherwise expanding, but in the Golden Age much the same could be said of almost any sport (in the spring of 1927, 40,000 were said to have attended an exhibition of Gaelic football at the Polo Grounds). More tangible was the amount of money now circulating in the ASL. Nat Agar claimed that the gross receipts of his Brooklyn Wanderers had risen from $5,388 in 1922-23 to somewhere between $120,000 and $150,000 by 1926-27. Some clubs were said to be paying out more than $1,000 a week in wages, and Bill Cunningham even boasted that 'soccer players here ... can make more money than in any country on earth'. Certainly it was more than in England, where the maximum wage was set at £8 a week in 1922 and remained there until 1945.

The New York *Evening Post* estimated that ASL clubs that season had spent $100,000 to obtain the services of about 60 players, but plenty of others had been whisked across the Atlantic for nothing, and by the summer of 1927 Europe had seen enough. FIFA summoned Andrew Brown to its congress in Finland and – under pressure from angry central European nations this time – demanded that the USFA crack down on contract-jumping. Fighting to keep his association in good standing, Brown and the evergreen Guss Manning spared the USFA any embarrassment, largely through diplomacy and contrition (to be fair, the jumping was not entirely in one direction). But they were far from out of the woods.

The ASL's tussles with the USFA were only just beginning, as was its pursuit of a more Americanised game. For 1927-28 it split the season into two halves, partly to reduce the number of meaningless fixtures and partly to instigate a showpiece championship match. Here again the league seems to have taken its lead from ice hockey and its Stanley Cup series, since the NFL's first play-off didn't take place until 1933, and until 1969 major league baseball simply sent the winners of its two leagues to the World Series.

The top two teams from each half qualified for the new post-season, which looked at risk of collapsing under the weight of a harsh winter. Some teams played as many as 57 league matches, with half a dozen or more Lewis and Challenge Cup ties to fit in as well. Players were certainly made to work for their wages. As one disaffected J & P Coats player recounted to the *Athletic News* after abandoning his American career:

Matches being played on Saturday and Sunday, we would leave Pawtucket at 6 on Friday evening, travel through the night, reach New York at about half-past six on Saturday morning, leave at 9am for, say, Philadelphia or Bethlehem, arrive about noon, play the match at 3, catch the return train to New York at 6pm, arrive New York at 10.30pm, stay the night, play again on Sunday in the New York district, leave at 11 on Sunday night, arrive home at 5 on Monday morning and then get ready for the day's work.

The most significant development that year was the purchase by the president of the New York Giants baseball club, Charles Stoneham, of the Indiana Flooring franchise just before the start of the season. Stoneham, described by one baseball historian as 'a multimillionaire whose fortune rested mainly on questionable legal securities operations', may have turned to soccer partly out of desperation. In 1918 he had bought what many considered to be the major leagues' most valuable property, only to see it eclipsed by the Babe Ruth-inspired New York Yankees.

Thwarted in his efforts to rename the Indiana franchise after his baseball team, Stoneham settled instead on the league they were members of. His New York Nationals shared residency with the baseballers in the Polo Grounds, abandoning the tiny New York Oval which many considered the worst facility in the league. That soccer was able to snare a big-wheel outsider made it seem a viable business enterprise, and it was hardly surprising that the baseball man was installed as league vice-president. But Stoneham was no paragon of virtue. He had recently been indicted by two federal grand juries for perjury and mail fraud (though he was cleared of the former, and the latter charges were dropped). The commissioner of baseball had also ordered him to dispose of dubious interests in a Cuban racetrack and casino, but did nothing to stop one of the most powerful figures in New York City's underworld, Arnold Rothstein – the man many regard as the pivotal figure in the 1919 World Series scandal – from making use of Stoneham's private Polo Grounds box.

With Indiana Flooring's Ernie Viberg installed as his business manager, Stoneham quickly learned the ASL routine, sending manager Bob Millar off to Scotland to fill up on imports. But his club began the season poorly and finished last at the end of the first half of the season, playing before disappointing gates in their major league home. In the Challenge Cup progress proved more immediate, both on the pitch and at the box office. Victories over the Giants at Starlight Park and the

Wanderers at Hawthorne Field came in front of packed houses, and 16,000 turned up for the final against the Bricklayers of Chicago, which the USFA helpfully staged at the Polo Grounds. The Nationals won, but only after a replay at Soldier Field, where two goals from George Henderson gave them a 3-0 victory. The *Chicago Herald-Examiner* claimed the one-time Rangers striker, 'formerly one of Scotland's greatest centers, and the best one seen in Chicago in many a year, was the principal factor in the downfall of the Brickies'. Stoneham's investment may not have reaped instant dividends, but some claimed that in his desire to keep the Polo Grounds occupied through the winter he had come to acquire a taste for soccer.

The situation in Bethlehem was far less encouraging. Travelling to one of the relative outposts of the league, to play before what even the local newspaper admitted was a 'corporal's guard' of spectators, continued to represent financial suicide for home and visiting teams alike. In March the club transferred a league cup-tie to Philadelphia for what it admitted were financial reasons. 'In other cities we are greeted by salvos of cheers for the other team, but in this city the stands are always quiet,' Luther Lewis observed. 'It is getting so bad that many teams are objecting to playing in this city because of the gate receipts ... Unless we can be assured of moral support and some financial assistance, I'm afraid that the Bethlehem Steel soccer team has played its last game here.' They hadn't, but they did stage almost all their remaining matches that season in Philadelphia, pulling in crowds as high as 3,000 as they pursued a berth in the championship series.

That series, and the entire play-off arrangements, proved to be ill-conceived and poorly managed enough to leave the league's 'professional' pretences in some doubt. Not much thought, it seemed, had been given to who would qualify for the post-season if, as in fact occurred, two clubs finished with the same winning percentage in one half of the season, or if the same team qualified from each half. The single-match championship final, between Boston and New Bedford, was staged on the latter's home ground, the desire for gate receipts swaying officials into abandoning neutrality. The Wonder Workers had reached the final largely thanks to the decision of president Cunningham to disqualify Bethlehem from the semi-finals for their unorthodox borrowing of the Brooklyn Wanderers goalkeeper. That the league's office was in Boston and that both Cunningham and his secretary, Dave Scott, wrote for Boston newspapers were picked up by incensed Steel fans. By this time, though, the season had encroached into June – ten months from its start – and bringing it to an end seemed to assume priority over ending it fairly.

On hostile soil, in front of the noisy New Bedford fans, Boston claimed a 4-1 championship victory thanks to a hat-trick from Barney Battles. The Musselburgh-born Battles, son of a Scottish international, returned home a few seasons later to sign for Hearts, and his 44 league goals for them in 1930-31 remains the club record. But this proved to be the last hurrah for the Wonder Workers, whose success on the pitch had never carried over to the turnstiles.

Under Cunningham the ASL had stagnated. Too many of its clubs still made their homes in humble venues such as Brooklyn's Hawthorne Field, with a capacity scarcely more than 6,000, or decaying major league baseball parks such as Philadelphia's Baker Bowl, part of which had collapsed in 1927 from rotting timber. The league had done almost nothing to develop native-born talent, improve the supply or standard of match officials, or expand into big cities outside its north-eastern strong-holds. It did not even produce a season-long fixture list at the beginning of the year. Yet it continued to perceive the USFA as the main obstacle to its success and the source of most of its misfortune.

In the run-up to the 1928-29 season, the *Fall River Globe* lamented:

> It is for the United States Football Association to assert its authority as the ruling power of soccer and take drastic measures in bringing the professional game back into favor with those who are helping to support it. It is known that those who own the franchise of the teams, figure that as long as they are backing the teams with the coin they will not allow outsiders to interfere ... Without doubt, the Amateur and Junior Leagues around the district are better managed than the American League and there is not a fraction of financial interest in them as there is in the big league.

Hope had arrived in the form of Tom Cahill, who was returned to the USFA secretary's post in 1927 after a three-year absence. Sympathetic to the professional cause, but more deeply to the sport, he bemoaned the absence of native-born talent in preference to overseas 'showmen'. It had, after all, been half a decade since a team of American origin had claimed the national title. The ASL was in no mood to listen, especially not with the considerable weight of Charley Stoneham behind it. Even before the Nationals had won the Challenge Cup Stoneham declared that his team would not take part in the competition in future. His rationale was easy enough to deduce. Baseball, after all, did not determine its national champions by pitting major league clubs against decidedly lesser entities, particularly not in one-off matches separate from the more demanding rigour of league competition. And it certainly did not require permission from state, national and international associations to carry out its affairs. While Stoneham may not have been the sole driving force behind the professionals' change of tack, his voice must have carried far – particularly as his championship-winning team had apparently lost money, a ludicrous outcome for a truly professional operation.

Determined to make the ASL plough its own furrow, Stoneham outlined – just days after the cup final – what the *New York Times* referred to as 'a new system of operation for the sport'. The ideas were undoubtedly radical for their time, but many of them were quite sensible: halting play for two months during the winter to stage an indoor tournament; scheduling late-season weekday games in the evening to attract people on their way home from work; moving franchises from smaller markets into those with major league baseball teams and stadiums; and creating a western league with which to contest a new form of national championship.

None of these suggestions was adopted (although the Nationals were already staging midweek 'twilight' matches), but another one was, and it would ultimately precipitate the most infamous of the soccer wars. Less than two weeks into the 1928-29 campaign, the ASL announced that 'because of the heavy schedule this season', its teams would not enter the Challenge Cup. Of course, the season wasn't any heavier than the one before; the league had simply grown more intransigent. At a time when the ASL believed it should have turned a financial corner, most of its owners were still losing money. Writing large cheques to the USFA in the form of gate receipts from Challenge Cup ties was now more than they could stand.

Or more than most could stand. Three teams – Bethlehem, Newark and the New York Giants – asked the USFA to keep their names in the draw. The ASL perceived this as mutiny and threatened the clubs with expulsion unless they changed their mind. When they did not, Cunningham hit them with a $1,000 fine. Then he threw them out of the league. The USFA sensed its nose had been tweaked. Its new president, Armstrong Patterson of Detroit, gave the ASL 24 hours to reconsider its decision, threatening 'drastic action' if it did not. It wasn't hard to guess how drastic the action might be: the ASL could be cast into renegade waters, left to sink or swim entirely on its own. This, though, was a fate it seemed prepared to accept. The war was on. The USFA revoked the league's membership and the ASL professed not to care. 'No club shall be punished for its loyalty to the parent body,' thundered Patterson, 'and if it is to be a fight to the finish, the USFA is fully prepared to defend its position, even to the extent of sanctioning a new organisation.'

Enter Cahill. Well before the ASL's suspension in October 1928, the USFA secretary had been furtively devising plans for a rival pro league. Now, less than a week after war was declared, he announced the formation of an Eastern Soccer League. It admitted the three ASL exiles, lured a few of the stronger teams out of the New York state leagues and established a 'Hakoah All-Stars' franchise which included a number of Viennese players. Within a month the venture was under way. The abrupt emergence of a competitor surprised the renegades and the immediate defection of many ASL players to safer waters – including Davie Brown, Pete Renzulli, Bob Millar and Murren Carlson – alarmed it as well. When 6,000 fans attended an early Eastern League doubleheader in New York, the new entry claimed a propaganda victory.

But the ASL fought back, bringing perpetually simmering feuds and rivalries to a rolling boil. Nat Agar, owner of the Brooklyn Wanderers, also happened to be vice-president of the Southern New York State Football Association, to which many of the Eastern League clubs were affiliated. He now spearheaded a move to pull that association out of the USFA, and when it did, he took over as its president. The ASL hastily formed a team in Philadelphia to square off with the Eastern League entry there and was rumoured to have planted an agent in Bethlehem to trawl for disaffected players (three in fact did leave for New Bedford). Impudently, it even appealed to FIFA to investigate the schism. FIFA, all too aware of the contract-jumping the renegade league had once condoned, unsurprisingly threw its weight squarely behind the USFA.

There were eight clubs in the Eastern League, but it soon became apparent that Bethlehem, the Giants and the Hakoah All-Stars were in a class of their own. In the hope of sustaining fan interest, player loans were hastily arranged. Bethlehem gave away virtually its entire reserve team and New York Hispano, a former state league team, were suddenly graced with the decidedly un-Hispanic presence of 'Wee Willie' Crilley, a veteran ASL forward who had come to the US not long after scoring 49 goals for Alloa Athletic in 1921-22, a club record which still stands.

As the autumn half of the season lurched to an awkward end, both factions stridently predicted victory and blamed each other for the conflict everyone agreed was ruining the game. In truth, neither league was prospering. The New York Celtics, a latecomer to the Eastern League, survived only a few weeks of the spring half before folding. In the ASL, Jersey City disbanded after playing only seven matches and the long-serving Coats team disappeared in March before reforming as Pawtucket Rangers. Rumours, claims and counter-claims abounded as the season wore on: Nat Agar had asked his players to take a 50 per cent drop in wages; Fall River fans had demanded that Sam Mark bring Bethlehem Steel back to New England; an Eastern League match in New York attracted a paid attendance of 39. Accusations that the two leagues were trying to poach each other's clubs (including, bizarrely, Stoneham's Nationals) also took wing – and as the season drew to a close New Bedford's ASL franchise actually did jump to the Eastern League. But the Whalers played only eight times there. Reportedly unimpressed by the standard of play and pining for derbies with Fall River, they jumped back.

The play-off system each league had originally devised was scrapped, largely because the winners of both halves were the same: Fall River in the ASL, Bethlehem in the Eastern League. A cash-strapped USFA turned the Challenge Cup final into a best-of-three series. The Hakoah All-Stars won the first leg against a St Louis entity known as the Madison Kennel Club – the image of a bounding dog sewn onto their shirts – in front of a healthy 18,000 in Missouri. For the second game Brooklyn's Dexter Park, a modest baseball facility, overflowed with eastern fans desperate for top-class action. The *New York World* reported:

> There were 21,583 persons in the enclosure, officially, and it is a safe estimate that approximately 150 of them, mostly policemen, saw all the game. The remaining customers had a look at the first ten minutes of the first half, if they were lucky, but very little after that. No soccer game ever played in the national championships in this country had drawn such a crowd before yesterday's performance. The sprawling green stands of the Dexter Park arena were packed with tugging and cussing humanity while the hills roundabout were black, white or indifferent, as the case may be, with canny neighbors who saw their soccer without the painful necessity of giving up a dollar. Probably those perched on the terraced reaches of Cypress Hills Cemetery saw more of the game than those in the box seats in the grandstand. Certainly they saw no less.

It was an unlikely conclusion to the most difficult year the profes-sional game had known. In staving off brickbats and threats, injunc-tions and lawsuits (including a $25,000 libel action from Agar, which was eventually thrown out), and the very real possibility of its own insol-vency, the USFA also seemed obsessed with vanquishing its enemies – especially Agar, whom it perceived as its chief nemesis. Interest in the association's professional offering had been patchy, since most clubs were unable to attract the crowds of 2,000 to 3,000 necessary to break even. Cahill's boast early in 1929 that 'the signing-off time for the ASL is near' proved wholly inaccurate as both leagues prepared for a second season in the trenches.

The ASL's position was no less tenuous. Its gates were just as poor and the entire league creaked under the weight of its outlaw status. In attempting to lure Motherwell across for a summer tour it learned the value of affiliation when the Scottish FA stepped in to block the visit. This lack of international support might have eventually placed the league in a more conciliatory frame of mind, but the sight of anxious players jumping to the sanctioned league only inflamed the antagonism. The case of ex-Hakoah Vienna star Josef Eisenhoffer, who didn't seem entirely sure which league he wanted to play in, was dragged through the New York court system. Clubs were as skittish as the players: the Eastern League lost its presence in Philadelphia but recruited a club in Bridgeport, Connecticut; the ASL soon moved its Bridgeport franchise to Philadelphia and Agar created a Hakoah team of his own in Brooklyn. New Bedford returned to the ASL in time for the new season. Fans could scarcely be expected to keep it all straight.

The breakthrough finally came in September 1930, by which time Cunningham and Cahill had disappeared from view and Sam Mark – who had assumed ownership of the struggling Boston franchise as well as his Marksmen – had stepped forward to help broker a peace. The reunified outcome, diplomatically branded the Atlantic Coast League, looked very similar to the ASL before the soccer war had started. All the outlaws were invited back in, including Agar, who merged his two clubs. Bethlehem and the New York Giants were included, while Bridgeport joined for a short time but ended up in Newark.

In November the reconciled factions began their season, but now outside events conspired to destroy the structures fatally weakened by the infighting. Two weeks earlier Wall Street had gone into free-fall, with consequences few could anticipate. The Great Depression would not reach its nadir until 1933, but soon even the most resilient of American sports were suffering along with the economy. Attendances at major league baseball fell from a record of more than ten million in 1930 to about 3.5 million in 1932, while even successful college gridiron teams saw their gate receipts drop by up to 40 per cent.

At first the ASL attributed its loss of revenue to the after-effects of the soccer war, believing fans were still disillusioned. In the main, they were broke. By 1932 more than a quarter of the national workforce was unemployed, a statistic keenly felt in most of the soccer enclaves. Disillusion did cause some to leave the game, most notably the Lewis brothers, whose Bethlehem Steel team played its final competitive match away to the Hakoah All-Stars on April 27, 1930, a 3-2 defeat watched by 3,500. It was enough, too, for the ageing Cahill, who resigned as USFA secretary days after the Steel disbanded in 1931. Unable to translate his energy and enthusiasm for the game into a lasting legacy, the man who St Louis newspapers still proclaimed as 'the father of American soccer' was mercifully left to witness the ASL's death-spiral from a distance.

The *Newark Star-Eagle* offered this less than glowing epitaph in 1931:

> After plugging along for twenty years in promoting soccer, the dream of Tom Cahill has failed to materialize. He visualised packed stadia in attending the championship finals – oh, yes, as high as 50,000, yet when the title contenders played the deciding game this season only 5,000 crowded a band-box park ... It was his belief that soccer would eventually become America's major winter sport. In the far distant future he saw organized teams grouped into leagues similar to major league baseball. In fact, he tried to put that idea across with cities now represented in the two big leagues. However, the necessary capital was not forthcoming with the result that the game's most ardent supporter was forced to clip his own wings. Whenever Cahill reviewed his plans he was told that the weather elements were the biggest handicap in the progress of soccer along the lines he had arranged. Nevertheless the old-timers refused to believe that even rain, snow or sleet could hinder the development of the sport. He always held out for weekly crowds of at least 50,000. Simply a matter of miscalculation on Cahill's part.

With only one defeat all season, Fall River comfortably claimed the first – and only – Atlantic Coast League championship, scoring 84 times in 27 matches. Part of their success was the result of a new striking partnership which featured two locally-born young men: Bert Patenaude and Billy Gonsalves. Both were destined for fame on an international stage, but the 44 league goals the pair scored that season was the first significant achievement of their celebrated careers. Gonsalves's name is indelibly linked to Challenge Cup finals of the 1930s, when he played in eight in a row, with five different teams. The first was in 1930, when Fall River easily disposed of the Bruell Insurance club of Cleveland – or the Cleveland Hungarians, depending on the newspaper – in the best-of-three final series. But the Depression had already bitten hard in the Spindle City (the city of Fall River filed for bankruptcy in 1931) and the halcyon days of the Marksmen were at an end. 'Despite the fact that the Fall River team performed a feat unheard of in American soccer, that of winning every title possible in one season,' the *Fall River Herald News* lamented, 'the fans have adopted a "don't care" attitude that does not make the future of the game here look any too promising.'

But had the Marksmen actually won the league that May? After the soccer war, things were often not as they seemed, and the 1929-30 season had not ended in the spring. It resumed in September – under the more familiar banner of the American Soccer League – as the second of two halves, even though Bethlehem had departed and a club from Newark had joined. The New York Giants were still there, but they were now Charley Stoneham's New York Nationals – the original Giants had been sold and become the New York Soccer Club. When Fall River won the second half of the league, on percentage points from New Bedford, the championship series was once again scrapped. It had been perhaps the longest season in the history of organised sport – 14 months, stretched across three years.

Amid the chaos, Sam Mark claimed one last hurrah. By February 1931 he had given up on Fall River and merged the Marksmen with New York SC. Hoping to catch some of Babe Ruth's mystique, he renamed the team the Yankees. With Mark's Stadium empty, it wasn't long before a consortium of businessmen – including Harold Brittan, now selling cars – bought the Providence franchise and shipped it down the coast as the Fall River Field Club. But within a few months both the Yankees and the Field Club disappeared. The relocation of the Marksmen had come too late for the Challenge Cup, with the USFA insisting the team play under their old name for as far as they progressed. Largely on the goal-scoring strengths of Patenaude (13 goals in eight games) and Gonsalves (nine) they reached the final, by which time everyone but the USFA had come to know them as the Yankees. Certainly on the day of the final they were Yankees down to their uniforms, with the New York press feting the club as its own.

The Yankees/Marksmen won the best-of-three final against Chicago's Bricklayers, but there were no spectacular crowds. Humble Sparta Field, in the heart of Chicago's Bohemian district, drew 4,500 for the deciding match, won by Mark's club with just ten players – captain Alec McNab broke his arm in a midweek friendly and the club had not brought along any reserves. Patenaude, who had scored five times in the first game, a 6-2 win at the Polo Grounds, added another in the third as his depleted team won 2-0. This, a fourth Challenge Cup triumph in eight seasons, was officially the Marksmen's last game, though virtually no one recognises it as such.

The desperate situation became still more fragmented the following year, with clubs merging and folding as the league struggled for breath. By the autumn of 1931 Mark had moved his failing Yankees to New Bedford, but in vain. He then turned his back on the game altogether, to spend most of the rest of his life operating nightclubs, leaving the stadium that bore his name to eventually fall into decay.

One of the last matches of the league's original incarnation also proved to be one of the most remarkable. The New York Giants won the spring half of the league and New Bedford the autumn, necessitating the first championship series in three years. Gonsalves, now with the Whalers, scored twice in an 8-3 victory in New England. Three days later the Giants, who had acquired Patenaude following the Yankees' demise, scored six without reply, overturning the five-goal deficit to claim the championship 9-8 on aggregate.

This amazing result – witnessed by just 3,000, and not at the Polo Grounds but the more humble Starlight Park – handed Stoneham what proved to be his only league honour. His colourful life, which came to an end in 1936, continued to be punctuated by court appearances and allegations of impropriety. Control of the baseball team passed to his son Horace, who infamously moved it to San Francisco in 1957. Partly as a result of this the Polo Grounds were demolished in 1964 – not without sentiment, but with scant acknowledgement from the nostalgic sporting fraternity that it still held the record crowd for a soccer match in America.

Another ASL, effectively a new organisation, emerged from the abyss of the Depression, devotedly propped up by hyphenated-Americans whose passion for the game far outstripped their financial wherewithal. But the

American Menace had long since been tamed, and no one was under any illusions about establishing the 'national pastime of the winter'. Soccer's bid for widespread acceptance, modest even at the height of the Golden Age, had failed, and other winter diversions such as basketball and ice hockey would soon cast it into decades of unremitting obscurity. The Golden Age had produced no bullion.

3. Strangers on a Boat
False dawns and hard landings for the national team

This is all we needed to make the game go in the United States.
Bill Jeffrey, Brazil, 1950

If any sporting occasion was tailor-made for Hollywood, this was surely it: the strange afternoon of June 29, 1950 when the United States upset England at the World Cup. In spite of its place in football history, and the worldwide attention it continued to receive, the match had remained stubbornly obscure to most of America – including, it seemed, its entertainment industry. Finally, in the spring of 2005, came a feature-length chance to enlighten the uninitiated: *The Game Of Their Lives*. Directed by David Anspaugh, who could lay claim to a number of popular sports dramas, the film was shot on location in St Louis and Brazil, and made use of a number of ex-professional players as technical consultants and extras. To soccer fans, it was all very exciting: the most famous day in America's World Cup history at last committed to celluloid.

Panned by critics, *Lives* proved to be a box-office disaster. In its first weekend it grossed only $175,000 – roughly 131 times less than the Nicole Kidman film *The Interpreter* and even five times less than the US release of a Hindi film, *Waqt: The Race Against Time*, both of which opened the same day. It sank without trace. The famous soccer episode may at last have been brought to a mainstream American audience – with the usual artistic licence – but the nation was not the slightest bit interested in hearing it.

Little seemed to have changed in 55 years. The day after Belo Horizonte, the country's reaction had been similarly underwhelming. US sports pages were, as usual, preoccupied with baseball: the Boston Red Sox had defeated the Philadelphia Athletics 22-14 to set an American League record for total runs in a game, and the Negro Leagues had impudently signed two white players to turn the tables on the majors. America had become a country which spoke of soccer in the same breath as fencing or water polo, and its interest in faraway international competition was largely limited to the Olympics. Although the White House had held receptions for sporting heroes and hopefuls from the time of Theodore Roosevelt, the US's humble World Cup entry received no presidential well-wishing on their departure and no congratulations on their return. (Admittedly Harry Truman did have rather a lot on his mind: the day after the match he had sent troops into Korea to resist the North's attack across the 38th parallel.)

The victory over England was all the more remarkable since it came at a time when the domestic game had fallen into one of its most barren eras. Belo Horizonte did not represent the culmination of a series of promising results, nor did it spark anything remotely comparable in the decades that followed. It was not planned and American soccer could not build on it, a missed opportunity that echoed those involving the national team at other momentous World Cups 20 years earlier and 20 years later. All of this was a matter for regret, but it served to make the achievement of its unheralded team all the more commendable – and incredible.

Some have argued that America's 1950 entry was a lot better than most give it credit for, and the result far less astonishing than, for example, North Korea's 1-0 defeat of Italy in 1966. Certainly that upset is far better documented. Most of those who witnessed the 1950 match are dead. The winning goal has not been preserved on film or even in a decent photograph; no one is even sure of all the jersey numbers worn by the US team. The North Koreans of 1966 were a well-drilled unit of pseudo-professionals who had prepared for the World Cup with the support of their government and the public. Their victory was aided by the fact that the Italians lost their captain to an injury before half-time, in the era before substitutions. America's result was achieved by semi-professional and amateur players who had played together only briefly, men who earned their living outside soccer and succeeded more in spite of than because of their country's infrastructure. And they had reached Brazil on the back of a single qualifying victory – the first for the US in a full international since 1934, it would later be determined. Whether the England team they faced in Belo Horizonte was in decline, propped up by reputation rather than form, is irrelevant. Had the Americans beaten anybody in Brazil, it would have been almost as astonishing.

England had played 256 internationals before stepping onto the patchy, bumpy pitch of the Independencia Stadium, but Belo Horizonte was their first against the US. No one knew how many matches the Americans had played, let alone how many had been official. Nobody had bothered to log them – and nobody would for some time to come. There had been only a few dozen, scattered thinly across the years, and two of them occurred before the United States Soccer Federation even existed.

The team which first represented the US, against Canada in 1885, 28 years before the current federation was formed, consisted entirely of players came from the Kearny area of New Jersey, including five from the famed ONT team. The match took place at ONT's field, before a crowd of 2,000 ('some 60 of whom were ladies', according to the *New York Times*). The Canadians won with the only goal of the match. A year later, on Thanksgiving Day, the two countries met again at the same place, and the Americans won 3-2. These were, by most accounts, fierce contests: the *Times* reported that in the inaugural game 'two of the players indulged in a regular fist fight'.

It was another 30 years before the United States played its first recognised international, and 38 before they contested one at home. In the meantime, soccer – with 30-minute halves – was played in a rather constrained fashion at the St Louis Olympics of 1904, where more than 80 per cent of the participants were from the host nation. Two American entries, one a local college, the other a local club, competed against Galt FC of Ontario, who took the gold medal.

The national team's official debut took place in the unlikely setting of Sweden during the First World War, with Thomas Cahill firmly in command. The visit came about after Cahill, in his capacity as USFA secretary, sent a copy of *Spalding's Soccer Football Guide*, the bible of its day, to the secretary of the Swedish National Gymnastic and Sporting Association, Christian Ludvig Kornerup. Replying in memorably understated prose, Kornerup confided that the thought had occurred to him that it would be a good thing if the United States could send a team to Sweden. Cahill took the comments at face value and, receiving belated confirmation from Stockholm, hastily arranged a tour. He accompanied the team as its manager and even served as a linesman on what was later recognised as its international debut.

But he did not choose the squad. The USFA's 'national and international games committee' was pressed into action for its first serious undertaking, and produced a selection far more national in scope than that which had appeared in Kearny three decades earlier, even including a representative from the west, Matt Diederichsen of St Louis. The *Brooklyn Daily Eagle* looked at the selections favourably:

> It is generally conceded that the team is about as good a combi-
> nation as could reasonably be expected to make the trip and
> will without doubt give a good account of itself. Emphasis has
> been placed on the speed of the Yankees to offset the superior

brawn of the Scandinavian players, who are noted for their muscular development and strength.

The unit was commonly referred to as the All-America Soccer Football Club – the phrase 'All-America' had become immensely popular through its use in college football, whose patriarchs selected a paper dream team each winter – but home-grown interest in these All-Americans was not nearly as keen. The team set sail in July 1916 from Hoboken, New Jersey, amid profound apathy and scepticism from the sporting public. 'So dubious were American followers of soccer generally as to the outcome of the enterprise,' wrote one newspaper, 'that hardly a handful of enthusiasts gathered at the Pier to bid the team good-by and wish it luck.' Once in Scandinavia, though, interest blossomed. The Swedes, whose humble national team had been competing as far back as the 1908 Olympics, were drawn to the presence of such exotic guests, and supported the tour in numbers far greater than their visitors were accustomed to at home.

Bolstered by a strenuous fitness regimen that included games of baseball on deck (leaving one to wonder how many balls the team might have blasted into the sea), the Americans arrived in Stockholm match-fit and eager. Aboard ship, and by the margin of one vote, they had elected their first captain: Thomas Swords, whose bustling, energetic style was perhaps indicative of the premium the team placed on speed and stamina. The only Fall River player on the tour, Swords had been on the losing side in the Challenge Cup final against Bethlehem Steel three months earlier, but would lead his Rovers to further final appearances in each of the next two years. Swords also claimed the distinction of scoring what has come to be recognised as America's first official international goal in the second match of the tour, a 3-2 victory over Sweden witnessed by King Gustav V and a crowd of 15,000.

The manner of this historic triumph was not especially well received. None of Sweden's 37 previous matches seem to have prepared them for the Americans' all-consuming desire for victory, manifested in such unsporting tactics as stalling to take a throw-in, playing defensively to protect a lead and even shouting for the ball. There were other clashes of footballing culture as well. The US's high-tempo, ball-chasing style seemed outmoded to a country which had grown accustomed to a less frenzied passing game. In defeating Örgryte 2-1 the All-Americans were roundly criticised for playing in the style of beginners, or belonging to a more primitive era.

A few, though, looked at things differently. The noted Gothenburg sportswriter Carl Linde observed how much ground the American forwards covered and how their sheer willpower often compensated for a lack of technique. Linde claimed this style represented 'a new way of playing' and that the visitors 'form a very dangerous team, mainly through their primitive brutality, through their speed and through their will to win at all costs'. Another writer remarked that such energetic play made the home side look as though they were engaged in 'exercise for older gents'.

Other manifestations of 'primitive brutality' were less welcome. Apparently incensed by their side's defeat – which had come in the dying minutes – some of the Örgryte fans attacked the American players as they left the pitch, pinning goalkeeper George Tintle of Brooklyn to the fence and kicking him. Half-back Charles Ellis of Brooklyn floored one assailant on the way to the dressing room. Trouble followed the team back to its hotel when one ruffian jumped aboard Cahill's limousine and attempted to make off with the secretary's prized American flag. The *Daily Eagle* noted the angry response:

> Calling to the chauffeur to stop, Cahill leaped out and, pursuing the vandal, delivered some well-aimed blows with his cane. He was making good headway toward the complete annihilation of his opponent when policemen with drawn swords interfered and drove Cahill back. The crowd gathered again and the Americans were lucky in making their escape.

The team refused to play another match in Gothenburg. King Gustav, said to have been 'vexed' at the incident, ordered a special commission to 'investigate and punish the offenders'. Cahill acknowledged his team had been treated well everywhere else, and candidly analysed its strengths and weaknesses. 'We were outclassed by the Swedish players on straight football. It was American grit, pluck and endurance that won,' he claimed. 'No great football stars were members of our team, but we had the pluckiest aggregation ever banded together.' The manager offered his highest praise for Norway, who in 19 outings had yet to record an international victory but had drawn 1-1 with the All-Americans in what Cahill considered the 'fastest and most exciting' game of the tour. The attendance of 20,000 was one of the largest crowds ever to gather for a sporting event in the country.

The Americans lost only one of their six matches and their robust, spirited play left an indelible impression. 'We have seen the fresh, breezy rushes of your men,' Kornerup wrote to Cahill – with further under-statement – 'and learnt to admire them and their tactics on the football field.' (The Swedes also developed an admiration for *baseball*, which the Americans had demonstrated against whatever local opposition they could find, impressing the king sufficiently enough for him to introduce it into Stockholm's schools.) The hosts reimbursed the USFA with $6,500 for expenses and the players – ostensibly amateur to a man – divided $1,000 in 'living expenses' between them.

Cahill returned twice more to Scandinavia, taking charge of teams representing Bethlehem and St Louis once the war had ended, but his pioneering initiative came to little. It was almost eight years before the All-America team kicked another ball – and 78 before the US faced Sweden again.

If America's first international outings had been understandably sparse, the 1920s offered good reasons to hope for a sustained and successful participation on the world stage. For one thing, there was now buoyant international competition – initially at the Olympics and then at the World Cup. For another, the rising powers of the world game for the first time included teams from outside Europe – specifically, the Americas. And third, the decade was one of the most promising, albeit fractured and stormy, in US domestic soccer. But it proved to be a lost decade for the national team, and the chance to flourish on what was a relatively uncluttered stage would never come again.

Mysteriously weighed down by apathy, the USFA did not send a soccer team to the Antwerp Olympics of 1920, a decision that incensed Guss Manning and deepened the animosity between himself and Cahill. The secretary claimed only $149 had been raised of the $10,000 the trip would require. Given the often farcical nature of the 1920 soccer tournament this was perhaps just as well, but it was disappointing all the same.

By the time of the 1924 Paris Games the American Soccer League was in full swing, and squabbling with the USFA. But Cahill, dismissed as secretary by Peter Peel, could only watch helplessly as George Matthew Collins, the soccer editor of the *Boston Daily Globe,* was appointed Olympics team manager. ('He is of Scotch birth,' Cahill wrote to a friend, 'and has a "burr" that would make Harry Lauder jealous.') While the thought of a journalist running a national team might seem ludicrous – except, perhaps, to journalists – the responsibilities of Collins and his contemporaries were perfunctory. Hours were whiled away writing meticulous reports for the masters back home and making speeches at formal banquets. Usually a 'coach' accompanied the manager, but he was chiefly concerned with conditioning and fitness. For 1924 this role was filled by George Burford, the 'physical director of the Pennsylvania Railroad YMCA'. Burford's credentials were not entirely irrelevant – he had helped to introduce soccer into Boston's public schools and while working in Poland had been named trainer of its aborted 1920 Olympic soccer entry – but the players were largely left to work out tactics for themselves. Little would change, in the US at least, for decades.

The same applied to the absurdly cumbersome process of squad selection. For 1924 the USFA solicited nominations from club officials, sportswriters, coaches and nearly everyone else prepared to offer an opinion. It then selected teams from this list for a series of 'tryout' matches, basing its final selection on personal prejudice and political favours as much as performance. The final squad was given no preparatory matches; their first appearance as a unit was the day they sailed to France.

They were hardly the best team the nation had to offer – only one player, goalkeeper Jimmy Douglas, came from the ASL – but to the USFA this was much less important than fielding a resolutely amateur team, even though by the mid-1920s it had become clear that Olympic soccer was being contested by nations with differing interpretations of amateurism. The fact that FIFA, which initially threw its weight behind the Games as a means of contesting a world championship, had already begun to contemplate an 'open' tournament suggested it had tired of the need to make a distinction.

The American taxonomy was strict: no payments to players, not even broken-time money in lieu of lost wages (the issue over which the British associations broke with FIFA once more in 1928). Douglas may have kept goal for the Newark Skeeters, but on an amateur contract. Eleven other clubs were represented in the squad, the most prominent among them Fleischer Yarn of Philadelphia, winners of the inaugural National Amateur Cup the previous year. There was also a rare early instance of west coast representation in the form of Dr Aage Brix, a forward with the Los Angeles Athletic Club.

In Paris, Europe once again shuddered at the ruthless American tactics. The French mood had been soured by America's failure to support the country's claims for war reparations against Germany (as well as the US's shock defeat of France in the rugby competition the day before) and the Americans' match with Estonia did little to sweeten their disposition. A penalty from Fleischer's centre-forward, Andy Stradan, gave the US an early first-half lead, but they chose to protect rather than build on

87

it. Amid catcalls and flying elbows they held on, though the unfortunate Dr Brix punctured a kidney to end his brief international career.

The narrow victory sent the Americans into the first round proper, where they faced the more sobering proposition of Uruguay, a team with an altogether more liberal attitude to amateurism and who had organised an extensive European tour to prepare themselves for the tournament. Against the US, the eventual gold medallists scored twice in the first quarter-hour and once more before half-time, coasting to a 3-0 win and prompting the *New York Times* to claim that 'no other team has shown anything like the same mastery of the game'. Collins took solace in the moral high ground. 'We did not win the championship of the world at soccer,' he noted in his report, 'but we did leave behind the impression that we played for the love of the game and sport only.' They had, in fact, played creditably, with the *Times* acknowledging that the scoreline 'was far from being a disaster'.

It also reflected a degree of tactical pragmatism. At half-time the team had abandoned the orthodox 2-3-5 'pyramid' system and pushed one of their full-backs into midfield. Uruguayan raids were thus thwarted by frequent offside decisions (the law at the time requiring three defenders between attacker and goal) and by the zonal marking which the Americans resorted to in midfield. The widespread use of such destructive tactics led the game's rulers to change the offside law the following year.

Chaste amateurs or not, the Uruguayans had produced one of the most powerful and exciting teams the game had yet seen, and four years later in Amsterdam they took gold again, their efforts aided by an extensive tour of the US the year before. Uruguay won ten of their 14 matches on American soil, though the quality of their football was rather less apparent than their irritability. The third match, against Newark, was abandoned after a frenzied pitch invasion which forced the referee to depart under police escort. The visitors, who had not endeared themselves to the crowd by turning up half an hour late, complained of biased officiating, but Newark's owner claimed they were piqued because his club had taken an early lead.

The matter proved embarrassing enough to gain the attention of the Uruguayan consul-general in New York, Don José Richling, who claimed the violence had been precipitated by differing interpretations of the laws. 'It is closer to American football than the European brand,' he said, promising the team's behaviour would improve or he would send them home ('I have explained the difference to them and they will play the American rules in the future'). But his words had little effect. A few weeks later, a match in Boston was abandoned after another fracas which left two of the Wonder Workers unconscious on the ground, and police were again summoned to break up a pitch invasion.

Uruguay met a number of ASL and 'all-star' aggregations as far west as St Louis that summer, but the one team they did not encounter was their American equivalent, largely because it hadn't yet been organised. Once again the US team for 1928 was designed by committee, and once again it reached its destination without playing a competitive match. But it was, of course, rigidly amateur, tightly conforming to the IOC mandate of two years earlier which outlawed broken-time payments. American officials may have patted themselves on the back for upholding the honour of amateurism, but the new regulation was far from universally heeded, and there was little sporting glory for the 11 Americans who found themselves drawn against Argentina, another South American collection of proto-professionals.

The USFA president, Andrew Brown, chose one of the association's vice-presidents, Elmer Schroeder of Philadelphia, to manage the Olympic team. Schroeder's interest in the game may have been wholehearted, but his appointment rankled with many. The day after it was made the USFA treasurer, expecting the position for himself, resigned in protest, while an annoyed Cahill declined an invitation to serve as an assistant. With the soccer war only months away, Brown's regime was already showing signs of the organisational incompetence that would plague the association's frail existence (twice he sought to resign, only to be talked out of it). Even the relatively straightforward task of selecting a team seemed beyond it. The *Fall River Globe* highlighted the case of Harry Farrell, an ASL forward who had gone to Paris with the 1924 team:

> According to information circulated in soccer circles Farrell wrote to and received from the Olympic Committee permission to absent himself from any and all trials, the official communications apparently indicating in clear language that Farrell was so far ahead of any other nominee that his selection was practically assured. But the committee on selections, when it met at St Louis – if it had not already compiled its team slate beforehand – failed to place Farrell, and the reason given was – despite its own official permission – that since Farrell did not participate in the Olympic trials his selection could not be approved.

Participation in Amsterdam lasted all of one match. By half-time, the Americans trailed 4-0, and this time there would be no tactical innovations to help keep the score down. Though an injury forced Argentina to play a man short for much of the second half, they still cantered to an 11-2 win. One version of why the unfortunate US goalkeeper, Albert Cooper of Trenton (an apprentice stage electrician for the Metropolitan Opera), let in so many goals that afternoon was that he had been rendered semi-conscious by a shot from point-blank range early in the match. Other reports, bizarrely, claim he was the best player in the team. But the embarrassing defeat, according to the *St Louis Post-Dispatch*, had hardly been the fault of Cooper or any of his team-mates:

> No one ever believed the aggregation sent across could beat any well organized eleven. Thrown together from various sections of the United States, sent aboard ship without even one practice game to weld them together, managed by a man who apparently did not know his stuff and pitted against teams like Uruguay … our puny, half-baked outfit was doomed in advance. Until America changes its 'amateur' definition to conform to European standards we cannot hope to battle on even terms; and the sending of teams to Europe under conditions like the 1928 team faced is a pure waste of time and money.

Argentina took the silver medal, behind their bitter rivals Uruguay. The 11-2 win remains the most one-sided in American Olympic history, although in decades to come the record would be sternly tested. Yet it marked the beginning rather than the end of Schroeder's spell as a national manager. Not even his election to the presidency of the USFA in 1932 could keep him out of the job.

He had to wait eight years to try to redeem his Olympic fortunes. With FIFA pushing for broken-time payments to be permitted – a stance opposed by the IOC and the USFA – and many nations finding it difficult to field a team during the Depression, no soccer was played at the Los Angeles Games of 1932. Some in the USFA regarded the amateur debate as merely an excuse for those objecting to the expense involved in reaching California, but the staging of the first World Cup two years earlier had also diluted the significance of the football tournament.

For the next few decades, American Olympic teams continued to suffer for their amateur rectitude (among other self-inflicted wounds) but the establishment of the World Cup offered a more suitable challenge.

Though the 1930 tournament was as noteworthy for the nations that didn't participate as those that did – England and Scotland were still out of FIFA, and Austria, Czechoslovakia, Germany, Hungary, Italy, Spain and Switzerland all stayed away – it at least made no pretension towards an amateur code. With the ASL firmly established as a professional entity, the USFA could at last dip into its sizeable pool of talent.

But the tournament came too late for Tom Cahill, probably more deserving than anyone of taking the team to Uruguay. After resigning as USFA secretary he had turned his attention towards developing the game in such soccer backwaters as Tennessee and Texas. The following year found him back in St Louis, attempting to revive its flagging professional league, which one local paper claimed had 'vanished into an apparently bottomless pit of indifference' by 1932. The country's changing attitudes and economic woes proved insurmountable, and Cahill, now in his late 60s, faced a desperate challenge. By the end of the decade, the St Louis League was no more and the 'father of American soccer' had faded into obscurity. 'I am sorry to say the outlook for soccer football, is, in my opinion, not bright ... with respect to its ever becoming a major professional pastime in this country,' he told a St Louis columnist in 1946. 'Years ago, we missed the boat.'

Cahill lived to see the US defeat England in 1950 – he died on September 29, 1951, an event which merited all of 62 words in the *New York Times* – and could take some credit for his country's World Cup debut. He and Guss Manning had advised FIFA of the US's intention to field a team in January 1929, with the soccer war still ablaze and parties on both sides haemorrhaging money. By the time the squad boarded the SS Munargo for Uruguay in June 1930, things had been patched up, but the financial consequences were severe. Without the hosts' offer to underwrite the travelling expenses of the invited teams it is unlikely the US would have appeared.

The players chosen to make the trip were not – as many writers who should know better later claimed – former British professionals squeezing out an extra few years' wages overseas. It is true some had been born in Britain and played for clubs there, but only one had arrived in the United States as a professional. Liverpool-born George Moorhouse had made two first-team appearances for Tranmere Rovers in the early 1920s, but he had played 200 times in the ASL and finished his career in America, dying on Long Island at the age of 42. Those two appearances in the Third Division (North) represented the total British professional experience in the US team.

Of the squad's 16 players, six had been born in England or Scotland, and a few did later return to Britain. Fife-born full-back Alex Wood spent time with Leicester City and Nottingham Forest, but then returned to Indiana where he had grown up, not far from where his American career had started with the Bricklayers of Chicago. The most famous of the foreign-born contingent was Edinburgh-born Bart McGhee, whose father had captained Hibernian and taken them to the Scottish Cup final in 1887 (he later became manager of Hearts). The younger McGhee emigrated to America some time after his father's arrival in 1910 and at 19 was playing in New York. By 1930 McGhee had become one of the stars of Charley Stoneham's New York Nationals, with more than 300 league appearances to his name.

But American-born players dominated the squad, and the ASL to which most of them belonged had developed them as capably as the imports. The captain, Tommy Florie of the New Bedford Whalers, was born in New Jersey to Italian parents and had scored 95 league goals. The goalkeeper, Newark's Jimmy Douglas, had turned professional after the 1924 Olympics and signed for Fall River in 1927. Rather more surprising was the inclusion of the 20-year-old striker Bert Patenaude, who had scored 57 times in two seasons with the Marksmen. His arrival was timely, since the prolific Archie Stark had opened a garage in Massachusetts and chose to stay at home. But a new Babe Ruth of Soccer was about to emerge in the form of Fall River's Billy Gonsalves. While Gonsalves's glory days did not arrive until the ASL and soccer had fallen into obscurity, he remains one of the heroes of the American game, and in the eyes of some still the greatest player the country has produced. 'As a reporter, I always asked the foreign players the inevitable question,' Dent McSkimming later claimed, 'and *en total* they agreed that Gonsalves would win a place and be a star in any team in the world.'

It is not difficult to see why. Gonsalves – christened Adelino by his Madeiran parents, nicknamed Billy by his English-speaking team-mates – was well over six feet tall and nearly 15 stone, and could strike a ball with breathtaking ferocity. Yet his ball skills and deceptive speed (in the unfortunate words of one Chicago sportswriter he moved 'like a light-weight despite his 200 pounds') belied his sturdy frame. Most remember him as a goalscorer, but in truth he was not especially prolific. Far more impressive were his close control and passing skills, and the intelligent and unselfish positional play which created goals for others.

Gonsalves played in Challenge Cup finals 11 times in 15 years, with clubs from four different states. Though such triumphs were largely ignored overseas, his appearances against foreign touring teams were not. Playing with a badly swollen ankle, he scored a hat-trick in a 4-3 win over Celtic at Boston's Fenway Park in 1931, two of his strikes coming from long range. Approached on more than one occasion to play abroad, he never went, and so unwittingly consigned himself to little more than a footnote in the notoriously unsympathetic annals of American sport.

Chosen to look after the intriguing mixture of native and Scottish-born talent were an American and a Scot. Wilfred Cummings, the manager, had been a player and coach in Chicago and, perhaps more importantly, treasurer of the USFA for several years. Bob Millar, the coach, had cut his managerial teeth in the ASL with Indiana Flooring and the New York Nationals after an exceptional playing career that included a stop at virtually every top team in the east. For once, the coach's role was not limited to callisthenics and rub-downs. While Cummings preened his blazer, Millar cast his mind towards tactics. Claiming the Uruguayans represented America's only obstacle to victory, he told one reporter how even they could be overcome:

> They are strategists, fast and game but they have that weakness of tiring themselves out, and we are going to be strategists with them. Just as a runner measures pace and lets the other fellow run as he wishes in the early part, we are going to estimate what is the winning pace over an hour and keep to it.

Millar was not given the chance to test his hypothesis, but his team acquitted themselves well, both on the pitch and with the public. Welcomed by a sizeable crowd in Montevideo (on what was said to have been the 92nd consecutive day of rain in the capital), Cummings wrote that a 'battery of cameramen, cartoonists and sportswriters dogged each and every individual of our party, seeking firsthand information as to our football status and abilities'. It wasn't long before the French contingent – presumably with memories of 1924 in mind – derisively branded the team 'shot-putters' for their emphasis on strength rather than technique. Had 5ft 3in Davie Brown not been ruled out of the squad through injury, their perspective might have changed.

As with most of the other nations, the Americans arrived in Uruguay not knowing which teams they would play, or where. The number of countries that refused invitations or declined at the last minute had forced the organisers to rethink their plans for a knockout competition. Hastily, the 13 nations that did turn up were put into four groups. Chosen as one of the four seeds, the US thus avoided Uruguay and Argentina, considered the two strongest sides. Instead they faced the less formidable Paraguay, and Belgium, a modest amateur team with a code so strict its star player, Raymond Braine, had been suspended for the unseemly act of opening a cafe.

Uruguay's miserable autumn had delayed the completion of its showpiece Centenary Stadium, so the early games were played in the two venues where the Americans had been training. At Central Park, the home of Nacional, a crowd of 18,500 (estimated by Cummings to have included 'some 80-odd' Americans) endured a pre-match snow shower to watch the US play Belgium, one of two matches on the first day of competition. Encouraged by a wet, sticky pitch of which many an ASL club would have been proud, the US were nevertheless 'struck with nerves' for the first 20 minutes. Just before half-time, though, Gonsalves thumped a shot against the post and McGhee netted the rebound. This helped to settle the team, and captain Florie scored a second before half-time with the Belgians vainly appealing for offside. Patenaude headed into an empty net for the third.

It was a comfortable win (Cummings noted toward the end of the match that his charges 'were wisely saving themselves'), and one characteristically achieved through strength and stamina. The Belgians were unable to cope with America's secure defence and incisive passes out to the flanks. A sympathetic referee may also have played a part. Cummings noted that the man in charge, the Argentinian José Macías, 'interpreted the rules more to European and our own standards', seeing fit to add that the 'young man was absolutely the class of the refereeing contingent, both in ability and dress'.

To Cummings's delight, the well-groomed arbiter returned for the US's next match. Paraguay were a much more formidable proposition than Belgium: they had recently beaten Uruguay and finished runners-up in the Copa America, and none of their players had been banned for running a cafe. But there is nothing in Cummings's report to suggest his charges were overawed ('the boys were on edge, simply raring to go') and within 15 minutes Patenaude had scored twice without reply. A second-half goal completed his hat-trick, the first in the competition's history.[*] Paraguay spurned chances and Aurelio Gonzáles's header hit the bar,

---

[*] One of Patenaude's goals is sometimes credited to Florie. But Cummings's report, the recollections of American players and the Argentinian newspaper *La Prensa*, which published diagrams of how the goals were scored, support Patenaude, as does FIFA.

but the US had again won largely on merit, to the delight of a crowd keen to see South American rivals beaten. Flair may not have been much in evidence – the *New York Times* reported that the team had played 'with a great confidence and in a business-like way' – though Cummings insisted his side had been 'flashy' at times. It hardly mattered: the Americans were through to the semi-finals and, stylish or not, it had been no fluke.

Now they faced the team which had handed them their worst-ever defeat, on a pitch twice as large as most in the ASL. Work on the Centenary Stadium had been completed and the Americans found themselves confronted by a playing surface which Cummings claimed measured 138 by 100 yards, 'eight yards over maximum length, according to the rules'. For a team relying on quick breaks out of defence, this was a considerable handicap, and against Argentina it proved insurmountable.

The Argentinians were a skilful attacking force, with considerable bite in the form of their notorious centre-half, Luisito Monti, whose sting had been apparent from the second minute of his World Cup debut when his tackle on Lucien Laurent left the Frenchman scarcely able to continue. No one could have blamed the Americans for feeling overawed by the occasion; certainly they had never encountered a crowd like the 73,000 who were about to watch them. Cummings noted that the teams arrived at the stadium under military escort and 'everybody, including the players, was frisked before entering the stadium gates'. Yet he claimed that only the referee, Belgium's John Langenus, 'appeared nervous and shaky ... the 22 players seemed as cool as cucumbers'. Langenus was a respected match official with a long career ahead of him, but he offered the Americans little protection. Centre-half Raphael Tracey of St Louis injured his leg badly enough to be removed from the game and Providence striker Andy Auld was kicked in the face so hard he finished the match with a cloth stuffed in his bloodied mouth. Worst of all, goalkeeper Jimmy Douglas twisted his ankle early on and hobbled the rest of the way.

Argentina took a 1-0 half-time lead (Cummings claimed 'the ball failed to bounce on the newly-sodden turf' and termed the goal 'quite undeserved') but in the second half the eight healthy Americans lost their way on the enormous pitch. Three late goals sailed past the incapacitated Douglas as Argentina coasted to a 6-1 win. The US had to be content with third place in the tournament, on the basis of their superior goal difference to the other beaten semi-finalists, Yugoslavia. As any fan knows, they have yet to do better.

The small number of entries, the size of their semi-final defeat and

95

their performance in subsequent World Cups have tended to minimise the achievements of America's 1930 entry. Yet they comfortably beat two solid teams and might easily have run Argentina closer. Certainly they were not the third-best team in the world, but equally clearly they had developed to the point where they could compete on the international stage. Sadly, that solid foundation was left to rot. There would be no further US internationals of any description until the next World Cup, by which time the ASL had been completely reorganised and was nothing like the league that had whisked top professionals away from Europe.

The quality of the original ASL is reflected not just in the admirable performance of the 1930 team, but also in the interest foreign clubs took in its players. While Gonsalves resolutely stayed at home, Kilmarnock-born Jimmy Brown, an ever-present in Uruguay, joined Manchester United in 1932. Many of the league's British mercenaries returned home to sign for big clubs, including Tom Devlin, Bobby Ballantyne and Steve Smith (all Aberdeen), Johnny Jaap (Hearts) and Bob McAuley (Rangers). Also heading overseas was a Montreal-born goalkeeper, Joe Kennaway, who had been capped by Canada. Kennaway, with seven ASL seasons to his name, played so well against a touring Celtic team that he was signed to replace John Thomson in 1931 after the Scottish goalkeeper's tragic death in the Old Firm match. He stayed in Glasgow for eight years and even made one appearance for Scotland before returning to Providence after the Second World War.

The legacy of the second ASL would be far less inspiring. By 1933 the Depression had eroded much of the bedrock on which the game existed: the mills, foundries, mines and other lodestones of immigrant labour. Yet in spite of dwindling resources the US made it to Italy in 1934. Schroeder had become the USFA's first American-born president and had learned from the inept Olympic showing in Amsterdam. The Philadelphia German-Americans, which he also managed, claimed the National Amateur Cup in 1933 and 1934, and went on to win the ASL in 1935 and the Challenge Cup in 1936. Schroeder now added managing the World Cup squad to his list of duties, choosing as his coach David Gould, a Scot who happened to be an assistant coach at his old university.

Qualifying for the 1934 World Cup was beset by confusion not only among the more numerous European entries – several of which subsequently withdrew – but also in the Americas, where it should have been simpler since only Cuba, Haiti, Mexico and the US (belatedly) entered. The Cubans advanced over Haiti in a three match-series in Port-au-Prince and progressed to another three-match series in Mexico, where they were beaten. Mexico were now required to take on the US and, for reasons known only to FIFA, played off in Rome just three days before the opening match of the tournament.

The USFA had granted its team a number of warm-up matches – one of them a 4-0 drubbing by an ASL selection which featured a hat-trick from the snubbed Archie Stark – but it sailed to Naples with just four members of the 1930 squad: Gonsalves (now playing in St Louis), Florie (Pawtucket), Moorhouse (New York) and Scottish-born Jimmy Gallagher (Cleveland). The club most heavily represented was, predictably, Schroeder's German-Americans, most of whom were amateurs. That only one of them got to play hints strongly at the politicking which undoubtedly influenced the selection process.

The star of the team turned out to be an amateur from the other side of the state: Aldo Donelli, known to all as Buff in homage to his hero, Buffalo Bill. Twice Donelli's Heidelberg club had won the National Amateur Cup – once over the enchantingly named La Flamme Cobblers of New Bedford – and he scored five times in the one-sided 1929 final. Contrary to some sources Donelli was born not in Italy but in Morgan, Pennsylvania. He was also a college football star, and it was not unusual for him to divide his weekends between the two sports until his gridiron eligibility at Duquesne University ended in 1929.

By 1934 Donelli the soccer player had joined the Curry Silver Tops of Pittsburgh, and he drove the length of Pennsylvania to attend the decisive tryout match between an eastern select team and, predictably, Schroeder's club team. Few expected him to be more than a squad player, but Gonsalves in particular lobbied hard for him to play (some accounts even claim he threatened to quit unless Donelli was picked). Both players lined up against Mexico and, with Benito Mussolini watching alongside the American ambassador, Buffalo Bill upstaged Babe Ruth, scoring all four goals in a 4-2 victory.

Mexico were still a few years away from becoming North America's dominant force. After making a curious international entrance by playing six games against Guatemala in 1923, their national team had gone into hibernation until the 1928 Olympics, and at the 1930 World Cup they lost all three games by emphatic margins. In Rome, the *New York Times* reported, the *Tricolores* 'appeared to be technically superior to the Americans, but they were of much slighter build and were obliged to yield to the more vigorous game of their heavier opponents'. So began competition with what would become America's fiercest and most frequent rival.

FIFA had chosen a knockout format for the surviving 16 teams, so while the luckless Mexicans returned home the Americans were guaranteed nothing beyond another 90 minutes. They found themselves paired with Italy, who had also been required to win a qualifying match – on home soil, naturally – against Greece. The hosts enjoyed other advantages too, particularly the fascist policy of *oriundi* which had given dual nationality to South American players of Italian descent. This allowed Luisito Monti, among others, to exchange his Argentinian stripes for Italian blue. Both Monti and Raimundo Orsi, a member of Argentina's 1928 Olympic team, lined up against the Americans in Rome.

The decline of the ASL and the USFA's decision to send a team liberally sprinkled with amateurs left the Americans in no position to compete with the fascist-backed *azzurri*. Buoyed by a partisan crowd and compelled by the ominous presence of *Il Duce* in his yachting cap the Italians galloped to a 7-1 win, with Donelli again the lone US scorer ('Only the fine goal-tending of Julius Hjulian of Chicago kept the score as low as it was,' claimed the *New York Times*). Once more the Schroeder regime had been found wanting. Scotty Nilsen, the Norwegian-born US forward, confided to one reporter:

> In our two games at Rome, we scarcely knew what positions we were playing. Half-backs were trying to play forward; an outside-left was at outside-right; we had to pull Gonsalves back to centre-half because we didn't have a regular man at that position, and things were pretty much messed up.

Oddly, those two games proved to be Donelli's only appearances in a US jersey. In spite of offers to remain in Italy (Napoli, among others, craved his signature) he turned his back on soccer altogether. His greatest fame came not as an international goalscorer, but as a professional and college gridiron coach.

Participation in two World Cups had done little to arrest American soccer's declining appeal, with neither tournament near enough to catch the attention of a country gripped by more indigenous pastimes. The *New York Times* even headlined one of its World Cup reports **US Soccer Squad Back After Successful Tour**, attaching considerable weight to victories in friendlies with German teams after the defeat in Rome. Having barely survived the Depression, the USFA remained perilously close to collapse. Receipts for Challenge Cup ties, which had been as high as $113,000 at the peak of the ASL's popularity, dropped to below $37,000 by 1937, leaving the association's share at less than $5,000. Schroeder's motion to levy a ten-cent registration fee was passed unanimously in 1933, but there were only about 50,000 affiliated players in the country.

Interest in the game had almost vanished. The deciding match of the 1935 Challenge Cup final between the Central Breweries club of St Louis and the Pawtucket Rangers attracted just 3,000 to Newark's City Stadium. Changing the name of the competition to the Open Cup scarcely improved its visibility. An embarrassing 1940 final paired the Sparta Athletic and Benevolent Association club of Chicago against Baltimore SC, the first leg of which ended goalless. Extra time in the second leg failed to break a 2-2 draw, but the USFA had instructed the referee to play further periods as necessary. Baltimore, though, ignored the order and walked off the pitch. Instead of awarding Chicago the match by forfeit, the USFA merely fined Baltimore $50, then ordered a third match to be played in New York. Sparta claimed its players could not get time off work to travel, and the championship was abandoned.

As its woes intensified, the USFA discovered a measure of salvation in the form of a Belfast-born linen salesman named Joe Barriskill, who replaced Schroeder as president in 1934. Schroeder continued to manage the German-Americans until 1948 and for a time became president of the ASL, but his life came to a grisly end in 1953, when he was brutally beaten and strangled in his apartment. His murder was never solved.[*] Barriskill, a long-distance cycling champion in his youth, migrated to New York in 1910 and befriended Guss Manning, rising through the ranks of the Southern New York Association. His two-year term as president marked the start of an autocratic relationship with the USFA that, incredibly, would stretch into the 1970s.

Early in his tenure Barriskill found himself confronted with the awkward issue of whether – and how – to send a team to the Berlin Olympics of 1936, a quandary which divided the US Olympic Committee as fiercely as the American public. Jewish groups and others who recognised the propaganda value of the Olympics to the Nazis lobbied hard for a boycott that would have deprived the Games of its biggest foreign participant. They were seen off largely by the efforts of USOC president (and future IOC president) Avery Brundage. No doubt influenced by Brundage's angry denunciation of the boycott movement (which he

---

[*] Schroeder was a bachelor, and two weeks before his death a man who had been living with him for several months had moved out. Newspapers reported that he was discovered bound around the neck, hands and feet with venetian blind cords, and with a sock and towel stuffed in his mouth. There were no signs of forced entry or robbery.

attributed to Jews and communists), Barriskill and Schroeder considered playing in Germany to be justifiable – so much so that Schroeder received a special award from the Reich in recognition of his efforts.

Getting a team to Berlin was another matter. With the USFA's funds nearly exhausted, Barriskill – in the brusque, tempestuous style which would become his trademark – collared and cajoled his associates for money. Once again Schroeder was named team manager and, as in 1934, the Philadelphian suffered the misfortune of a first-round draw against the eventual winners (Italy, again). However, he did redeem himself somewhat on the international stage. With no fewer than seven of his German-Americans on the teamsheet (including the captain Francis Ryan, nicknamed 'Hun'), Schroeder's team was only narrowly defeated, though in a match far removed from the Olympic ideal. One report referred to 'a bruising game in which the German referee, Weingaertner, frequently was forced to warn the Italians for rough tactics' and noted that when the referee tried to send off Italy's Achille Piccini, 'a half-dozen Italian players swarmed over the referee, pinning his hands to his sides, and clamping hands over his mouth. The game was formally finished with Piccini still in the line-up.' Italy, its team laced with Serie A 'students', won by a single goal.

Such determined efforts on the field weren't enough to save American soccer from its indigence. After a three-match tournament in Mexico in September 1937, the US did not play another full international for 12 years. The American squad in 1937 bore no resemblance to the one which had appeared in Berlin, nor did it face the same opponents it had trounced in Rome three years earlier. The Mexicans had discovered how to cope with American muscle and won all three matches by embarrassing margins. Not until 1980 would they again lose to their northern neighbours.

If, as some claim, the 1920s had produced American soccer's golden age, the 1930s represented more an age of balsa wood: flimsy, fragile and not much to look at. But it had hardly been the only sport to struggle through the penury of the decade. Baseball's attendances did not fully recover from the effects of the Depression until after the Second World War. Babe Ruth retired in 1935 and proved irreplaceable as an icon. Player salaries dropped to levels last seen in the early 1920s and poorer clubs from smaller cities flirted with bankruptcy. All manner of innovations were introduced in an effort to drum up interest. Some – the All-Star game, floodlights and a Hall of Fame – endured, though as late as 1934 radio broadcasts were still banned at certain clubs.

Professional football, still an uncertain prospect in the 1930s, also suffered badly, its image still tarnished in relation to the theoretically simon-pure collegiates. The Heisman Trophy, awarded annually to the nation's top college player, was instituted in 1936, but its first five winners all declined to turn professional. Very few NFL franchises made money, and the Depression all but wiped out the small-town teams (save for Green Bay, Wisconsin, whose Packers grew into a formidable success). The NFL, too, staged an All-Star game, pitting its league champions against a selection of top collegiates in an exhibition which often proved the biggest draw of the season. Attitudes began to change during the war, but it wasn't until the late 1950s that pro football seriously began to rival baseball for attention.

College football's head seemed a little further above water, buoyed by its relatively affluent fan base and the pristine reputation the media had affectionately cultivated for it (about 50 full-length motion pictures with a football theme were made in the 1930s). 'King Football' reigned most proudly in the south, where very little soccer had ever been played and where major league baseball had yet to venture. Yet there was no part of America where the rah-rah spirit of the gridiron had failed to take hold. The game's popularity transcended mere college loyalty or state pride, arousing passions even along sectarian lines. At many Catholic schools, prayers were said each Friday for the University of Notre Dame to win the next day.

Against such forces, college soccer could make only modest gains. The game had clawed its way back on to campus largely through intra-mural and recreational competition, although by 1937 about 80 schools – almost all from the northeast – played at a recognised intercollegiate level. In the midwest, universities as prominent as Ohio State and Illinois fielded teams, but soon became frustrated at the journeys required to play other colleges and gave up after only a few seasons. The story was much the same further west, where only a few institutions (most notably the University of San Francisco) took soccer at all seriously. In the south, beyond Maryland, there was King Football.

By 1944, the reality of the American sporting landscape had finally reached the USFA, which renamed itself the United States Soccer Football Association. The name change sparked no revolutions. Barriskill worked without pay for most of the 1940s, drafting in his wife as a stenographer and frequently paying staff out of his own pocket. Though the association proudly claimed to be the governing body of soccer in America, in truth its powers were minuscule. It was more akin to a fellowship or fraternity, a safe haven for those hyphenated-Americans too stubborn or too passionate to abandon such a patently foreign pursuit.

The game as a whole fared only marginally better. The war proved more of an opportunity for Americans to introduce their own pastimes to the world than the other way around. Baseball was embraced by the Japanese and rapidly displaced soccer in Cuba and other Latin American countries (particularly Panama, Nicaragua, Venezuela and the Dominican Republic). Soccer did enjoy a few returns in branches of the military, most conspicuously in the navy, where it was introduced largely for its fitness value. But at the same time wartime budgets and travel restrictions removed it from many universities.

Where the sport survived, it did so under peculiar conditions. Most college players had little experience of watching the game and their technique was often primitive. Kicking the ball as if attempting a gridiron field goal – straight on, with the toe and as hard as possible – was a common sight. Others struggled with throw-ins (as did some referees), a frustration which led at least one collegiate league to allow them to be taken with one hand. For a number of years the NCAA even abandoned them altogether in favour of kick-ins. This proved rather more successful than the rash decision to abolish the offside rule, which predictably created enough mayhem in the penalty area for them to quickly change their minds. Well into the 1960s curious deviations – including modifying the penalty box into a penalty semi-circle, which it did in 1958 – were sanctioned by industrious 'rules committees' which did not share FIFA's proclivity for moderation. The absence of restrictions on substitutions – surely the greatest blasphemy – handed even the most neophyte coach an opportunity to win matches through the copious use of fresh legs.

One could snootily argue that this wasn't really soccer at all, but no real attempt had ever been made to force the colleges to toe a more international line. The USSFA scarcely had the resources of the collegiate association and in any case carried no real influence on how it chose to play the game. What political clout could Joe Barriskill possibly carry, running the association's affairs in his spare time from a broom-cupboard office borrowed from his employer?

In any case, the USSFA was much more at home with its own kind: men with colourful first names who still spoke with affection about 'the old country'. It was a world far removed from the American mainstream, and far from a homogeneous one. By the 1940s the ASL consisted of one group of clubs seemingly intent on retaining their ethnic heritage

(Brooklyn Hispano, Kearny Scots) and another attempting to distance themselves from it (New York Americans, Philadelphia Nationals). Yet nothing seemed able to transform the game's appeal. The Open Cup final of 1946 between the Viking club of Chicago and Ponta Delgada – who returned the city of Fall River to the national championship series after a 15-year absence – attracted just 5,000 to the decidedly mainstream surroundings of Chicago's Comiskey Park.

Still, some thought the game deserved better, and even in the immediate postwar years there were people either brave or foolish enough to try to get professional soccer off the ground. In 1945 an attempt was made to establish a multi-city professional league in the midwest. Including as it did an entry from Toronto as well as Detroit, Pittsburgh and Chicago, it called itself the North American Soccer Football League, but it only ever sputtered along, playing a modest schedule in largely empty baseball parks. Partly out of desperation, a team in St Louis was added for 1947, but it ran into difficulty almost from the start. The new Raiders sold just 2,360 tickets for their first home match and a month later drew only 500 on a pleasant Sunday afternoon. When one of the Chicago clubs revealed it was sinking in debt, the league suspended operations. By the autumn some clubs had folded and others had left for more local leagues.

Two decades would pass before anyone summoned the courage to attempt another pro league, by which time the Open Cup had fallen into even more pitiful obscurity. The first leg of the 1956 final, between the Schwaben club of Chicago and the Hamarville Hurricanes of Pittsburgh, produced an attendance of just 941 at Chicago's Winnemac Park. Gates of less than 3,000 became typical throughout the Fifties for what the USSFA still touted as the national championship.

The few people who had been paying attention after the war could scarcely have failed to notice the mercurial striker Gil Heron, who helped the Detroit Wolverines win the North American league championship in 1946. Neither this league nor its rivals to the east had produced many black players: Cuba's Pito Villanon is said to have broken the colour barrier in the ASL but he remained a conspicuous presence. It was hardly a surprise. The 'gentlemen's agreement' barring black players from major league baseball was not breached by Jackie Robinson until 1947, about the same time that black players were allowed to reappear in professional gridiron.

Heron was a Jamaican emigrant who earned his living as a photographer and had played for a number of midwestern teams in the 1940s before joining the North American league. He was also an accomplished sprinter, boxer and cricketer. During an American tour in 1951 Celtic were impressed enough by his footballing skills to offer him a trial, and that year he became the first black player to appear in the Scottish League. Heron scored 15 times in 15 reserve matches, but made only one league appearance before moving on to Third Lanark and, in 1953, Kidderminster Harriers. His football legacy may not have become familiar to Americans, though his son Gil-Scott Heron, the musician and poet, certainly did.

In those gloomy decades it was often the charity and bloody-mindedness of Barriskill that kept the USSFA from collapse, though not without periodic challenges from other quarters. In his 1983 book *US Soccer vs the World*, the sportswriter Tony Cirino gives a colourful account of one such confrontation, with the ex-Hungarian international winger Erno Schwarcz, who by the 1940s had become business manager of the ASL and a key figure in the American game:

> 'Ernie came to the office one day,' recalled Barriskill, 'and he said, "We understand you are broke. We are taking over." I said, "Who's broke? Who's taking over?" "You're broke," he said. "You owe us money." I said, "How much money do we owe you?" "So and so and so." I wrote him a check and I said, "Here, put that in your pocket and get the hell out of here and don't come back again or else I'll break your neck."'

Barriskill proved rather less confrontational towards the chairman of Liverpool, Bill McConnell, when approached about the possibility of a summer tour. In 1945 McConnell had spent three months in the US studying industrial cafeterias (he owned several dozen on Merseyside). The time he spent sampling the decidedly less austere American cuisine soon led him to make a inspired proposition. 'If I could bring my team to play a few games while sampling American malted milks and ice cream, American meats and vegetables,' he was reported to have said, 'they'd go back to Liverpool and win the first division championship.'

That, strangely enough, is exactly what happened. How much of an edge such hearty eating actually provided McConnell's team is difficult to gauge, but the month they spent on tour – at a time when even the best English clubs were still hamstrung by rationing and other wartime restrictions – would certainly have given them a head start. The tour must have also bolstered Liverpool's confidence, since most of the American opposition represented little more than target practice. A local all-star unit lost 12-0 in Philadelphia; the ASL's Baltimore Americans went down 9-0; a combined Chicago-St Louis team was beaten 9-3 at Soldier Field. Soon manager George Kay was admitting that 'the terrific hospitality we are receiving is the only thing likely to beat us', while the correspondent of the *Liverpool Echo* added:

> Apparently the Americans, in an effort to repay some of the hospitality extended to their servicemen in this country, are being exceptionally lavish in the entertaining line – and they were never behindhand in that even before the war ... British clubs, harassed by the difficulty in getting gear and balls, will envy the Americans, where there is apparently no shortage. At any rate, Mr Kay says they used six balls in the floodlit game in Baltimore. 'It was wonderfully clear under the lights,' he said, 'but the main trouble is that the white ball soon gets discoloured and has to be changed.' One other snag was the press photographers letting off their flashlights behind the goal.

Their appetite sated in every sense of the word, Liverpool returned to Anfield with ten victories out of ten. Their nine US matches had attracted about 100,000 fans and grossed nearly $93,000, earning the USSFA a cut of about $7,000. Nearly 20,000 saw the opening match in New York, with 16,000 returning a week later; 12,000 turned out in Kearny and even 7,000 braved a miserably chilly day in Chicago. 'If an epidemic of foreign soccer team visitations develops in this country,' one St Louis sportswriter joked, 'just charge it to our United States food ... soccer elevens, it appears, are like armies – they travel on their stomachs.'

Liverpool were the country's first significant postwar visitors, and the success of their tour encouraged others to follow. The next summer 43,000 were at Yankee Stadium for the visit of Hapoel Tel-Aviv, even though the match was shown on local television (possibly a first for American soccer). But like the interest in Hakoah Vienna two decades earlier – and with the added intensity given to Jewish-American identity by the Holocaust – interest stemmed more from ethnic solidarity than soccer. The following year 25,000 turned up to watch the new national team of Israel play at the Polo Grounds.

Liverpool came back in 1948 for another helping of malted milks and created a new landmark. Their 3-2 win over Djurgården at Ebbets Field in Brooklyn was the first time two foreign professional clubs had played each other on US soil. The 18,000 in attendance helped confirm what some had begun to suspect: fans were more interested in top-quality soccer than the presence of a local team to cheer for.

The following summer Newcastle United, Internazionale and Belfast Celtic came across, with the Geordies even playing several matches in the hinterland of the Pacific northwest. Organisers began scheduling what were sometimes referred to as 'dream doubleheaders', two matches in the same stadium on the same day. Amid such keenly promoted exhibitions the ASL quickly learned its place. In May 1949 Belfast Celtic, who had just withdrawn from the Irish League over sectarian tensions and would soon disappear altogether, took part in one such event, facing a local all-star team in New York. The preliminary match happened to be the ASL's play-off final. When that ended 2-2, necessitating extra time, Belfast's match still kicked off as scheduled, leaving the New York Americans and Philadelphia Nationals to settle the fate of the league championship later in the day.

Another doubleheader, played in New York in June 1949, drew 17,000 to see a somewhat incongruous assortment of teams. Newcastle defeated IFK Gothenburg (or Kamraterna as the local press referred to them – the 'K' in IFK meaning 'comrades') in the second game, but the first attracted most of the support. A Scottish XI – the full national team, by most accounts – survived what the *Glasgow Herald* perceived as the 'over-robust and irritating tactics' of a US national selection to win 4-0 in what was very close to a full international. (Probably because it agreed to allow substitutes, the Scottish FA don't recognise it as such, but since at that time an American national team didn't really exist outside formal tournaments the point is academic.)

Yet Scottish football's exceptionally strong ties to the States were loosening. Though they had sent across teams of various descriptions in 1935 and 1939, four decades now passed before they did so again. The 1949 tour was the most extensive of the US ever undertaken by a British national team and a convincing representation at that. The squad included Derby's Billy Steel and Rangers' Willie Waddell in attack, and hardly anyone who was not either an international or about to become one. Needless to say, they won without much trouble – even in the 35-degree heat of Philadelphia they claimed an 8-1 win over the local all-stars. Here too, competition seemed to be of less importance than gastronomy. The *Herald* correspondent noted that the touring players were more often than not 'in a paradise of food ... The helpings are enormous compared to our austerity standards.'

Of course, not everything was as impressive. The 'generally narrow and bumpy' pitches with their 'great bare patches caused by the exertions of the baseball players' left the *Herald* to ruefully conclude that soccer in America would 'never attain world ranking until the pitches are developed exclusively for football'. Other native predilections were treated with similar disapproval:

> The Scottish players have now become used to the American pre-match ceremonial which involves a procession with the players included and then their announcement one by one via the loudspeaker. Each man comes out to the applause of the crowd ... the Scots, however, cannot become accustomed to the announcer who every few minutes during a game bawls out some elementary (to the Scots) commentary about a decision or the identity of the man who just kicked the ball.

The modest success of the foreign tours may have helped put a few dollars in the USSFA's pocket, but they did little to raise the standard of domestic play. At the London Olympics of 1948, the performance of the US team was not nearly as noteworthy as that of the association, which by the usual excruciating means unveiled yet another ill-prepared squad. A shortlist of about 5,000 players, whittled down through several months of trial matches and committee decisions, resulted in the final unit arriving in Brentford without so much as a training session to its name. Poland's withdrawal from the tournament left the Americans once again facing Italy (a startlingly recurring opponent) and another heavy defeat. The USSFA Olympic Soccer Committee's post-mortem is an archetype of austerity and naivety (not to mention poor grammar):

> Naturally, that 9-0 score is discouraging but the USSFA should be proud of the US Olympic soccer team. All of them conducted themselves as gentlemen and sportsman and made many friend for the United States in London and the other places they visited ... If at all possible, the US Olympic team should be assembled several weeks prior to sailing so that combination play could be developed. Our team can compete on a equal basis with most of the countries entered in the Olympics but we must give the team a chance to practice as a unit.

The report pointed with pride to a 2-0 defeat of a Korean XI in a friendly ('much to the surprise of many of the teams from other countries') but was less forthcoming on the trouncings the team received on the journey home: 11-0 to Norway in Oslo, a loss described only as being 'by a one-sided score', and 5-0 in Belfast to a Northern Ireland XI which 'fielded six professional players'.

It hardly suggested that the national team's greatest achievement was just around the corner, although when the time came to qualify for the 1950 World Cup in Brazil there was at least the nucleus of an Olympic team to work with. Midfielder Walter Bahr had grown up in Philadelphia's soccer-friendly Kensington district, becoming a star for Temple University before joining the ASL's Philadelphia Nationals. Charlie Colombo, an archetypal tough-as-nails centre-half, came from the Italian section of St Louis known as The Hill or *La Montagna* (sometimes denoted as Dago Hill on city maps of the time), and helped the Simpkins Ford club to an Open Cup triumph in 1948. Inside-forward John Souza of Fall River, better known as Clarkie, was probably the most talented player in the team, exceptionally agile and unusually comfortable with the ball at his feet.

To get to Brazil, all the Americans had to do was finish first or second in a three-team North American qualifying tournament, albeit one which took place entirely in Mexico in the space of 17 days. With the Mexicans likely to qualify no matter where they played, both the US and the other participant, Cuba, were apparently happy to play away from home for the extra gate money.

Finishing second in a three-nation tournament may have seemed achievable, but this was an American team that hadn't scored a goal in a full international since the war. Hopes receded further after the opening match, a 6-0 trouncing by the hosts in the thin air and midday heat of Mexico City, a result which quickly ruled out any thoughts of first place. But what really mattered was how much further Cuba had succumbed to baseball. In an attempt to revive their country's flagging soccer interest, the Cubans had in 1947 staged a North American Championship, but attendance was so pitiful the tournament was abandoned. The US had sent a 'national' team in the form of Ponta Delgada, the Fall River club that had won both the Amateur and Open Cups that year, but they were hopelessly outmanned. Such was the USSFA's gratitude that Ponta found themselves financing the trip out of their own pocket.

Now, two years later, those championships were revived with World Cup berths at stake. In their first match against Cuba the Americans managed a goal – their first in more than nine hours of international play – and held on for a 1-1 draw. More importantly, they discovered that the Cubans were beatable. Although a 6-2 defeat in the return match with the *Tricolores* wrapped up the North American championship for the hosts, it offered further signs of US progress – some reports even claimed the scoreline had flattered the winners. By the time of the final, decisive match, the American team had grown used to the Mexico City air, and to each other. Largely through the eccentricities of a reserve Cuban goalkeeper, they scored four before half-time and held on for a 5-2 win, qualifying for Brazil on the back of what would ultimately be recognised as their only international victory in 15 years.

The novel experience of an extended run of matches for the same group of players had helped, but the American team had not spent its days in Mexico as one big, happy family. Its manager, Walter Giesler of St Louis – the author of the misleading 1948 Olympic report – was also president of the USSFA, and, as with Elmer Schroeder decades earlier, team selection carried a pungent whiff of favouritism. One Chicago soccer paper bitterly insisted that 'full-time use of four St Louis players killed all chances of harmony on the team ... Only loyalty to their country prevented a walkout and an early return home by certain players and officials.'

Striker Jack Hynes of the New York Americans, an ever-present in Mexico City, harboured similar reservations but made the mistake of voicing them to a journalist friend. When his mild criticism – 'A postcard from Jacky Hynes in Mexico thinks that we could have fielded a better team' – accidentally ended up in print, the USSFA responded hysterically. Hynes, who had played well in Mexico and was certainly one of the country's best forwards, was never chosen again.

One of Hynes's striking partners, Ben McLaughlin of Philadelphia, didn't go to Brazil either, but only because he couldn't get time off work. Pete Matevich of Chicago, who had scored twice in the win over Cuba, also stayed at home. In fact, only six players from Mexico ended up at the World Cup. Even those who were selected had other jobs to work around: delivering the mail, designing carpets, stripping wallpaper. Six of the final 17 were from St Louis, the city in which the final trial match had been staged, and from where Giesler also obtained his trainer, Bill 'Chubby' Lyons.

Bahr, Colombo and Souza were in the squad, as were striker Gino Pariani and Harry Keough, a St Louis amateur full-back who later admitted he owed his place to Giesler. Of the other three St Louisans, goalkeeper Frank Borghi and forward Frank Wallace had played in Mexico. Christened Valicenti, Wallace was better known as Pee Wee.

He, Colombo, Pariani and Borghi all played for the Simpkins Ford club that had claimed the Open Cup that year. Two of them had something else in common: Wallace had spent more than a year in a German POW camp after his tank had been set on fire at Anzio and Borghi had been decorated for his actions as a field medic in Normandy, having enlisted at 19. Wide-eyed youngsters they were not.

All of them played every minute in Brazil, as did an eccentric 25-year-old centre-forward named Joe Gaetjens, who had not gone to Mexico. Born in Port-au-Prince, Gaetjens had come to New York on a scholarship from the Haitian government to attend Columbia University. He was not an American citizen, though he had obtained papers denoting an intent to become one. That was enough for the USSFA – that and the 18 goals he had scored for Brookhattan in the ASL over the season. And, at the time, what was good enough for the USSFA was good enough for FIFA.

Gaetjens was joined by two others in similar circumstances: Scottish-born Ed McIlvenny, who had been on Wrexham's books before joining the Philadelphia Nationals; and Joe Maca, who had played in the Belgian Third Division and emigrated to New York after the war. Few of the others were foreign-born. The most notable was Adam Wolanin, once of the Polish first division but now a naturalised American citizen playing in Chicago, and who in any case featured in only one match.

This motley collection did not suffer the usual fate of meeting each other for the first time on their way out of the country, though the two test matches arranged by the USSFA hardly amounted to methodical preparation. Against touring Besiktas in St Louis, before barely 2,000 fans, the Americans lost 5-0 in a match which saw several of the eastern players substituted early in the second half to enable them to catch flights home. 'Coach Eric Keen of the Turkish team said he expected to find more skill in the American players,' reported Dent McSkimming, who also remarked that 'few individuals in the United States team appeared to advantage'. Things changed when the team reconvened a few weeks later in New York. Fielding the same line-up that would begin their World Cup campaign, the US held a touring English FA XI – which included Nat Lofthouse and Stanley Matthews – to a 1-0 victory (a result achieved in blue-and-white quartered jerseys emblazoned with an 'H', thought to have been borrowed from the ASL's Brooklyn Hakoah team). It was true that the English tourists had played 12 games in little over a month, though scorelines like the 19-1 defeat they handed a team in Saskatoon suggest they were far from taxed, and four of their players who had been named in the World Cup squad had left for home early.

The US coach, Bill Jeffrey, did not set much store by the result. Chosen from the university ranks and appointed less than two weeks before the team set out on its 30-hour, six-airport expedition to Brazil, he was a hasty replacement for the original candidate, Erno Schwarcz. Born in Edinburgh, Jeffrey might have ended up playing in the Scottish League had he not suffered the double misfortune of an injury and a disapproving mother. Sent to live with an uncle in Pennsylvania, he found work as a railway mechanic and became involved in the works team. His success there eventually led to a coaching position at Penn State College, where he stayed for 27 years. His 1935 side – which had benefited from an enlightening, if humbling, tour of his native country the year before – went through the entire season without so much as conceding a goal, and in 1951 he honoured a request from the US State Department to send his team on a goodwill tour of Iran.

Making waves in the peculiar world of college soccer may not have qualified Jeffrey to run a World Cup team (Penn State conceded 64 goals during their eight-match 1934 Scottish tour), but in American circles few coaches were more widely respected, or would leave a greater legacy. Well after his death in 1966 – from a heart attack at a coaching conference – the instructional book Jeffrey wrote during the early part of his tenure, *The Boys With the Educated Feet*, could be seen in the offices of novice American coaches desperate for college-friendly instructional material.

The soft-spoken Scotsman freely admitted his team stood no chance in Brazil, and his squad, unashamedly aware of its amateur standing in a world of professionals, seemed to be characterised by a gallows humour. Team-mates christened Borghi 'the Six-Goal Wonder', and with no trace of irony – holding opponents to half a dozen goals was considered a mark of his talent. A lanky man with huge hands, Borghi was a hearse driver by trade. By his own admission he was not much of a soccer player, and had aspired to play professional baseball. His name did not appear on the USSF's initial shortlist, and many expected Gino Gardissanich, the Most Valuable Player of the National League of Chicago, to make the starting line-up. But Borghi's natural hand-eye co-ordination and ball-handling ability, honed by his brief career on minor-league baseball diamonds, overcame many of his technical deficiencies, and that spring they had helped Simpkins Ford to the Open Cup.

Before the mighty upset of England there was Spain – a match largely forgotten in the light of what followed, but one remarkable enough in its own right. Pariani gave the US an early lead, which they held for over an hour before tiring and, in the last ten minutes, collapsing: Spain scored three times to win 3-1. The capitulation might partly be attributed to the 30-minute halves the St Louis leagues still adhered to, but for a team used to losing to lesser opposition by margins two or three times as great, it was a creditable performance. Not only had the team shown its tenacity and spirit, the scoreline had flushed them with confidence. Without this, it's hard to imagine the US not being overwhelmed by England.

Only one member of the American press corps turned up in Brazil, on his own time and largely at his own expense. Dent McSkimming, steadfast 53-year-old correspondent of the *St Louis Post-Dispatch*, was one of the few US journalists even aware of the significance of the competition. A well-travelled, erudite man, McSkimming had covered soccer for decades, and with a devotion few could match. In the 1920s, he had taken leave of absence from his newspaper job and worked in the engine room of a merchant ship bound for England, home of the Football League. McSkimming preferred watching from an isolated part of the ground to the disconcerting chatter of the press-box. ('I never meant to be anti-social, but I couldn't cover a game while listening to a political argument, a baseball discussion or anything else ... Turn your head a second and you've missed what could be important action.') His presence in Brazil was similarly inconspicuous, since the *Post-Dispatch* ungratefully printed his reports without a byline.

In the run-up to England's encounter with the US, the altogether more abundant English press corps had taken up a familiar refrain, with the correspondent of the *Daily Herald* boasting that 'sportswriters here consider England to be more superior scientifically than any visiting team seen to date'. A 2-0 win over Chile had done nothing to dispel such claims, and against a team of part-timers begging to be termed plucky there was no reason to expect anything short of a cakewalk. When the Americans arrived at the Independencia Stadium – some wearing Stetsons, some chomping on cigars – they were largely a source of bemusement to the international press, who knew virtually nothing about any of them.

The Americans, in turn, knew almost nothing about international soccer. Indeed, their greatest weapon in this match, as Maca later claimed, may have been their naivety. While the full-back from Brussels might have fretted over the prospect of facing Finney, Wright and Mortensen, such names meant little to his US-born team-mates. Even the puzzling – or, as some claim, presumptuous – absence of Stanley Matthews from the England team-sheet may not have carried much weight. Few of the Americans, after all, had ever seen him play.

The scoreline carved out on the bumpy, barren surface of the Independencia, with its treacherous cinder track hugging the touchlines, owed as much to woeful English finishing as to American grit. Borghi, in a curious combination of short sleeves and knee-pads, saved impressively from Wilf Mannion early on, but was a helpless spectator during several near-misses. That his sheet remained clean with half an hour gone seemed something of a fluke; even after he clawed Tom Finney's header over the bar, a deluge of England goals seemed inevitable. England may have been profligate, but they underestimated their opponents' resolve. They also had to contend with a predominantly hostile crowd whose affections for the underdog grew with each scoreless minute. Even the tamest of shots from Pariani, flying straight into the arms of Bert Williams, drew lusty cheers of encouragement.

The goal came seven minutes before half-time. Bahr received a throw-in on the right and, under pressure from Billy Wright, took aim from 25 yards. The next anyone knew, Williams had been wrong-footed and the ball was in the net. Prostrate on the ground lay Gaetjens, who may or may not have deliberately flung himself at the speculative effort. Whether he stumbled or launched himself headfirst is not clear and doubtless never will be. But he had made contact – if only just, with the side of his head – and his team entered the dingy dressing-rooms a goal to the good.

The English later complained of 'gremlins in the goal', but for all their good fortune the Americans had marked tightly and defended capably. They were anchored by two decent full-backs: Keough, wise beyond his 22 years, and Maca, who had lined up for Belgium against Jimmy Mullen and England in 1946 (allegedly prompting the Wolves star to ask him in Belo Horizonte: 'How many countries do you play for?'). There was also the bruising presence of Charlie Colombo, an amateur boxer who eccentrically wore an old pair of boxing mittens whenever he played. Cursing, spitting, kicking and scratching, the mean streak he carried onto the pitch had been made known to Roy Bentley and the other England forwards almost from the first whistle, but he is best remembered for his second-half rugby-tackle on Stan Mortensen, for which he was spared a sending-off by the Italian referee, Generoso Dattilo (conspiracy theorists claim Dattilo was keen to see England lose to boost the chances of his own country, though as it turned out they were eliminated on the same day). Mullen headed the ensuing free-kick goalwards but Borghi scrambled the ball to safety – after it appeared to have crossed the line.

With that, England had fired their last arrow. Seemingly resigned to their fate, they almost suffered the ignominy of a second goal, Alf Ramsey clearing Pee Wee Wallace's tame shot off the line. By then American confidence had grown enough for Clarkie Souza – perhaps the best player on the pitch – to engage in an impish dribble through several frustrated opponents. The American public may not have been collectively perched beside their radios, but the locals sensed the magnitude of the occasion. In the stands, firecrackers and bonfires were lit, and what had originally been a crowd of about 10,000 had grown to maybe 40,000 – no one really knows. When it was over, many of them rushed on to the pitch to hoist the two heroes of the game, Gaetjens and Borghi, on their shoulders.

In his match report, prosaically headlined **U.S. Upsets England in Soccer: Gaetjens Scores the Only Goal**, McSkimming admitted that England 'in their general play appeared superior to that of the winners except on the scoreboard', but also claimed that 'the underdog Americans dominated the attack during the entire game'. Years later he compared the result, not without justification, to a baseball team from Oxford University beating the New York Yankees. But his countrymen responded with no more than a shrug of the shoulders. Not even the *New York Times* seemed terribly bothered, printing a wire service report which credited the goal to the wrong player. (It was hardly alone in conveying such inaccuracies: both the *Daily Telegraph* and the *Manchester Guardian* referred to Gaetjens as 'Argentine-born' and the *Telegraph* even claimed he 'scored with a lovely shot from 20 yards in the corner of the net'.)

It would require the efforts of a baseball player a year later for the full irony of Belo Horizonte to be realised. With typical self-reverence, the dramatic last-ditch home run struck by Bobby Thomson that won baseball's National League championship for the New York Giants came to be referred to by the American press as the 'shot heard round the world'. Yet international interest in Thomson (born in Glasgow) or the Giants was, of course, no greater than what America had afforded the 'shot' from Gaetjens.

English witnesses could not agree why or how the Americans had managed to win. Stanley Rous, the secretary of the Football Association, tactfully conceded his country had been 'beaten by a fitter and faster team'. The manager Walter Winterbottom claimed his forwards had been 'far too eager'. The *Daily Mail* correspondent blamed 'bad shooting, over-anxiety in the second half and failure to settle down on the small pitch'. The *Daily Telegraph* pointed to 'the small ground and the close marking of the defenders' which 'seemed to spoil the Englishmen's close passing game ... repeated switches in the front line brought no results'. Whatever the long-term significance – if indeed there was any – the defeat certainly precipitated a collapse in England's fortunes that summer. A 1-0 defeat by Spain three days later put them on the boat home, sending the press into the first of its many hyperbolic states of indignation.

That result gave Spain a perfect record – they had also beaten Chile 2-0 – and with only one team to go through from each group, the US's final match was meaningless. In any case, they could not maintain the momentum in Recife against the Chileans, who took the lead with two first-half goals. Wallace and Maca, with a penalty, levelled the score early in the second half, but within six minutes their opponents reclaimed the lead, and the Americans soon wilted on the leaden pitch, conceding two further goals to finish, on goal difference, at the bottom of the group. Strangely, they had ended up exactly where they had been expected to.

Some in the team received offers to play overseas, but the only takers were the three who had not become citizens, none of whom played for the US again. McIlvenny joined Manchester United but soon found himself in Ireland with Waterford. Maca returned to Belgium as something of a hero, but his time in the Second Division there was brief and he came back to America for good, fathering a son who spent several seasons in the NASL. Gaetjens moved to France, spending two seasons as a professional before going home to Haiti, opening a dry-cleaning business and even earning a cap for his native country. Fatefully, in 1957 he declared his support for Louis Dejoie, the political opponent of François 'Papa Doc' Duvalier, who became president that year (Gaetjens's brother had been an adviser to Dejoie). In July 1964, less than a month after Duvalier declared himself president for life, Gaetjens was forced into a car at gunpoint by two men. His family never saw him alive again; in all likelihood he was shot dead by Duvalier's militia, the Tontons Macoutes, two days later.[*]

The rest of the US team returned to their familiar mixture of day jobs and weekend soccer. Colombo turned down $8,000 a year to play in Brazil and stayed with Simpkins Ford. Souza moved to New York and played for the German-Hungarians, making as much money on the field as he did in his day job designing patterns for women's jumpers (the factory and the team were owned by the same man). Borghi became a funeral director. Bahr and Keough played for their country for another seven years and eventually became doyens of the college coaching world.

---

[*] The football world was slow to honour Gaetjens's memory. In his autobiography Stanley Rous cheerfully recounts the 'overwhelming' hospitality he received on a visit to Haiti as FIFA president for their World Cup qualifiers in 1973, which included armed escorts from his hotel courtesy of the Tontons Macoutes.

Decades passed before the American sporting fraternity began to acknowledge what had happened in Belo Horizonte, by which time many in Jeffrey's squad, and the coach himself, had died. American soccer continued to exist in a vacuum, presided over by the acerbic Barriskill – who, it is said, saw fit to conduct its affairs in his underwear when the summer heat of his cramped Manhattan office became too much to bear. The USSFA pursued what it perceived as its Holy Grail – a rematch with England on American soil – only to be continually rebuffed by the FA. So for two years they contested no internationals at all.

They did send a team to Helsinki for the 1952 Olympics, a competition which was still far more important to them than the World Cup. Changing attitudes towards amateurism permitted Colombo and Souza to travel to Finland, where they played alongside Keough. This, though, was a team amateur in both name and nature. The new chairman of the Olympic soccer committee was William Hobson, a long-serving USSFA official who had taken part in the 1932 and 1936 Olympics as a member of the field hockey team. He had accompanied the 1948 soccer squad to the London Games, but his grasp of the game seemed terrifyingly fragile. Keough recalled Hobson's advice to the 1948 side in Geoffrey Douglas's 1996 book *The Game Of Their Lives:*

> So he says to his players before the game, 'Now anytime your man gets away from you, what you gotta do is, you gotta yell "Check!"' ... 'How come?' the players want to know. 'Well,' the coach tells 'em, 'because that's how they do it in field hockey, that's why.' 'Field hockey? Field hockey?' – Keough fairly shrieks now. 'What the goddamn fuck's field hockey got to do with anything?'

In Helsinki, the US lost 8-0 in the opening round against perpetual nemesis Italy and yet again headed home after 90 minutes. Familiar recriminations over a lack of preparation ensued. Giesler, still the team manager (Bill Jeffrey had worked under him in Brazil) claimed the US were 'comparable to Italy as individuals but as a team lacked the understanding of each other's play'. He recommended sending the US amateur champions in future; there weren't enough resources to do anything else. One final Olympic humiliation, a 9-1 defeat to Yugoslavia in Melbourne, came in 1956 before the introduction of qualifying competitions began to keep American teams at home. By this time, though, Olympic soccer had lost much of its relevance.

Though still pining for England, the USSFA accepted an invitation from Scotland to play at Hampden Park in 1952, but sent a team with no manager, coach or even a trainer. Bad weather forced their only practice match to be cancelled, although the day before kick-off the coach of Queen's Park – on the way to finishing second from bottom of the Scottish League – was persuaded to organise a training session. None of this dissuaded the Scottish FA from hyping the match as a major international event – the Americans, after all, were the conquerors of England – and more than 107,000 turned up. The 6-0 victory, though, was little short of a farce, and left the *Glasgow Herald* correspondent fuming:

> [Scotland] thrashed [the US] without expending effort comparable with what they would have employed had they been opposed by a team of Scottish juvenile players. In saying that, I do not wish to be too critical of the juvenile section of Scottish football ... When Scottish followers are eager to see how our failing standards compare with those of countries such as Austria, they have to be content with such rubbish as they saw in what must be Hampden Park's most irritating match in all the great history of the famous ground ... Both backs, Bahr (the most consistent American player) and John Souza might conceivably be considered for one of our moderate Division A teams. The others were merely triers and far from successful triers at that.

The telegram the USSFA officials are alleged to have sent to New York after the match – '107,765 in attendance; score secondary' – may be apocryphal, but the $14,000 it took from the gate receipts, not including $6,300 in expenses, was certainly more useful to its survival than another celebrated upset.

Another year passed before the English FA finally agreed to try to avenge its World Cup humiliation, almost three years after Belo Horizonte and just five months before its portentous date with the Hungarians at Wembley. Anticipating a huge crowd, the USSFA secured Yankee Stadium for a Sunday evening kick-off, but succeeded in attracting only embarrassment. When gentle rain began to fall late that afternoon, the stadium's proprietors abruptly postponed the match, fearing damage to the baseball surface. British journalists, many of whom were due back in London for a boxing match, were flabbergasted; even Rous thought the decision 'inconceivable'. Only 7,200 returned the next day to watch the

Americans lose 6-3. 'No England team has ever played before so miserably sparse an attendance,' complained the *Daily Herald*, maintaining that 'it will be a long, long time before another representative England soccer team sets foot in New York'.

It would in fact be nearly 11 years, and on more expendable turf. Soccer in New York City typically found refuge in modest Triborough Stadium, a facility on tiny Randall's Island, whose greatest claims to fame were that Jesse Owens had qualified for the Berlin Olympics there and that it was the home of the world's largest sewage treatment plant. Both Liverpool's 1946 and 1948 tours had started at Triborough, Scotland had played three of its 1949 tour matches there, and it had been the venue for the narrow England XI victory a month before Belo Horizonte. By the time England returned to New York in 1964, the facility had been renamed Downing Stadium, and the goal-gremlins had long since disappeared. In front of fewer than 5,000, against a makeshift American team foreign-born almost to a man, England scored ten times without reply. They had also defeated the US 8-1 in 1959 – Billy Wright's last appearance in an England shirt – at a Los Angeles baseball stadium in which the groundsman had apparently not bothered to flatten the 15-inch high pitcher's mound.

World Cup football was leaving America to choke in the dust. Mexico had become the region's standard-bearer, and a more demanding qualification process, combined with tighter eligibility restrictions, prompted the USSFA to treat the event more as a financial liability than a bid for glory. It opted to play all its 1954 qualification rounds away from home, a decision which netted it a welcome $21,000 but virtually ensured the team would not reach Switzerland. As quickly as the hotchpotch American squad was assembled, it was being dismantled: the Mexican FA had identified four players who failed to meet the new eligibility rules and the USSFA was forced to scratch them from the team. After Mexico won their two matches against the US by a combined score of 7-1 the association tried to back out of its remaining two fixtures with Haiti, but was made to send a team to Port-au-Prince three months later. The two matches, both won by the Americans, were played on consecutive days.

The USSFA meekly defended its decision to play away by pointing to the cost of hiring a New York baseball stadium, and noting that the Randall's Island pitch was too narrow for FIFA's liking. By 1957 it had realised there were places to play outside New York, but choosing to take on Mexico in Long Beach, California, was tantamount to playing away. Almost all of the 12,500 in attendance came to support the visitors, and took pleasure in the 7-2 hammering of yet another slapdash American collective. As the US had lost 6-0 in Mexico City three weeks earlier, the USSFA disbanded the team, sending the Kutis club of St Louis – prophetically sponsored by a firm of undertakers – to fulfil the remaining fixtures against Canada, both of which were lost. Hardly a newspaper in America bothered to print the final table.

Well into the 1970s the USSFA continued to stage its qualifiers with Mexico in California, where it could count on a large crowd. That it was a predominantly hostile one, frequently basking in weather more familiar to the opposition, seemed an unavoidable necessity. For the 1962 World Cup, the Americans held Mexico to a 3-3 draw in a Los Angeles baseball park – a result somewhat rashly judged by the *LA Times* to be 'the biggest international upset since the Alamo' – but a week later were eliminated 3-0 in front of 100,000 in the Olympic Stadium. The *Times* noted that in the first leg 'Uncle Sam fielded a pick-up team composed of fellows gathered up from around the country, many of whom had never seen each other before'. Nor would they see each other again before the return leg. But this was not necessarily the USSFA's fault, as the chairman of its selection committee took pains to point out:

> Many of the so-called critics are constantly harping on the fact that the team is not together for a period of two to three to four weeks prior to playing. One instance about players playing beyond one or two days was the one in Los Angeles where we invited the team to stay one week there prior to going to Mexico. Out of the entire squad of 15, only five players were able to get time off from work. Our Association will gladly spend extra money for preparatory practice, however, it is the players who cannot get the necessary time from their jobs.

And here was the root of the problem. Though there were deficiencies in almost every facet of the American set-up – fitness levels, coaching acumen and certainly organisational competence – a full-time professional set-up might have remedied most of them. But big-time American soccer remained an oxymoron. The ASL's collection of Uhrik Truckers and Ukrainian Nationals, playing in their spartan ovals to people who spoke in foreign tongues, was not professional sport as America recognised it. And playing through the winter, which the league continued to do until 1969, was intolerable. The experience of Arthur Daley, the *New York Times*'s Pulitzer Prize-winning sportswriter, writing in 1960, spoke for many:

About 30 years ago this reporter was assigned to cover a soccer championship on the outer fringes of Brooklyn. It was a grim day in the dead of winter with no transportation, no shelter, no spectators and no score. They played three overtime periods. It was enough to scar a man for life. This reporter hasn't witnessed a soccer game of his own free will since.

Yet the country's sporting landscape was starting to experience seismic shifts it had not known since the Golden Age of the 1920s. Television – on a global scale – made the difference and soccer was not immune from its effects. As early as 1961 the ABC network had taken a crew to Wembley to televise the FA Cup final, possibly the first time armchair sports fans from coast to coast had been given the opportunity to watch a top foreign match. Images of enormous crowds at places like Wembley and the staggering popularity of the game's top talent – in particular, the youthful Pelé – left a lingering impression on a number of ambitious promoters. Before the 1960s came to an end, soccer in the US had begun its flirtation with the big time, and the country's ambivalence towards the game began to dissolve – for better, and for worse.

4. 'We will become phenomenal'
Ambition and folly in the Sixties

Here is a viable product, they feel, and the whole operation is to be tackled as a promotional and merchandising effort on a scale comparable to what – to use their own words – a major automotive or soap company, for example, undertakes when it attempts to 'condition' the public to its new product.
Geoffrey Green, The Times, February 25, 1967

By the mid-1960s, the value of television to big-time sport was unmistakable. Gridiron's NFL and its upstart rival, the American Football League, had each signed lucrative long-term contracts with commercial networks. This virtually assured them not only of a sound financial footing – as early as 1960 all but five NFL teams would have lost money without TV – but a captive national audience. Baseball, with its *Game of the Week*, had also become a familiar living-room guest, as had college gridiron and basketball. In golf, tennis, boxing and other individual sports, the medium had begun to 'personalise' sportsmen such as Arnold Palmer and Cassius Clay. The way America chose to watch its sport had been transformed.

When the NBC network bought the national rights to the fledgling AFL in 1964, it paid a whopping $36 million for the privilege. Almost at a stroke, the future of the league was assured. 'People have now stopped asking me if we are going to make it,' league commissioner Joe Foss proclaimed, and by 1966 the AFL found itself in the remarkable position of being able to hammer out merger terms with the NFL.

Baseball was not immune from such entrepreneurial spirit. In 1959, one of its most famous executives, Branch Rickey – who in 1947 had broken the 'gentlemen's agreement' banning black players from the major leagues by signing Jackie Robinson – announced the formation of a Continental League, which intended to place many of its franchises in growing cities such as Houston and Atlanta which faced no major-league competition. Rickey's league never got off the ground, largely because he had alarmed the major leagues enough for them to move into many Continental League markets, killing off the challenge before it had arrived.

Towards the end of the Sixties attention turned to the other two big-time sports. In 1967 the National Hockey League – which consisted of only six teams, two of them Canadian – doubled in size and established its first presence on the west coast, pandering to television executives who had indicated its limited geographic appeal was a barrier to more lucrative exposure. The following year, an American Basketball Association was introduced as a rival to the NBA; it too would force a merger of sorts a decade later.

But there were only so many established sports to go around, and the sudden rush to make money as a big-league owner – or at the very least reduce tax liabilities – soon required aspirants to think in broader terms. Some began looking closely at soccer. The development of jet travel and the creeping influence of television meant the game's worldwide popularity had never been so apparent. It is not difficult to imagine an American executive in Rome or Buenos Aires switching on the television in his hotel suite and marvelling at the enormous crowds.

The attraction was mutual. Jet travel had enticed increasing numbers of foreign teams to spend part of their summer in North America, since they could now complete tours in weeks instead of months. The late Fifties and early Sixties saw a remarkable influx of famous clubs – most from Europe and many of them happy to play from coast to coast: Manchester United, Tottenham Hotspur, Celtic, Rapid Vienna, Napoli, Sampdoria, Red Star Belgrade, Munich 1860, VfB Stuttgart and a host of others. As had become the pattern, when the weather and venue were favourable and the competing events few, fans responded in large numbers.

The success of these tours was not lost on promoters from outside the incestuous American soccer world. In the early 1960s, New York-born Bill Cox became the most conspicuous of them. A one-time art dealer and lumber company executive, Cox had dabbled in sport for decades, and not without controversy. In 1943 he purchased baseball's Philadelphia Phillies but was forced to sell up after only eight months when authorities discovered him betting on his own club. A few years later he operated a team in a short-lived professional gridiron league. But by the late 1950s Cox had turned his attention to soccer, having ventured to big matches in London, Madrid and Rio de Janeiro and marvelled at the size of the gates. 'I've never been able to understand why soccer hasn't caught on here,' he confessed. He was not alone.

Cox was convinced the reason for the Americans' indifference was that they had never seen the game played as foreigners did: in a big-time, high-calibre competition. He also suspected that the New York sporting public would welcome a new summer diversion after two of its three major league baseball teams, the Giants and the Dodgers, moved to California in 1957. (The city did, but it turned out to be the New York Mets, who filled the baseball gap in 1962.) By inviting foreign clubs to participate in a summer competition, Cox hoped to offer fans an attractive standard of play through something more than a series of meaningless exhibitions.

His International Soccer League, as it was christened, lasted from 1960 to 1965. From time to time, it proved capable of attracting sizeable crowds: the first final, between Kilmarnock and Bangu of Brazil, drew more than 25,000 to the Polo Grounds. It also brought across the odd talented team, none better than the young Dukla Prague side that won the competition in 1961. Dukla were soon to dominate Czech soccer, and their touring team included Josef Masopust, 1962's European Footballer of the Year. More commonly, though, the ISL featured middling teams that often left their stars at home, playing before modest crowds.

Cox usually included an 'American' all-star team in his venture, but its presence had little impact at the turnstiles – not even in 1965 when an aggregation called the New Yorkers managed to reach the championship series. They lost to Polonia Bytom of Poland with a team that included a free-spirited English import named Bobby Howfield, who had recently been released by Fulham. Most Americans remember Howfield as one of the NFL's early 'soccer-style' place-kickers.

While the ISL didn't make Cox any money, it didn't lose him much, either, and its ambitions towards becoming a proper domestic league grew more transparent. By 1964 it was staging games in Los Angeles and Chicago, among other cities, and was said to have approached basketball star Wilt Chamberlain – all 7ft 1in of him – with $100,000 to keep goal for an American team. But Cox had begun to incur the wrath of the USSFA, whose own leagues had been underwriting foreign tours for decades – in 1965 they had drawn a crowd of more than 23,000 to see AC Milan and Santos, a national record for a floodlit match. Almost inevitably, the two parties wriggled their way toward a lawsuit.

The USSFA had been contemplating a glittering new future of its own. Discreetly, it had put the word out that it would look favourably on anyone interested in underwriting a coast-to-coast, bona fide professional league, of the type likely to excite television networks and elevate the game to a loftier status. It didn't take long for three groups to come forward, each claiming they had the means to take soccer into the stratosphere: major-league venues, interest from TV, trolleyloads of money and, of course, the benefit of their commercial acumen.

Behind the proposals stood some of the most famous sports promoters in North America. One syndicate was fronted by Jack Kent Cooke, the Canadian communications tycoon and a former business partner in the publishing empire of Lord Thomson of Fleet Street. In 1960 the flamboyant Cooke ('sports is my life now') had bought an interest in the NFL's Washington Redskins; more recently he had purchased basketball's Los Angeles Lakers and the rights to an expansion NHL team, and he was building a $10 million arena for them both to play in.

Alongside Cooke was Judge Roy Hofheinz, the colourful proprietor of Houston's wondrous Astrodome (opened in 1965), and Lamar Hunt, the Texas oilman and self-confessed sport junkie who had been a crucial figure in the formation of the gridiron AFL and would soon sell big-money tennis to network television. The other two groups also contained men with interests in other professional sports – baseball's Atlanta Braves and Baltimore Orioles, football's Los Angeles Rams and Pittsburgh Steelers – and high-flyers from the business world. They also included Bill Cox, who some had credited with dreaming up the idea in the first place.

The USSFA appointed a three-man committee to look at the proposals. It was to make its recommendation in time for the annual convention in San Francisco, in July 1966. How the association would cope with the sudden profusion of interest in its game was anyone's guess. FIFA were naturally eager to see soccer take wing in the US, but the idea of promoting a sport from the top down, creating a league before it had any players, left Sir Stanley Rous, by now president of the governing body, and his colleagues treading on unfamiliar ground. Rous's suggestion was to sanction individual clubs according to their merit, rather than *en masse*. But each group had banded tightly together, and insisted that a merger of any kind was out of the question. The USSFA ignored Rous and decided to sanction one league.

A few months before the convention, the Cox group decided to take matters into its own hands. It announced that it had formed an 11-team 'North American Professional Soccer League' and would begin play in the autumn of 1967. Cox had decided to 'take the bull by the horns and make our announcement now', bypassing the USSFA's collection of volunteers and part-timers in favour of direct contact with FIFA. Convinced a trip to London had produced a green light from Rous, he thumbed his nose at the USSFA.

The association had demanded a pound of flesh for its seal of approval: $25,000 per franchise, plus four per cent of all gate receipts and ten per cent of the revenue from any television contract. This was rather more than the \$25 a year the ASL paid for its professional licence. Two of the groups balked at such demands, but Cooke's agreed. Not surprisingly, the committee recommended that his consortium, the 'North American Soccer League', be approved. In San Francisco, the delegates duly obliged. Yet before the convention had ended, the two rebuffed leagues suddenly decided they could merge after all and asked to put their case forward. But it was too late. The association did not wish to go back on its deal with Cooke's syndicate, or on the decision to sanction only one league. The NASL believed it was paying for exclusivity – including the right to host foreign tours, seen as critical to their venture's success.

Quickly, the renegades began to fight back. In August, they announced that their merged 'National Professional Soccer League' was not only going ahead, but would begin in April 1967 – a full year in front of the NASL. They even dangled \$30,000 in front of Alan Hardaker, secretary of the Football League, to help them direct their operations. Hardaker declined, but Sir George Graham, the straight-laced former secretary of the Scottish FA, took up the offer. The NPSL then played its trump card: a long-term, \$1 million-a-year television contract with the CBS network. While the agreement was tilted in favour of the broadcaster ('It's a unilateral contract,' sniffed one rival owner. 'As I read it, CBS doesn't even have to put on one game'), the money wasn't nearly as important as the ability to be seen in living rooms across the nation. In spite of its uncertain status – to say nothing of the fact that it scarcely knew where its players would be coming from – television had given the NPSL a decided advantage.

The league continued its overtures toward FIFA, who in turn urged Joe Barriskill to broker some sort of merger of the millionaires. But the association had placed itself squarely behind the NASL. Its president, Frank Woods, was named as an executive of the San Francisco franchise, and former president Jim McGuire, a member of the three-man committee who had recommended the NASL in the first place, was chairman of the league. 'We opened the door to the other league,' McGuire later insisted, 'but it takes two to tango.'

There would be no tango, only a sort of moshpit. Realising the NPSL was not going to go away (and was in fact about to have 1967 all to itself) the NASL announced it too would sponsor a competition that year. It would do so by importing entire foreign teams – the very practice which had helped to alienate Cox from the USSFA – and rebadge them as American clubs. But of course it could only do this once the European and South American leagues had finished. This made for a rather short season (12 matches, as it turned out), but it would prevent the NPSL from stealing too much of a march.

The outlaws had given themselves very little time to put their operation together, but they seemed convinced that their sporting know-how and bulging wallets would put everything right. Certainly, neither league was short of money. New York's NPSL franchise had been nicknamed the Generals in deference to its well-heeled owners, RKO General, Inc. The club's directors included John Pinto, an 'entertainment and cable-vision tycoon' who was an executive vice-president of the corporation. In the NASL, the Detroit franchise had the weight of the Ford Motor Company behind it, to the extent that the club named itself the Cougars, after Ford's newest model. Dallas's ownership group even included a millionaire fruitcake seller in the form of William McNutt, proprietor of the Collin Street Bakery, who wisely chose not call the team after his firm's principal delicacy.

The only thing the groups seemed to lack was much of a clue about the game itself. Only a handful of investors professed to be actual soccer fans. The most conspicuous of them was Dan Tana, the Hollywood actor (*Peter Gunn, The Enemy Below*) who formed part of the Los Angeles NPSL group. As a teenager named Dobrivoje Tanasijevic, Tana had been with Red Star Belgrade before embarking on a strange career that took him to Los Angeles, where he ran a restaurant popular with celebrities, and later to Griffin Park as chairman of Brentford.

Virtually everyone else, though, seemed startlingly blasé. Both leagues took a very clinical approach to what for them was a simple business proposition. The NASL commissioner, Dick Walsh, was a baseball executive who turned up at his first press conference and boasted almost insolently: 'I don't know the difference between a soccer ball and a billiard ball.' Walsh had been vice-president of the Los Angeles Dodgers, a position he left to 'create a sports organisation', the mechanics of which he claimed were 'the same regardless of what sport you're in'. The NPSL did not appoint its commissioner until its season was less than two months away – and bizarrely chose a man named Ken Macker, who had spent the past few years publishing newspapers in the Philippines.

By then, NBC had brought the World Cup into American living rooms for the first time, broadcasting the 1966 final via satellite within hours of its conclusion. With the match starting at noon New York time, the country was able to witness one of the biggest sporting events it had never heard of. Extra time forced NBC to edit the match to fit its timeslot, but Germany's last-gasp equaliser and the suspense of the outcome made for compelling viewing – particularly as the images of Bobby Moore receiving the cup from the Queen were transmitted well before the opening pitch of the day's first baseball game.

The broadcast attracted an audience of about nine million– not earth-shattering, but eye-opening for a programme which had begun at 9am on the west coast. Perhaps more importantly, it also attracted an unprecedented level of interest from the American media. Even football-obsessed Texas woke up to find a photo of Germany's equaliser gracing the sports pages of the *Dallas Morning News*. While the World Cup certainly did not lead to the formation of big-time professional soccer, as many claim, it did help to reinforce the belief that it was a sound investment. And the game's international appeal seemed to point to unprecedented, lucrative streams of revenue which would surely substantiate the boastful words of John Pinto: 'As soon as we get some stature, we will become phenomenal.'

There was further cause for optimism later in the summer when Pelé made his first appearance in the US. As the highest-paid sportsman in the world, his name was already well known, and when his Santos club arrived for a close-season tour, the level of his popularity was plain to see. On Randall's Island, Downing Stadium filled to its 28,000 capacity for a match against Eusebio's Benfica, with some locked-out fans taking up restricted vantage points along the busy Triborough Bridge. The appearance of the two stars was somewhat overshadowed by an over-exuberant crowd, whose behaviour delayed the second-half for a quarter of an hour (leaving organisers to attempt to quell the disturbance by playing polka music over the public address system). Santos eventually claimed a comfortable 4-0 win, the 17-year-old Edu overshadowing his more feted team-mate with two goals. Two weeks later, more than 41,000 turned up in Yankee Stadium to watch Pelé lead his team to a 4-1 win over Internazionale ('although tripped, mauled and kneed' according to the *New York Times*). In Los Angeles, Pelé's presence was enough to shatter the city's record soccer crowd, as 31,291 at the Coliseum watched Santos lose 4-2 to River Plate of Argentina.

America's new soccer executives might have been able to appreciate the genius of a Pelé, yet their pitiful knowledge of the game soon left them embarrassingly exposed. Telling good players from ordinary ones proved beyond them, and many were taken in by wily agents and intermediaries. One exasperated NPSL executive sighed: 'There's more experts in this game than any sport I've ever seen.'

Though there was little chance that the world's top players would join an outlaw league, the NPSL's melting-pot squads owed as much to haste and incompetence as any formal restrictions. The Atlanta Chiefs developed an African connection through an English contact, Jack Sewell, who had managed Zambia's national team. They also found room for three Jamaicans, a slew of Britons and a Swedish goalkeeper. The Baltimore Bays picked up players from Haiti and Israel as well as Europe and South America. And the squad of Dan Tana's Los Angeles Toros, managed by Polish goalkeeper Max Wosniak, included players from England, Germany, Mexico, Israel, Yugoslavia, Paraguay, Turkey, Austria, Uruguay and Costa Rica.

Amid the international flotsam and jetsam, a few stars could be found, though most had reached the tail-end of their careers. Pittsburgh numbered amongst its collection of Dutchmen, Germans and Maltese the former Netherlands international Co Prins, who had played for Ajax and Kaiserslautern (and later appeared in *Escape To Victory*). Chicago recruited Horst Syzmaniak, capped 43 times for West Germany, but who had more recently figured in Tasmania Berlin's infamously inept 1966 Bundesliga campaign. The Toronto Falcons coaxed Hungary's Ladislao Kubala, formerly of Barcelona, out of retirement by pairing him with his son Branko, while the St Louis Stars fielded Yugoslavs Bora Kostic and Dragoslav Sekularac. And, portentously, the former Wales international Phil Woosnam left Aston Villa to play for and manage the Atlanta Chiefs. 'This is a challenge to me, an opportunity to return something to the game,' he declared. 'We're really spreading the gospel now.'

One nationality was, of course, conspicuous by its absence: the United States. Even its foreign-born contingent, which still represented the best of what talent the country possessed, was largely overlooked. The most notable exception was German-born Willy Roy, who had learned the game not in Europe but in Chicago (his family had emigrated when he was six). Two years earlier, playing in the city's top league, Roy had been capped by the US; now he became the property of the NPSL's Chicago Spurs. The Spurs also signed the league's only US collegiate, the Ukrainian-born Nick Krat, who, according to the NPSL press guide, 'was a great center halfback on the Michigan State team which he brought into the college finals almost single handed'. Apart from Joe Speca, a Baltimore native signed by his hometown club, the only other American-born players in the league were Carl Schwarzen, Carl Gentile and Pat McBride, all local products signed – fittingly, given the city's historic attachment to the game – by the St Louis Stars.

Of course there were no American players at all in the rival NASL, a fact which became particularly ironic when, less than three months before its season was due to begin, the league changed its name to the United Soccer Association – USA. Officials claimed this was to 'make it easier for fans to remember that the league is sanctioned', although the patriotic overtones were more than a happy coincidence. As the NPSL busily recruited its players, the USA scrambled after entire teams, only to find most of those it was interested in had other commitments. Commissioning Jimmy Greaves and the BBC's Kenneth Wolstenholme to help with the search, it ended up with a host of representatives from the British Isles. League officials tried to place teams in cities with matching ethnic populations: Boston hosted Ireland's Shamrock Rovers, christening them the Boston Rovers; Los Angeles, assigned Wolverhampton Wanderers, ditched Cooke's preferred nickname of Zorros in favour of Wolves; the Cleveland Stokers (Stoke City) adopted the club's red-and-white striped jerseys, which to Americans made them look like the gridiron referees of the AFL. Cagliari of Italy went to Chicago as the Mustangs, Bangu of Brazil to Houston as the Stars, while New York, which could have taken just about anybody, ended up with Cerro of Uruguay and renamed them the Skyliners.

Nobody was sure which league would prove the more popular, or which teams were likely to attract the most fans, but there was certainly no shortage of tickets to sell, for venues even a casual fan recognised as major league. Inner-city ovals and high school premises were out. Even the smallest ballpark (Temple University's stadium in Philadelphia), held 20,000. Both New York clubs rented Yankee Stadium, accepting the baseball team's insistence that games should be postponed when it rained to protect the playing surface. In Los Angeles, the Wolves and Toros shared the 93,000-seat Coliseum. St Louis, Oakland and Atlanta all occupied freshly constructed, 50,000-seat multipurpose stadiums.

As the 22 professional clubs began their quest for the leisure dollar, major league baseball looked anxiously over its shoulder. Commissioner William Eckert spent much of the spring pondering the implications of baseball owners dabbling in soccer. The presence of a new summer game had divided his fraternity. The New York Mets refused to allow soccer on their diamond, fearing, among other things, damage to the playing surface (no mean feat considering the club didn't even own the stadium). Others, including Eckert, were more concerned about the potential conflict of interest – described by the *New York Times* as 'public relations damage in "downgrading" the relative importance of baseball'.

The *Times* was sufficiently alarmed to claim: 'If soccer thrives under the projected set-up, it can do so only at baseball's expense.'

But this was a tangled weave of financial interests. CBS, which had the contract to televise the NPSL, had also taken ownership of Yankees, then a poor team at a time of slumping spectator interest. In 1966, average Yankees crowds barely reached 14,000, the worst the club had experienced since the war. Yet this was still better than many – longstanding teams in Chicago, Philadelphia and Cincinnati were drawing fewer than 10,000 at home. To some baseball owners, 'economic diversification' was seen as a necessity. These were, after all, men whose bottom-line mentality had attracted them to soccer in the first place.

For the time being, baseball would need to co-exist with its new rival, and the stadiums which accommodated both sports posed the same idiosyncratic problems soccer had endured from its earliest days. The dirt of the baseball infield was not turfed over, meaning that play in certain areas could disappear into a cloud of dust. Playing dimensions and sight-lines were often compromised. The layout at Forbes Field in Pittsburgh produced particularly awful vantage points, especially from the coveted seats behind baseball's home plate. Baltimore's Memorial Stadium had trouble fitting even the gridiron pitch (considerably narrower than soccer's) into its playing confines, and at such a skew that two of the corners verged perilously near the stands.

These were familiar problems to CBS, which had shown NFL contests at many of the facilities, and indeed had telecast every league game since 1962. The network had developed a variety of innovations to engage the viewer, including the action replay, which it introduced at a college game in 1963. Now they proclaimed their soccer telecasts to be the first anywhere in the world to be regularly broadcast in colour. This was no public relations puffery, since even the NFL was still often shown in black-and-white. For NPSL matches, CBS deployed six cameras: two covering the majority of play from near the halfway line, one behind a goal, two level with the edge of the penalty area and one roaming the touchline. This was more than had been used for even the biggest matches abroad, but it wasn't far removed from what gridiron viewers had come to expect. The network paired the versatile Jack Whitaker, one of its top commentators, with the Northern Ireland international Danny Blanchflower, who had turned to journalism after finishing his career with Tottenham in 1964. They were faced with the daunting task of educating and entertaining a potentially enormous audience of neophytes.

CBS faced another substantial problem: where to fit in its commercial breaks. In the late 1950s, television had persuaded the NFL to concoct 'TV time-outs', stoppages designed solely for commercials. But these had been accommodated simply by lengthening the breaks that were a conventional part of gridiron. Soccer offered no such possibility, leaving the league to contemplate some limited form of innovation. Indeed, the NPSL was keen to make its product as television-friendly as possible, plastering enormous numbers across the front as well as the back of the playing strips and adopting squad numbers (if anything was likely to alienate US fans, it was numbering players by their position). Some teams even stitched players' surnames across the back, as was becoming common in other sports. The New York Generals chose their club colours advisedly: dark green and gold, matching the dominant gridiron team of the era, the Green Bay Packers (they were 'good colours for television', John Pinto claimed). And for the millions still without colour sets, the league even adhered to the American tradition of opposing teams wearing light and dark coloured jerseys.

Who would be wearing them still wasn't entirely clear a few weeks before kick-off. The Generals conducted their pre-season training on a high school pitch in Florida, guided by Freddie Goodwin, a one-time county cricketer and former manager of Scunthorpe United, whose playing career had included spells at Manchester United and Leeds and who later took Birmingham City back to the First Division. Goodwin's polyglot team, with its Italian, Danish, West Indian, Yugoslav and English unknowns, was little different from others in the league. While it was pointed out that almost all of them knew at least some English, it was rather less clear how well they could play. For the Generals in particular this was critical, operating as they did in a city which knew good soccer from bad, and whose hugely influential media was likely to make or break the entire venture. Yet the haste of the NPSL in advancing their start-up date had forced the Generals and their rivals into a mad, desperate rush for players.

Marketing departments shifted into high gear. The Stokers took out a full-page advertisement in the *Cleveland Press* to introduce the city to their team and the sport ('soccer is partly football, partly hockey, totally exciting'), while in the *Chicago Tribune* the hometown Spurs promised 'Excitement! Thrills! Bone-bruising action at Soldier Field!' Both *Time* and *Newsweek* ran features on what one of them termed 'the most popular sport in the world, outside of girl watching'. Yet it was hard to know just what buttons to push. In his book *Nice Guys Finish Last*, Paul Gardner observed:

In the midst of this uncharted sea, there were just two signposts that everyone recognised. One read 'Pelé', the other 'World Cup'. The idea was to use them as much as possible in publicity releases, even if it meant dragging them in by the scruff of their necks. Players were described as 'Haitian World Cup stars' or 'Jamaican World Cup stars', countries that had never got past the preliminary rounds of that competition ... The Baltimore Bays described their new player, Hipolito Chilinque, as formerly of 'Cruzeiro in Brazil's first division. Cruzeiro pulled the Brazilian soccer upset of the year last season when they beat Santos in the Brazilian Cup Final. Pelé, the greatest soccer player in the world, stars for Santos.'

With less than three weeks to go before his team's first match, John Pinto openly confessed to the *New York Times*: 'I hope by opening day I'll know enough about the game to enjoy it.'

The build-up reached its peak on April 16, 1967, the most ambitious day soccer in America had ever seen. All ten NPSL teams took to the field – and were greeted by largely empty seats. Those who turned up in Philadelphia to watch the Spartans play the Toronto Falcons came closest to representing a capacity crowd, though the attendance of 14,200 still left the stadium one-third empty. Amid threats of tornadoes at Soldier Field, the Chicago Spurs drew just 4,700. The Generals attracted 7,800, half of what they had expected for their first match, if close to what they professed would be an acceptable season average. Presciently, the *New York Times* noted those who had turned up included 'a large percentage of young marrieds, as well as fathers and sons', which contrasted with the 'older group of fans' who usually turned out for soccer.

The signs were more encouraging in St Louis a week later. Although the city's professional league had long since collapsed (one source claims the 'entire soccer structure disintegrated' after 1953), the 34,000 tickets sold for the home debut of the St Louis Stars hinted at a latent interest. But rain spoiled the big day, and since the match doubled as a charity fund-raiser it wasn't clear how many had really considered going in the first place. The 21,000 who attended the Stars' first match turned out to be the club's biggest gate of the season.

The league put on a brave face, declaring itself 'pleasantly surprised and frankly delighted by the size of the crowds which have turned out'. This might have been true, and certainly any early disappointments could have been overcome if television had established itself as a strong promotional tool. CBS had boldly anticipated an audience of seven million for their weekly broadcasts. Yet their first game, Baltimore v Atlanta, saw Whitaker and Blanchflower trying to play up a catastrophically low-scoring contest, won by a single goal from the hometown Bays. The arrival of warmer weather to the snow belt produced no rush to the turnstiles. In fact, the league's expectation that interest would grow over the season proved entirely unfounded. By June, the Generals were playing to a crowd of only 2,000 against Toronto; Pittsburgh v Atlanta drew less than 2,500; and the pitiful Chicago Spurs attracted just 870 to a match with the Los Angeles Toros.

Two weeks into the NPSL season, the USA began its sanctioned 'minileague'. Yet it, too, found it hard to sustain attention. The 34,965 who visited the new Astrodome for the Houston Stars' first match against the Los Angeles Wolves might have been an impressive figure (for the first league match anywhere in the world to be played on plastic grass), but the real attraction was not soccer but the stadium itself: the 'Eighth Wonder of the World', with its $2 million scoreboard, padded seats, bar and restaurant, and space-age glamour. The Astrodome proved to be the biggest draw in either league, though by the time of the Stars' final home game crowds had dropped to 12,000 – a reasonable average, but one nurtured more by the promotional antics of Judge Hofheinz than his Brazilian tenants.

Elsewhere, the New York Skyliners struggled along with the Generals. Nearly 21,000 turned up for the team's first appearance in Yankee Stadium, but fewer than 6,000 returned for the next, and by early July the figure had dropped to 3,500. In Detroit, attendance at Cougars matches slumped from 11,600 to just 648, while Boston's gates twice dipped below four figures. The Chicago Mustangs, no more able to attract fans to Comiskey Park than the Spurs had to Soldier Field, thought that promising to field a team full of Americans the following season might boost their plummeting gates (it didn't). Even in Washington, where attendance was expected to be boosted by soccer fanatics on Embassy Row, the Whips – Aberdeen in disguise – failed to exceed 10,000 for any of their six games.

Thus did pro soccer lumber through 1967, left with little more than gimmicks to redress its fortunes. Baltimore featured roving trad-jazz combos at Bays games; the Whips offered babysitting services, free soccer hosiery and even female 'Whipettes' to roam the stands (if proof were ever needed of the relative innocence of the 1960s, the presence of 'Whipettes' at a sporting contest is surely it). Shocking pink uniforms, half-time penalty competitions, ticket discounts, 'ethnic nights' – the owners clutched at straws, and the public steadfastly kept away.

To make matters worse, uneven refereeing and the muggy summer air fuelled a number of on-field melees and pitch invasions, particularly in the USA. Pitting Glentoran of Northern Ireland against Shamrock Rovers of the Republic, as the league had done in the form of the Detroit Cougars and Boston Rovers, always carried the potential for trouble, though when sparks flew the first time the two clubs met, sectarianism was not to blame. After a last-minute Cougars goal was disallowed for offside, Detroit player-manager John Colrain was reported for punching a linesman, an offence which produced a hefty suspension from league commissioner Walsh. (The affair is said to have so enraged Colrain, who denied striking the official, that when the club travelled to San Francisco a few weeks later he sent Walsh a postcard of Alcatraz on which he wrote 'Wish you were here'.)

Two weeks later the Cougars were in trouble again when a spiteful match with the Houston Stars disintegrated into a free-for-all. When fans stormed the pitch and players began uprooting corner flags to use as weapons, the match was abandoned ('in the interests of life and limb' according to the *Detroit Free Press*). There was rarely a dull moment with the Cougars. The Northern Ireland champions later found themselves entering Yankee Stadium behind an Irish tricolour, grinding pre-match festivities to an embarrassing halt. Despite all this the official centenary publication of the Irish Football Association rated Glentoran's presentable results as 'a highly successful series' and they were welcomed home to a 'phenomenal' reception from crowds lining the streets from Belfast City Hall to their Oval ground.

In New York, a match between the Skyliners (Cerro) and Mustangs (Cagliari) was abandoned after fans took to the field in protest over a referee's decision and began chasing him around the pitch. 'Fleeing for his life, like some rabbit caught in the headlights of a car, the referee stumbled and fell at first base on the baseball diamond,' read an account in the London *Times*. 'There was a small, grotesque riot. The match was abandoned while the subway trains rumbled by and the music blared out *The Stars and Stripes [Forever]* to restore order. And all the while the truncheons of the cops were flying.' However unsavoury, the incident wasn't enough to chasten the Mustangs. Two days later, away to Toronto City (Hibernian), they found themselves at the centre of more crowd trouble. When the home team scored from a quickly taken free-kick, manager Manlio Scopigno removed his team in protest, prompting another pitch invasion and another abandonment. Scopigno was dismissed as Cagliari's manager on the team's return to Italy, allegedly because of his team's behaviour in America that summer.

While the USA struggled with the competence of its match officials and the behaviour of just about everyone else, the NPSL had problems of its own. CBS had figured out how to work in commercial breaks for its Sunday *Game of the Week*, but these had not been as seamless as expected. The network had equipped the referee with an electronic device which it activated whenever it wanted to cut away for an advert. The referee was to comply by prolonging the next stoppage in play, only resuming when a man on the touchline signalled the all-clear. This somewhat cumbersome system seemed to work for a few weeks until the English referee of the match between Toronto and Pittsburgh, Peter Rhodes, admitted to having 'made up' 11 fouls to help fit in the breaks. Rhodes later claimed to have been misquoted, insisting that he had merely extended genuine stoppages, though at least one report alleged he had been seen holding down a prostrate player. Rhodes also divulged that league referees had been told to speak to both teams before the match to emphasise the need for 'co-operation'. The incident was serious enough to arouse the attention of the Federal Communications Commission, but CBS was eventually cleared of misleading its audience.

Not that there had been many to mislead. As the NPSL season wound down, the game's novelty appeal vanished. Pittsburgh's last match attracted just 892. The Toros ended their home campaign before 2,339 – or 90,661 empty seats. And the Generals, who had spent much of the season with the worst record in the league, finished up in front of 2,821. CBS's audience, reasonably encouraging at first, had nose-dived. Armchair viewers found the game hard going, and the temptation to change channels difficult to resist. After the first telecast, Arthur Daley wrote in the *New York Times*:

> The soccer game whisked into view sharp and clear, with the orange uniforms of Baltimore – or did they wear the red? – and the other uniforms of Atlanta in sharp contrast to the deep green grass of the Baltimore Stadium field. Everyone was an unknown and the action had no compelling interest. A flick of the wrist, and Richie Allen was hitting a home run for the Phils, Charlie Smith was making a super-spectacular stop of a liner and [Wilt] Chamberlain was wolfing in rebounds.

The paper's TV critic was similarly dismissive:

> Occasionally there were moments of exotic footwork and team co-ordination that explain the success of soccer elsewhere. But on the whole the patches of tension and excitement were so infrequent that it took a notable sense of duty not to sample competing sports attractions on other channels.

Such discontent had not yet produced the sort of bilious antipathy the game would soon provoke from more reactionary elements of the media, perhaps culminating in Dick Young of the *New York Daily News* referring to it as a 'game for commie pansies'. Soccer in the 1960s was not yet to be feared, it was merely strange. Devoid of natural stoppages, with no readily discernible tactics or 'plays' and – worst of all – notoriously low scores, it bewildered more than it annoyed. Those whose curiosity had been pricked found it difficult to see what each team was trying to do with the ball or discern a pattern to the game, deficiencies made all the more apparent in near-empty stadiums and amplified by the comments of CBS's Blanchflower, who, to the horror of both league and network, openly disparaged the standard of play.

Though some gates had been more reasonable than the owners' expectations, recriminations were not long in coming. The 'foreign' nature of the sport was called to account. Could real Americans get behind a team with players named Trond Hoftvedt and Zeev Zeltser, who spoke English only haltingly or with largely impenetrable accents? (Baltimore's match programme had even resorted to offering a pronunciation guide to the names of the Bays' players.) And it lacked scoring. Would fans learn to enjoy the more subtle elements of play – running off the ball, perhaps, or the telepathy of a strong central defensive partnership? Could they come to appreciate a 1-0 victory, the way they could for baseball?

The tactics of the day did them no favours. In Europe, cautious, dull football had propelled ultra-defensive teams such as Eintracht Braunschweig and Juventus to league championships in 1967, when both secured their honours by scoring less than a goal and a half per game. Liverpool's 1966 championship had been won with a scoring rate poorer than any English title holder since 1950 and a defence meaner than any since 1948. It was a similar story with Atlético Madrid's Spanish title that year. Modern soccer had come to mean defensive soccer.

The NPSL attempted to remedy this through a convoluted system which awarded six points for a victory and three for a draw, with additional points for each goal up to a maximum of three. While this ultimately produced an average of 3.4 goals a game (compared with 3.0 in the English First Division and 2.9 in the Bundesliga that year), it did little to address the fundamental problem of away teams holding out for a draw. Some clubs responded to the system with greater enthusiasm than others. The Baltimore Bays, coached by Englishman Doug Millward, ground out three 1-0 home wins and four goalless away draws on their way to one of the league's two division titles.

It wasn't just a mind-set at fault – with such hastily assembled teams, it was far easier to destroy than create. Few NPSL managers ever seemed content with the teams they put out. Freddie Goodwin changed the Generals' line-up 14 times over the course of the season; as early as the third match he was making new signings just hours before kick-off. The Chicago Spurs fielded 26 different players from 14 nations, four of whom were used only once. Virtually every club in the league found itself discarding players after only one or two games. But in spite of its hetero-geneity, or perhaps because of it, the NPSL proved to be a reasonably competitive league, if a rather anonymous one. The deciding match of the two-legged championship series between division winners drew just 9,000 to Oakland, with the Clippers overturning Baltimore's 1-0 first-leg victory with a 4-1 win to claim the league title.

The USA managed to end its brief season with a bang: a free-scoring and drawn-out championship match between Los Angeles and Washington, seen by 17,800 in the LA Coliseum. When 30 minutes of extra time succeeded only in turning a 4-4 draw into 5-5, the two exhausted teams lined up for the first 'sudden death' extra time professional soccer had ever staged – a forerunner of FIFA's 'golden goal' experiment. Six minutes later, a Whips defender put through his own net to hand the Wolves the title, 6-5.

The USA's league had played the better football, even if some of its clubs treated the competition as more of a close-season holiday than a fully fledged competition. Neither venture, though, had emerged with much credibility, and both factions spent the autumn licking their wounds. For many, these ran deep. Average attendances in the NPSL had failed to reach 5,000, saddling nearly every club with troubling debts. St Louis had paid the colourful Bundesliga manager Rudi Gutendorf $50,000 to manage its team and had lost more than ten times that amount. Pittsburgh, who had lured Co Prins from Holland by more than doubling his salary and were everyone's tip for the title, finished as the worst team in the Eastern Division and $745,000 in the red, with Los

Angeles ($692,000) and New York ($600,000) nearly as drained. All told, the ten clubs had lost nearly $5 million.

The USA fared little better. Apart from the initial flurry of interest in the Astrodome, apathy was rampant. None of the other clubs averaged as much as 9,000, and their gates looked all the more embarrassing in the light of the crowds the league had attracted for many of its pre-season friendlies. In addition to the 33,351 who had seen West Ham play Real Madrid in the Astrodome (the first proper soccer match ever played indoors), they had included Benfica v Manchester United in Los Angeles (20,380) and Sparta Prague v Glasgow Rangers in Toronto (21,940). The USA's own regular season ended with just 4,000 scattered across San Francisco's 59,000-seat Kezar Stadium for a match that – almost inevitably – ended 0-0.

All of this suggested emphatically that pro soccer was a long-term proposition, unsuited for making a quick buck. But this wasn't what the owners wanted to hear, and nor were criticisms of their haste, short-sightedness and the almost total absence of soccer expertise which doomed their projects from the start. Seeking to redress its financial plight and still irritated by its outlaw status, the NPSL filed an $18 million lawsuit against FIFA, the USA, the USSFA and the Canadian Football Association, claiming the four had conspired to drive them out of business. Such was the level of their paranoia that they even alleged the other parties had encouraged rumours that foreign players joining the NPSL would be drafted to serve in Vietnam.

Eventually the antagonists gave in to common sense and a merger, taking up the discarded North American Soccer League name and declaring an amnesty on the NPSL outlaws. British players wishing to return home, though, found themselves confronted with a one-year ban – a considerably harsher punishment than that which had been handed down a decade earlier to the much more prominent players tempted by unauthorised transfers to Colombia. Four players were told by the FA their applications would not be considered until September 1968, and only Barry Rowan, later of Exeter City, played more than a few games again in the Football League. Brian Eastham is described as having 'slipped unnoticed through the official machinery', though only to the extent of 13 further appearances for Rochdale.

By January 1968 not nearly as many seeds had been planted as club officials had once so enthusiastically pledged. The Chicago Mustangs, who had seen off the threat of the rival Spurs (moved to Kansas City) did not stock their team full of Americans and remained as international a collective as the other 17 survivors. The NASL did hold a mid-season college draft – akin to those used by professional basketball and football teams – but it was a hollow exercise. Most managers weren't in the slightest bit familiar with or interested in the college game, and few considered any of its players to be close to the required standard.

With the development of the American player abandoned for another year, preparation for the 1970 World Cup – an event capable of trans-forming the league's fortunes – suffered. Between 1961 and 1965 the only full international the US had played was the 1964 debacle against England. Yet in attempting to qualify for the 1966 tournament, the American team, which was still selected by the USSFA through Byzantine means, had performed reasonably well, especially given the chaos under which it operated. The players were not even sure who was managing the team. Geza Henni, who had kept goal for Hungary and later managed the New York Hungarians to some success in the German-American League, had been appointed as an assistant, but soon clashed with Chicago-born manager George Meyer. Meyer had also been in charge of the 1964 Olympic team, which had managed to lose one of its qualifiers to Surinam.

On a preparatory tour of Bermuda the players were eventually exposed to what had been a private feud between the two men. Yet they still managed a 2-2 draw against Mexico in hostile Los Angeles, before a record 'home' crowd of 22,500. Defeat in Mexico City five days later rendered the two remaining matches with Honduras meaningless. Both were played away, within a week of each other and in stadiums with no dressing rooms. Because the USSFA had made no provisions for local transport, the team even needed to find its own way to the game. Though qualification for Mexico 70 was due to start after the 1968 NASL season, the USSFA did not appoint a new manager until it was almost over.

Meanwhile, the surviving USA clubs found themselves in much the same position the NPSL had been in the season before: needing to find players as quickly as possible. Some did so with surprising success. Cleveland – still calling themselves the Stokers even though they were no longer Stoke City – brought in the Argentinian Reuben Navarro from disbanded Philadelphia and Enrique Mateos from Seville. Henni left the national team to take charge of the Houston Stars, who now became largely Yugoslav, augmented by players from the manager's homeland. The Washington Whips were no longer Aberdeen but a curious blend of Danes and Brazilians, coached first by a Hungarian and then a Turk. Ferenc Puskas took over at Vancouver (though Bobby Robson had been lined up for the job before the merger), and offered playing time to citizens of Cyprus, Hong Kong and Luxembourg as well as one Canadian.

While each of these teams scrambled to a level of respectability with their hastily formed squads, the same could not be said of the club who had been Dundee United in 1967. The Dallas Tornado hired as their manager a Croatian migrant named Bob Kapoustin who had settled in Canada. Kapoustin – or Kap as he came to be known – claimed to have played professionally in Yugoslavia for ten years before emigrating to Hungary and fleeing during the 1956 uprising. More recently he had been editor of a short-lived soccer magazine in Toronto.

The Tornado's preparation for the 1968 season bordered on the surreal. Kap flew to Europe to search for a team and emerged with a collection of mostly English, Norwegian and Dutch players, none married, most barely 20 and all utterly anonymous. 'There will not be a star system,' he declared. 'The only name here is mine.' Then, with the club's blessing, he took them on a 45-match, seven-month pre-season tour, before any of the players had even set foot in Dallas (a blemish the club attempted to remedy by supplying everyone with ten-gallon hats and western-style outfits). From August to February, the Tornado played two and sometimes three matches a week on a globe-trotting odyssey that sent them as far afield as Ceylon, Burma and even war-torn Vietnam. They lost 2-1 to the Iranian Air Force, 5-1 to a team from Bombay, 2-1 in Manila, and finished with a 3-0 defeat in Tahiti – 19 different countries in all, losing nearly everywhere they went.

The thinking was that exposure to modest and varied opposition would help the young bachelors – who were apparently very popular with the ladies – fuse into a cohesive unit. Yet it seemed only to exhaust them. 'We won't finish last,' Kap had promised after being hired, but his team lost its NASL debut 6-0 against Houston and played another 21 times before managing a victory. By then Kap had been replaced by an Englishman, Keith Spurgeon, who had briefly managed Ajax and was now fresh from a stint with the Libyan national team. 'As a Tornado, you couldn't have blown out a candle,' Spurgeon grumbled to his apparently ill-conditioned charges, but he could supply no extra lung-power. Dallas managed only two victories all season, and most of the 35 players it ran through were never heard from again.

There were other curiosities that season. The Oakland Clippers, who won as many games as any other team in the league, scored the most goals and compiled the best goal difference, didn't even qualify for the play-offs. The NASL had opted to retain the NPSL's bonus point scheme and as a result Oakland finished second to the San Diego Toros. The Toros, though, faltered in the play-off final, losing to the Atlanta Chiefs, a largely British team whose top scorer was a 23-year-old South African named Kaizer 'Boy-Boy' Motaung. (After returning to his own country several years later Motaung used his American experience to found the club he named after himself and his former team: the Kaizer Chiefs.) Once again Atlanta had been managed by Phil Woosnam, his star rising brightly amid the gloom. Assuming the role of general manager had given the university-educated Welshman a seat at league meetings and helped to acquaint him with the machinations of American sport. The enthusiasm, optimism and energy of someone who understood soccer stood out at a time when the league's future seemed bleak.

Woosnam later claimed league owners had not begun to address their financial difficulties until the season had almost finished, but the yawning expanses of empty seats had been obvious from the start. The Chiefs averaged less than 6,000 in Atlanta. The Toros drew home crowds as low as 2,200, and didn't even manage 10,000 for their leg of the play-off final. Even Houston now found themselves playing in front of just 3,200 in the Astrodome.

In the larger cities, interest was even more pitiful. The Chicago Mustangs succeeded in luring only 336 to an early-season match; the Los Angeles Wolves often played in front of fewer than 2,000, which looked more like 20 in their colossal home. Worst of all, fans in New York had all but given up on the Generals. One late-season match drew 1,554 to Yankee Stadium, rather fewer than the baseball team attracted for pre-game batting practice. New York City still teemed with soccer fans, but they were not interested in paying to watch a polyglot unit – of whom Cesar Luis Menotti, the future World Cup-winning manager of Argentina, was one – even if it was now comfortably off the bottom of its division. Nearly 37,000 attended the Generals' fixture with Detroit, but only because it was part of a doubleheader. Almost all had come to see the match that followed, a friendly between Santos and Benfica on a pitch limited by Yankee Stadium management to a width of just 60 yards. Two months earlier the Generals themselves had played Pelé's club – and won – in front of more than 15,000, a figure which dropped to just 3,000 for their next home game.

That a mid-table NASL team had beaten one of South America's top clubs may seem surprising, but the 1968 version of American pro soccer was considerably better than what the NPSL had managed to throw together the year before. Manchester City, the reigning English champions, lost a friendly to Woosnam's Chiefs that summer, a defeat their manager Malcolm Allison dismissed as a fluke, insisting Atlanta were little more than a fourth division side and would never beat them in a rematch. After one of City's other fixtures was cancelled – and after the club had also lost to the Oakland Clippers – a rematch was arranged and the Chiefs beat Allison's side once again. Elsewhere, the Cleveland Stokers duplicated the Generals' achievement of beating Santos, and the Kansas City Spurs held Europe-bound Dunfermline Athletic – fourth in the Scottish League and holders of the Scottish Cup – to a draw. Not surprisingly, friendlies against such high-profile opposition often outdrew league contests, and reinforced the limited appeal of the NASL. Within weeks of Atlanta's championship victory – the deep south's first in national professional sport – the league began to haemorrhage.

The Detroit Cougars were the first to go, slipping away less than three weeks after their final home match. Losses, officials claimed, were $1 million, far in excess of their most pessimistic projections. Others followed in ominously rapid succession. Sensing an apocalypse, the league fled from its high-rent offices in New York, and sadly shed much of its documentation. Those willing to try to stem the tide were few. As early as September, Baltimore manager Gordon Jago (later of QPR) warned: 'The NASL is one week away from having a strong league or no league at all. They've got to come up with strong leadership, a commissioner who is almost a dictator.' But it would take months for such a dictator, or even a leader, to emerge.

CBS, which had given the NASL the benefit of the doubt by renewing its contract for 1968 (and replacing Blanchflower in the commentary box), decided it had seen and shown enough. Removing soccer – or, more precisely, the chance to see it – from the nation's living rooms made an already gloomy prognosis all the more disheartening. Before the year ended, six clubs had disbanded. Dick Walsh and Ken Macker, named as the divisional overlords at the start of the season, threw in the towel, never to dirty their hands with the sport again. Many of the remaining franchises teetered precariously, including Woosnam's own Chiefs.

The clubs that remained were hardly united in their appraisal of what had gone wrong. Eugene Scott, a former Davis Cup tennis player and a director of the Generals, was appointed temporary chairman of what was left of the NASL. 'Sure we're in trouble,' he admitted, 'but give us time. Remember what a slow start professional football had? Soccer can make it, too.' Down in Georgia, Woosnam was expressing similar views, but the two men had completely different ideas on how to take the game forward.

Woosnam wanted the remaining clubs to merge temporarily into one 'all-American' unit and take on teams like Santos, the theory being that this would generate sufficient interest to reconstitute the league. Scott and the Generals – whose weary coach Freddie Goodwin had long since resigned, expressing doubts that Americans would ever warm to soccer – favoured an eight-team league, playing a short, weekends-only fixture list at more humble venues.

To Scott's cost, power in the league had shifted from New York to, of all places, Atlanta, where Woosnam emerged as the new chieftain. 'The whole problem of soccer in this country goes deeper than playing a few professional games,' he pointed out, to those who were still listening. 'You don't start with pro soccer and wind up with eight-year-olds playing soccer in grammar school. You start with the eight-year-olds and end with highly competent professional teams. Americans have got to learn the value of playing soccer before they can enjoy watching the finished product.'

Woosnam was right, but like so many others who became captivated by the dream of selling soccer in the US, he would soon lose patience waiting for the eight-year-olds to grow up. The adoption of his philosophy, though, meant that clubs now needed to devote as much of their energy to promoting the sport as selling tickets, something generally overlooked in the rush to make millions. In Atlanta, soccer had been as alien a game as cricket, but Woosnam and his colleagues had visited schools and youth groups, often without much support from the club and sometimes because the players' own children had no place to play. Perhaps not coincidentally, few teams matched the attendances of the Chiefs over the two seasons.

Building for the next generation was a reasonable strategy, but it hardly solved the immediate problems of the league. Some clubs had let their players' contracts expire, some were unsure whether they wanted to continue, and the USSFA was not at all happy with the all-American, single team approach. It wanted the franchises – which were still granted exclusive rights to professional soccer in their city – to remain as separate teams. What eventually materialised was a strange hybrid that drew its inspiration from the United Soccer Association's mini-league of 1967. The 1969 campaign would begin with foreign teams playing in NASL strips, which would then be handed over to the club's own players, who would contest a shortened season. Not everyone was enamoured of the idea, and when Woosnam was appointed league commissioner, Scott and the Generals disappeared.

The new leader spent much of the winter attempting to convince the remaining clubs of the viability of this plan. The Chicago Mustangs decided their future was best represented by their city's National League and opted out. Oakland decided to go part-time as the California Clippers and gained a small measure of distinction a few weeks later when they played host to Dinamo Kiev, the first American visit by a Soviet club. But they, too, would vanish. By March the NASL's numbers had withered to five. 'Like Tantalus reaching vainly for the plums, soccer here has seemed doomed to perpetual frustration,' wrote the *New York Times*. 'Like Tantalus, though, the soccer promoters keep trying.'

Woosnam's startlingly quick rise to power had surprised many, but by 1969 few had any appetite to prop up what seemed a futile endeavour. Yet his efforts had not been restricted to squeezing blood from the NASL stone. Unlike many of his cohorts, Woosnam recognised and deferred to the authority of the USSFA and this, combined with his international credibility, led him to be given a crack at the national team, imminently facing its 1970 World Cup campaign. The manager was even granted the unprecedented freedom to pick the team himself. For a man who had only recently faced international sanction as a member of a renegade league, it was a surprising reversal of fortune.

America's World Cup hopes were better than they had been for decades. The traditional obstacle of Mexico had been removed by their automatic qualification as hosts, and the USSFA's financial position was bolstered by the hefty franchise fees it had levied on the NASL and USA. At the time of its 1968 convention, the association had about $225,000 sitting in its treasury, probably more than it had ever seen, and it had moved its offices into the Empire State Building. Now it could comb the world for players worthy of a place in national team. The eligibility of Coventry City striker Gerry Baker, born in New York state to English parents, had been known for some time, but during the 1966 qualification series, when Baker was with Ipswich Town, the USSFA claimed it couldn't afford to fly him across. (It said the same to Andreas Maté, a German-American League player who had joined Hamburg of the Bundesliga.) But in 1968 Baker, nearing the end of his professional career, became the first European first division player to earn a US cap.

Baker was unable to play in the series of warm-up games the USSFA had consented to, and the results suggested they needed him. The Americans lost 4-0 to Israel in Philadelphia and won only 4-2 against an ASL club. Even Baker's presence in the first qualifying match, away to Canada, couldn't prevent a 4-2 defeat. But Woosnam was given the opportunity to keep the team together until the return match ten days later, and in the space of four days managed to stage no fewer than three friendlies against Haiti. Returning from Port-au-Prince to a crowd of less than 3,000 in Atlanta, the US squeezed out a 1-0 victory over the Canadians, keeping themselves in contention.

They advanced to the next stage a month later by making a clean sweep of Bermuda (Baker scored twice in a 6-2 rout in Kansas City), while Canada dropped a point against the islanders. But five months passed before the US faced Haiti in the semi-final round, by which time Woosnam's hands had been tied by the NASL. The job was left to his assistant, Gordon Jago, who himself was still managing the Baltimore Bays. Now there were no warm-up matches, only bad timing: the semi-final fixtures in late April 1969 were too early in the NASL season, and too early for Baker to fly in from relegation-threatened Coventry. In Port-au-Prince, the Americans were overwhelmed and lost 2-0. To reach the final round against either Honduras or El Salvador – whose tie would spark the infamous 'soccer war' – they needed a decisive win in the return match.

The city of San Diego, celebrating its 200th anniversary, had approached the USSFA about staging a national team match; now it was handed one of the most pivotal in the country's history, albeit one which attracted only 6,500 to the home of baseball's Padres. Baker rejoined a US team rather different to the one he had left in November. Several players had been drafted in from the National League of Chicago, while others carried injuries or weren't match-fit. Jago had little option but to throw his team into attack from the kick-off, but the Haitian defence – and goalkeeper Henry Francillon in particular – were in inspired form. The only goal came just before half-time, scored for Haiti by Guy Saint-Vil, who had spent the previous season with Jago and the Bays. Baker blasted a close-range effort over the bar, but it was as near as the Americans came. Once again, they were out.

It is tempting to imagine how a victory in this match – surprisingly unheralded, even in American soccer circles – might have altered the development of the domestic game. Would the US have defeated El Salvador in the final round and qualified for Mexico? If so, who back home would have noticed? Would American television have deigned to broadcast the tournament – and might the public's response to World Cup soccer have picked up where 1966 had left off? And what would the knock-on effects have been for the beleaguered NASL? As it was, only Americans living in big cities saw any of Mexico 70, and then only if they were willing to pay to watch it on closed-circuit television in cinemas. The nation missed out on what many regard as the greatest team the game has produced, captained by the only soccer player it knew, claiming sport's greatest prize only a few hundred miles from its border. The USSFA's post-mortem smacked of despondency:

> We are still playing soccer in a country where the native American has little or no interest and we are still largely dependent on ethnic groups as spectators, who, unfortunately would rather go and see foreign teams play than their own United States Team ... Unless we can find a method of acquiring money from other sources in the game, the economics of the World Cup may some day preclude us from being participants.

Keeping the NASL alive in 1969 proved just as daunting, but Woosnam had found two especially useful allies. One was Clive Toye, a former sportswriter for the *Daily Express* who had come to the US to oversee an NPSL franchise in Hartford, Connecticut, and ended up as vice-president and general manager of the Bays. Like Woosnam, Toye had seen the potential of the American game and thought the original owners had miscalculated in their approach. In Dallas, the Tornado's abysmal season had not tempted Lamar Hunt into folding the club, and his continued presence gave the league some credibility. As for the others, the owners and general managers who claimed to be 'in it for the long run' and who had supposedly braced themselves for early disappointment – they had fled. Hunt, Toye and Woosnam would emerge as the constants of what turned out to be a tumultuous decade.

The five remaining clubs brought in British teams to masquerade as American ones for the first part of the 1969 season. Aston Villa became Atlanta; West Ham United Baltimore; Wolverhampton Wanderers the Kansas City Spurs; Kilmarnock the St Louis Stars; and Dundee United the Dallas Tornado (again). The scheme avoided the need for another winter of hasty signings, but it also meant the season couldn't begin until Britain's had ended. And it did not whet many appetites. The opening contest of what was optimistically billed as the 'International Cup' drew a crowd of just 5,000 to see West Ham and Wolves, and it proved to be one of the largest of the competition.

There were other novelties. A season earlier the New York Generals had audaciously petitioned the NASL to scrap the offside rule, claiming it made the game too slow. Now the league seemed to agree. Nodding faintly toward the original ASL's desire for 'Americanisation' 40 years earlier – and desperate to introduce a more attacking brand of play than the *catenaccio* that was about to send Italy into the World Cup final – they applied to FIFA to waive offside in the penalty area, then settled for eliminating it at free-kicks. The league's own research found that under the rule change '72 per cent of the free-kicks with no offsides resulted in a goal-mouth situation'. It also claimed that 70 per cent of its fans saw the rule change as 'creating more excitement' and 94 per cent as 'creating more action'. Not surprisingly, then, 63 per cent favoured the rule change.

But that was still 63 per cent of not many. The International Cup may have offered soccer of an acceptable quality, but it was played in front of an unacceptable number of empty seats (one match in Dallas drew fewer than 200). National media coverage had all but disappeared and the small subset of the local community that embraced their strange new teams did so as much out of curiosity as passion.

With a side featuring Peter Knowles and Derek Dougan, members of the 1967 champions Los Angeles Wolves, Wolverhampton won the Cup for Kansas City, closely followed by West Ham, with World Cup-winners Geoff Hurst, Martin Peters and Bobby Moore masquerading as Baltimore Bays. Wolves' success, though, did little to strengthen interest in Kansas City when the real Spurs began their campaign. An average of 4,200 filed into the city's Memorial Stadium – the best in the league, but less than one-tenth of what gridiron's Kansas City Chiefs drew to the same venue on their way to a Super Bowl triumph that season. The Spurs ended up laying claim to a peculiar double by winning the 'real' league with their own players – among them such luminaries as William Quiros, Fons Stoffels and Ademar Saccone. But few had noticed.

If this was because the Spurs were chock-full of foreigners, then the approach adopted by the St Louis Stars seemed no more hopeful. The Stars had moved out of high-profile Busch Stadium and on to the unassuming playing field of a local university, hiring a native-born local coach and sourcing players largely from local clubs and colleges. This was a bold move, one that St Louis more than most cities might have been expected to warm to. The season started encouragingly enough with a victory, but only 2,800 turned up, and after a number of embarrassing defeats, interest evaporated. Summers in St Louis were spent supporting the baseball team; the Cardinals had won the World Series in 1967 and only narrowly lost it the following year.

If there was a legacy to the 1969 season, it was probably nothing more notable than the playing strip of the Dallas Tornado, whose 'Columbia blue and burnt orange' had left an impression on Dundee United. After finishing third in the International Cup, United took the burnt orange back to Scotland (blue, of course, being strictly for their city rivals) and added it as 'tangerine' to their traditional black and white strip.

In merely surviving the season, Woosnam, Hunt and Toye had beaten the odds, but with just five teams and no presence in New York, Los Angeles or Chicago – to say nothing of a television contract – the NASL was no longer big-league. Yet it was far from a total failure. Little by little, America was learning the new game. Seeds had been planted by the various community initiatives, where NASL representatives had diligently tried to educate all who would listen on the game's rudiments: how to head the ball, where to stand for a corner. Perhaps more significantly, CBS's coast-to-coast telecasts had taken soccer into virgin territories, and though most of the country had never tuned in, some liked what they saw.

By the end of the 1960s, gridiron had emerged as the new national pastime, a development for which television could take the credit. The flamboyant Joe Namath led his upstart New York Jets to a shock Super Bowl triumph, spawning a gridiron frenzy in the nation's media capital. College football produced a much-hyped 'game of the century' between the universities of Texas and Arkansas, with President Richard Nixon, a huge fan, appearing in the winners' dressing-room to offer his congratulations.

But not all of America was swept away by the pigskin. The celebrated counter-culture of the Sixties left its impression on sport as much as any other area of society. Namath himself, a long-haired bachelor, was portrayed as something of an individualist in the manner of George Best, famously 'guaranteeing' his team's Super Bowl victory and threatening to retire when the NFL insisted he divest his interests in a nightclub. Yet his reputation as a rebel paled in comparison with a small group of disaffected players who wrote controversial, soul-searching books questioning their commitment to such a violent and sometimes dehumanising sport. Their views, and those of other critics, came to prominence in the national press. Loosely borrowing from George Orwell's view of soccer, some referred to gridiron as 'war without the killing'– an incendiary simile with the nation knee-deep in Vietnam. How much soccer benefited from such shifting attitudes is difficult to say. Though it was certainly less violent and dangerous than its distant cousin, its appeal in schools and universities rested primarily on the fact that it was cheaper.

Yet many parents – to say nothing of their children – approved of a game where every player got a touch of the ball and there was no overwhelming advantage to being bigger or brawnier.

It would be an exaggeration to claim soccer for the counter-culture, yet the sport often found its most fertile soil among those with egalitarian leanings. In 1964 a Californian named Hans Stierle founded the American Youth Soccer Organisation, which treated the game more as a highly participative, fun activity than a competitive sport. Its 'everybody plays' motto contrasted sharply with the win-at-all-costs philosophy of other youth sports. Kids were guaranteed to appear in at least half of every AYSO match, and to avoid lopsided scores leagues spread their talent equally across the teams. Though many perceived this as patently un-American, others were inspired. Soon soccer organisations with similar philosophies emerged across the country, signing up children by the thousands.

Schools and colleges experienced similarly astonishing growth for their more competitive programmes. An NASL survey indicated that the number of high schools fielding soccer teams had grown from 800 in 1965 to 2,800 less than five years later. By 1970, nearly 500 colleges and universities were playing the game at a varsity level, even in the most unlikely states: West Virginia, Kentucky, Tennessee. A few started to take the game very seriously, offering scholarships just as they did for football and basketball.

There were other straws in the wind. Clay Berling, an insurance salesman in Oakland, California, whose interest was aroused by the NASL, was prompted by frustration with the media's haphazard coverage to create a newsletter, *Soccer America*, destined to become the nation's most enduring and reliable soccer publication. And in 1971, the largest crowd the college game had ever produced, a match between Harvard and Penn, drew 12,000 to Philadelphia's Franklin Field. Yet this modest figure was still eclipsed each week by scores of football (and many basketball) contests across the country. College soccer continued to be staged on anonymous, vacant fields in front of a handful of onlookers, with none of the marching bands or cheerleaders of gridiron. Growth was largely limited to participation. Watching one's son – or even daughter – chasing and occasionally making contact with a ball was one thing; turning up to support the local team out of love for the sport was another. Soccer, it seemed, was wonderful to play, but not so wonderful to watch.

Before the 1969 season had even finished the Baltimore Bays, drawing no more than a few hundred to their modest new home, an inner-city high school football field, told the NASL they were folding, leaving it with just four clubs. As children across the country began fiddling with round, spotted balls and strange new goalposts began appearing in public parks, the league which had done much to help put them there was in danger of disappearing.

5. Moving the Goalposts

Pelé and the Cosmos

I can't explain how I feel. When we drew the 62,000 I cried. This I can't explain. You can bring Maracana here and you will probably fill it with people.

Pelé, August 14, 1977

The largest crowd to watch a soccer match in the United States in 1970 was not the 2,000 who saw the Elizabeth Soccer Club of New Jersey beat Los Angeles Croatia in the Open Cup final, nor was it the 5,543 on hand for the deciding leg of the NASL championship game. It wasn't even the 20,000 or so who filled Madison Square Garden and its adjacent Felt Forum to watch Brazil triumph in the World Cup final on closed-circuit TV. It was the 22,143 who squeezed into every available space in Downing Stadium to see Pelé and Santos draw 2-2 with West Ham in a meaningless late-summer exhibition.

The man celebrated as the 'world's highest-paid athlete' had become a regular visitor to the US, and his triumph in Mexico that summer only heightened America's fascination with him – especially in New York. This particular September evening on Randall's Island found fans perching in the aisles or wherever they could find space, boisterously chanting *Pérola Negra!* in homage to their hero. Against a West Ham team that included Bobby Moore, Geoff Hurst, Jimmy Greaves, Trevor Brooking and Clyde Best, Pelé was in top form, scoring both Santos goals to send the crowd home happy. New York had seen a number of star players and clubs that season, but only 7,000 watched George Best and Manchester United at Downing Stadium several months earlier, and Milan, Celtic and Racing Club of Argentina had drawn similarly modest crowds. *Pérola Negra* was in another league.

The paradox facing US soccer as it entered the 1970s was obvious: the boom in scholastic and youth participation had not produced much of a response at the box office. The NASL had scraped together enough teams to get it through the 1970 season, but only by raiding the ASL for the Rochester Lancers and Washington Darts, and keeping the demise of the Baltimore Bays quiet through the winter. Its clubs were kept to shoestring budgets. The highest-paid player was probably the one-armed

Argentinian striker Victorio Casa, who made $15,000 with Washington, an amount baseball's top earners could blow on a good night out. While Rochester won the two-match championship series against Washington, the NASL's biggest triumph that season was simply surviving.

Radiating confidence and enthusiasm, the triumvirate of Woosnam, Toye and Hunt steadfastly promoted their stripped-down, pragmatic league, now operating out of a spare room at Atlanta-Fulton County Stadium. 'The people in it this time know the business inside out,' the commissioner claimed. 'They are the best you can find anywhere.' Only in terms of geography, though, did the NASL represent much of a step up from the ASL and other regional leagues. The biggest ethnic leagues could almost certainly lay claim to stronger teams.

Unable to find a place to play – and with their 1968 average attendance of 8,500 still a league record – the Kansas City Spurs folded in 1970, briefly paring membership to five before the arrival of three new franchises. Two of 1971's arrivals turned out to be Canadian: Montreal and Toronto. The third marked the return of a team to New York, one which would eventually transform the fortunes of the league.

Woosnam had been told of two Turkish brothers working in the city who were big enough soccer fans to have flown to Mexico for the World Cup. Ahmet and Nesuhi Ertegun were also record producers and serious players in the entertainment industry – Nesuhi was a senior executive at Atlantic Records, and had produced albums for Ray Charles, John Coltrane and Aretha Franklin. With the might of the Warner Communications conglomerate behind them, the Erteguns agreed to the league's revised $25,000 franchise fee – more than double what Rochester and Washington had paid the season before – and hired Toye as their general manager. Woosnam in turn moved the league's offices back to New York. The darkest days seemed to be over.

There would be no reappearance of the Generals – two high school coaches won a trip to Europe for suggesting the team call itself the Cosmos – though the club revived their green and gold colour scheme, and took up residency in Yankee Stadium. But the first-year Cosmos were a far cry from the celebrated team who would emerge at the end of the decade. They chose as their manager Gordon Bradley, a Sunderland-born emigrant who had led New York Hota (a Bavarian ethnic club) to the Open Cup title that season. Bradley's rather anonymous playing career had included stops at Bradford Park Avenue and Carlisle United, and a spell with the Generals in 1968. Still only 32, he doubled as his team's full-back and recruited the rest of the squad largely from local contacts.

The most conspicuous member of the early Cosmos was a Bermudan named Randy Horton, an economics student at Rutgers University with an impressive afro that added several inches to his already-imposing 6ft 2in frame. The club's top scorer, Horton was named league Rookie of the Year that season, though fans strangely developed a less charitable attitude towards his somewhat gangly presence. Though the Cosmos qualified for the post-season play-offs – as did half the league – Yankee Stadium remained just as empty as it had been for the Generals and the Skyliners. A crowd of 19,000 was announced for the visit of Rochester, but virtually everyone had come for the second game of the evening: Pelé's Santos against Deportivo Cali of Colombia.

Signs of heightened interest were modest. The St Louis Stars, persisting with an American-heavy team, again finished with a woeful points total and crowds of only a few thousand, while the American-less Washington Darts completed their season in front of just 1,224. Rochester were probably the league's best team, but even they averaged just 7,500 at the high-school football facility they called home. One of their stars was a Brazilian émigré named Carlos Metidieri, a striker who supplemented his soccer wages by working at a local supermarket.

The Lancers proved to be gluttons for hard work that season. They were eliminated in the semi-finals by Dallas over three games, the first of which took 176 minutes to resolve. Six 15-minute periods of 'sudden death' extra time – nearly the equivalent of another entire match – were played before Metidieri finally found the net. (Woosnam missed the goal in his efforts to reach the pitch; he was about to instruct the officials to abandon the match at the end of the period.) Rochester lost the remaining two matches, one of which required 58 minutes of extra time, and Dallas went on to defeat Atlanta in the championship series, taking the decisive game in Georgia before fewer than 5,000.

The Lancers recorded another footnote by agreeing to participate in the Concacaf Champions Cup as American champions of 1970. Whether they actually were the best team in the country – as opposed to winners of its most visible league – was a matter of doubt, but they sneaked past Pembroke Zebras of Bermuda and Mexico's Guadalajara, who forfeited, and then finished fourth in the final group of six. No NASL club ever entered the competition again. International commitments seemed to matter little to a league stubbornly ploughing its own furrow, often against all convention. The league remained wedded to its bonus points scheme, even over the objections of some of its own clubs ('this system has proved to be successful because the teams in the league come all out to score,' Woosnam contended), and for 1970 and 1971 it counted the results of matches against selected touring teams – including Coventry City and Hearts – towards the league championship. (Relatively poor performances against the likes of Vicenza of Italy and Bangu of Brazil cost Washington a play-off berth in 1971.) It saw no reason to accept the sanctity of the laws of the game, many of which it regarded as outmoded and restrictive. 'The entire world of soccer recognises that changes in the laws that produce greater goalscoring opportunities must be considered,' Woosnam claimed. 'It is our belief, shared by many European officials, that the ultimate answer is to make a change in the offside rule and the size of the goal.'

FIFA balked at tinkering with the goalposts, but proved more pliable on the other 'answer'. The NASL believed that restricting offside to a smaller zone would open up play in the middle of the pitch and create more scoring chances. To the open-minded, this was food for thought, since in many countries the game remained blighted by negative, defensive play. Smack in the middle of the 1972 season, the NASL was given permission to remark its pitches, extending the long line of the penalty area to the touchline, meaning a player could be offside only if he was 18 yards or less from the goalline. The experiment didn't work as intended. The next three matches produced just three goals (one even ended 0-0), and the average number of goals per game actually fell, from 2.87 before the change to 2.68. Defenders simply dropped further back, crowding the penalty area and making it even more difficult for attacking teams to get behind the defence. The new markings were erased at the end of the season, but soon gave way to a more enduring 35-yard line which – again with FIFA's consent – appeared on NASL pitches the following year.

The spirit of co-operation between the league and its governors contrasted sharply with the more combustible attitudes which had given rise to the outlaw NPSL. Gone, Woosnam insisted, was the turmoil of half a decade earlier when 'the pros looked in one direction, the colleges and the semi-pros in another, and on top of all that, the USSFA wasn't looking at anybody.' This may not have been entirely true, but the NASL was certainly making progress. For the first time, all its franchises returned the following season, although not necessarily to the same city. Washington's move to Miami, where they renamed themselves the Gatos in an attempt to attract the city's Hispanic fans, proved a failure. From their opening match, played in a downpour in front of just 1,700 at a local college, the Gatos lumbered through a dismal season, managing just three victories.

Other relocations were more successful. In Dallas, Lamar Hunt had moved the Tornado into Texas Stadium, the gleaming new home of the NFL's Cowboys, and found a crowd of 24,700 turning up to watch Moscow Dynamo hold his team to a goalless draw on the artificial surface. By some measure, this was the club's largest gate of the season, well in excess of anything it had ever produced for the NASL. The St Louis Stars moved back into big-time Busch Memorial Stadium and ended up with the league's best average attendance, nearly 7,800. Only the Stars and Tornado remained from 1967, but they seemed to have little else in common. While St Louis continued to field teams which drew heavily on local talent, Dallas manager Ron Newman preferred bringing in British veterans. Newman, a journeyman English striker once of Gillingham, had joined the Tornado from Atlanta as a player in 1968, having decided to stay in the US after being banned by the FA for a year for joining the outlaw NPSL. Not a single native player appeared for the Tornado in his first three seasons in charge.

Bradley's Cosmos were more tolerant of North American citizens, though most had been born elsewhere. Standards remained fairly modest: the club's biggest name was Josef Jelinek, who had appeared for Czechoslovakia in the 1962 World Cup but more recently had been playing in Mexico. New York posted the best record in the league and won the championship, but local scepticism still ran high. Vacating Yankee Stadium for the cosier (and cheaper) Hofstra University Stadium on Long Island, the club still drew only around 5,000 a game. A crowd of 6,102 turned up at Hofstra for the championship match with St Louis, won by Jelinek four minutes from the end with a penalty.

While the NASL continued to be dominated by foreign imports, it had always been assumed that in 'a few years' the league would become predominantly North American. As the Seventies unfolded, though, the playing time given to even the best of the American-born collegiates – names such as Otley Cannon at Dallas, Steve Twellman at Atlanta and Barry Barto at Montreal – remained derisory. The league's managers, almost all of them British, were much more comfortable rummaging through the Football League for durable tradesmen looking for summer work than they were traipsing across North America in pursuit of unproven and unfamiliar names, be they young collegiates or capable semi-professionals.

Even at college level, the temptation to stock a team full of imports often proved irresistible. In the 1971 NCAA final, Howard University of Washington DC – whose coach, Lincoln Phillips, doubled as an NASL goalkeeper – ended St Louis University's hopes of a third consecutive championship with a team consisting solely of foreign players, primarily from Africa and the Caribbean. When five of them were subsequently deemed to be ineligible, the NCAA – amid allegations of racial discrimination from Phillips – stripped Howard of its title.

Nicknamed the Billikens after an Asian good-luck figure popular at the turn of the century, St Louis were coached by Belo Horizonte hero Harry Keough. They had won the previous two national college championships, and after the forfeit claimed the next two as well. The Billikens even set a new attendance record in 1973 when more than 20,000 saw their local derby with Southern Illinois-Edwardsville. But the college game was maturing, and when Howard put a legitimate end to the St Louis streak in 1974, their 2-1 victory marked a turning point. St Louis's collection of home-grown players and their native ball-chasing style had always held sway over the college ranks, and helped to turn Keough into the doyen of university coaches. But an influx of gifted players and coaches, many of them imported, now produced powerful teams that relied more on guile and finesse. The consequences proved disastrous for Keough, who never won another title, and for the St Louis area, which hasn't reached the final of the major college championship since 1979.

The University of San Francisco soon displaced St Louis at the top of the collegiate tree with a largely imported team and no competition from gridiron, which had been dropped from its programme in 1972 (St Louis had done the same in 1950). A few other colleges took similar decisions as soccer became better established on campus, though spectator interest remained negligible. Most games, even those involving top teams, did well to attract more than few hundred. The weather didn't help. Although the college season had long since been moved from winter to autumn, it meant crucial late-season matches often consisted of players skidding across pitches in sub-freezing temperatures. In 1967, bad weather forced the abandonment of the national championship game.

For those who were watching, though, the improvement in standards was palpable. By the 1972 Munich Olympics it had helped to rescue the US from a decade-long qualification slump. Four years earlier, the Americans had been eliminated over two legs after losing in Chicago to Bermuda, a nation whose entire population could comfortably fit inside Soldier Field. To reach the 1972 finals the US had to play no fewer than 11 times in six countries (and three American states) – and needed to beat El Salvador on penalties in a play-off for the final qualifying round.

The best-known member of the team was its goalkeeper, a brash, long-haired Harvard graduate named Shep Messing, destined to become one of the first 'personalities' in the American game. Messing was a sportswriter's dream. Outspoken and articulate, he claimed to have eaten glass and taken his pet boa constrictor to lectures, and his insolence even led him to demand that the university dismiss its ageing head coach, Bruce Munro, who had run the team since the late 1940s. Messing's Olympic performances were no less outlandish. In the crucial tie with El Salvador he flew into a mock rage during the penalty shoot-out, tearing off his shirt and screaming profanities before slapping his bewildered opponent on the back and urging him not to miss. 'The guy was so confused he made the worst penalty kick I have ever seen,' he recalled.

The rest of the team may not have been quite as flamboyant, but most were also American-born collegiates, and many ended up in the NASL. In Germany, though, they were outclassed. They failed even to register a goal in their three matches and went down 7-0 in front of more than 65,000 in Munich's Olympiastadion to a West Germany team that included Uli Hoeness, Manfred Kaltz and Ottmar Hitzfeld. American television, preoccupied with Mark Spitz, Olga Korbut and other gold medallists, barely acknowledged their existence, but fans – led by *Soccer America* – successfully petitioned ABC to broadcast a few highlights.

In the spring of 1972 the NASL reinstated its college draft which, though not treated seriously by every club, at least demonstrated a desire to take advantage of whatever talent the universities might produce. Twelve of the 35 players selected that year did make league appearances. The Cosmos found room on their roster for Stan Startzell, a US-born striker from the University of Pennsylvania. The following year they drafted a goalkeeper from Cornell University named Bruce Arena, but did not sign him. Arena, probably never dreaming of the contribution he would make to American soccer in decades to come, joined a professional lacrosse league instead. Appropriate noises were made in the league's offices. Woosnam talked of a 'tremendous pool of skilful young Americans' and even approved a rule forcing each team to include two North American citizens on its roster, though there was no requirement for them to play.

In truth, native participation was less important to the league than professional credibility. With gates gently rising and costs reined in, four clubs – Atlanta, Toronto, Rochester and St Louis – claimed to be nearing profitability. Yet the NASL had no presence on the west coast, nor in midwestern cities the size of Chicago and Detroit. If television was ever going to offer the kind of riches it bestowed on the NFL – a prize the commissioner eagerly sought – it needed to expand. During the 1972 season, Woosnam announced that his owners were seeking to double their membership to 16 by 1975 and 'ultimately to 32 clubs capable of participating in tournaments on a worldwide basis'. No one could accuse him of not thinking big.

There was only one new arrival in 1973, but it was a spectacular one: the Philadelphia Atoms, an entity which had arisen from a chance meeting between Lamar Hunt and a construction tycoon named Tom McCloskey. Itching to get his hands on an NFL franchise, McCloskey was said to have bought into the NASL only after Hunt plied him with Super Bowl tickets. The Atoms stormed to the league championship in their first year with a team liberally sprinkled with local players and coached by a Pennsylvanian. It seemed to offer proof of the giant strides the American game had taken in a few short years. Yet the club would soon meet a sad end, the first of the NASL's riches-to-rags stories.

For whatever reason – naivety, patriotism, expediency or a combination of the three – McCloskey had hired Al Miller, the coach of tiny Hartwick College in upstate New York, to manage his team. Miller was a hero at Hartwick, whose campus was as soccer-mad as any in the country. Sceptical of the NASL at first, he eventually surrendered to the allure of becoming its first American-born coach. 'Soccer needs a final touch,' he claimed. 'It has everything but a professional image. I plan to change all that.'

His strategy was to blend American and foreign players in much the same way the St Louis Stars had been doing with limited success. The imports came largely on loan from Britain, including the future Liverpool manager Roy Evans and striker Jim Fryatt, who had played for seven clubs and held the Football League record for the fastest goal (four seconds, for Bradford Park Avenue). The combination proved surprisingly fruitful. Combined with the Atoms' fan-friendly approach – which, among other things, permitted supporters to hold pre-match picnics on the artificial playing surface and mingle with the players – it captured the imagination of a city starved of sporting success. The Atoms lost only two of their 19 league matches, with their stingy defence, the 'no-goal patrol', conceding just 15 goals. More significantly, their average attendance of 11,000 was easily the largest the NASL had ever seen.

Through to the championship final, both the Atoms and their opponents, the Dallas Tornado, discovered a drawback to taking players on loan – namely, the start of the English season. Dallas strikers Ritchie

Reynolds and Nick Jennings and defender John Collins all went back to Portsmouth, while Philadelphia lost Fryatt and 5ft 5in Scotsman Andy Provan to Southport of the Fourth Division. The Atoms were left with six Americans in their starting line-up and played defender Bill Straub, only recently acquired from Montreal, as a striker. Straub scored the clinching goal in a 2-0 victory, his first match for the club. Philadelphia was the NASL's first real success story, one which attracted an unusual level of media interest. *Sports Illustrated* featured the championship match on its cover – the first time soccer had received such attention – and the honour fell not to Pelé or some other international icon, but to Bob Rigby, the Atoms' 22-year-old Pennsylvania-born goalkeeper.

In Dallas, the largely British Tornado had surprisingly thrown up an American hero of its own. Hardly anyone in gridiron-crazy Texas wasn't familiar with the name Kyle Rote, who a generation earlier had starred at Southern Methodist University in Dallas before helping the New York Giants to NFL success. Now his namesake son, who had begun his college career in the same sport before securing a soccer scholarship from Tennessee's University of the South, became an overnight NASL sensation. Drafted by Dallas in 1972, Rote junior spent the whole of his first season on the bench, but the following year he claimed the NASL's scoring title by virtue of the ten 'assists' which supplemented his ten goals. (Like other sports in the US, soccer counted both towards its 'scoring' titles, so that the leading goalscorer was not always the top 'scorer'.) Rote's modest, humble demeanour and family pedigree quickly established him as a role model, even if his talent was unexceptional and his status as Rookie of the Year had been achieved largely through graft and an utter lack of pretension. Dallas, it seemed, had found an acceptable face of American soccer – and a winning team. The Tornado's attendance climbed to 7,500 a game.

Yet most of Rote's fame stemmed not so much from his soccer performances as the more conspicuous feats he undertook for the benefit of television's *Superstars* competition. Three times in four years – to the astonishment of the audience – he finished as the overall champion. For the first time, mainstream America was able to name an American-born soccer player, even if most had never seen him at work. Superstar though he may have been, Rote's salary was strictly minor league: he made $1,500 with the Tornado in 1973. Bob Rigby supplemented his Atoms earnings by working as a supply teacher. Randy Horton commuted from Bermuda, where he worked at a private school. Others more conventionally spent the close season coaching or playing for other teams.

And, of course, many of the league's most capable players earned the bulk of their income from the British clubs who had loaned them for the summer.

Playing in major-league facilities, though, made the NASL look for all the world like the real thing. In 1974 Joe Robbie, owner of the NFL's Miami Dolphins, bought the ailing Gatos and moved them into the 80,000-seat Orange Bowl as the Toros. St Louis, Philadelphia and Dallas also occupied NFL facilities, leaving the Cosmos in the league's smallest ground. Frustrated in their bid to move to the Singer Bowl, a facility built for the 1964 World's Fair (and later revived for tennis as the home of the US Open), they headed for Randall's Island.

Meanwhile, league officials kept their eyes fixed on what they saw as their salvation: network television. The obsession was understandable. The success of professional gridiron, in which Dallas's Hunt and Miami's Robbie emphatically shared, was plainer than ever, and it had been fuelled almost entirely by staggering amounts of TV money. The experiment of *Monday Night Football*, launched in 1970, proved a phenomenal success, and the marketing savvy of league commissioner Pete Rozelle – the interests of televisual paymasters never far from his mind – was widely celebrated. Woosnam's impatience to measure up to this new sporting colossus was obvious. 'If we can do the job properly, we can have greater revenue than football, with less expenses,' he claimed, boasting that in ten years his league would have the most valuable franchises in sport. But in 1974 the income NASL clubs derived from television was about what NFL teams had earned two decades earlier: virtually nothing. Most clubs received some local coverage, but the quantity varied considerably. A Miami channel devoted half an hour to the Toros every Monday night, while the Cosmos found some of their matches being broadcast two or three days after they had occurred. 'Doing the job properly' meant, in part, convincing the networks of what they were missing. But that wasn't easy for a league with just nine teams, none further west than Dallas.

As with ice hockey a decade earlier, expansion was the key to the NASL's case, and a strategy which brought in lots of money in its own right. Whereas $10,000 once secured a franchise, by 1974 prospective owners were being asked to part with $250,000 – on top of about $450,000 a season in operating costs. Few seemed deterred by the fact that none of the clubs was making money; it was surely only a matter of time before the millions of youngsters playing soccer would start paying to watch it. But television continued to give the game a wide berth. American fans wanting to watch the 1974 World Cup once again needed to seek out a cinema or sporting arena in a big city and stump up for closed-circuit broadcasts. Of course, the fact that the US had again failed to qualify did little to whet the networks' appetite. The campaign started in a rainstorm in Newfoundland, with a 3-2 defeat to Canada leaving the US bid in a familiar hole. The USSFA again meddled in squad selection and reneged on promises to team boss Bob Kehoe, the one-time manager of the St Louis Stars. Kehoe was asked to prepare for qualification by pitting his team against an aggregation from New York's German-American League (they lost). The squad he took to Canada looked nothing like the one which had assembled at a preparatory training camp. But the USSFA was preoccupied with the Olympic team's debut in Munich, which took place just a week later – and which for years afterwards it naively assumed had been a full international.

The return fixture with the Canadians, on the same day the Olympians lost 3-0 to Malaysia, was staged in Baltimore's Memorial Stadium, whose tiny pitch the Salvadoran referee noted was narrower than FIFA's required minimum. The tie went ahead only because neither team objected, but the 2-2 draw in front of 3,273 (more than 48,000 empty seats) meant American hopes of qualification dimmed even before a ball was kicked against Mexico. A familiar dose of administrative incompetence left full-back Werner Roth, whom the Cosmos had released for the match, unable to play, since the USSFA had failed to register him for the game. Two meaningless defeats against Mexico followed, the second of which portrayed an American team in free-fall. With some players injured and others unable to go to Los Angeles, no one knew who, or even how many, would play. In the event 'Barney' Djordjevic, a German-American League winger who had been seen loitering in the stadium before kick-off, was drafted in for his first and only international call-up. That this assemblage somehow took an early lead and ended up losing only 2-1 suggests the Mexicans were not entirely concentrating.

The pathos continued into the following year, when the USSFA bizarrely decided to stage a European tour after its World Cup horse had bolted. Suddenly the national team was provided with more competition than in any other year of its history: 18 matches in eight countries. Team selection was made through a revolving door – 61 men, most of them foreign-born, played at least once, many of them picked up and discarded more according to occasion than form. The US played seven times in less than three weeks and lost their first six matches by a combined score of 28-2, including a 4-0 defeat against Poland and a 7-0 loss to Lazio.

There was still no full-time manager. Max Wosniak, who had carved out a reputation in the Greater Los Angeles League after the demise of the LA Toros in 1967, was the temporary choice, but he was so unfamiliar with most of the players he had to ask them what positions they played. When the USSFA staged a further series of matches later in the year, Gene Chyzowych, a high school coach who had spent several years in the ASL, was left to reassemble the team. But with many NASL clubs refusing to co-operate, Chyzowych was left trawling lesser leagues in a frantic search for material. The Poles arrived in Chicago for the first of three matches and faced a team different in every position except goalkeeper from the one they had trounced five months earlier in Poznan.

Beaten 1-0 in Chicago, the US met Poland again in San Francisco a week later, with half the team recruited locally. They lost 4-0, then travelled more than 2,500 miles – or at least some of them did – for a third match in New Britain, Connecticut, two days later. With the NASL season nearly over, more players were now available, allowing Chyzowych to make nine changes to his team. One can only wonder what the Poles made of it all. Matters were scarcely helped by the men in the blazers. At half-time of the third game the manager and his team were ordered by a USSFA official to come out of the dressing room to pose for a photo with the association president. When Chyzowych refused, pointing out that his team held a 1-0 lead and was preparing for the second half, he was paged over the tannoy and reprimanded.

The US held on to their lead – on a pitch whose unlawful narrowness did not escape censure from the visitors – to claim what might have been the most credible result the country had produced since Belo Horizonte, particularly as the Poles proved such a formidable force in the World Cup the following summer. Chyzowych exclaimed that it was 'one of the happiest days of my life', but only about 8,000 were there to share in it, and most were cheering for the visitors. The nation's press continued its diet of late-season baseball and pre-season football without lifting an eyebrow.

It proved to be one of only three US victories that year and the goal – a rasping strike from St Louisan Al Trost – one of only eight the team scored. The year ended with yet another loss to Mexico and two emphatic defeats in Israel. Chyzowych's pleas to employ a full-time manager were ignored; the USSFA borrowed the Cosmos' Gordon Bradley to oversee the final few games of the year. By this time, players were appearing in American colours who were not entitled to do so. Canada had lost to a team containing two of them and complained to FIFA.

Far from taking the game forward, the USSFA seemed to be holding it back. Without a national manager or any idea of what its best team looked like, reaching the World Cup was a flight of fancy. The association might have taken up residency on Fifth Avenue and distanced itself from the impecunious days of Joe Barriskill, but it still referred to itself as the United States Soccer *Football* Association, the only people in the country who still understood football to be played with a round ball.

Two events in the summer of 1974 pointed toward a more enlightened future. The association changed its name to the United States Soccer Federation – perhaps a half a century too late – and at last appointed a permanent national team manager. The choice seemed astute enough: the international coaching guru Dettmar Cramer, who only weeks earlier had helped Helmut Schön to win the World Cup for West Germany. Cramer had performed a similar role in 1966, and in between had toured the world as FIFA's chief coach. It was said he could conduct training sessions in six different languages. Perhaps more relevant for the US was his achievement in leading Japan to the Olympic bronze medal in 1968.

Having helped the US Olympic squad in the run-up to the 1972 Games, and serving as an adviser on other occasions, Cramer was enormously respected (Phil Woosnam described him as 'undoubtedly the best qualified man in the world for this position'). But he was also forlorn. Widely expected to succeed Schön after the 1974 World Cup, he was passed over when Schön was persuaded to extend his contract. Hertha Berlin attempted to lure Cramer into the Bundesliga, but without success. The USSF's offer – reportedly $220,000 over four years – was timely and tempting, effectively handing him control of the American game. Accustomed to the arcane politics of the USSF, Cramer's observations on other aspects of American soccer were equally perceptive. Coaching and refereeing, he observed, had not kept up with the boom in participation and greater emphasis needed to be placed on the national youth teams. Few could argue with him – or with the selection of Al Miller, the NASL's first American-born coach, as an assistant.

The regime began brightly with two matches against Mexico. A gate of 22,164 in Dallas was more than had ever seen the US on its own soil. Playing on the same Texas plastic where the Atoms had clinched the NASL title the season before, the American team – which, naturally, bore little resemblance to the one that had beaten Poland – lost 1-0, having been defeated 3-1 in Monterrey three days earlier. It was at least a team flag-wavers could identify with: Rigby, Rote and Trost all got to play, as did a number of other American-born, college-bred youngsters. More importantly, it was something like a permanent selection, available to the manager whenever required and – Cramer having put his foot down – free from the whims and prejudices of USSF officials. It all seemed a credible leap forward, a time of palpable optimism. But it did not survive beyond the end of the year.

The root of the trouble was the form of the Bundesliga's leading team. Bayern Munich had staggered into the winter break near the bottom of the league, with faith in manager Udo Lattek having all but evaporated. Twelve years earlier, Cramer had befriended Franz Beckenbauer when it was revealed the latter had fathered a child out of wedlock and helped to save him from being thrown off the national youth team. Now Beckenbauer was making overtures towards the new US boss about taking over at Bayern. For all the feathers in Cramer's cap, he had never held the reins of a Bundesliga club, let alone the reigning national and European champions.

Six months into his American assignment, he jumped ship. Taking over from Lattek, Cramer steered Bayern to mid-table safety and another European Cup triumph, against Leeds United. An open-mouthed USSF threatened to sue him for $10 million for breach of contract, only to realise they had never managed to put his signature to one. Patrick Keohane soberly reflected in *Soccer America:*

> Cramer was unlike any other foreign coach. He had been in the United States for five years previously. He had put together a highly successful course of instruction for coaches based on years of experience that only he had. He seemed to be highly motivated to acquire the job as America's national coach. He had a well acclaimed international reputation as one of the most superior minds in soccer, one of only a handful of people so widely respected. More than that, he had studied intensively the problems of American athletics and the psychology and sociology of the American player. The latter is really the rub. Dettmar Cramer knew the sailing wasn't about to be smooth. He was aware of our administrative and organizational problems. The very reason he never signed a contract with the USSF was an apprehension about the organization.

Within eight months of Cramer's departure, the Olympic team lost 8-0 to Mexico and failed to qualify for the Montreal Games, while the full national team lost 7-0 to Poland and 10-0 to Italy on a spring trip. Bayern even cancelled a midwinter American tour, one presumably arranged to ease their conscience.

It took two years for the USSF to appoint a full-time replacement. Gordon Jago, back in England with Millwall, turned the job down, so the national team was left in the hands of interim coaches, with all the familiar impediments: hastily assembled squads, poor preparation and few objectives apart from the rather lofty ones of qualifying for major tournaments. Little of this ever appeared in the national press. The US team's profile was so low as to be almost non-existent – even Cramer's shock departure scarcely warranted a mention in the *New York Times*. Consequently, not every budding soccer fan who had cheered Kyle Rote to his *Superstars* victories was aware that the Tornado striker also played for his country, or even that the country had its own team.

The more immediate future of the game seemed to rest with the NASL and, to a lesser extent, the ASL, which by 1972 had grown to 14 clubs and expanded into the midwest for the first time. In 1974 the last of its ethnically named clubs, the Philadelphia Ukrainians, disappeared, leaving membership to the likes of the Boston Astros and Cleveland Cobras. In the hope of drawing attention to itself, the ASL had hired an ex-basketball star, Bob Cousy, as its commissioner. 'I am what you call the "name" commissioner,' Cousy admitted. 'When we reach the point where we have a good product, I will be the man to pick up the phone and call [ABC-TV sports supremo] Roone Arledge and say, "Hey Rooney-baby, I've got something for you," and I think he will listen.' Yet as Cousy's league dreamed of network exposure, its teams continued to play in minor league parks before a sprinkling of fans.

To most of the country, professional soccer meant the NASL, and in 1974 its aggressive expansion policy produced a batch of new teams and a coast-to-coast presence for the first time since the 1968 collapse. Suddenly talk of reaching 32 clubs – more than any of the other major leagues – seemed credible. Soccer arrived in Denver, San Jose and Seattle, and returned to Baltimore, Boston, Los Angeles, Vancouver and Washington DC. Almost at a stroke, the league had grown to look more like its basketball, football and ice hockey counterparts, with 15 clubs split into four regionalised divisions. Six would qualify for the championship play-offs, supposedly limiting – in increasingly popular fashion – the number of meaningless end-of-season matches. 'We are gaining stability and nationwide respect,' Woosnam claimed as he moved his league into plush new offices on Sixth Avenue.

Respect, though, was not forthcoming from the millions of Americans put off by the game's relative lack of scoring. Even Tom McCloskey confessed he found an indoor exhibition the Atoms had staged 'much more exciting' because of the frequency of 'goal kicks' (attempts on goal). Another popular notion, exacerbated by the demands of television, was that every sporting contest needed a winner and a loser. Draws, the catch-phrase claimed, were 'like kissing your sister'. Thus, a sport ending not only with a level score but without any score at all was an abomination. Baseball and basketball games always produced a winner, playing on for as long as it took to get one. Even professional football, whose last 0-0 match took place in 1943, had succumbed to the obsession with winners and losers – in 1974 the NFL instigated a period of 'sudden death' to reduce the number of draws.

NASL owners responded in kind that same year. Having already persuaded FIFA to allow them to paint 35-yard lines across their pitches and amend the offside rule accordingly – which they continued to perceive as a liberating innovation – they now announced that in their brand of soccer any match ending in a draw would be settled by penalties. UEFA had been using spot-kicks to settle drawn ties in European club competitions since 1970, but it scarcely needed to contemplate such a thing for league fixtures. America, though, had never cultivated the soccer mindset which could consider an away draw as a form of victory – a dilemma which was compounded by the fact that NASL coaches, most of them European, had not fully embraced the idea of attacking soccer. Even the American-managed Atoms' championship had been predicated on the 'no-goal patrol'; its attack produced barely a goal and a half per game.

The new scheme forced the league to modify its points system. The winner of a match decided on penalties now got three points instead of six. This gave rise to the somewhat surreal concept of a 'tie-win', a victory achieved not in open play but on spot-kicks. It may also have raised the question in the minds of purists as to whether a game with a 35-yard line and no draws could still call itself soccer.

Whether because of these innovations or in spite of them, the 1974 season seemed to justify the league's bold expansion and boundless optimism. Rote's winning performance in *Superstars* had given the Tornado an early publicity boost: nearly 23,000 turned up in Dallas for the opening day and watched their hero score the winner against St Louis. In Miami, more than 18,000 attended the Toros' first home game, while Philadelphia claimed 24,000 for the Atoms (though McCloskey privately admitted of his club's figures: 'We purposely blow 'em up to give the sport the impetus it needs. If it's 5,000 and we say 8,000 does that offend anybody?')

The attendance success story of the season was the San Jose Earthquakes, a newcomer to the league. Hoping to place a team in San Francisco, the NASL was persuaded to settle for a smaller market 50 miles south by a Serbian-born entrepreneur named Milan Mandaric, who had made a small fortune manufacturing computer parts (and who decades later would turn his attention to English football, becoming chairman of Portsmouth in 1999). Mandaric's insistence on playing in San Jose – virgin territory for a professional sports team – proved farsighted. The Earthquakes at one stage attracted seven straight capacity crowds, and their record home average of 16,500 was all the more remarkable for coming in a tiny 18,000-seat stadium. The Quakes also laid claim to the league's top scorer, Paul Child, an Aston Villa reserve who had been loaned to Atlanta in 1972 without ever appearing in the Football League.

Interest was nearly as promising in Seattle. Named after the Puget Sound on whose shores the city was founded (3,000 other entries had been submitted in a name-the-team contest), the Sounders were created with an eye cast intently on the domed stadium being built for the city's forthcoming NFL franchise. Fielding an almost entirely English team, they soon drew crowds of more than 12,000. Similar stirrings were apparent just over the border with Vancouver's new franchise, the Whitecaps.

After fruitless years of yearning for a breakthrough in the biggest cities, the NASL had stumbled on unexpectedly fertile ground in smaller markets, particularly in the north-west. Big-time Los Angeles, with a thriving ethnic league, took little interest in the expansion Aztecs, who chose a small local college for their home and limped along on gates of 5,000 – even though they finished ahead of the Earthquakes, Sounders and Whitecaps and won the Western Division. Largely Hispanic (though top scorer Doug McMillan had migrated from Scotland), the club won its opening play-off match with Boston to reach the championship game in their first year. Their opponents, the Miami Toros, were no more popular, often luring fewer than 4,000 to their enormous gridiron home. There were a less embarrassing 15,500 in the Orange Bowl for the final, played in a searing heat which laid low the referee, among others. Though the league persuaded CBS to broadcast the match, armchair fans were few. Yet the Toros and Aztecs did their best to produce an exciting contest with an American twist: the visitors produced a dramatic late equaliser and claimed the title on penalties.

For supporters of home-grown talent, the affair was altogether less exciting, as not a single American-born player appeared in the match. That season, only St Louis, Philadelphia and Vancouver offered native players much of an opportunity, and all three fared poorly. Most managers took an openly sceptical or even disdainful view of the domestic pool. Ron Newman may have broken in Kyle Rote junior at Dallas, but he showed little appetite for further experiments, even suggesting St Louis's dismal season was partly attributable to the fact that manager John Sewell – a Londoner – had played too many Americans. So wide had the schism become that when the Stars met the Tornado later in the season, St Louis players presented their opponents with miniature US flags during pre-match introductions.

Regardless of where the players came from, many discerning fans took little interest in the league. Nowhere was this more apparent than in New York, where the Cosmos continued to founder. Deeming Hofstra Stadium 'too far away from the ethnic fan', officials sank $75,000 into improving Downing Stadium, but crowds became worse than ever, trailing even those of the unlamented Generals. Asked by the *New York Times* to rationalise the club's predicament, one ethnic league official replied: 'The number one reason is the field conditions. The number two reason is that people are too ethnic-minded. And the number three reason is the calibre of play.' Three years on from their championship-winning season, New York was anything but a flagship club. The city may have been home to a multitude of soccer fans, but only around 3,500 of them – the worst average in the league – turned up for the NASL. That was all about to change.

As early as 1971, the NASL had been courting the one man they knew would send fans streaming through the turnstiles. Pelé's response had always been the same, never saying yes without actually saying no. By the autumn of 1974 he had left Santos and, he insisted, played his last competitive match. Woosnam and Toye thought otherwise and, more significantly, Warner Communications were prepared to bankroll sport's most recognised figure. By the end of the year they had drafted a package they believed would convince him to lace up his boots again.

As the 1975 season began, the Cosmos were also attempting to convince George Best to restart his tumultuous career. The value of Best to the league was manifold: his skills were obvious and easily appreciable, and his lifestyle was capable of writing headlines for even the most soccer-averse newspaper. Yet his name scarcely sold tickets the way Pelé's did. On tours with Manchester United, the former European Footballer of the Year roamed American streets in anonymity. Introduced at a press conference in which Woosnam unveiled what would become a lasting symbol of the league – a star-spangled soccer ball – Best appeared to have capitulated, but he ended up not signing. Another European Footballer of the Year did begin the season in an NASL jersey: Eusebio, who found himself with the Boston Minutemen after a deal intended for him to join the ASL fell through.

In June the four-year, 75,000-mile expedition Toye claimed to have made in an effort to land Pelé, with stops in Bermuda, Sao Paulo, Munich and Rome, finally reached a fruitful end. For a package approaching $7 million, the richest deal in American sports, Edson Arantes do Nascimento was coming out of retirement. A string of press releases, personal appearances, government statements and even the inter- vention of Henry Kissinger were credited with minimising the backlash in Brazil, as was Pelé's diplomatic tact. 'I think my countrymen will be proud of me helping soccer in the biggest country in the world,' he declared. 'My contract is not to just play for the Cosmos, it is to promote soccer in America.' It wasn't just Brazil which had to be placated. In borrowing a national treasure, the Cosmos had summarily destroyed the NASL's salary cap. Now they proposed that the league renegotiate the allocation of away gate receipts to help finance their acquisition. The rival owners, with images of packed stadiums no doubt dancing in their heads, consented. Here, they sensed, was the turning point in their fortunes. Pelé would lead fans to the turnstiles; the game would do the rest.

Though he appeared only in a white leisure suit, the league's new icon was greeted by more than 20,000 on the Cosmos' visit to Philadelphia. His first match, a hastily arranged friendly against Lamar Hunt's Tornado (chosen because they weren't on New York's list of league fixtures that season) drew 21,000 to Randall's Island, four times as many as had seen the club's previous home game. CBS, having snapped up worldwide broadcast rights for a mere $50,000, relayed the game to the rest of the country, and 11 others. They painted green the bare patches of the frail Downing Stadium pitch and, in the event that any sports fan might have spent the summer under a boulder, relentlessly promoted their telecast as 'The Return of Pelé'.

Five million Americans tuned in – and every one of them missed his debut goal as the network cut away for a commercial break. What CBS lacked in timing, though, it more than made up for in hyperbole, according to the *New York Times*:

The announcers were unyielding in their hero worship. If Pelé merely touched the ball, he touched it as no other mortal could. If he looked around the field casually, the audience was told 'that's that great peripheral vision ... proved by medical tests'. If, for a moment, the superstar was caught doing something that appeared less than graceful or even downright clumsy, an announcer would quickly start reciting his records ('has scored eight goals in a single game').

It was a taste of what was to come as American soccer and Pelé became inextricably linked. Headlines such as **Pelé Here Saturday** or **Cosmos Win, Pelé Scores**, or even **Local Team Has Pelé of Its Own** emerged with monotonous regularity. Suddenly pro soccer was awash with media coverage, and all because of one man: Pelé in the White House, juggling a ball for President Ford; Pelé on the *Tonight Show*, practising his halting English for Johnny Carson's amusement; Pelé on the cover of *Sports Illustrated*; Pelé striking an exultant pose on the features pages of newspapers that had never printed a soccer photograph before.

His performances on the pitch were almost a side-show to his mere presence in the country. The Cosmos remained a mediocre team, but they were now a staggeringly popular one. Toronto, whose previous two home matches had attracted a total of 5,200, found 22,000 wanting to see Pelé on his league debut. In Washington two weeks later, 35,520 – the largest crowd in NASL history – saw New York overwhelm the Diplomats 9-2, Pelé scoring twice. Interest turned to frenzy in Boston, where an unruly if adoring crowd invaded the pitch after Pelé had apparently scored, mobbing him to such an extent that he was taken off with a minor injury. The desperate Boston owners had sold close to 20,000 tickets for a stadium that held 12,500, and security arrangements were so poor that Pelé's own minders had to rush on to the field to protect him. While all of this might suggest the appeal of the NASL was concentrated in one player, Pelé actually put only a small bump in overall attendances. On the west coast, a new franchise in Oregon was pulling in crowds similar to those in San Jose, Seattle and Vancouver. By the end of the season more than 20,000 were following the Portland Timbers as they swept to the Western Division title with the best record in the league.

On the basis of having more teams than ice hockey's NHL or basketball's NBA or ABA, the NASL now boasted of being 'the third largest pro sports league in America'. It had expanded into Chicago; San Antonio, Texas; Hartford, Connecticut; and Tampa, Florida. Seven of the nation's ten biggest metropolitan areas now played host to professional teams. There was no doubt, Woosnam insisted, that the league was here to stay. Yet none of the clubs was making money, and many continued to skate on thin ice. There was only so much Pelé could do to prop up the likes of the Baltimore Comets, who opened their season before just 4,000 at a local college and saw those numbers drop to about 1,000 by mid-season. Hartford had fought off competition from an ASL entry called the Connecticut Yankees for soccer rights to their stadium, but soon found only a few thousand willing to enter it. In Toronto, the Metros were rescued from oblivion by the local Croatia club, but with strings attached – though the NASL had strict rules against ethnic nicknames, they made an unwieldy exception for the Toronto Metros-Croatia.

Exceptions, of course, were nothing new to a league so willing to tinker with rules. For 1975, the NASL decided to include a period of sudden-death extra time ahead of the penalty kick tie-breaker, a development which predated FIFA's use of the 'golden goal' by a couple of decades. The arrival of five more clubs also forced an overhaul of the championship play-offs. Eight teams now qualified for post-season play, a format likely to bewilder fans in other countries but which had now become common domestic practice. And, in the most overt indication yet of its fixation with the NFL, the league relabelled its championship game the Soccer Bowl.

However much sentiment might have demanded it, not even the obliging play-off format could accommodate Pelé and his pedestrian team. The winners of the inaugural Soccer Bowl were yet another first-year entity, the Tampa Bay Rowdies. Managed by the South African-born Eddie Firmani, whose playing experience had been drawn from Italy and England, the Rowdies lost just six of their 22 league matches with a collection of largely British and South African youngsters. Here, too, the novelty of the sport, combined with a successful team, produced appreciable crowds. But the Rowdies were also armed to the teeth with marketing weaponry, enough to attract the attention of their peers outside soccer. They had an odd nickname – apparently chosen by someone blissfully unaware of the game's international reputation for fan violence – but emblazoned it proudly across the front of their strip, which itself was a puzzling combination of plain white shirts and shorts with green-and-yellow-striped sleeves and socks.

The Rowdies installed a Wurlitzer organ in their stadium and commissioned a team song to accompany their ubiquitous slogan, 'Soccer is a kick in the grass'. Home turf was referred to as Rowdiesland; the nubile cheerleading corps were Wowdies; fans, however inappropriately to British ears, were Fannies. The gimmickry attracted plenty of attention, but not all of America was impressed, nor was the club simply grafting accepted American sports practice on to soccer. One of the top baseball teams of the period, the Cincinnati Reds, prided themselves on offering little more than the game to ticket-holders.

A 3-0 win over Miami in front of nearly 23,000 put the Rowdies in the Soccer Bowl. There they met Portland, a team even newer than they were – less than two months before the start of the season, the Timbers hadn't signed a player or a manager. Vic Crowe, whose NASL experience included three years alongside Woosnam in Atlanta, but who more recently had been dismissed as manager of Second Division Aston Villa, filled the coaching spot, and hastily brought in a fleet of British pros, some of whom went on to greater success in their native country. One was Peter Withe, scorer of 16 of the club's 43 goals, whom Timbers fans fleetingly referred to as the 'Wizard of Nod' for his aerial prowess. By the time of Portland's final home game, 33,500 were turning up at Civic Stadium and supporters had taken to proclaiming themselves residents of 'Soccer City, USA', a strange boast given that their team was entirely imported. Not a single minute of play had been granted to an American-born player.

At Soccer Bowl 75 in San Jose – the first time the league had dared to choose a neutral venue for its championship game – Tampa claimed a 2-0 victory over the Timbers with goals from Clyde Best and Haitian defender Arsene Auguste. Yet it was their defence, led by the Crystal Palace centre-half Stewart Jump, that drew most of the praise. It didn't help Portland that the Earthquakes' home pitch was considerably narrower than the all-British Timbers were used to, but with CBS again televising the match, the crowd of 17,000 that nearly filled tiny Spartan Stadium projected a far more attractive image than the vast expanses of empty seats at the two previous championship games.

For all the promising signs, the NASL was still fragile, as the Philadelphia Atoms were about to make painfully clear. Singularly unable to regain their championship form of 1973, the Atoms were haemorrhaging fans and by the end of 1975 had completely lost their way. Tom McCloskey's construction empire had crumbled and he put the club up for sale, while Al Miller left for Dallas. Even the Atoms' principal accomplishment of 1975 proved bittersweet. Their top goalscorer, Chris Bahr, was named the league's Rookie of the Year, an award with which he strangely chose to end his pro soccer career. The son of 1950 World Cup half-back Walter, Bahr was a student at Penn State University and place-kicked for its powerful gridiron team. His proficiency hadn't escaped the notice of NFL clubs, who of course could pay him more in a week than the NASL could in a year. 'I'd like to be able to play soccer also,' Bahr pleaded to his wealthy suitors, but his foot was too valuable to be risked. Upon signing for the Cincinnati Bengals that spring, Bahr left the NASL and spent the next 14 seasons in the NFL.

His predicament was hardly unique. Many of the nation's top college soccer players found themselves courted by the NFL as much as the NASL thanks to gridiron's recent discovery that soccer-style kickers – 'sidewinders' – were far more effective than their toe-jamming forerunners. Oddly enough, Bahr's predecessor at Cincinnati was a German goalkeeper named Horst Muhlmann who had played in the Bundesliga for Schalke and had originally come to the US to play soccer (he joined the Kansas City Spurs in 1968). The loss of Bahr to the NFL cast an even longer shadow over the Atoms. Deadlines came and went for a new owner, then at the 11th hour a Mexican consortium stepped in and predictably created an almost entirely new team. But *los átomos* were a failure on the pitch and at the gate, ending the season with six straight defeats and an almost deserted stadium. They were finished.

It was a media relations disaster: the first soccer team to appear on the cover of *Sports Illustrated* extinct after just four seasons. But awkward questions about why the surge of interest at schools and colleges was not producing a more tangible fan base were buried under an avalanche of Pelé-fuelled optimism. The NASL was not prone to looking back. It was selling more tickets than ever, and it had no shortage of wealthy patrons willing to stake a claim in the game's future. Not many tears, then, were shed in Colorado over the failure of the Denver Dynamos – it was merely a case of new owners stepping in and moving the franchise to Minnesota. Hampered by similar apathy, Baltimore migrated 3,000 miles west and became, of all things, the San Diego Jaws, after the recent Hollywood blockbuster. Any member of the new team was to suffer the ignominy of being referred to as a Jaw.

Nicknames were not the NASL's long suit. Another film, *The Sting*, was the inspiration for the Chicago franchise, whose logo featured an angry, boater-wearing bee buzzing beneath a soccer ball. More than one careless newspaper referred to them as the Stings; another, perhaps more mischievously, as the Stink. Hartford were christened the Bicentennials, a clumsy patriotic reference to the nation's 200th birthday that journalists preferred to shorten to Bi's (though it did not carry quite the sexual connotation it would today). Headline writers also enjoyed reforming the Washington Diplomats into the Dips and Toronto's Metros-Croatia into the M-Cs. And for the few who still had no idea what the sport involved, the new Minnesota team created the most inane name of all: the Kicks.

The one franchise which did not dare move, of course, was the Cosmos, yet their underachievement remained the most worrying. Warner Communications' investment in Pelé had put Clive Toye under pressure to produce a winning team, but Gordon Bradley's polyglot squad was not the answer. It was also clear that unassuming Downing Stadium was hardly the venue to convince a jaded New York media that big-time soccer had arrived, particularly when Yankee Stadium had just been given a $48 million refurbishment for its famous baseball tenant. At considerable expense – roughly more for a single game than an entire season on Randall's Island – the Cosmos moved back into the Bronx's sporting cathedral. They also began refashioning their team from the top down, shepherding Bradley into an administrative role and filling the vacancy with Teessider Ken Furphy, recently dismissed as manager of Sheffield United.

The self-assured Furphy (who the *New York Times* noted had often been accused of being 'domineering and confident, almost to the point of arrogance') unsurprisingly brought in a collection of no-nonsense English veterans, among them Tony Field, Terry Garbett, Dave Clements and Keith Eddy. The Cosmos also signed Bob Rigby and defender Bobby Smith from the fading Atoms and a small contingent from South America, headed by Ramon Mifflin, the former captain of Peru.

The biggest acquisition, and probably the most significant in the league's history, came after the start of the season. Word reached Furphy that the Italian striker Giorgio Chinaglia, who had led Lazio to their first championship in 1974, had become disillusioned with Italian football following the death of the club's manager, Tommaso Maestrelli, whom he had befriended. Though only 28, Chinaglia's international career had ended abruptly at the 1974 World Cup after he made an obscene gesture upon being substituted against Haiti, and it was clear he did not figure in Enzo Bearzot's plans for Argentina. Furthermore, his American wife had returned to the US and wanted to raise their children there. For $750,000 ('the cheapest purchase in the history of the game', boasted Toye) Warner Communications had found not just a player capable of stirring New York's Italian fans but a first-rate striker who could feed off Pelé's creativity. Still the idol of the *Biancocelesti*, with a personal fan club said to consist of 21,000 members, Chinaglia took out a full-page advert in *Corriere dello Sport* outlining the reasons for his departure, and took up residence in a 14-bedroom mansion in New Jersey. The money, he claimed, was secondary to the opportunity for a new life in America, though his $80,000-a-year salary – about an eighth of Pelé's – was said to have been paid in advance.

Few other NASL clubs could afford that level of expenditure. Geoff Hurst, now 34, left West Bromwich Albion for Seattle on a free transfer, and a disenchanted Rodney Marsh cost Tampa Bay no more than $80,000. Other British stars also turned up for the 1976 season, some in very unlikely places. The close-to-anonymous San Antonio Thunder, a second-year team owned by potato crisp heir Ward Lay, took Bobby Moore, 35, on loan from Fulham and Scotland goalkeeper Bobby Clark, 30, from Aberdeen.

The acquisition of such ageing international talent may have improved the quality of play, but it had little impact at the gate, as the Thunder quickly discovered. Few Texans had heard of Bobby Moore, and if they had it was bound to be the one who played wide receiver for the Minnesota Vikings and changed his name to Ahmad Rashad. The English Moore found himself answering to a soft-spoken New Mexican coach named Don Batie, who had spent eight years at humble Chico State University in California and tried to instil an effusive collegiate spirit into his largely British troupe, gathering them into gridiron-style 'huddles' where they held hands and exhorted each other to victory. Neither Batie nor the Thunder, with its lurid tricolour playing strip of lightning bolts, stars and stripes, remained in the league for long. Two seasons spent wandering among high school football stadiums in search of fans proved enough for Lay, who packed his franchise's bags for Hawaii.

The fortunes of another ex-college coach, Terry Fisher, entering his second season in charge of the Los Angeles Aztecs, proved less fleeting. The 26-year-old Fisher had developed his interest in the game while working in Europe. Now his responsibilities included George Best, still not yet 30, who had apparently walked away from the Cosmos because the prospect of living in New York frightened him. Enticed to less terrifying Los Angeles during a month-long stint at Stockport County, some expected Best to transform Fisher's Aztecs into a sort of west coast Cosmos – though it was of course anyone's guess as to which George Best would turn up in California. In between signing for the Aztecs and arriving for pre-season training, he had been released by Cork Celtic of the League of Ireland for a 'failure to show any enthusiasm'. His debut season in LA proved a happier story. Touted by the owners as the second highest-paid player in the league, Best played in every match but one and finished among the NASL's top scorers, while demonstrating that much of his skill remained. Mercifully, his flamboyance had been given a sympathetic home (Elton John part-owned the franchise) and in Fisher he found an understanding coach. Nevertheless, crowds still failed to exceed 10,000 for any of the 12 home matches.

In Tampa Bay, the Rowdies offered Marsh a similar platform for his showmanship, and a much larger audience. Fannies continued to respond to the club's marketing nous; a record 42,611 saw their team dismantle Pelé and the Cosmos 5-1. Eddie Firmani fashioned what was probably the country's best team that season. Tampa scored 58 times in 24 matches, with a league-leading 20 from Derek Smethurst, a South African who had played briefly for Chelsea. At the back they were shored up by the celebrated hard-man Tommy Smith, on loan from Liverpool, and Brooklyn-born goalkeeper Arnie Mausser, the former Hartford Bi.

In Seattle, performances were largely eclipsed by the Sounders' move into the city's imposing new Kingdome. Few could have imagined that in the club's first appearance there, a pre-season friendly with the Cosmos, the national attendance record set by Hakoah Vienna 50 years earlier would fall, but the gate of 58,128 exceeded the figure comfortably. Soccer had the novelty of the Kingdome more or less to itself that summer, and Seattleans responded in record numbers. The Sounders averaged nearly 24,000, a figure unembellished by a league visit from Pelé's team. Not far behind were the Kicks, who drew more than 46,000 to see the Cosmos and 42,000 for the visit of the Aztecs.

As in other apparently soccer-mad communities, much of the attention in Minnesota was generated by clever marketing and a loss-leading sales philosophy. The family-conscious Kicks sold tickets cheaply and offered free car parking, discounts from local merchants, and even complimentary soft drinks for fans queuing for tickets. 'Don't tell me this is a soccer city and this one is not,' insisted president Jack Crocker, a supermarket tycoon who had never seen a professional soccer match before he bought the club. 'You have to do things for people, and that's what we have done in Minnesota.' By the time of the Kicks' play-off showdown with San Jose, few were prepared to argue. A crowd of 49,572 squeezed into Metropolitan Stadium and, after an emotional victory, carried their new heroes away on their shoulders. That Minnesota, with a modest soccer heritage, had produced the second-largest gate the American game had ever seen seemed incongruous, but to the NASL it was inspirational.

Despite success on the field, and their natty outfits, the imported Scots of Bethlehem Steel never won the hearts of their home town. Here the first genuinely professional team in the US marks its 1-0 win over Fall River Rovers in the 1916 National Challenge Cup final.

Thomas Cahill with Thomas Swords of Fall River Rovers, the first captain of the US. Though his efforts ended in frustration, Cahill could claim credit for the first real governing body, the first professional league and the first serious steps of the national team.

SIUE*

SIUE*

The prolific Archie Stark, above, hit 253 goals in 293 ASL matches mostly for Bethlehem. Billy Gonsalves, far right, may have been even better. His best days came after the league had passed its peak but, unlike Stark, he played in the first two World Cups.

FMPICS

Bert Patenaude, right, in action during the 3-0 win over Belgium at the 1930 World Cup. Patenaude scored four goals in Uruguay, including the tournament's first hat-trick, more than any American has managed at a World Cup since.

They stunned England in 1950, though the result did little for US soccer in the long term. Back row: Bill Lyons (assistant manager), Joe Maca, Charlie Colombo, Frank Borghi, Harry Keough, Walter Bahr, Bill Jeffrey (coach); Front row: Frank Wallace, Ed McIlvenny, Gino Pariani, Joe Gaetjens, John Souza, Ed Souza.

Harvard and Princeton illustrate the irrelevance of college soccer in 1963, with the referee dressed as a gridiron official (and signalling a touchdown), a goalkeeper in a sweatshirt, and at least one spectator responding with profound indifference to the winning goal.

Slick marketing, 1960s-style, failed to win over the public in Baltimore, whose Bays folded three seasons after the optimistic rebirth of professional soccer in 1967. The baseball scoreboard was in no danger of becoming redundant.

Glentoran line up before a match against the Vancouver Royal Canadians (also known as Sunderland) during their turbulent summer masquerading as the Detroit Cougars. John Colrain, the central figure in their controversies, is second from the right.

ACTION IMAGES

Steve Hunt celebrates with Giorgio
Chinaglia and Pelé after his cheeky goal
for the Cosmos against Seattle in the
1977 Soccer Bowl. Pony footwear gets a
namecheck too.

Only the NASL could have brought together
Henry Kissinger and Rodney Marsh, seen
here getting a consolation after his final
game for the Tampa Bay Rowdies, the 1979
Soccer Bowl, ended in defeat.

EMPICS

Franz Beckenbauer relaxes on the artificial turf of Giants Stadium. The Kaiser's
performances for the Cosmos were suitably imperious, but he was disparaging about
American fans and blamed the plastic pitches for his injuries.

Even God cried, they said. Pelé survives with dignity intact despite the hype, hoopla and hangers-on at his farewell match between the Cosmos and Santos in 1977. But his departure turned out to be the high water mark of the NASL.

New Jersey's finest come under cultural attack during the 1994 World Cup, which inspired welcome enthusiasm among neglected soccer fans, but provoked derision from many devotees of America's other sports.

John Harkes and Jeff Agoos of DC United claim the first MLS Cup after their rain-soaked triumph in 1996. Alan Rothenberg, left, entrusted with the creation of the league, has reason to smile too.

By the end of the 1990s the days of US teams facing hostile crowds at home were largely over. The transformation owed much to the creation of Sam's Army, on display here in Washington DC at a World Cup qualifier against Guatemala, September 2000.

Fans give Bruce Arena some helpful advice as his team defeats Portugal 3-2 at the 2002 World Cup finals, a victory that kickstarted the most successful tournament for the US since 1930.

Lamar Hunt, the perennial optimist of US soccer, who began his involvement by bankrolling the Dallas Tornado in 1967 and was still around to see FC Dallas move into their own stadium in 2005.

Young female fans clamour for the autograph of their idol, Mia Hamm. But the demand for women's soccer did not prove strong enough to sustain a professional league.

For every well-supported club, though, there were twice as many in various states of distress. As the Philadelphia Atoms disappeared from view, the league runners-up in 1974, Miami, found themselves similarly endangered. Worst of all was the situation in Boston, whose owner openly gave up on the Minutemen and threatened to fold them in mid-season. Offloading former Portuguese World Cup winger Antonio Simoes and Bayern Munich midfielder Wolfgang Sühnholz among others helped to keep them afloat, but coach Hubert Vogelsinger had left in despair, as did most of the fans. Just 583 witnessed the season-ending defeat by Miami, a dismal note on which the Minutemen rode off into the night.

It was, then, a two-faced NASL, far from the 'phenomenon' some proclaimed, and one which had yet to conquer New York. By leaving Downing Stadium the Cosmos nearly doubled their average gates, but at just over 18,000 they still lagged behind the likes of Portland and San Jose. In June Gordon Bradley returned to replace Furphy, which galvanised the team enough for them to win eight of their last ten matches, though it wasn't enough to overtake Tampa Bay in the division. Still, under the league's protracted championship play-off – seemingly devised to ensure even a middling Cosmos performance would land Pelé in the play-offs – New York were able to reach the quarter-finals before losing to the Rowdies.

Though not an outright embarrassment, the elimination of the Cosmos represented a disappointment to a league desperate for its principal star to be put on show. The regret was compounded by the fact that the winners of Soccer Bowl 76 were one of the least popular teams in the league, the Toronto Metros-Croatia, whose unashamed ethnicity all but ensured them of a limited audience. Far from the proponents of attacking football the NASL's points system supposedly encouraged, the M-Cs scored just 38 times in 24 league matches, at one stage going seven games without a goal yet still earning 21 points for winning three times on penalties (tie-wins now being worth six points). Eusebio, acquired from Boston during the winter, offered some inspiration, producing 16 goals in his 22 appearances and scoring in an improbable play-off semi-final victory at Tampa.

The more marketable face of the game, Minnesota, won the other semi-final, meaning that a first-year team had reached the championship match four years running. Discovering that Freddie Goodwin had come unstuck at Birmingham City, the Kicks lured the former Generals manager back to the US, but the melting-pot recruitment tactics that had plagued his time in New York were consigned to the past. Almost the entire Minnesota team was English, and its top goalscorer was a Middlesbrough reserve, Alan Willey.

The league hired the spacious Kingdome for Soccer Bowl 76, but CBS insisted on a 11am kick-off to accommodate other programmes. Embarrassing though this was, the match produced 25,000 fans, and one of Toronto's most measured performances of the season. Eusebio's delightful free-kick opened the scoring, with two further goals taking the championship to Canada for the first time. Celebrations were short-lived: both Eusebio and Sühnholz, the man of the match, found themselves offloaded to other clubs and the humble M-Cs quickly reverted to the more familiar status of also-rans.

If the Soccer Bowl was still a relatively undistinguished event, a tournament earlier in the year with tenuous connections to the nation's 200th birthday gave fresh rein to the more fevered imaginations of the sport's proponents. The NASL and USSF arranged for the national teams of Brazil, Italy and England to square off with a multinational NASL selection erroneously billed as Team America in a 'Bicentennial Cup'. Press boxes, desolate places for even the most keenly anticipated NASL contest, groaned under the weight of foreign journalists, while overseas television obsessively tracked the progress of the visiting entries, pausing occasionally to deride the synthetic nature of the host team.

It turned out to be a feast for even the most discerning fan, the first time three top national teams had converged on American soil. In Washington 33,000 turned up to watch Italy overwhelm the 'home' side 4-0. The result came as little surprise, since Team America's hotchpotch of naturalised citizens, fading international stars and token Americans – the NASL in microcosm – had never played together before. Marsh and Best withdrew from the squad, reportedly because they had not been guaranteed places in the starting line-up (though Marsh later claimed he thought only Americans should have been selected), but Pelé, Moore and Chinaglia all turned out. Team America also lost 2-0 to Brazil in Seattle and 3-1 to England in Philadelphia, but the opposition seemed to be selling most of the tickets. England returned to Yankee Stadium for the first time since their infamous 1953 rainout and drew a crowd of more than 40,000 for a 3-2 win over Italy.

The Bicentennial Cup clearly illustrated the guarded – if not contemptuous – attitude both the NASL and USSF had taken towards the development of the American player. Only four natives were selected for Team America (or 'USA' as it said on the jerseys) and two were goalkeepers. Citizens of ten other countries, most no more yankee-doodle than the teams they lined up against, were granted places in the squad. Though the real US team faced crucial World Cup qualifying games later in the year and would unquestionably have benefited from run-outs against top-class opposition, it didn't play a single game that summer.

The only area in which American players seemed to be advancing in any numbers was in goal. Heading the list was the Rowdies' Arnie Mausser, soon to become a national team mainstay. Shep Messing had come through the Olympic ranks to become Boston's first choice and was now snapped up by the Cosmos, where he replaced an injured Bob Rigby. Half a dozen others found regular spots in the NASL, among them local product Dave Jokerst at St Louis (in competition with the Englishman Len Bond, who was permitted to wear jersey number 007). By 1976, only St Louis could be said to have fielded anything approaching an American-flavoured team, and they again finished with the worst points total in the league, playing to worryingly small crowds. The Stars survived just one more season, unable to keep pace with the rise in quality of the imports. While league clubs had been ordered to increase the number of North Americans in their squads to at least six, there were no constraints on 'naturalised' citizens making up the numbers, and no requirement for any of the six to appear on the pitch.

The league's Americanisation efforts seemed to be focused more on the laws of the game than the nationality of its participants. Having increased the number of substitutes to three, and added 'sudden-death' to its tie-break procedure, the NASL now unveiled its wildest innovation yet: a reworking of the penalty kick tie-breaker which it hoped would generate more excitement and show off more skill. The device was to be called the Shootout, and it was perhaps the most flagrant indication yet that the league had no intention of capitulating to international protocol. The Shootout arose partly as a result of work the Washington Diplomats had carried out for the league, filming various interpretations of ice hockey's penalty shot, in which the attacker was permitted to bear down on goal before trying to score. Officials were excited by the prospect of a scoring attempt in which the goalkeeper played a more active role, and where the shooter needed to do more than merely pick his spot. So in 1977 they moved the ball out to the 35-yard line and allowed the attacker five seconds to find the net, with the goalie free to come off his line.

It was undeniably more dramatic than standard penalty kicks, but whether it belonged in the sport was less clear. 'This thing is not part of the game of soccer,' fumed Gordon Bradley after the Cosmos had lost their first of the new tie-breakers. 'One hundred and forty-eight countries around the world are smart enough not to put things like this into the game,' Eddie Firmani warned. 'We're getting further and further away from the game as it is played in the rest of the world ... Soon we'll have five or six rules to change when we play against foreign teams.' Most of the favourable views seemed to come from the Americans. 'We are all about showbiz,' Al Miller claimed, 'and you have to please your audience.'

Thirty of the 234 regular-season matches were decided by the Shootout in 1977, some rather ignominiously. Artificial pitches provided the greatest potential for embarrassment, cruelly exposing any unfamiliarity with the super-quick surface. Many an unwary player would race towards goal only to find the ball running away from him and into the arms of a grateful goalkeeper. Players – and the occasional referee – often forgot that the attacker was allowed five seconds to shoot, not find the net, and that scoring from a rebound was not allowed, even if time remained.

Fortunately, the most significant event that season had little to do with tie-breakers or refereeing controversies. It wasn't even related to CBS's decision to cancel the final year of its Soccer Bowl contract (the 1976 finale had been another ratings flop). The biggest news that winter, with the benefit of hindsight, was the decision of the Cosmos to abandon New York City. For this, they had the NFL's New York Giants to thank. Five years earlier the Giants had declared their intention to leave the city for a new stadium to be built in East Rutherford, New Jersey. It was a contentious decision. No big-league club had crossed state lines before, at least not without changing its name. The outcry among New Yorkers was fierce, with mayor John Lindsay vowing to 'restrict the right of the Giants to call themselves by the name of the city they have chosen to leave'.

But by 1976 the Giants' new home – actually part of a 'Meadowlands Sports Complex' which included a racetrack, an indoor arena and possibly the body of Teamsters boss Jimmy Hoffa – was ready for occupation. It was in fact no further from Times Square than Yankee Stadium, but to New Yorkers New Jersey was still New Jersey, and their bitterness did not readily subside. (When the team, name intact, won its first Super Bowl in 1987, mayor Ed Koch denied them the satisfaction of the customary ticker-tape parade through the city.) Giants Stadium was a $75 million, 76,000-seat structure designed expressly for football, but its artificial surface made it more amenable to ground-sharing. Toye signed up for ten years. The agreement offered a happy degree of latitude in fixture selection and few conflicts with other sports, since the NFL and NASL seasons barely overlapped. Perhaps more importantly, the facility, surrounded by 25,000 parking spaces, was within easy reach of soccer-friendly communities. Less than four miles down the New Jersey Turnpike stood the city of Kearny.

Thus, The Cosmos, as they were now officially called (not the New York Cosmos, and with a pompous capital 'T') entered a new era, the one most of the world would remember them for. 'We are going to fill this stadium again and again for soccer,' Toye declared, though when the 1977 season kicked off his boast seemed distinctly idle. The Cosmos remained an unseemly tangle of egos and a mishmash of playing styles, and the disenchantment of their marquee player, now in the final year of his contract, was plain for all to see. Pelé did not report for duty until two weeks before the season, almost a month and a half later than most of his team-mates. Bruised pride wasn't hard to find. Chinaglia, firmly ensconced as the resident *prima donna* (it was said he had once paid two team-mates to stand throughout a crowded flight so he could stretch his frame across three seats), said: 'I don't feel a part of this team ... sometimes I feel like it's just a waste of my time playing here.' A beleaguered Gordon Bradley began the new campaign with two Americans, five Englishmen, a Yugoslav, a Peruvian, an Italian and Pelé on the field – and lost 1-0 to a team playing its first league game.

But Woosnam, now given to longer hair and flashier suits and having lost much of his Welsh accent, still burned with ambition. By 1985, he predicted, the NASL would have 32 clubs and its wages would begin to match those of the NFL. And that was only the start. 'I am totally confident,' he insisted, 'that soccer will be the biggest sport in this country, and that the United States will be the world centre of soccer.' This might have seemed ludicrous, yet anyone who had witnessed local baseball diamonds being perforated with soccer posts, and the hordes of youngsters monopolising Saturday morning playing fields, could scarcely discount it.

TV still represented the linchpin of his strategy, and for 1977 Woosnam turned to a syndicated network with a presence in most of the major markets. While the new package was modest – only four regular-season games, plus two play-off matches and the Soccer Bowl – it was more than a nationwide audience had been able to see for some time. The aloof relationship between TV and soccer showed other signs of thawing. Public television, which had offered live NASL matches in 1975, began presenting weekly hour-long highlights of West German matches under the banner *Soccer Made in Germany*. (For a time it also carried an English equivalent, *Star Soccer*, bought from ITV.) Audiences were minuscule, but non-commercial television could afford to be more forgiving, relying as it did on donations rather than ratings. *Soccer Made in Germany* endured in various guises for more than a decade, providing the American fan with a window on German football few other countries could match at the time.

The Bundesliga would make an even more indelible impression on the Cosmos. Having convinced Pelé to come out of retirement for an unprecedented amount of money, Warner saw no reason why a similarly hefty offer wouldn't entice the European Footballer of the Year, Franz Beckenbauer. The move was not quite as preposterous as it might seem. Beckenbauer's private life had become a perpetual source of fascination to the German media after a series of extra-marital relationships, and his club's inability to reclaim its Bundesliga superiority had helped to sour relations with Dettmar Cramer. Initially, Beckenbauer insisted the earliest he would leave Germany was after the 1978 World Cup, but an offer of about $2.8 million, spread over four years, helped change his mind. He arrived in New York in May 1977.

Few could see it, but the Cosmos and the league had begun to take leave of their senses. If Pelé's arrival had boosted the NASL, Beckenbauer's signalled one club's intention to overwhelm it. Some were sceptical of his appeal. 'He's a great player, don't get me wrong,' Chinaglia brooded. 'But is he going to help us with the crowds? No. He won't draw in this country.'

As it turned out, fans flocked to see the Cosmos that season, with or without their new star. More than 45,000 witnessed Beckenbauer's league debut, a 4-2 defeat in Tampa. When the two teams met a month later at Giants Stadium, Pelé scored a hat trick in front of an eye-popping 62,394, a figure which prompted the head of the USSF to claim, somewhat thoughtlessly: 'When they write the history of soccer in this country, that afternoon will be Day One in all the books.' It wouldn't, because Day Ones kept cropping up throughout the summer. On one memorable Sunday the Cosmos even outdrew the Yankees with a gate of 57,000. Admittedly, they did not play 81 times at home as their baseball rivals did, but the Yankees went on to win the World Series that year, and there wasn't a serious sports fan in the nation who couldn't recite most of their starting line-up. The Cosmos, on the other hand, used 26 players during the season, some famous, like Brazilian World Cup defender Carlos Alberto, some unheralded, like English striker Steve Hunt – an emerging star – and others, like Yugoslav Jadranko Topic and Brazil's Rildo, who disappeared after a handful of matches.

The key man was Chinaglia, and not just for his prowess in front of goal. His relationship with Warner chairman Steve Ross had become so intimate that many considered him to be the club's real general manager. It was no coincidence that two of the officials Chinaglia disliked most, head coach Bradley and president Toye, were removed from their positions by the end of the season. In July Bradley gave way to Tampa's Eddie Firmani, who only weeks earlier had mysteriously quit the high-flying Rowdies for 'personal reasons'. Shortly beforehand, eyewitnesses claimed to have seen Firmani dining with Chinaglia.

The unprecedented number of fans flocking to see the Cosmos in their posh new home at last established a presence where the NASL needed it most. Elsewhere, a familiar ratio of failures remained. Membership had declined to 18 clubs with the passing away of Boston and Philadelphia, and the league began to show its proclivity for hasty franchise relocations and daft nicknames. Miami moved up the coast to a smaller market in Fort Lauderdale and renamed themselves the Strikers. Hartford became Connecticut after a move 40 miles south to Yale University (with Bill Cox as their new president and general manager, his last significant involvement in the game) but remained the Bicentennials even though the nation was now well past its 200th birthday. The San Diego Jaws migrated to Las Vegas as the Quicksilvers – or was it the Quicksilver? – and Ward Lay's San Antonio Thunder moved to Honolulu, where they gave up on nicknames altogether and called themselves Team Hawaii.

Most of the new entries were short-lived. Hawaii, a logistical nightmare, became a dismal one-season experiment. Las Vegas finished last in their division and then left Nevada, while Connecticut disappeared after playing to the league's smallest crowds. Only Fort Lauderdale showed any real promise. Ron Newman, their coach, gave the club a predictably English look, emphasising fitness and a tight defence. Gordon Banks came out of retirement in spite of having the lost sight in one eye as a result of a road crash, and played capably enough to be named in the league's all-star team – though not without misgivings ('I felt like a circus act: "Roll up, roll up to see the greatest one-eyed goalkeeper in the world"'). Seemingly headed for Soccer Bowl 77 as the latest first-year success story, they were undone on the soggy artificial pitch of Giants Stadium by a Cosmos team at its free-flowing best. With Beckenbauer – moved from sweeper into the midfield role where he had started his career – playing in front of Carlos Alberto, and Chinaglia, Hunt and Tony Field combining up front, the home side pumped eight goals past Banks, all but eliminating the Strikers before the return leg even began.

The wild 8-3 scoreline was witnessed by an audience even the Cosmos'

NFL cohabitants failed to match that year: 77,691, a figure soon to assume iconic status in American soccer. (It even set a new North American record, eclipsing the improbable 71,619 who saw the 1976 Olympic final between East Germany and Poland in Montreal.) For years to come, the illuminated proclamation of the Giants Stadium scoreboard that August evening would be reproduced whenever the NASL's 'meteoric' rise was charted – something which now began to happen with increasing frequency.

Often misconstrued as the new incarnation of American soccer, the exceptional Cosmos and their sudden throng of fans distracted attention away from more earnest upsurges elsewhere. An appreciable proportion of Dallas began to follow the Tornado, whose combination of American and imported talent, skilfully blended by Al Miller, claimed a divisional title. Yet average crowds of 16,500, respectable as they might be, did not make for good copy when three or four times as many were turning East Rutherford, New Jersey, into the soccer capital of the continent. Nearly 74,000 returned to the Meadowlands for the Cosmos' next home play-off match against the Rochester Lancers, and the 4-1 victory sent them into Soccer Bowl 77. The next day, Seattle drew more than 56,000 to the Kingdome and reached the final by beating Los Angeles 1-0.

Suddenly, the modest 27,000 capacity of Portland's Civic Stadium, which the league had selected as the venue for Soccer Bowl 77, seemed utterly inadequate. Temporary seats accommodated an extra 8,500, but with the match promoted as Pelé's last competitive appearance, they were scarcely enough. It was a mistake Phil Woosnam would not make again.

A mistake – as big as they came – handed the Cosmos an early lead. Tony Chursky, Seattle's Canadian goalkeeper (who attracted the attention of sportswriters by admitting to practising ballet to help his game), rolled the ball to the edge of his penalty area, only for Hunt to steal in and whack it into the net. The Sounders quickly equalised, but ten minutes from time Chinaglia won the match with a rare headed goal. Pelé's American sojourn had ended as most had hoped. 'God has been kind to me; now I can die,' he declared, having exchanged his jersey with the Sounders' Seattle-born defender Jim McAlister, a torch passed to the nation's own young talent.

Two months later, a friendly in the Meadowlands between the Cosmos and Santos saw Pelé 'returned to the people of Brazil', playing a half for each team in a rainstorm that failed to dissuade 75,000 from saying farewell. ABC television got in on the act, broadcasting its first live soccer match and stage-managing proceedings with the help of such theoretical soccer fans as Danny Kaye, Barbra Streisand and Robert Redford, and an elaborate ceremony involving Muhammad Ali and a host of others that threatened to supplant the actual game. But the charisma of the retiree shone through. Pelé scored, waved to the soggy crowd, burst into tears and was carried off the pitch as, some poetically claimed, 'God cried'.

His mission seemed accomplished. Soccer had never been so popular. While the joy of playing it had been obvious for some time, Pelé had heightened interest in watching it and reading about it. Newspapers across the country now carried NASL results and wrote features on college and high school teams, printing photos invariably captioned with a reference to players 'getting their kicks'. Magazines with titles such as *Soccer Corner* and *Soccer Express* – and, for a time, even a weekly soccer tabloid – appeared on newsstands. Bookstores made space for *All About Soccer, Inside Soccer* and *The International Book of Soccer;* Shep Messing even found a publisher for his autobiography, *The Education of an American Soccer Player,* written before his 29th birthday. The unfailing cultural barometer of television advertising now featured soccer players muddying their clothes or working up a thirst for the benefit of commerce.

What some had prophesied in 1967 as 'instant major league' had come to pass – it had just taken a few years longer than expected. Yet the handsome mansion the NASL had built for itself still lacked a sturdy foundation. Nobody had made any money yet, least of all the Cosmos, and most of the league's membership remained anonymous outside a tiny circle of obsessive fans. But in the infectious spirit of the times, these seemed little more than bothersome details. Surely, soccer's time had finally come.

6. Shootout to the Death

The collapse of the NASL

I tell you, those Cosmos were the best and the worst thing that happened to this league.

Atlanta Chiefs official, 1980

S occer in America had never experienced anything like the late 1970s. By 1978 more than 350,000 boys and girls had registered with youth associations, and 5,800 high schools fielded teams. White, middle-class suburbia provided the most fertile ground for this frenzied growth. Soccer moms and dads fervently pointed out that other sports were often dominated by children with exceptional height or strength, or who had simply matured faster than their peers. In Little League baseball, some players could go through a whole game without touching the ball. But there was no overpowering pitcher in soccer, no sitting in a dugout waiting for the next turn, no being told when to swing or when to run. Just about anyone could kick a ball – and nearly everyone kicked it with the same uncultured naivety.

It seemed inevitable that this innate appeal would soon help to establish the professional game. Pelé's departure was widely perceived as timely and appropriate, leaving behind an NASL capable of standing on its own feet. 'The crowds went out to see Pelé in 1975 and 1976,' Clive Toye claimed, 'but in 1977 they went out to see soccer.' The optimism reached its peak in the winter of 1977-78. Woosnam and the owners brought in six new franchises, insisting that expansion to 24 clubs – from just nine five years earlier – was both measured and justified. Indeed, prospective owners were queuing up for a stake in the NASL even if it meant, by Woosnam's own estimate, losing the odd million over the first few seasons. Two years earlier the commissioner had insisted that 'everyone in the league understands we are ultimately going to 32 or 40 teams', and it was now clear why: the steady stream of franchise shifts and new arrivals had earned the league plenty of money. With 27 full-time employees and a spacious office in midtown Manhattan, the NASL looked convincingly established.

The entry fee, now an even $1 million, did little to dissuade a host of new owners from chasing riches. Rick Wakeman, Paul Simon and Peter

Frampton backed a new team in Philadelphia – not the Atoms, but the Fury. Pro soccer also returned to Detroit, where Jimmy Hill, the British TV football pundit and Coventry City chairman, sought to reinvest the tidy sum he had made from ventures in Saudi Arabia. Hill joined forces with a local consortium to bring a team into the 80,500-seat Pontiac Silverdome, the league's largest venue.

The NASL reappeared in the Boston area, as well as Denver, Houston and Oakland; it spread to Memphis, Tennessee, and Tulsa, Oklahoma, two cities with no competition from major league baseball. There was a new assortment of gauche nicknames and logos, the most lamentable in San Diego, the city which found itself with the remains of Team Hawaii. It called its franchise the Sockers, choosing as its logo a bruised boy named Socko with a ball tucked under his arm. The new entry in the north-east was named the New England Tea Men in homage to its backers, the Thomas J Lipton Corporation, as well as the Tea Party of 1773; its badge featured a clipper ship sailing in rough seas. Detroit were nicknamed the Express and distilled their identity into a cartoon automobile poised to head a soccer ball (if an automobile can be said to possess a head). Milan Mandaric, having sold his interest in the San Jose Earthquakes, bought the Connecticut Bicentennials and moved them into Oakland as the Stompers (a ball soaring in front of a bunch of grapes), while the St Louis Stars were now the California Surf, a name dreamt up by an 11-year-old.

There were also, regrettably, the Caribous of Colorado, who played in Denver's 75,000-seat Mile High Stadium. The Caribous would be known not so much for their bizarre logo – a reindeer with an oversized soccer ball stuck in its antlers – as their tan, brown and black strip with a western-style fringe strung across the chest. For better or for worse (certainly worse in the Caribous' case), an unprecedented amount of attention was now being paid to team colours and kits, with fashion designers occasionally roped in to apply the finishing touches. Ralph Lauren inspired the Cosmos to scrap their green-and-white scheme in favour of an all-white ensemble with the shirt collar and socks striped in navy and yellow. Sal Cesarani designed the Philadelphia Fury's shorts to be shorter and the shirts tighter, with three buttons down the front. Club president Frank Barsalona, who managed Frampton and Wakeman, was perhaps influenced by the wife of one of the Fury owners, who professed to being turned on by watching footballers dash about in what she likened to underwear.

NASL matches had never been especially solemn occasions – some clubs did not give a second thought to offering match commentary over the tannoy or piping in music whenever the noise level dropped. But as the decade neared its end the hoopla scaled new heights, embracing fireworks displays, parachute landings and other sideshows. The Cosmos recruited a troupe of scantily-clad cheerleaders and men dressed as Warner Brothers cartoon characters to patrol the touchlines. Seattle released a soccer ball from the roof of the Kingdome and invited fans to predict how high it would bounce. A Dallas radio station scattered $40,000 across the pitch at half-time and selected six fans to pick up as much as they could in 99 seconds (each of the notes was tied to a small stone to prevent them being blown into the crowd). A lion performed a ceremonial kick-off in San Jose, then proceeded to observe play from behind one of the goals – much to the horror of a player who came close to colliding with it. And in Tulsa, a half-time show featured a man calling himself Mr Dynamite, who locked himself in a wooden box and then blew himself out with a few sticks of well-placed explosive. Everything seemed to go according to plan until the smoke cleared and Mr Dynamite was discovered to be unconscious.

The most noticeable feature of the 1978 season, though, was how transparent the league's obsession with professional gridiron had become. The NASL saw nothing wrong with copying the NFL's six-division, two-conference format, or even its names. The Soccer Bowl, like the Super Bowl, was now to be contested by the winners of the American and National Conferences, each of which consisted of three divisions: East, Central and West. This, Woosnam claimed, provided 'excellent television marketing opportunities', though the networks did not seem to agree.

The Cosmos, at last, became the team to beat, and invested heavily in foreign talent: $500,000 for Manchester City's Dennis Tueart and a similar amount for Vladislav Bogicevic of Red Star Belgrade. Chinaglia was the league's deadliest striker, Hunt a willing runner, Beckenbauer and Carlos Alberto without peer. New York swept all before them, destroying Fort Lauderdale 7-0 to start the season and attracting 71,000 to Giants Stadium for a 5-1 defeat of Seattle on 'Franz Beckenbauer Day'.

But the league's bizarre new play-off format put their superiority to a strange test. Sixteen of the 24 clubs qualified for the post-season, reducing the 30-match regular season to an almost meaningless exercise. Furthermore, the first round of the play-offs consisted of a single, winner-take-all contest – meaning that a club like Philadelphia, which had finished last in the American Conference Eastern Division, needed only to put together a decent 90 minutes to eliminate the Detroit Express, winners of the American Conference Central Division. As it happened the Express squeezed through by a single goal – but the New England Tea Men, who finished first in the Fury's division, 22 points in front of Fort Lauderdale, lost to the Strikers and went out.

Then it got much more complicated and even more unfair. The second round was over two legs, but if each team won one of them, the outcome was decided not on aggregate goals but on a further 30 minutes of play immediately after the second leg. The league called this its Mini-Game and claimed it would encourage teams to attack instead of protecting first-leg victories. But it also caused players to wilt. In searing late-summer heat, on unforgiving artificial surfaces, the Mini-Game often made for a grim spectacle. Play could stretch to more than three hours if all the possible permutations were called upon: a draw after 90 minutes of the second leg requiring extra time, then (if scores were still level) a Shootout; if the team that had lost the first leg won the second, then another Mini-Game; and if that did not break the deadlock, one final, winner-take-all Shootout.

This cumbersome system was a ludicrous outcome for a league that had begun its tinkering to provide a quick winner in every game. It was also manifestly unjust. It meant that the remarkable 9-2 second-round, first-leg win the Minnesota Kicks claimed over the Cosmos – in front of 46,000 delirious home fans – counted for little. Two days later, New York won the return by a less dizzying 4-0. When the ensuing Mini-Game failed to produce a goal, the outcome came to rest on the Shootout. Few of the fans in the Meadowlands would forget the sight of Carlos Alberto scooping the ball up with his instep and bouncing it on his thigh as he jogged towards the goal, then letting it fall lazily to the ground and nonchalantly prodding it past the goalkeeper to clinch the victory.

The Cosmos went on to an emphatic semi-final victory over Portland and a 3-1 defeat of Tampa Bay in Soccer Bowl 78, which the league obligingly staged in Giants Stadium. The Rowdies-Cosmos rivalry had become the most celebrated in the league, with Rodney Marsh and Chinaglia its two most prominent characters. But now Marsh was absent with a shin wound, as was Derek Smethurst (traded to San Diego after failing as a place-kicker with the NFL's Tampa Bay Buccaneers). Up against a partisan crowd, the Rowdies acquitted themselves well, but they were unable to rein in Tueart, who scored twice and set up the third for Chinaglia. It marked a bittersweet return to the US for Gordon Jago, who had left Millwall to take over at Tampa.

Chinaglia's 34 goals and 11 'assists' secured him the league scoring title, comfortably ahead of an impressive collection of Englishmen obtained largely on loan and in the prime of their Football League careers. Among them were Trevor Francis (Detroit), soon to become Britain's first million-pound signing, Kevin Hector (Vancouver) and Charlton Athletic's Mike Flanagan, whose 30-goal output for New England (including five in one match against California) prompted the league to name him its Most Valuable Player. Minnesota's Alan Willey weighed in with 21 goals on his way to an NASL career total of 129, more than any other British player.

This reliance on imports, fuelled by rapidly rising salaries, kept Americans off the pitch, or confined them to defensive duties. The top American-born scorer in 1977 was Al Trost, with just ten goals for California, while the fading Kyle Rote managed only six for Dallas. The most American team in the league, the Tornado, now found themselves losing more often than not, and the city's glory-hunting fans drifted away. Enough was enough for some. One of the oldest native-born hands, the Cosmos' Bobby Smith – who was suspended by the club in 1977 after an incident which stemmed from his being left out of the team – pulled no punches when a magazine asked for his comments on the NASL's Americanisation policies:

> We have owners who don't know what's going on, who are being influenced by British coaches and a British commissioner. The British coaches don't feel any obligation to develop American players. They expect an American to walk straight into the first team after he's drafted. If he doesn't do that, they don't want him.

Smith had a point, but one could not fault NASL coaches for wanting to win matches. Many saw too much risk in giving home-grown youngsters even the most cursory run-out. The Cosmos, who had featured Smith and other North Americans sporadically, were far from the guiltiest party – of the 18 players Portland's Don Megson used in 1978, only two were native-born. The Football League put a stop to the loan practice in 1979, but England remained the most common source of NASL talent.

US players typically filled peripheral roles. Virtually anonymous except to the most devoted fan, they usually arrived on the professional stage at 21 or 22, far from polished by their college experience. The college season lasted scarcely four months – fewer than 20 fixtures – meaning that entire university careers often equated to little more than a proper season elsewhere. College coaches continued to exploit the liberal substitution rules, some brazenly adopting 'line change' principles similar to ice hockey, where an entire group of players – or even the whole team – was replaced simultaneously. Such crass latitudes did nothing for the development of top-class talent. The NASL persisted with its college draft, but the absence of what Americans came to call 'impact players' was obvious. The Cosmos drafted seven in 1978, but only one ever played for them. The New England Tea Men, situated in probably the most fertile collegiate area in the country, traded two of their four draft choices away; the other two never made a league appearance.

Thus, the emphasis remained on bringing in foreign players and elite ones at that, whose transfer fees and salary demands were commensurate with major-league crowds and megalomaniac owners. 'The Cosmos have created a monster,' lamented the owner of the Rochester Lancers, the league's humblest team. Now native stars were beginning to demand their share as well, and a few even received it. Oakland agreed to pay Shep Messing $100,000 a year and whisked him away from the Meadowlands. Reports estimated the average NASL salary to be $19,000 – about a third of major league baseball's and a quarter of the NFL's, but considerably more than the $1,500 Kyle Rote had earned in 1973.

It was a lot of money for a league whose financial viability remained doubtful. The mere signing of famous names guaranteed neither a successful team nor popularity at the gate, as the Philadelphia Fury were quick to discover. The club's racy strip had been handed to some of English football's most familiar names: Chelsea idol Peter Osgood, World Cup hero Alan Ball and Leeds legend Johnny Giles. But Osgood managed only one goal in his 22 appearances, while Ball finished the season as the club's manager but was unable to steer them out of last place. As the Fury's gates suffered (averaging fewer than 8,500) some suggested that post-match concerts from a few of their musical owners might be the best way of filling the empty seats.

The Chicago Sting entered their fourth season with the poorest support in the league, faced with two major-league baseball teams and pronounced scepticism from the local media and fans. The club's most promising player, Miro Rys, a Czech-born product of the local leagues, was traded in 1977 to Los Angeles, then signed for Hertha Berlin, only to be killed in a traffic accident the day he arrived in Germany. Although they raided the Bundesliga and elsewhere for fresh blood, the Sting began the 1978 season with ten straight defeats, trimming crowds to as low as 1,500. There was hardly any greater enthusiasm for the Sockers, the NASL's third attempt at winning over San Diego. Hispanic fans showed little interest in the club's largely central European entourage, while the only North American to see much action was five-year veteran Alan Mayer, a New York-born goalkeeper who had suffered so many concussions he had taken to wearing a protective, if perhaps illegal, plastic helmet.

Fan indifference wasn't hard to find. The Memphis Rogues, who parted company with manager Malcolm Allison before the team had even conducted a training session, played before crowds as low as 3,800 in the city's 50,000-seat Liberty Bowl. Houston typically lured no more than 5,000 to watch the Hurricane in the Astrodome. More acutely embarrassing was the situation in Los Angeles, where the woeful Aztecs had moved to the 104,696-seat Rose Bowl and frequently played to more than 100,000 empty seats. George Best served a suspension for failing to turn up for training and no longer seemed to be enjoying himself. Nobody in the team scored more than four goals all season.

In truth, there were only a handful of teams on which to build a league, and even sensational attendance figures in Minnesota and Seattle had been created as much by enterprising marketing as any passion for the game. Entry to an NASL match often entitled fans to eat cheaply at a nearby restaurant, obtain discounts from local shops or see a post-match concert or fireworks display, and it wasn't difficult to buy tickets at a discount for what was increasingly referred to as an 'experience'. While this helped to fill stadiums, it didn't bring in money, and though the gates looked good in the newspapers, the crowds had often assembled to see matches of no particular significance.

Still, if some teams wobbled dangerously, it seemed inevitable they would simply be rescued by people with deeper pockets and sharper promotional skills. The Toronto Metros-Croatia entered the 1979 season with a new nickname, the Blizzard (oddly, for a summer sport), having been purchased by the less ethnocentric Global Television empire. Immediately, crowds nearly doubled. Even more promising was the sale of the Washington Diplomats to Madison Square Garden Corporation, a subsidiary of the enormous Gulf and Western conglomerate. In 1963 Sonny Werblin, the corporation president, had bought the New York Titans, the laughing-stock of the American Football League, and renamed them the Jets. Six years later, with Joe Namath at the helm, they won the Super Bowl. It was a story Woosnam was intimately familiar with – indeed, he claimed that turning soccer into a big-time sport was 'nothing more than the Titans of '63 becoming the Jets of '69'. The

Diplomats, until then persistent under-achievers on and off the pitch, suddenly looked capable of competing with the Cosmos. One of their officials boasted: 'I guess you can say we are not held back in anything we want to do because of money.'

NASL crowds reached 5.3 million in 1978, the best figure yet, and the Cosmos' average of nearly 43,000 was surpassed in Britain only by Manchester United. The syndicated television ratings were largely poor, but in October 1978 a beaming Woosnam emerged with his prized possession: a network contract. ABC announced it would televise nine matches a season, including the Soccer Bowl, for the next three years. While each club received less than $30,000 from the deal – rather less than the $6 million a season each of the 28 NFL teams got from TV – revenue was perceived as less important than 'visibility'.

Not everyone shared the commissioner's obsession with network television, or the enthusiasm for rapid expansion. The league's planning committee had recommended adding just two clubs for 1978 and then one a year, taking membership to 28 by 1987. In 1979, though, such prudence was made to look over-cautious. All 24 franchises were retained, albeit with the usual assortment of ownership changes and relocations. 'The league appears to have reached a period of consolidation and stability,' observed the *New York Times*, proclaiming that the NASL had 'enough things going for it to overshadow the few shaky franchises'. The 1979 season began with an unrivalled sense of anticipation: a presence in nine of the ten largest markets in North America (with only Montreal missing), unprecedented levels of corporate ownership, big-time national television and a rising tide of famous imports.

The assertion that the NASL now started to skim off the cream of the soccer world, though, is largely incorrect. Most of the brightest stars of the era – Alan Simonsen, Zico, Mario Kempes, Kenny Dalglish – never set foot in it. Beckenbauer was an exception, not the rule; in Germany, the NASL had come to be known as *die Operetten-Liga*, a mickey-mouse league. This was a notion largely shared by the British, who viewed the 'razzmatazz' with a mixture of curiosity and disdain. Thus Sweden's evergreen international Bjorn Nordqvist joined Minnesota at 36; Alex Stepney came to Dallas at the same age, after he had lost the Manchester United goalkeeper's jersey to Gary Bailey. Fort Lauderdale claimed West Germany's prolific goalscorer Gerd Müller, but at 34 he was giving way to a promising Karl-Heinz Rummenigge at Bayern. Arsenal's Alan Hudson, though only 28 when he signed for Seattle, had already squandered his English career, while Toronto acquired Peter Lorimer not from Leeds United but more unassuming York City. The backbone of the NASL remained a mix of journeymen and untried youngsters, largely European, primarily British, and almost all unknown outside – or even inside – their own country. Playing alongside Müller and Peru's Teofilo Cubillas in Florida were striker Tony Whelan, who had joined from Rochdale, and Wigan defender Maurice Whittle. The club's top scorer, David Irving, came from Oldham Athletic. In Portland, ex-Rochdale goalkeeper Mick Poole began his third season with the Timbers, playing behind the likes of Graham Day (Bristol Rovers), John Bain (Brentford) and Clive Charles (Cardiff City).

Only the Cosmos – now officially the New York Cosmos again, though they still played in New Jersey – were truly rife with international talent. They had signed the Dutch World Cup pair of Johan Neeskens and Wim Rijsbergen, as well as Andranik Eskandarian, who had come to prominence in the same tournament by scoring an own goal in Iran's draw with Scotland. The signings did little to bring about a more settled side; by the end of the season they had run through 30 players of 14 different nationalities. It was a level of extravagance few other clubs could afford. The one possible exception was the Diplomats, where new coach Gordon Bradley at one stage found himself needing to deny that he would simply fly down to Argentina and buy the team that had just won the World Cup. Bradley did spend a few turbulent days in Buenos Aires trying to sign captain Daniel Passarella, but the club balked at the asking price, and in fact spent relatively frugally that season.

Los Angeles made the league's biggest catch, luring three-time European Footballer of the Year Johan Cruyff out of retirement and linking him up with his mentor Rinus Michels, the Aztecs' new manager. Everyone had expected Cruyff to sign for New York, since the Cosmos had an agreement binding him to their club should he decide to play again. The Aztecs bought out the agreement for $600,000 and then found themselves fighting off a $1.5 million bid from, of all people, the New Jersey Americans of the ASL, a league still searching for a Pelé of its own. Cruyff's decision to play in California seemed at least partly fuelled by self-image, and he made it clear where he saw himself fitting in: 'The Cosmos drew well when they had Pelé, and even after he left they still had a lot of people in the stands,' he noted, 'so I thought my job should be on this coast.'

But the number of Californians who knew his name was considerably less than those in New York who had heard of the other fellow. Compounding difficulties were the expansion plans of the ASL, a league which had broken into the west coast in 1976 and contributed three of the five aspiring professional teams in the Los Angeles area. (In addition to the NASL's California Surf, who played in nearby Anaheim, there were the ASL's Los Angeles Skyhawks, Santa Barbara Condors and the California Sunshine, in the promising location of Villa Park, near Anaheim. Apart from the Aztecs, all folded within four seasons.)

On his league debut, in midweek against Rochester, Cruyff could not entice 10,000 to the Rose Bowl; a week later, just 5,900 saw him play in New England. Michels soon turned the Aztecs back into a contender, but could do little about the empty seats. Average gates rose to a club record 14,000, but this was still only a third of what the Cosmos pulled in on a typical day at the Meadowlands. Cruyff, for all his impressive performances on the pitch, proved to be no Pacific-coast Pelé. By the end of the season the Diplomats, having failed in their bid to tempt Trevor Francis away from Nottingham Forest, took him to Washington. It scarcely transformed their own attendance difficulties, and by 1981 Cruyff was out of the league.

The departure was probably hastened by his well-known aversion to artificial turf – it may even have influenced his decision not to sign for the Cosmos – which by the late Seventies had spread across the country with abandon. For British veterans whose careers had been built on strength and aggression and who felt at home in ankle-deep mud, playing on a carpet laid over concrete was a challenge. Others considered it downright treacherous. Beckenbauer missed 12 weeks of the 1979 season with a knee injury he blamed on the Giants Stadium pitch. Others wrestled with shin splints, ingrown toenails and ugly abrasions. But it would be years before ailments such as 'turf toe' passed into the American sporting vernacular, and gridiron and baseball teams had not yet begun to attribute serious injuries to their playing surfaces. Astroturf was still seen as the future, particularly in stadiums expected to cope with more than one sport.[*] Winning in the NASL now meant not just overcoming the Cosmos, but coming to terms with their pitch as well. Of the 20 teams who reached the championship game (or series)

---

[*] The Monsanto Corporation, which had been testing synthetic pitches in the mid-1960s, gained its initial breakthrough through rather bizarre means. Houston's Astrodome was originally built with a grass surface, but baseball teams found it impossible to track flying balls under the dome's glass. When the glass was painted over, the grass died. After Monsanto rolled out their synthetic solution in 1966, Judge Roy Hofheinz, the owner of the Dome, persuaded them to call the surface Astroturf, a name which quickly passed into generic use, although the product has long since been superseded.

after the first Soccer Bowl in 1975, 13 played on plastic. Of the 20 losing semi-finalists, 16 played on grass.

Or part-grass. The NASL was no more successful than its predecessors at addressing the familiar problem of laying a soccer pitch over a baseball diamond. The Chicago Sting's relief at leaving Soldier Field was tempered by their need to use baseball parks. Six other clubs shared their home with teams in the major leagues, leaving them to cope with dirt infields and awkward sightlines. Some struggled to accommodate a rectangular pitch, a limitation even the mighty NFL had recognised and compromised over. (When Milwaukee's baseball stadium hosted Packers games the corner of one end zone was lopped off slightly, sending the occasional touchdown-scorer crashing into the perimeter wall.)

The problem was far worse for the NASL. American football required a field exactly $53^1/_3$ yards wide, a distance set nearly a century earlier because it was all Harvard University's new stadium could accommodate. The dimension had been hampering soccer ever since. Rochester played on a pitch 65 yards wide, Minnesota just 63. Though a field of 100 by 50 yards passed muster with FIFA, the minimum for international matches (110 by 70) was – suspiciously – only just met by most teams. Soccer played on pitches marked out for gridiron, with all manner of lines, numbers and graphics stencilled across the field, helped to reinforce notions of inferiority, and even provided moments of low comedy when inexperienced players failed to interpret the lines correctly. It was clear the NASL needed its own homes, or at least more sympathetic ones, but the league was not prepared to plant its roots to such a depth.

Not much thought, and certainly little media attention, was given to this particular growing pain. While some Cosmos players complained about the dimensions and surface of Giants Stadium, the two-time champions were in no mood to leave what they now regarded as their home, frequented as it was by the likes of Henry Kissinger and Mick Jagger. Soccer was hip, and it was hippest in the Meadowlands. They had become an international phenomenon, touring the world and filling stadiums from Indonesia to Ecuador. Almost 40,000 turned up at Stamford Bridge in 1978, the Cosmos boosted by the addition of Cruyff as a guest player, during a season when Chelsea averaged barely half that.

Not all the attention was favourable. FIFA, happy to bless bold experiments like an 18-yard offside line for an anonymously tiny league, had begun to feel differently now that the NASL had apparently grown up. Their strongest objections were to the use of three substitutes instead of two and the 35-yard offside line, both of which contravened its laws of the game (the Shootout and elaborate points system did not). As early as April 1978 FIFA threatened to blacklist the NASL if it did not start toeing the line and warned the USSF that staging the World Cup or other large tournaments would be out of the question. But the league did nothing.

This was not the only source of heat. The huge salaries offered to foreign stars increasingly dwarfed those that even the best native talent could hope for. In the late 1960s and early 1970s pro baseball and basketball players had beefed up their unions (or 'player associations') to gain a much greater share of the television riches. Baseball's salaries more than doubled between 1967 and 1975, while basketball's increased five-fold to an average of $107,000. These facts were not lost on NASL players, particularly native ones. Yet as the 1970s drew to a close they had yet to even obtain union recognition from the owners. Frustration reached simmering point as the 1979 season began. Scarcely had a ball been kicked than the NASL Players Association declared a strike, in the emphatic belief that a majority of colleagues would support it. Indeed, 69 per cent of players had voted for action. Even the Cosmos, who ostensibly stood to gain the least, voted overwhelmingly in favour. But the owners refused to back down and ordered coaches to begin searching for 'replacement' labour as a contingency.

The issue was clouded by the federal government's stance on resident aliens working during a recognised labour stoppage (an issue which certainly set the NASL apart from the country's other professional leagues). At first, it seemed the foreign players might be deported if they continued to work. Then the Immigration and Naturalisation Service, influenced by the Justice Department, changed its mind. Three-quarters of the players crossed picket lines, including the entire Cosmos team, who were in the middle of a three-match road trip. Only a few clubs, such as New England and Portland, found themselves dependent on new labour. When 72,000 turned up for the Cosmos' first home game – a new national record for a regular-season match – any chance the strike had of success evaporated. 'A majority of the foreigners really don't care about the league or protection of the players,' concluded Bobby Smith, the Cosmos' union representative who found himself traded to San Diego by season's end. It was true that among the foreign imports who, enthusiastically or otherwise, promoted the game through endless public appearances and freely dispensed advice to young team-mates, there were many who had come to the NASL for an easy life. Spending a few lazy summers earning a hefty paycheque alongside some of international football's household names, before a largely naive public, was a lot more comfortable than toiling in the Football League.

The Cosmos and their nemesis Tampa Bay seemed the likeliest candidates for Soccer Bowl 79 and both turned in strong seasons. Gordon Jago had bravely parted company with most of his British contingent, save for Rodney Marsh and Tottenham full-back John Gorman. Oscar Fabbiani arrived from Chilean club Palestino to worry Chinaglia at the top of the scoring charts and average crowds in Rowdiesland exceeded 27,500. But the reigning champions remained a step ahead of everyone else. They lost just two of their first 14 games and scored in every regular-season match. In fact, the club's greatest enemy seemed to be itself, its list of egocentrics topped by the irrepressible Chinaglia. New York's impressive start did not prevent Eddie Firmani from being sacked just two months into the season. While the club blamed his departure on a failure to develop the younger players, most believed he had fallen out with the one player he could least afford to. Firmani disappeared, briefly, into the obscurity of the ASL, replaced by a New York college coach, Ray Klivecka, and a 'technical director', Julio Mazzei, whom most had known as Pelé's interpreter.

Chinaglia's 26 goals once again made him the league's top scorer, and his temperament was still very much in evidence. During one mid-season practice he jumped into the stands to fight with heckling members of the clean-up crew at Giants Stadium, an altercation which left one man in hospital. As a goalscorer, though, the NASL knew no equal. In 100 matches over four seasons, Chinaglia scored 94 times. Even more impressively, he managed 20 goals in 20 play-off games. The following season he scored seven in a match against Tulsa.

Few expected the Cosmos to come unstuck in their semi-final against Vancouver, even if the Whitecaps had beaten them twice, by considerable margins, during the regular season. Tony Waiters, a former England goalkeeper, had become Vancouver's coach in 1977 after parting company with Plymouth Argyle and quickly replaced a team of Canadians with a blend of experienced and ambitious English pros. In mid-season he acquired Alan Ball from the flagging Philadelphia Fury to solidify an already impressive midfield. Canadian fans responded in record numbers: the Whitecaps' average attendance of 23,000 was nearly twice what it had been two years earlier.

The first leg in Vancouver produced a crowd of nearly 33,000, and ample evidence of the Cosmos' petulance. Carlos Alberto's famously explosive temper earned him suspension from the second leg after he assaulted a linesman and Eskandarian received a similar fate after being sent off in the dying seconds. Trevor Whymark and Willie Johnston scored in a 2-0 Whitecaps' win. Three days later, the return match produced what many regard as the jewel of the league's history. Ahead 2-1, the Cosmos seemed to have the match wrapped up until Johnston headed a last-minute equaliser. Fifteen minutes of extra time produced no further score, leaving the match in the hands of the Shootout, which the Cosmos won. The outcome of the tie now depended on the 30-minute Mini-Game. Though both teams had apparent goals disallowed – New York's in the penultimate minute – neither scored. Left with a new Shootout to determine the winner, the Cosmos' hopes came to rest on Nelsi Morais, a seldom-used Brazilian defender, who failed to get his shot away within the five seconds. After three and a half tense hours of soccer of varying descriptions, Vancouver had upset the Cosmos to reach the Soccer Bowl.

As their fans scowled, the losers did little to dispel their reputation as prima donnas, claiming the officiating in Vancouver had been 'inadequate' and bizarrely suggesting that the referee should not have been selected for the match because he was Canadian. 'I think this is the way the league wants it,' Mazzei sniffed. 'I don't think they wanted the Cosmos in the final.' The sense of persecution was acute enough for the club to consider legal action over what they deemed an 'anti-Cosmos feeling' among NASL executives. The league's preparation for Soccer Bowl 79 suggested otherwise. It had again chosen Giants Stadium as the venue, in the reasonable expectation that the home team would be there to fill it. But 16,000 fans who had bought tickets now decided to bin them. Only 50,000 turned out to see Vancouver take on Tampa Bay, who had seen off San Diego in a Mini-Game of their own.

The final thus became something of an anti-climax. Rodney Marsh made his last appearance for the Rowdies, his career coming to an end with an ignominious substitution 12 minutes from time. Vancouver claimed a 2-1 win, but when Woosnam and Kissinger, the league's nominal 'chairman', stepped forward to present the championship trophy, chants of 'Cosmos' filled the air. Boos cascaded from the stands as the Whitecaps attempted their victory lap. 'It was like, "forget the rest of the NASL, it's only the Cosmos",' Waiters complained.

Is it time to break up the Cosmos? one New York newspaper asked, inviting San Diego manager Hubert Vogelsinger and Woosnam to argue whether the franchise had grown too big for the league. Vogelsinger said yes:

The plan was for a slow, gradual development of the teams and the league, a soundly-based plan that wouldn't cause some owners to lose their shirts. Now the whole thing is upside down. The player market has been totally upset by the Cosmos, whose owners have been going around the world luring players to New York with outrageous salaries ... The creation of a team like the Cosmos violates a basic American axiom – fairness.

Woosnam, not surprisingly, defended the Cosmos partly with references to pro gridiron:

I think the rate of achieving success always varies within the league, as demonstrated with the American Football League in the early 60s. Initially the (Oakland) Raiders and (Kansas City) Chiefs made the league go. Then, ultimately, other teams like the Patriots, Broncos, Jets – everyone caught up.

The NASL's catching-up process had a long way to go. While average gates broke 14,000 for the first time, it was not the resounding figure the NASL had anticipated, and a few warning signs began to appear. Crowds had dropped significantly in Minnesota even though the Kicks continued to field one of the strongest teams in the league. In Houston, Finnish-born Timo Liekoski, who had been Al Miller's successor at Hartwick College, had turned the Hurricane into division champions, yet they entertained crowds of only a few thousand. Other big-city clubs – Detroit, New England, Chicago, Dallas and the woeful Philadelphia Fury – played to similarly empty houses. ABC's television ratings compounded the disappointment. Viewing figures for the Soccer Bowl were hurt by the absence of the Cosmos, but even when the club had been featured during the regular season, audiences were small. There was no evidence that the NFL-style divisional line-up had transformed the NASL's appeal, and still no sign that all those children meant anything to the box office.

When the 1980 season began with exactly the same teams from the season before – an unprecedented feat – many assumed the league had stabilised. But five franchises had changed owners and a number of clubs were on shaky ground, some to the tune of several million dollars. Calls for austerity fell on deaf ears. Even the reasonably pragmatic Lamar Hunt found himself signing Bundesliga scoring ace Klaus Toppmöller from Kaiserslautern for $1 million and moving his Tornado back into the enormous Texas Stadium. The Cosmos' thirst for top-class international talent now extended into management. They brought in Hennes Weisweiler, the architect of Borussia Mönchengladbach's rise to German football supremacy, who more recently had led Cologne to the West German championship. It was their sixth managerial change in less than four years and, combined with the arrival of Cor van der Hart at Fort Lauderdale, meant British managers were no longer in the majority.

While Toppmöller's contribution in Dallas proved less than spectacular, an influx of Germans had transformed the Tornado, and did much the same for Chicago. The Sting's new hero was Karl-Heinz Granitza, the top scorer for high-flying Hertha Berlin who had arrived on loan in 1978. Dick Advocaat, the future manager of Rangers and the Dutch national team, also joined. They and other imports finally helped the Sting attract a modicum of attention, not only from the city's disinclined soccer fans, but also from success-starved Chicagoans. Inevitably, though, attention centred on the Cosmos, and whether their new manager could exert enough influence on his charges to stop them from self-combusting. With the rampant Chinaglia scoring 32 regular-season goals, an average of one a game, and the elegance of Beckenbauer and Bogicevic, New York swept into Soccer Bowl 80 with little resistance. But in moving Beckenbauer back to his familiar libero role, the manager had affronted Carlos Alberto. Left out of the 3-0 win over Fort Lauderdale in Soccer Bowl 80, Alberto vowed never to play for the club again. The following season he joined the California Surf.

Kaiser Franz departed too, back to the Bundesliga to win another title, this time with Hamburg. Though his spell in New York drew plaudits – he made the league's all-star team in each of his four seasons – he was not the successor to Pelé the club had hoped for. Beckenbauer considered his style of play too subtle for his new audience:

> The Americans loved it when a guy dribbled around three or four people. Then they would be very nice and disregard that the fifth man took the ball away from the guy. They'd cheer like crazy. In Europe, you'd be whistled out of the stadium for that kind of foolishness. Reversing the flow of play, building a rhythm, consistency … these are harder things to get excited about.

Of course, one could no more blame American fans for their lack of sophistication than blame Germans for not understanding how a baseball pitcher worked the strike zone. But Beckenbauer's point was largely lost on an American soccer media which saw little point in insulting its audience, regardless of how accurate his claims were.

The 1980 season proved to be the NASL's watershed. Sonny Werblin's Diplomats, whose average attendance had exceeded 19,000 – far more than Washington had produced before – lost $5 million in two years. Jimmy Hill later claimed the entire three-year budget of his Detroit Express, about $3 million, had been spent in the first 12 months. In total, the 24 teams were said to have lost about $30 million over the season. Average crowds increased only marginally – in New York they fell by 4,000 – and television coverage was a flop. ABC declared it was no longer interested in the NASL and would show only the Soccer Bowl in 1981.

Owners spent the winter squabbling over strategy. Werblin advocated consolidation, weeding out the weaker teams and smaller markets and giving the Cosmos more of a run for their money. Clandestinely, some of his colleagues agreed, and even hatched plans for a 12-team league. But there would be no breakaway and, since decisions to reduce the number of participants required the consent of all the owners, no radical restructuring. So Werblin pulled out. The Diplomats turned in their franchise certificate, with Rochester and Houston following suit. The Lancers ended an 11-year affiliation with the league, their demise hastened by competing sets of owners seeking to gain control of the team. One faction had hired Ray Klivecka from the Cosmos; the other sacked him just hours after a match against Toronto.

These were far from the only losses. The New England Tea Men, who in 1979 had been forced out of their NFL home, returned in 1980 but under a restrictive lease which forced them to play most of their matches on Saturday afternoons or Monday nights. When gates promptly slumped the owners moved the club to Florida, christening them (with little regard for history or logic) the Jacksonville Tea Men. In Philadelphia, new coach Eddie Firmani sent the club's top scorer, former Scottish international striker David Robb, to Vancouver, and loaned the charismatic Frank Worthington to Tampa Bay. Neither was adequately replaced, consigning the Fury to another last-place finish. With gates now approaching 2,000, the showbiz owners baled out, selling the franchise to a Canadian brewery, who moved it to Montreal. The Memphis Rogues, who had once sought to be the second franchise in New York – a move inevitably vetoed by the Cosmos under the league's 'territorial rights' provisions – also fled the country after being bought by Nelson Skalbania, a self-made Vancouver millionaire who seemed to collect sports franchises as a hobby (he would later be convicted of embezzlement). His Calgary Boomers, with Al Miller as manager, went bust after a year.

Though fingers were pointed in all sorts of directions, many of them were suddenly aimed at Woosnam. Owners had been happy to collect the handsome entrance fees that rapid expansion had brought, but they were less thrilled with seeing their clubs playing before four-digit crowds, particularly when wage bills had soared. Those who did not share the commissioner's obsession with the NFL and network television pointed to the survival of ice hockey's NHL for decades with minimal national television exposure.

'Americanisation' was another bone of contention. A generation of Americans had now grown up with soccer balls at their feet, yet none had really progressed to the highest level. The Cosmos had touted a Denver-born college product, Rick Davis, as the country's next superstar, and featured him in almost all their matches in 1979. But injury limited his appearances in 1980, and the best American performance that season probably came from St Louisan Steve Moyers, whose 13 goals in 26 matches for California didn't even place him among the top ten. The NASL had increased the minimum requirement for North Americans on the pitch from two to three, but it was a change most clubs easily accommodated with their cadre of naturalised citizens. In their semi-final play-off with the Cosmos, the Aztecs fielded a team consisting entirely of foreign-born players, while Fort Lauderdale's Soccer Bowl 80 representatives contained just one player born in the US.

This did not point towards a fruitful national team, and neither did the 4-0 defeat with which the US began its qualification for the 1980 Olympics in Mexico (where the teams lined up to the strains of the German national anthem instead of *The Star Spangled Banner*). They ended up qualifying for Moscow through the back door, after Mexico were banned for fielding professional players, but never played there because of the American boycott over the Soviet Union's invasion of Afghanistan.

In 1976, the federation had hired only its second full-time manager, Ukrainian-born Walt Chyzowych (brother of Gene, who had been in temporary charge a few years earlier), naming him to lead both the Olympic and full national team. Denied a trip to Moscow, Chyzowych focused on qualification for the 1982 World Cup, which began only a few months after the Olympics. With 24 nations now invited, including two from Concacaf, the United States no longer needed to finish ahead of Mexico, a hopeful note soon to be soured through the usual arcane machinations of the USSF.

Some were baffled as to how Chyzowych had managed to keep his job after the US failed to reach Argentina four years earlier with a reasonably well-prepared team. USSF officials had even lobbied Standard Liege to release Hungarian-born Gyula Visnyei, whom NASL fans would soon recognise as Julie Veee, probably the only player in the world whose name featured three consecutive identical vowels. Before Veee's arrival, the Americans had taken a point in Vancouver against Canada and held Mexico to a goalless draw, with the USSF once again effectively conceding home advantage by staging the game in Los Angeles (the crowd of 33,171 set a national team record). The group ended with all three teams on the same number of points. Mexico advanced to the final qualifying round with a superior goal difference, but Concacaf ordered a play-off to separate the other two – in Haiti, three days before Christmas.

The federation had begun to pay attention to all those reports it had written which implored its World Cup teams to be given time to train and play together. In preparation for the showdown in Port-au-Prince it arranged a series of test matches, including three against the full Haitian team, all of which ended goalless. After witnessing Canada's feeble 3-0 warm-up defeat to that country, a confident Chyzowych boasted: 'I think the score could be 3-0 to us.' Instead, the Canadians took a surprise first-half lead when one of their efforts struck an American defender, then a post, then the crossbar and then the net. The US's familiar lack of scoring punch was exposed as Canada marked Veee out of the game and scored two late goals to win 3-0.

Three years later Chyzowych was still at the helm and the USSF was more than $1 million richer from sponsors such as Coca-Cola, which had invested heavily in the nascent World Youth Cup (the Under-20 championships). The US played host to the Concacaf qualifying round of the 1981 competition, the first time it had staged an international tournament of any consequence, and qualified for the finals, where the team flopped. When it came to qualifying for the 1982 World Cup the federation again contributed to the team's downfall, this time by securing a sponsorship deal requiring national team players to wear Adidas boots for a preparatory European tour. Many players refused, since they were under contract to rival firms, and had always kept such money for themselves. When they demanded compensation, USSF officials flew over from New York, told the players no more money would be made available and advised those who were unhappy to pack their bags. Bobby

Smith did. Those who stayed were still divided, over what amounted to a few dollars a day, and a helpless Chyzowych found his plans in tatters.

The tour drove a wedge through the team. The US began qualification with a damaging 0-0 draw against Canada in Fort Lauderdale, then lost the return in Vancouver, which all but eliminated them before they had even faced the Mexicans. A 5-1 rout in Mexico City doused remaining hopes and Chyzowych bore the brunt of the criticism. His regime had generally produced defensive, regimented teams rife with poor discipline (three sendings-off in nine qualifying matches, two of them for the captain, Steve Pecher). In most other countries the dismissal of a national team manager who had failed in two World Cup campaigns would be inevitable, yet the USSF seemed to think progress had been made. Less than a year earlier, the performance of the Olympic team led Chyzowych to boast: 'People think we are bad, but I've got news for you: look out for us, because we've arrived.' Now, in the aftermath of Mexico City, he was left to mutter: 'Let's not have illusions – we're not even close.' At times his team selection reeked of desperation. He played Davis, a midfielder with the Cosmos, at centre-forward against Canada, then moved him to sweeper for the Mexico game. The Cosmos stepped forward to accuse Chyzowych of destroying progress, with Chinaglia, never short of an opinion, leading demands for his resignation.

Chyzowych retorted that the NASL hardly offered much of a foundation for his team, since clubs had failed to develop American players. Nor did it help to have a Cosmos official appear in the dressing room immediately after the Canada match, tickets in hand, to take players away for a winter tour. The coach duly departed, but his points remained valid. For all the NASL owners' pronouncements, their attitude towards a foreign competition which earned them no revenue and merely ran the risk of injuring their employees could be easily surmised (some clubs even bridled at excusing players from a training session in order to play for their country).

While the Cosmos featured more native players in their team than most, they also stood accused of hoarding American talent, acquiring players just to keep them away from other clubs. In 1980 they signed a Maryland high school prospect, Daryl Gee, tipping him to become America's first black soccer star, then waited two years before putting him in the team. Larry Hulcer, named the league's Rookie of the Year in 1979 with Los Angeles, was traded to New York in 1980 only to sit on the bench. By 1981 he was out of the league altogether. Boris Bandov, Angelo DiBernardo and David Brcic were important parts of Chyzowych's set-up, but with the Cosmos all three were usually second-choice.

If the NASL was failing to bring along American players, it was faring even worse with American coaches. Including the NPSL of 1967, 112 men had been in charge of NASL teams for at least part of a season, yet only ten were American-born and three of those had been in charge only briefly. The country remained pitifully short of quality coaches. Yet there was little incentive for them to leave the relative safety of a college empire, often built over many years, only to discover, as Ray Klivecka had at the Cosmos, they had very little influence on team affairs.

NASL budgets now started to tighten, and by 1981 most teams found themselves struggling. The league could have made things easier by requiring them to use more American players, but it still believed imports created a more attractive product. Consequently, while some marquee names departed, new talent continued to arrive as if nothing was wrong. San Diego signed the Polish international Kazimierz Denya; Fort Lauderdale picked up three-time South American Footballer of the Year Elias Figueroa of Chile and West German international Bernd Holzenbein; and Montreal brought Manchester United's Gordon Hill back into the league after a five-year absence (he had played for Chicago in 1976). Brian Kidd left Bolton Wanderers for Atlanta while Steve Daley, Britain's record signing two years earlier, joined Seattle for nearly $1 million. No one seemed willing to contemplate what might lie ahead – certainly not the Cosmos, who were said to earn $1.2 million a year from their close-season international tours, and whose participation in a 'Trans-Atlantic Challenge Cup' during the early part of the season drew more than 60,000 for a Giants Stadium double-header involving Vancouver, Roma and Manchester City.

Sensing a loss of interest, some owners – among them Freddie Goodwin, now president of the Minnesota Kicks – pushed for more radical changes to the game. Winter meetings saw wild ideas bandied about by Goodwin and others, including an even more confusing scoring system which allowed teams to claim 15 points by winning a match with at least three goals in open play. This was voted down, as were proposals to widen the goals, or even narrow the posts, reduce matches to 70 minutes to permit time-outs for coaching (and television commercials) and, interestingly, to restrict back-passes to the goalkeeper.

Much of the reluctance to experiment further could be traced to threats from FIFA, which remained unyielding towards its laws. The NASL's rejoinder was that it produced more goals – 3.37 a game – than any other league in the world (the English First Division average in 1979-80 was 2.51, but the Bundesliga was up to 3.39 a year later) and attributed this in part to its 35-yard line and extra substitution. By 1981 FIFA had grown tired of such rationalising. It demanded the NASL scrap the two changes by March 31 or the federation would face expulsion.

But the NASL counted in its ranks plenty of headstrong owners who did not take kindly to ultimatums from foreign lands. The season approached without any changes. Caught in the middle was the USSF, which pleaded with the league not to take FIFA 'for fools'. Finally, with the first of the new season's matches just hours away, the NASL capitu-lated – if only for a fortnight. On April 9 it received a message from FIFA President João Havelange which it claimed gave the league permission to revert to its own rules for the rest of the season. That was debatable – the message was confusingly worded and led some USSF officials to claim the NASL misconstrued it on purpose.

The NASL did rescind the two rules for 1982, and restricted most of its future tinkering to infrastructure. The NFL-style divisional formats and the Mini-Game were scrapped in favour of five divisions and best-of-three play-off series; a 32-match regular season eliminated only six of its 21 clubs. But none of this halted the decline in attendances and growing uncertainty over the league's very existence. Almost every club reported a drop in gates: the Cosmos were down to less than 35,000, their worst average in four seasons, and Minnesota's had alarmingly fallen below 17,000. Vancouver, its list of goalscorers headed by 20-year-old Peter Beardsley, lost 3,500 a game after four straight years of increases. The Aztecs moved out of the Rose Bowl and back into the Coliseum, only to find even smaller crowds – 2,300 at one point – watching a reasonably successful team under the former Brazil manager Claudio Coutinho. Neither party would survive another year: the Aztecs folded and soon afterwards Coutinho drowned in a fishing accident off Ipanema Beach.

The happy exception to the misery was Montreal, where the new Manic played to enthusiastic crowds which grew steadily over the course of a promising season. A play-off encounter with Chicago drew more than 58,000, better than anything the Cosmos could manage that year. The Manic finished with the second-highest attendance in the league, a badly needed sign that all hope was not necessarily lost. Chicago ended the season as champions, but the city only took an interest once a title loomed into view: 39,600 saw the deciding match of their play-off semi-final with San Diego. At Soccer Bowl 81 – held outside the US for the first time, in Toronto – fewer than 37,000 saw the Sting beat New York in a Shootout after a 0-0 draw, becoming Chicago's first professional sports champions since 1963. The match took place on a Saturday night (Toronto's Canadian Football League team occupied the stadium the next day) and since the television contract specified a Sunday kick-off, ABC did not show it live. Still, 7,000 fans greeted the Sting on their return from Canada as soccer reached the front page of that city's newspapers for perhaps the first time. The adulation would prove short-lived.

In fact, the afterglow began to fade the next day, when three clubs announced they were folding and two others agreed to merge. The deaths of the flagging Atlanta Chiefs and California Surf were no great surprise, but the demise of Washington set alarm bells ringing. After Gulf & Western's withdrawal the Diplomats had been rescued by Jimmy Hill and other owners of the Detroit Express, who had folded that club after three seasons of empty seats. In spite of the losses incurred in Michigan, Hill daringly invested £500,000 of Coventry City's money in his new team. But with Cruyff playing only five times in 1981 and the club stuck in the same division with New York and Montreal, the Dips struggled. By June they were up for sale and in August the *New York Times* reported that Hill was virtually bankrupt (his son Duncan, the club's general manager, claimed: 'All we have left is our home'). Hill angrily denied this, insisting he had lost only the money he had earned in Saudi Arabia, and that Coventry's stake in the Diplomats – a figure described by City's secretary as 'sizeable' – was only equivalent to 'a moderate player'. But it was gone, and so was the franchise.

So, too, were the Minnesota Kicks, who only three years earlier had averaged more than 30,000 but whose 1981 season was played out against a backdrop of uncertainty. Their multipurpose home, shared with the baseball Twins and gridiron Vikings, was about to be demolished – eventually making way for the largest shopping mall in the world – and the club had not secured a right to use the new domed facility being built in central Minneapolis. Chairman Ralph Sweet, a former executive at Notts County, accused the Vikings of complicity, but the stadium was only half the story. The ticket discounts and giveaways had failed to create the expected mass of loyal fans, or any income. The club's last home match, a play-off defeat by Fort Lauderdale, took place in front of fewer than 12,000.

The cruellest blow of all came with the demise of the Dallas Tornado, lone remnant of the league's first season. Lamar Hunt's pleas for austerity had fallen on deaf ears. His suggestion that each club's losses be kept to a maximum of $400,000 contrasted sharply with the $35 million the league was said to have lost in 1981. The Tornado's season, in which they won just five matches, rivalled the Kap/Spurgeon regime for futility. Merging Dallas with Tampa Bay, Hunt became a Rowdies director for a time, but in effectively folding his tent the man who had helped prop up the league during its darkest hours in 1969 and who had always forecast sunshine for soccer, now sent dark clouds scuttling across the skies. There would be no more expansion teams in the NASL, only casualties.

Where had all the fans gone? Why was the league losing its appeal when soccer continued to encroach on the conventional pastimes of American youth? The league's exposure had never been greater – ABC might have all but given up on it, but two national cable networks and numerous local stations had put more matches on the air than ever before. The summer of 1981 had even produced a strike by major league baseball players, handing the NASL seven weeks of undivided summer attention. But the league had neither been able to attract bored baseball fans nor increase the size of its TV audience. Pro soccer seemed to have been a fad. Attending a match had always carried a certain novelty appeal, particularly when tickets were cheap and the atmosphere was festive. While the NASL produced a clique of native fans who warmed to the game, and even embraced it, the result wasn't nearly enough to fill big-league stadiums. The awful truth was that most of the 77,691 who had packed Giants Stadium that famous August evening in 1977 were never potential season ticket-holders. Many, in fact, were not likely to pay to watch a soccer match again.

All of which left Phil Woosnam in a precarious position, particularly after his disastrous decision to play the Soccer Bowl on Saturday night left the league without live TV coverage of its showcase game. Though he stayed on as commissioner for another season, the owners created a new post of league president which effectively displaced him. The position was filled by Howard Samuels, a 62-year-old New York entrepreneur whose greatest sporting success had been as chairman of the city's new and hugely successful Off-Track Betting Corporation. 'It's absolutely true that soccer hasn't made it commercially here,' Samuels admitted, 'but I'm sure it will make it – and I say to the NFL, watch out because ten years from now we'll be the leaders, on the field and on television.'

The words had a depressingly familiar ring to them, one that seemed especially hollow now that the NASL had no presence in seven of the nation's ten largest markets and an enormous pile of debt. Increasingly the 'phenomenon' of soccer seemed to be giving way to the new 'phenomenon' of indoor soccer, an enterprise apparently unable and unwilling to cultivate interest beyond its own narrow peripheries.

In July Samuels outlined his priorities for the season in the *New York Times*. Near the top of the list was a reconciliation with the Major Indoor Soccer League, whose 'Americanised' game had caught on like a virus in cities such as Baltimore and St Louis which the NASL had never managed to crack. He also drew attention to developing native players and qualifying for the 1986 World Cup. But his biggest priority was injecting some semblance of financial realism into a league which had somehow survived for 15 years without making any money.

The boom was over. In 1982 gates fell in every city except Toronto. Plenty of famous names had departed, Cruyff, Müller, Best and Figueroa among them. But the Cosmos, even playing before crowds as low as 18,000, were still a formidable team. Victories over Tulsa and the luckless San Diego Sockers – defeated in the semi-finals for the fourth straight year – put them in their fifth Soccer Bowl in six seasons. There they faced Seattle, who squeezed through two nail-biting play-off victories over Fort Lauderdale partly thanks to their new striker Peter Ward, acquired from Nottingham Forest. But Soccer Bowl 82, staged in San Diego, was, in Samuels' words, 'a disaster', 23,000 turning up in one corner of the country to see teams from two of the others. It wasn't broadcast on national TV and the media, which began to circle the league like a vulture, used the event primarily to speculate about its future. A Chinaglia goal handed the Cosmos their fifth title. They would not get another.

More teams fell by the wayside that winter: the Portland Timbers, whose days as 'Soccer City, USA' now seemed a long time ago; the Edmonton Drillers, whose largely Canadian team compiled the league's worst record; and the incongruous Jacksonville Tea Men, who decided to jump to the ASL, a league whose own future scarcely looked any more secure. Having abandoned the west coast, the ASL had concentrated its efforts in the deep south, creating teams such as the Georgia Generals and Carolina Lightnin' (possibly the first club in the world to end its name with an apostrophe). Such was the ASL's wanderlust that it abandoned New York altogether after 1981. Its past 11 seasons had produced ten different champions, only three of which still existed. Jacksonville and five other clubs signed up for 1983, the most senior being the five-year-old Pennsylvania Stoners (Pennsylvania being the Keystone State), based in Allentown and as close to professional soccer as nearby Bethlehem had come since the demise of the Steel. The Stoners reached the 1983 championship final, where they lost to the Tea Men, but that season – the

ASL's 51st since its re-emergence in 1933 – proved to be its last. Its death was not widely mourned.

Far from in rude health itself, the NASL sputtered into 1983. Even cable television now abandoned interest, a particularly cruel blow after an unprecedented number of foreign matches had appeared on American screens. The ambitious ESPN network transmitted the 1982 FA Cup final live for the first time (it was 'Breakfast at Wembley') and continued its diet of English highlights and even the occasional college contest, something no commercial network had dared attempt. The all-sports channel became a soccer fan's delight that summer, carrying a number of World Cup matches from Spain, including Italy's thrilling 3-2 victory over Brazil. Public television also carried edited highlights of World Cup matches via *Soccer Made in Germany* and ABC showed the final live. Yet none of this seemed to rub off on the NASL.

If the league could be saved, most agreed Samuels was the man to do it. Having seemingly brokered a peace plan with the insolent MISL, the commissioner turned his attention to Americanisation, an especially topical issue in a World Cup year. The US's absence from the tournament was more conspicuous than ever, and owners had begun to recognise the value of a strong national team. Samuels saw no reason why that team couldn't become a member of his league, however odd a concept it was both to the rest of the soccer-playing world and American professional sport. Samuels was convinced part of the NASL's lack of appeal was down to what he referred to as 'nationalistic interest', and since only the most devoted fan could name more than a handful of native players, that was hard to stir up. The country had taken a fiercely patriotic turn with the election of Ronald Reagan in 1980, and waving the flag had become fashionable again. Sport had played its part with the gold medal-winning performance of the US ice hockey team at the 1980 Winter Olympics, the 'miracle on ice' in which a team of plucky collegiates defeated the Soviet Union, and a victory which lingered in the national psyche.

It was this type of thrill Samuels was seeking to reproduce for his league, and in January 1983 the proposal, with the blessing of the USSF, became reality. Team America, consisting solely of US citizens, would occupy the vacant slot in Washington DC. But the venture was doomed from the start, requiring more co-operation and goodwill than the various parties were willing to provide. Some players, like Rick Davis of the Cosmos, felt it was more beneficial to play alongside foreign stars than against them; others were not released by their clubs. Team America ended up looking nothing like the national team it was meant to represent. Most of its players had never been capped and some were naturalised citizens with little hope of appearing in a World Cup. Nottingham-born goalkeeper Paul Hammond, a nine-year NASL veteran, and two other Englishmen, Alan Merrick and Alan Green, were winding down their careers. Hammond never earned a US cap, while Merrick and Green managed one each. Even Alkis Panagoulis, the successor to Walt Chyzowych, who as national team manager became Team America manager by default, was himself a naturalised citizen. Panagoulis had led the New York Greek-Americans to three Open Cup triumphs in the early 1960s and was later manager of the Greek national team at the 1994 World Cup, but earned his living selling real estate.

Beleaguered by the club-versus-country (or club-versus-Team America) dilemma, Washington ended up with the worst entry in the league and little in the way of 'nationalistic interest'. More than 50,000 attended Team America's 2-1 win over Fort Lauderdale, but only because the match was the curtain-raiser for a Beach Boys concert; just 8,200 had been at the same ground three days earlier for the visit of Tampa Bay. Panagoulis wondered aloud: 'Where are we going? What the hell are we doing? Why do these people keep paying me?' In the end, they didn't – the experiment came to an embarrassing end after just one year.

Such appeals to patriotism worked no better in Seattle, whose franchise had been purchased by a consortium headed by Bruce Anderson, a former NFL defensive lineman. The Sounders' gates had fallen to an average of 12,500, a record low which the new owners seemed to blame on the club's lingering Anglophilia. Virtually the entire team was English, as was their coach, the former Derby winger Alan Hinton, whose use of words like 'pitch' and 'lads' rubbed Anderson up the wrong way ('lad is what I call my dog, and pitch is something I get on my hands when I put up the Christmas tree').

For 1983 Hinton was replaced with Birmingham-born Laurie Calloway, whose half-season in charge of the California Surf had been no roaring success, but who displayed greater sympathies toward native talent. The Sounders were given a new logo, a new playing strip and a lamentable new marketing slogan: 'Red, white, black and blue.' But all the fresh thinking and flag-waving merely sent the remaining fans away. The Sounders ended up with the second-worst gates in the league, one-third down on even the previous season's dismal figures. Anderson lost about $1 million, and with that the city lost its franchise. Of all its collapses, this was the NASL's most spectacular – no Soccer Bowl participant had ever gone out of business the following year.

A similar miscalculation led to the demise of the Montreal Manic, whose owners had alienated much of the city's fan base by declaring their intent to field a Team Canada for the 1984 season. In a city whose French-speaking *Quebecois* had harnessed a particularly strong separatist movement, this was suicidal. Almost at a stroke, crowds at the Olympic Stadium dropped by more than half, and the Manic followed the Sounders into extinction. Problems in San Diego were of a different nature. Allowed to spend the winter in the MISL, the Sockers ended up as champions, and often found themselves attracting more fans indoors than out. Club owners claimed they had lost $7 million during their six NASL seasons. Chicago, too, joined the MISL that winter and found it easier to recruit indoor fans, as did San Jose, who had changed their name to the Golden Bay Earthquakes in an effort to widen their geographic appeal.

All this seemed to point to another Cosmos championship, particularly with Beckenbauer back from Germany. But Chinaglia, playing in his last season, featured in less than half the club's matches and Giants Stadium was now frequently three-quarters empty. Even the once-fierce rivalry with Tampa Bay attracted fewer than 20,000. Paired against Montreal in the first round of the play-offs, the Cosmos received the shock of their life, losing 4-2 at home before fewer than 18,000. Six days later the Manic knocked them out in Montreal, and New York television did not even bother to broadcast the misfortune live. It was Chinaglia's final competitive game. His 193 goals in 213 league appearances over eight seasons put him comfortably atop the league's scoring ladder, although his 49 goals in 45 play-off matches were perhaps even more significant. In a league which emphasised attack and abounded with famous strikers, he was the NASL's greatest asset, a player fans loved or hated but could not ignore, and one whose talent and statistics easily impressed the fans.

With the Cosmos eliminated and Toronto knocking out a Vancouver team which had lost only six of 30 league matches, Soccer Bowl 83 was up for grabs. Few could have predicted its eventual winner. The Tulsa Roughnecks operated in a small market with one of the league's lowest payrolls, and during their seven-year history they had changed owners four times. But their prudently run franchise, bolstered by tireless promotional work and an absence of big-league competition, attracted consistent if unspectacular crowds. In 1983 the Roughnecks claimed their first division title with a starless collection of largely British imports managed by former Wales international Terry Hennessey. They eliminated Montreal with a 3-0 victory in the deciding match of their semi-final, and produced a goalscoring hero of their own in former Manchester City striker Ron Futcher, an NASL veteran of eight years. In the five games leading up to the Soccer Bowl, Futcher scored five times, but acquired one too many yellow cards and was suspended for the championship game. Appeals to let him play were waved aside until, late in the day, Samuels took it upon himself to overrule his office's own decision 'in the best interests of the game'. Futcher, naturally, scored as the Roughnecks melted the Blizzard 2-0, bestowing professional sports success on the state of Oklahoma for the first time.

Though more than 60,000 turned up in Vancouver's indoor BC Place to see it, Soccer Bowl 83 could not conceal another miserable year, one which Samuels admitted had run the league close to collapse. In Tampa, attendance at Rowdies matches had dwindled to about 11,000, about the same as were now turning up to see the Earthquakes in San Jose. Infatuated with the MISL, the Chicago Sting sought to pull out of the NASL, while Fort Lauderdale moved to Minneapolis, largely because it wanted an indoor arena. Even the champion Roughnecks were in danger of folding. They were saved partly by a cable television executive and partly by an enthusiastic disc jockey who orchestrated a door-to-door fund-raising drive. With Montreal, Seattle and Team America disbanding, membership fell to nine, fewer than at any time since 1973.

Other events also conspired against the league, though in some cases the owners had only themselves to blame. The NASL had responded energetically in the wake of Colombia's decision to withdraw as hosts of the 1986 World Cup, sensing an opportunity to bolster their sagging fortunes by stepping in to stage the tournament. The refusal of USSF president Gene Edwards to make a bid didn't stop them from turning to one of the vice-presidents, Werner Fricker, a Serbian-born Philadelphia property developer, who had played for the US in the 1964 Olympic qualifiers. Flushed with optimism, and competing only against Canada, Mexico and Brazil, they even received encouraging noises from João Havelange, who described the US as a 'healthy candidate'. Of course, with an abundance of huge stadiums, an enviable infrastructure and American promotional savvy, this was merely stating the obvious. But when, in August 1982, nearly 77,000 filled Giants Stadium for a FIFA benefit match featuring most of the stars from that year's World Cup, America's – or at least greater New York's – interest in top-class international soccer seemed hard to deny. Yet FIFA had not forgotten how the NASL had irritatingly bickered over its idiosyncratic rules. Politically predisposed towards Mexico anyway, they rejected the US proposal, not even extending the courtesy of an inspection of potential sites. Falling at the start of the 1983 NASL season, the blow sent the league reeling.

Punches were being thrown from all directions. America's seemingly insatiable appetite for gridiron had led to the creation of the United States Football League, which defied convention by operating during the spring. It placed a franchise in the Meadowlands opposite the Cosmos and also went head-to-head with the NASL in Chicago, Washington and Tampa. The league had secured high-profile television contracts with ABC and ESPN, hired a former network TV executive as its commissioner and animated the national press with a series of big-name signings, kicking off in March to crowds soccer had little hope of replicating. 'We haven't had a good year,' sighed Samuels as 1983 came to an end. 'We haven't had a really bad year, either, but since it wasn't better than last year, I consider it a bad year.'

It would only get worse. After 48 straight quarters of record profits, Warner Communications reported a loss of $424 million over the first three quarters of 1983. Sales in its lucrative Atari electronics division had nosedived, leaving chief executive Steve Ross – whose management style was condemned as 'lackadaisical' – in a compromised position over his soccer plaything. Although continuing to tour the world and hosting an assortment of international friendlies (including European champions Hamburg, whom they beat 7-2 in June), the Cosmos lost $5 million in 1983. Beckenbauer did not return for 1984; nor did Rick Davis, who defected to the MISL.

Samuels continued to sober up the league, trimming its expenditure by millions on the assumption that gates would remain modest. He put in place a new collective bargaining agreement which included a player salary cap and agreed to slash administrative costs. He increased the requirement for North Americans on the pitch from four to five. And he scrapped the Soccer Bowl in favour of a best-of-three match series on the contestants' own turf. Yet he still found himself with too many opponents to fight: the owners, whose interest in his league continued to suffer at the hands of the indoor craze; the intransigent MISL, who steadfastly refused all invitations to merge; the media, whose interest in a shrivelling league amounted largely to *Schadenfreude*; and the labyrinthine politics of the USSF, whose president saw nothing wrong with directing operations from Wisconsin.

The NASL staggered through 1984 with few hopeful signs. San Diego, champions of the western division but destined to be defeated in the play-off semi-finals for the fifth time in six years, continued to draw pitifully. Gates in Tampa Bay slumped to as low as 4,900. Minnesota attracted more than 52,000 to a bank holiday game with Tampa Bay, but it was the Beach Boys at work again. League champions Tulsa drew only 7,300 for their opener, lost six of their first seven matches and before the season had even ended announced they were pulling out. So did Chicago, who, along with San Diego, pledged allegiance to the MISL. The championship series between Chicago and Toronto, won by the lame-duck Sting, drew just 8,300 to Chicago's Comiskey Park and 16,800 to Toronto's Varsity Stadium.

The Cosmos staggered through their worst season in more than a decade, failing even to make the play-offs. Warner handed Chinaglia a controlling share of the club, effectively ending its interest, the last of the corporate benefactors. But Chinaglia had also taken control of Lazio, leaving him with little money to sink into a second team, particularly with the *Biancocelesti* about to be relegated to Serie B. Suddenly even the league's flagship franchise sought comfort in the flashing lights of the MISL. Brash as ever, Chinaglia threatened to pull his club out of the NASL if it couldn't spend the winter earning money indoors ('They're a sinking ship right now, and I refuse to go down with them').

The ship was indeed sinking, but no one knew just how quickly. Less than a month after the league crowned its 18th champions, the heavy-smoking, 64-year-old Samuels died of a heart attack. Clive Toye stepped forward to assume control, but by then just four teams had expressed interest in another season. Chinaglia duly stuck his team in the MISL but found its strange game difficult to master. Before the season ended, the Cosmos had run out of money and were forced to withdraw. Clutching at straws, they expressed an intention to contest a series of friendlies with top foreign clubs. But their charisma had vanished, and the few matches they managed to stage in Giants Stadium in the summer of 1985 were played out in front of ghosts. Just 8,700 turned up to watch Chinaglia's two teams face off at the Meadowlands. A fight broke out and the match was abandoned. The Cosmos never played again.

The NASL was finished. By March, it had been reduced to just Toronto and Minnesota. Toye politely expressed the hope it would be back, or at least that 'a good pro league will be in operation for the 1986 season'. But it would take a good deal more than a year for the professional game to find its feet, and by the time it did, 'soccer' in America would come to carry two meanings.

7. A Foot in the Door

Harsh lessons at Italia 90

If we lived in another country, we would ask for political asylum. But since we're American, we'll stay in New York and nobody will recognise us.

Tab Ramos

I n the summer of 1968, a 36-year-old Hungarian refugee named Joe Martin turned up on Randall's Island with a hefty stack of plywood and an idea for a new type of soccer, one he hoped would attract the kind of crowds the country's two professional leagues had sought in vain the year before. Inspired by the speed and constant action of ice hockey – living in Ontario he would have seen plenty of it – he ringed the Downing Stadium pitch with a three-foot wall to keep the ball from going out of play. Other elements of the game were also modified: corner kicks were replaced by penalties taken from 23 yards, the goals were enlarged and the offside law scrapped. Martin called his new game American Soccer System, and he had sketched out ambitious plans for it. After the New York debut, his show would move to Toronto and then to 25 other cities before venturing overseas. In a few years, he boasted, teams from around the world would be competing for millions of dollars in prizes.

The world premiere of American Soccer System, a match between teams representing the US and Canada, produced a final score of 14-11 – and an attendance of 243. Martin claimed to have spent $40,000 perfecting his idea, and another $1,000 to use the stadium, but the meagre ticket sales didn't even cover his rental fee. American Soccer System was never played again.[*] The humiliating experience did not stop other promoters with similar ideas from tinkering with the sport, and the collapse of the NASL in 1985 seemed to vindicate Martin's point of view: soccer as played by the rest of the planet could not be translated into American, at least not in a way that made any money. Even the most familiar indigenous sports underwent periodic rule changes – some quite dramatic – to address perceived shortcomings and sustain fan

---

[*] Martin persevered. In 1973 he unveiled plans in an adult cinema for an indoor league that would pay George Best $2,000 a game. He also tried to promote indoor matches with go-go dancers on the crossbars before settling for running a brothel in Toronto.

interest. That soccer should remain sacrosanct as competition for the entertainment dollar grew ever fiercer struck some as terribly naive.

So it was that during the 1980s the game came to mean something rather different to many Americans. It was played indoors on a small, boxed-in pitch, and by rules completely its own. Its aims were little different from American Soccer System – to speed up the game and increase scoring. Subtle artistry and flair would seldom be celebrated in this new enterprise, yet to those turned off by soccer's potential for lethargy, the new invention was far more palatable.

Playing indoors was hardly a novel idea. The harsh winters of the northern US had taken the game inside as far back as the 1880s, when Boston newspapers reported on contests of 11-a-side. Charles Stoneham's radical proposals for the ASL in 1928 had included forsaking outdoor play during December and January for more hospitable venues. Though the idea never came to fruition, the creation of large indoor arenas in the 1920s and 1930s helped other leagues to escape the elements for brief periods, devising rules to suit both the venue and the whims of the promoters. One such tournament, staged in Madison Square Garden in 1941, saw teams of seven compete ferociously on a bare concrete floor. Two players were taken to hospital and the crowd of 8,000 was treated to what one newspaper described as 'the fiercest free-for-all fight seen here in many a moon'.

After one or two other brief experiments it was 17 years before indoor soccer returned to the Garden, by which time the organisers had at least accepted the need to cushion any awkward landings (with topsoil from the National Horse Show). In 1950 Chicago's National Soccer League held an indoor competition popular enough to feature on local radio and TV. Other ethnic leagues also took their teams inside and on favourable days played in front of thousands. But these were largely wintertime diversions, not to be treated with the same gravitas as the genuine article. It was only as the impact of televised sports became apparent during the 1960s – and bona fide soccer emerged as a loser – that the indoor game developed into a serious commercial proposition.

The NASL had tested its teams indoors as early as 1973, keen to derive maximum value from the year-round contracts it was offering its players, but there was no exceptional zeal behind the venture. Support for the outdoor league was still blossoming, and Pelé had yet to arrive. Many give the credit (or blame) for spawning the game's bastard child to a pair of indoor exhibitions the league organised for the touring CSKA Moscow side in February 1974. For the first match, in Toronto, the NASL cobbled together an all-star team, which the Russians easily defeated. The second, in Philadelphia, involved the league champion Atoms.

It's easy to forget how rare American-Soviet sporting confrontations were outside the Olympics. Professional ice hockey's first visit from a Soviet team – an occasion far more widely acclaimed – was still two years away, while big-league basketball abstained from such challenges right up to the fall of the Iron Curtain. This left American flag-wavers with relatively esoteric events such as the figure skating world championships to compare East with West.

Partly because of this, and partly because the Atoms had become an overnight sensation in a city with few recent sporting successes to its name, the Russian match drew a crowd of nearly 12,000, an impressive figure for a contest whose rules were largely unfamiliar. An artificial pitch was laid over the ice rink, and the match was split into three 20-minute periods. With six players on each side and unlimited substitutions, the game resembled ice hockey as much as soccer. The Atoms fielded a number of guest players and performed creditably, conceding three third-period goals to lose 6-3. Ultimately, though, the result proved less significant than the conventions by which it had been played. To many, this was better than the sport they had seen during the summer.

That was certainly true of Ed Tepper, a local businessman and owner of an indoor lacrosse franchise who had turned up ostensibly because he was interested in something other than plywood for his team to play on. Tepper later claimed the match convinced him of the potential of indoor soccer, though two years later he became president and general manager of the Atoms, suggesting at least some attraction to the established game. But after the club met its ignominious end in 1976, Tepper joined forces with another disillusioned ex-NASL figure, Earl Foreman, who had forsaken the Washington Whips in favour of a franchise in the American Basketball Association several years earlier. The two may have believed they had discovered professional sport's next big opportunity, yet their intuition was far from reliable: Tepper's lacrosse league folded in 1975, and Foreman's struggling basketball entity ended up being sold back to the league. Meanwhile, the NASL had staged a successful indoor tournament as a preamble to its 1975 season.

The first rumblings of a big-time, dedicated indoor league came from two other former NASL executives, Rick Ragone and Norm Sutherland. 'The indoor game is a great product for television,' they declared in September 1975, announcing that their venture, the Major Soccer League, would begin the following summer and go head-to-head with the NASL. The league never materialised, but the conditions to create it remained: there were dozens of arenas with empty dates to fill, and lots of cheap college talent frozen out by the NASL's Anglophilia.

Even without the Major Soccer League, by the spring of 1978 – with eerie parallels to a decade earlier – it looked as though three new leagues would be competing for the sports fan's dollar. The Major Indoor Soccer League, the brainchild of Tepper and Foreman, announced it would start in November. Another offering, the Super Soccer League, with links to Ragone and Sutherland's aborted effort, was to begin six months earlier. It was fronted by Jerry Saperstein, whose father Abe had founded basketball's Harlem Globetrotters. Meanwhile the NASL, ears suitably pricked, announced its indoor tournaments – largely contested by reserves and young American hopefuls, and only some of its teams – would be replaced by a fully-fledged winter league.

In the end, the MISL had 1978 to itself. Unable to prop up all its transient franchises, Super Soccer collapsed, while NASL owners, against the wishes of Phil Woosnam, opted to sit out a year and see what happened to their rival. The USSF, delighted to collect around $25,000 from each of the MISL teams, hastily christened the new game soccer and welcomed it to the family. With only six franchises, the MISL began in relative anonymity, but coasted with self-assurance into uncharted waters, cheerfully devising rules without the restraint of FIFA or the USSF. At a meeting in a Philadelphia apartment Tepper stood in a doorway and declared that the eight-foot frame would determine the height of the goals. Ice hockey dasher boards and Plexiglas screens would ring the tiny pitch – in certain situations, players could be bundled into them without penalty. Serious transgressions would result in banishment to a sin-bin. Unlimited interchange meant managers could bring on an entire new team if they so desired and replace it a few minutes later.

There were no international superstars to raise the MISL's profile, but the league did pull off an early publicity coup by signing a disgruntled Shep Messing to spearhead its New York franchise. True to form, the voluble goalkeeper promptly declared the outdoor game dead and soon abandoned it. Most of Messing's team-mates came from the Rochester Lancers, delighted by the prospect of close-season employment, but few other teams signed up names even the most devout NASL fan would recognise. The appeal of the MISL's brand of soccer, though, and its proprietors' masterstroke, was that in such a hybrid game accomplished internationals were no more experienced than fresh-faced youngsters. As long as the action kept moving, technical deficiencies could be readily accommodated. Errant shooting could produce a goal on the rebound; hammering the ball against the dasher board made for an effective pass. Even the poorest player could endear himself to the crowd by charging an opponent into the wall.

And, of course, it had goals, more goals than anything calling itself soccer had ever seen. The league's top marksman, Slavisa Zungul (rechristened Steve), who two years earlier had been helping Yugoslavia to a European Championship semi-final, scored 90 in 32 matches. The best goalkeeper let in more than four a game. Contests routinely ended 8-3 or 9-6; the championship final finished 7-4. The MISL's bright red ball took more abuse in one match than most NASL models did across an entire season, whacked as it was against everything from the intrepid goalkeeper's outstretched limbs to the occasional head of an unwary fan. Indoor soccer, with its wailing sirens, flashing lights and thumping music, represented almost everything traditional soccer was not: it was frenetic, undemanding, brash – and unapologetically American. The real thing, Foreman maintained, would never succeed in the US because it was 'too European'.

That this might not actually be soccer was of far less importance than whether fans would come out to watch it. In many places they did. What initially seemed at best a credible accompaniment to the NASL's summer fare had by 1980 grown into a 12-team, coast-to-coast enterprise that threatened to upstage the outdoor game. The bellwether New York club, the Arrows, obligingly claimed the first four league championships, by which time two and a half a million fans a season were passing through MISL turnstiles.

The NASL had little option but to join in, which it did in 1979, replicating the MISL formula right down to the size of its goals. Yet only ten of its 24 teams took part, mostly the weaker ones. Even without the possibility of a lucrative Cosmos visit, the league competed well with its rival, so much so that struggling franchises in Memphis and Atlanta often found themselves with bigger gates indoors than out. The latter even threatened to jump to the MISL.

By 1983 the rot had set in. A foundering NASL scaled down its summer fixtures to accommodate more indoor ones and continued squaring off with the MISL for talent and attention. While attempts by Howard Samuels and others to end the feuding failed, the USSF meekly shrugged its shoulders. For those who bothered to notice, the game in America had all but capitulated to its mutant offspring, to little if any outcry from the public and scarcely a whimper on the sports pages. Even the participants didn't seem terribly bothered. Rick Davis, probably the most visible native-born player in the country, left the NASL for the MISL after the Cosmos tried to trim his wages. 'You still kick the ball with your feet,' he said of his new vocation. 'You still can't touch it with your hands, you're still trying to score goals by shooting the ball and heading the ball, you still have defenders, midfielders and forwards ... and unless they've changed something, to me that's soccer.' As the number of NASL teams shrank and budgets tightened, others had little choice but to join him.

Once again, American soccer lay in the hands of the wrong people. There were no working arrangements or compromises between the two leagues, only escalating competition for fans and players. In the end, the MISL's intransigence caused problems for itself as well as the NASL. The Arrows went bankrupt in 1984, shortly after the new title-holders, the Baltimore Blast, revealed that they had lost millions of dollars in spite of filling their arena to capacity for nearly every home game. Tickets had been too cheap, promotions too costly.

Yet it was the MISL's brand of soccer that proved to be the 'sport of the Eighties'. Its rock-concert atmospherics were soon mimicked by the established professional leagues, and even the Super Bowl. Minor copycat circuits germinated across the country, giving birth to the likes of the Garland Genesis and Philadelphia Kixx. Some stood even the most sacrosanct rules on their head; for a time, one league doubled and trebled the value of goals scored from certain ranges.

By 1986, as the MISL entered its eighth season, the last vestiges of optimism that had helped to propel the NASL for more than a decade had vanished. Entrepreneurs abandoned any expectation of a decent financial return from soccer, and turned their attention to hybrid offerings in other sports, most notably the Arena Football League, an indoor gridiron concoction inspired by one man's visit to an MISL all-star exhibition. Signs of outdoor recovery were modest. The Pacific northwest formed a four-team semi-professional competition, but team names like FC Seattle and FC Portland pointed towards rather provincial ambitions. Hopes were briefly pinned on a United Soccer League, romantically based in Bethlehem, Pennsylvania, and pieced together partly from remnants of the ASL, among them the peripatetic but enduring Jacksonville Tea Men. It wheezed into life in 1984 with nine teams in the east and south, preaching fiscal responsibility and the promotion of American talent. But with no mainstream media exposure and trifling fan support, it stumbled through its first season, then saw seven of its teams fold. Six matches into its second year, the USL ran out of money and collapsed.

That left the college game, with all its idiosyncrasies, as the country's most prominent offering. The 1986 final between the University of California at Los Angeles (UCLA) and American University of Washington DC saw the two teams play for 90 minutes with scarcely a scoring chance, then engage in 76 minutes of extra time, the longest match in college history. Indiana and Duke universities had played almost as exhausting a contest for the 1982 title, the year France and West Germany had contested the World Cup's first penalty shoot-out. Some college coaches continued to import the bulk of their talent from overseas or pushed for closer adherence to FIFA's laws, while others persisted with outmoded tactical formations and substituted players as if through a revolving door. Arguably the most successful college coach of the era, Indiana's Jerry Yeagley, frequently made his four or five at a time.

It may have been oddly fascinating, but it was largely irrelevant. The college game's showpiece event, the NCAA Division I championship final, never attracted more than 10,000 in the Eighties. On campuses across the country, soccer was still played before a sparse collection of parents, friends and scouts from rival teams. Dreams of filling the mighty football stadium with hordes of newly converted fans were gradually abandoned. Some institutions consented to build modest soccer-only facilities with proper pitches and a few rows of seats.

During this bleak period, one momentous occasion cast an unexpected beam of light on the game, an event which would play a much more pivotal role in shaping its destiny than the self-absorbed colleges. More than 1.4 million fans – an average of nearly 44,500 – scrambled to sites on both coasts in support of the 1984 Olympic football tournament. All manner of attendance records fell. At a college gridiron stadium in Palo Alto, 30 miles north of San Francisco, 78,265 turned up to watch the US play Costa Rica, topping the record home attendance for an American national team – by 45,000 – and the celebrated 77,691 set by the Cosmos. Nor was it simply about the home team. The gold medal match in which France beat Brazil 2-0 drew nearly 102,000 to Pasadena's Rose Bowl.

It seemed unfathomable. The country might have been gripped by a particularly virulent strain of Olympic fever, hosting the event for the first time in more than half a century and returning to competition after boycotting the 1980 games, but for it to have suddenly capitulated to the world's favourite sport seemed ludicrous. The most plausible explanation was that the public had been enticed simply by the prospect of witnessing an Olympic event. With soccer tickets among the cheapest and most plentiful of the Games the competition became strangely attractive – even on the east coast at Harvard University and the US Naval Academy where, bizarrely, first-round matches took place.

Soccer fans were ecstatic. Here, they exclaimed, was evidence of America's continued appetite for the game, evidence that Pelé had not worn a Cosmos jersey in vain. But they were also furious. ABC television's wall-to-wall Olympics coverage all but ignored the event, favouring gold-medal performances from Americans and the traditional staples of athletics, gymnastics and basketball. Though its presenters sometimes teased viewers with references to the latest enormous soccer crowd, its coverage of even the gold medal match was best measured by a stopwatch.

The Olympics could not rescue the NASL, but the Games did give impetus to a long-held dream of the USSF. Shunned two years earlier in applying to host the 1986 World Cup – a process which nearly bankrupted it and sent president Werner Fricker reaching into his own pocket – the USSF had not abandoned hope. Looking towards the 1994 tournament, FIFA took note of the popularity and organisation of the Olympic tournament, but the credit for this belonged not to the USSF (whose penury soon forced them to abandon New York for rent-free offices at US Olympic Committee headquarters in Colorado) but to Alan Rothenberg, the millionaire Los Angeles lawyer assigned to run the event. For the time being Rothenberg returned to his law firm and the NBA's Los Angeles Clippers, of which he was president, but FIFA did not forget his name.

Only a few months after France claimed its gold medal in the Rose Bowl, the NASL kicked what proved to be its last ball, casting big-league soccer into the wilderness. By 1987 the humble Western Soccer Alliance had stretched itself as far south as San Diego, but its abrupt, ten-match season, playing to crowds often bettered by local college teams, was little more than a modest refuge for those fans and players who found the MISL's idea of soccer wanting. In May, Toye announced that a new league would begin on the east coast in 1988. Yet the enterprise, a third incarnation of the American Soccer League, was of limited ambition and not surprisingly found itself playing to rows of empty seats and indifference from the national media.

Yet however depressing the professional collapse might have been, it did not leave the US where it had started. Too many youngsters had grown up with the game – an entire generation – and for some of the most talented it had become their preferred sport. With improved funding, facilities, and coaching helping to expand the talent pool, by the mid-Eighties some of the best players were able to contemplate a modest career overseas. During the decade, their ranks grew, helping to sustain the credibility of the American game and ultimately to bring it back home.

As early as 1974, Bobby Smith of the Cosmos had spent a winter with the Irish side Dundalk. The Cosmos' reserve goalkeeper David Brcic went to Morton in 1978, where one Scottish newspaper named him 'player of the day' after his debut against Motherwell. But these were loan spells rather than career decisions. Things were different by 1987 when the country's top college player, John Kerr, a Canadian striker who had helped Duke University to its first national championship, chose to pursue his career with England's semi-professional Harrow Borough. (Kerr's father, an eight-year veteran of the NASL, had been born in Glasgow, which allowed his son to play without a work permit.) Kerr eventually signed for Portsmouth, but after a few appearances and a loan spell at Peterborough he returned home and joined the ASL, leaving as his English legacy the doubtful honour of being the first substitute in the First Division to be substituted himself (against Watford in September 1987).

That same year another top collegian, Paul Caligiuri of UCLA, signed for Hamburg, a feat momentous enough to be featured by *Sports Illustrated* – though apparently not momentous enough for the magazine to spell his surname correctly. Having been named the Most Valuable Player in the Western Soccer Alliance the previous summer, Caligiuri was invited to play alongside Diego Maradona and others at a benefit match at the Rose Bowl, an event which put him in touch with Hamburg officials. Arriving in Germany he found himself loaned to lower-division Meppen, where he played creditably for two seasons. Not until 1995 did he crack the Bundesliga – the first American to do so – with Hamburg's local rivals St Pauli.

Both Caligiuri and Kerr featured in the US team which seemed to stand a fair chance of reaching the 1986 World Cup finals, particularly since Mexico qualified automatically as hosts. But again the campaign ended in failure. It began nervously on a pitch devoid of grass in the Dutch Antilles, where the Americans produced few chances and came home with a pitiful goalless draw. In the return leg their modest opponents finished the match with only nine men, but kept the score at 0-0 until the second half, when the US eventually found the net four times.

In the second round the Americans were drawn against Costa Rica and Trinidad & Tobago, with the winners progressing to a final group of three. Two victories and a draw left them needing only a point at home to Costa Rica, but they were betrayed by a rare error from veteran goalkeeper Arnie Mausser, whose failure to reach a low cross yielded the only goal of the game. Moreover, the largely hostile crowd of 11,800 in Torrance, California, provided a familiar lack of home advantage. 'We were down in the locker room at half-time and we could hear the music,' one player recounted. 'We were wondering, "What the hell is this? Are we in Costa Rica, or what?"' George Vecsey wrote in the *New York Times*:

> In the litter of empty soda cans and empty dreams, Gregg Thompson had a question burning across his face. The young defender from Minnesota strode across the rudimentary locker room and blurted at the American soccer coach, Alkis Panagoulias: 'When are we ever going to play a home game?' The answer from Panagoulias was equally blunt: 'Never.'

Next time, a USSF official promised, they would play in Alaska. Yet the defeat had much less to do with the fans than with the collapse of the NASL and rise of the MISL, a lethal combination which riddled the team with players ill-equipped for international duty. Panagoulias refused to be drawn into talking about the indoor league and its commissioner, 'because I'll say bad things about them'. Three of the starting line-up in Torrance still played for university teams but the others – apart from Mausser, who was without a club at all – were beholden to the MISL.

The ignoble exit came just two days after the Heysel Stadium disaster, which, combined with the fire at Bradford City's ground a few weeks earlier, prompted the American media to develop a certain road-crash fascination with the perils of soccer, reporting in some detail on the events in Belgium and the strange breed of fans who were drawn to such occasions. Though one sociologist had counted more than 300 sport-related riots in the US over a 12-year period, and after-match disturbances on the streets of Detroit the previous autumn had visibly marred the Tigers' World Series victory, such domestic outbreaks rarely received the kind of sensational coverage reserved for soccer's woes. The game was being kicked when it was down. Even ESPN, which had secured the rights to the crucial Costa Rica qualifier, opted to show it on videotape. On the east coast its broadcast ended just before 2.30am, leaving only the odd insomniac to observe how the Americans had dominated play but once again lacked a clinical finisher.

Its hopes of a World Cup payday dashed, the impoverished federation declined to renew Panagoulias's contract, and that of its director of coaching, Karl-Heinz Heddergott, the former manager of Cologne. No full-time successors were appointed. Panagoulias's eventual replacement, Lothar Osiander, continued to work as a waiter in a San Francisco restaurant. Born in Germany, Osiander had led the Greek-American club of San Francisco to Open Cup success the year before his appointment. Now he had to get the Olympic team to South Korea with virtually the same players who had failed in the World Cup. The IOC's increasingly relaxed stance on amateurism had effectively turned the US's qualifying rounds into full internationals.

Though the state of Alaska was not called upon, the federation did schedule most of its home fixtures in a small, soccer-specific facility just outside St Louis, where appreciable numbers of visiting fans were less likely to venture. The biggest transformation in America's fortunes came in the form of Brent Goulet, the Western Soccer Alliance's Most Valuable Player that summer. Heralded as the country's first natural goalscorer since Billy Gonsalves – for those who had heard of him – Goulet's finishing scaled impressive heights during qualifying, and his hat-trick against Trinidad & Tobago was only the third an American had managed in 80 years of Olympic competition.

Yet the team struggled at first, losing the away leg of their first-round tie with Canada 2-0. Only an unlikely 3-0 win in Missouri put them through to the group stage. Goulet complemented his hat-trick with another two goals against El Salvador as his team went on a rare scoring spree, netting 13 in four games against the Salvadorans and Trinidad & Tobago to qualify comfortably. By that time the ambitious young striker had left Portland for Bournemouth of the English Second Division. 'I was a first-round pick in the MISL draft, but that wasn't what I wanted,' he declared. 'You don't know how much I love the outdoor game.' His stay at Dean Court was brief. As with Caligiuri in Hamburg and Kerr at Portsmouth, Goulet found it difficult to force his way into the first team. Briefly loaned to Fourth Division Crewe (for whom he scored three goals in three games), he found greater success in Germany, where he remained for several seasons.

The American performances in Seoul (or, more precisely, Taegu and Pusan) were respectable, if not stunning: a 1-1 draw with Argentina which they might have won; a goalless encounter with the hosts, played to an often eerie silence from a crowd of 30,000; and a comprehensive 4-2 defeat by the eventual winners, the Soviet Union, by which time Goulet's form had faded badly enough to relegate him to the bench.

Five MISL clubs folded in 1988, suggesting the wheels were starting to fall off Foreman's juggernaut, but it did little to help proper soccer. Though the two emerging pro leagues, one on either coast, agreed to pit their top teams against each other in a sort of national championship, interest remained modest. The following year they merged and took to calling themselves the American Professional Soccer League – although 13 of the 22 clubs promptly folded. Officials promoted this as a necessary housecleaning, but there was only so much attention a league devoid of franchises in New York, Chicago, Philadelphia and other metropolises could command. While APSL officials remained convinced that big-time soccer needed to be built slowly from the ground up, the way the major leagues in other sports had done, critics argued that sport in America didn't work that way any more. This, they insisted, was a country which now responded only to the big time. Television's obsession with the major leagues had helped to decimate the number of minor-league baseball clubs and semi-professional gridiron leagues, and it would hardly be any kinder to a modest soccer undertaking.

There was at least one big-time event that US soccer could look to for salvation, and as the Eighties progressed the chances of landing the World Cup developed into a near-certainty. With Europe due to stage the 1990 tournament and the blossoming of Japanese football still some years off, American competition for 1994 was limited to two shaky prospects. Brazil had submitted a proposal which its own government refused to support, while Morocco's stadiums existed largely on paper. Colombia's embarrassing withdrawal as hosts of the 1986 tournament left FIFA in no mood to take any chances on bids backed by doubtful economies or rickety infrastructure. The Americans, on the other hand, had included in their application a supportive letter from President Reagan – a feat which one USSF official claimed had 'stunned' both the selection committee and the international media – and a shortlist of 15 of the country's best gridiron facilities, all apparently soccer-sympathetic. So FIFA's announcement, on Independence Day, 1988, seemed a foregone conclusion. In the weeks leading up to the decision, American officials oozed confidence, although as it turned out their bid defeated the North Africans by only ten votes to seven. Yet however predictable, the decision was still momentous enough to reach the front page of the *New York Times*.

The success of the tournament, on the other hand, was far from certain. This was a nation which had not qualified for a World Cup in 38 years, and one without a genuine professional league. Most of its inhabitants exhibited at best indifference and at worst cold-blooded hostility to what they still saw as a foreign game, one they had never seen played to any standard. FIFA, with options limited, found itself committed to a tournament that would have to be run in part as a brazen promotional tool.

It did not take long for cynics to flinch at the thought of how the game might be compromised for the sake of the native population. Rumours of larger goals, of play being split into quarters, of time-outs and other indigenous fetishes soon appeared in the international press. FIFA's primary concern, though, was not to win over the American infidels. Nor was it, as its secretary Sepp Blatter claimed, to help get a professional league off the ground – had this been true, FIFA would not have summarily rejected the US bid for the 1986 tournament, at the very time the NASL was listing. On the contrary, the choice of host reflected the prevailing attitude towards top-drawer sport. As one member of the Brazilian delegation noted: 'A lot of people can make a lot of money if the games take off.'

A lot of people had made a lot of money in 1984, when the Olympics came to Los Angeles and the IOC had to rewrite its constitution to sanction a privatised organising committee. The Games quickly became a hostage to commercial enterprise. Corporate tie-ins and media deals left the LA organisers with a 'surplus' of $200 million (from which the president of the organising committee, Peter Ueberroth, awarded himself a bonus of $475,000). The following year, the IOC began selling the rights to display its five interlocking rings on nearly anything that could be bought. With scarcely a whimper of protest, the Olympics became an event geared to realising maximum commercial gain. FIFA had been heading in a similar direction since the election of João Havelange as president in 1974. The 1986 World Cup turned a profit of more than $30 million, but in the hands of powerful Yankee entrepreneurs such a figure was bound to pale.

On the field, reaching Italy in 1990 was now imperative if the US were to carry any credibility as a host. The Americans began their qualifying campaign in Jamaica with Goulet missing through injury. After a worryingly impotent 0-0 display in Kingston, the team was left needing a return-leg victory to avoid an embarrassingly early exit. Three weeks later, with less than half an hour to play in St Louis, the Americans stood on the brink of elimination, their opponents clinging to a 1-1 draw. Only a late flurry of goals, sparked by the second-half insertion of Hugo Perez, produced a comfortable 5-1 victory – and a radical change to the operation of the national team. Five of the starting line-up in Missouri, including captain Rick Davis, were without a club, a situation largely created by the contraction of the MISL. Within hours of the victory the USSF announced that it would sign players to contracts of its own, assuring them of a modest salary and committing them to the national team, though still allowing them to be loaned to other clubs. 'Playing regularly on the highest level is of the utmost importance for the players,' maintained Werner Fricker – an aphorism uttered by many of his predecessors which, at last, seemed more than simply rhetoric.

However different it may have been to the way other national teams operated, the arrangement had its advantages, notably in guaranteeing the availability of key talent. It also enabled the US to create a busy fixture list, with a team as experimental as it wished. The month before the draw in Kingston had seen American teams of varying strengths contend with a frenzied schedule. One squad represented the US at a tournament in South Korea while another was engaged in a series at home, playing seven times in a fortnight. Four dozen players earned caps.

This was too much for a part-time manager, particularly one unwilling to give up his day job. Osiander resigned, and the USSF handed the reins to its Under-20 coach, 47-year-old Hungarian-born Bob Gansler. Gansler's father had been imprisoned by the Soviets during the Second World War before the family fled to Germany, then to Wisconsin. As a teenager, the young immigrant tried his hand as a baseball catcher before earning a master's degree in German and teaching history at a local high school. His performances at centre-half for Milwaukee's Bavarian club helped earn him the captaincy of the 1964 and 1968 Olympic teams and several international call-ups, and in 1968 he joined the NASL's Chicago Mustangs. By 1984 Gansler had taken charge of the team at the University of Wisconsin-Milwaukee, a position he was now forced to relinquish.

Though well known in the guarded circles of the USSF, Gansler's international pedigree was limited. Admittedly, his Under-20s had reached the 1989 World Youth Cup finals in Saudi Arabia and finished second to Brazil in their group, as good a performance as the US had ever produced. He had also filled in for Osiander when the manager couldn't be excused from his restaurant work. Yet the bulk of his coaching experience had been at college level, where he had been only moderately successful. This was perfectly acceptable to Werner Fricker, who ruled out an approach for a foreign manager and cited Gansler as the only logical candidate. It was also good news for Walt Chyzowych, whose failings as national manager had not stopped Fricker, a fellow Philadelphian, appointing him as national director of coaching. Gansler and Chyzowych had often worked together, most visibly in getting the US to the 1981 World Youth Cup. Now the duo would lead the senior team through its most conspicuous campaign yet.

The US got their best break before the group stage even began, with the expulsion of Mexico for fraudulently using overage players at the 1989 World Youth Cup (a breach helpfully exposed by the Mexican federation's yearbook, which listed their real birthdates). Conspiracy theorists suggested FIFA's harsh punishment was designed to help the Americans. If so, they certainly looked as though they needed it. Over the next 12 months the US stumbled through a qualifying group lacking not only the Mexicans but also Canada, who had been eliminated by Guatemala in a preliminary round.

Thrust into the unusual role of favourites, the Americans' incoherent and sluggish play produced a string of disappointing results, while fans struggled to provide the team with any sort of inspiration. After losing 1-0 in Costa Rica, the US found itself playing the return fixture before 1,000 or so visiting fans among a capacity crowd of 8,500 in St Louis. The raucous support for the visiting *Ticos* even produced pleas from the public address announcer to 'remind the players what country the game is being played in'. The hosts produced little worth shouting about, escaping with what one writer termed a 'nightmare victory' only after goalkeeper David Vanole blocked a last-minute penalty. Two weeks later, an 88th-minute goal handed Trinidad & Tobago a share of the points in California, a match again enlivened by boisterous support for the visitors.

Gansler came under fire for his team selection and ultra-cautious tactics, which favoured protecting narrow leads and restrained counter-attacks. In fairness, he was hampered by injuries to key players, including captain Davis, whose knee troubles put a sorry end to a frustrating career, and Goulet's alarming loss of form. There were other irritations: a boot-endorsement dispute turned acrimonious enough for several players to file suit against the federation and a feud between Fricker and Hugo Perez resulted in one of the team's most gifted players refusing a new national team contract in favour of one with Red Star Paris of the French Second Division. ('Fricker told me to take it or leave it,' Perez complained. 'It was like he didn't need me.')

Differences between the USSF that had languished in obscurity for decades and the USSF selected to stage the world's most prestigious sporting event were often difficult to discern. The Trinidad match was staged at a college venue in Torrance, California, described by one promoter as 'one of the nastiest, dirtiest stadiums I have ever seen'. Its pitch, barely 70 yards wide and mismarked (a fact which didn't come to light until a few hours before kick-off), was a bumpy mess, in part because a vandal had driven across it the day before. Officials who had expected no more than 5,000 fans found themselves scrambling to accommodate twice as many, and explaining to them that the numbers on their tickets did not correspond to any numbers on the stadium seats. A month later, in New Britain, Connecticut, the US took on Guatemala, where promoters couldn't cope with a surge of interest from foreign journalists and ended up housing most of them in a tent behind one of the goals. The public address obligingly provided announcements in Spanish for fans of the visiting team. The US won narrowly and unconvincingly with Bruce Murray's impressive first-time volley eclipsed by the surely unprecedented news that police had arrested several ticket touts outside the ground.

One hundred years on from their unofficial debut, the national team was finally acquiring an appreciable level of support. Healthy crowds for friendlies peaked in Philadelphia, where 43,356 turned up for an exhibition with Dnepr Dnepropetrovsk of the Soviet Union (and, more pertinently to Philadelphia, of Ukraine). Results, such as a 3-0 defeat of Peru, were also creditable, but when the outcome was more important, goals proved harder to come by. The US's final home qualifier against already eliminated El Salvador – whose team was almost entirely replaced by a club from Usulután, and who arrived in St Louis at 9pm the night before kick-off – ended 0-0, a scoreline as profoundly disappointing as the one in Guatemala City a month earlier. In only one of seven group matches had Gansler's team produced more than a single goal. Caution had evolved into fear.

It meant that the US's fate rested on a victory in Trinidad, where they had always won, if never with the stakes so high. A draw would be enough to send the hosts through as the smallest country ever to reach the finals. Gansler claimed that he had known all along qualification would hinge on the last match, yet few had expected his team to limp into it so lamely, and their indifferent form left the USSF in a precarious position. Elimination would not only erode the federation's credibility as a World Cup host but also threaten its financial position – it had borrowed half a million dollars to underwrite the national team, with the clear expectation of reaching Italy. Meanwhile, the noises about a professional league which had echoed in the afterglow of the USA 94 announcement (Fricker had proposed that a three-division national league begin in 1989) had been reduced to whimpers. Nobody, it seemed, was interested enough to underwrite the project. Far more than qualification, then, rested on a victory in Port-of-Spain. As the new captain, Mike Windischmann of the ASL's Albany Capitals, impressed on his team-mates: 'Don't you realise if we lose some of us will have to go out and get jobs?'

Neutral sentiment favoured the home side. Its sea of fans displayed an exuberance for their team Americans had yet to produce, and their government had benignly declared the following day a national holiday, win or lose. Moreover, Trinidad & Tobago had been scandalously robbed of qualification in 1974, when four of their goals were curiously disallowed in a 2-1 defeat by Haiti during a final qualification round held entirely in Port-au-Prince. Some 35,000 red-shirted, umbrella-wielding fans now jammed the National Stadium to see their 'Strike Squad' make amends.

The US flew to Port of Spain from Miami in relative anonymity – an announcement over the airport public address referred to them as 'the Miami Soccer Club' – but media interest in the team had reached a modest new peak. About 40 American journalists travelled to Trinidad, with almost all the major dailies sending reporters. Even the most hard-hearted of them found the atmosphere and the do-or-die stakes irresistible. 'This game was an example of what international soccer is all about,' raved the *Los Angeles Times* correspondent, 'if not at its best then at least at its most thrilling.'

The draw with El Salvador two weeks earlier turned out to be a blessing in disguise. Forced to field an attacking team, Gansler made four changes, naming Caligiuri as a starter. Ultimately, though, it was not tactics so much as fear that won the match – a fear which this time crushed the opposition under the weight of national expectations. 'When we were with them in the tunnel before the game they were scared,' Windischmann recalled. 'You could tell by looking in their eyes. They didn't want to play.'

Half an hour into the match, Caligiuri produced what American soccer fans would soon refer to affectionately, if misguidedly, as the 'shot heard round the world', an awkwardly dipping, left-footed effort from 25 yards which somehow deceived the goalkeeper and planted itself in the net. It was his team's first goal in nearly four hours and only the fifth in eight group matches, but it proved enough. Though the Americans had demonstrated a worrying inability to protect such scorelines, and there were one or two anxious moments in the hour that followed, their nervous opponents could offer no real response. The US qualified for Italy with perhaps their most poised performance of the campaign.

It did not earn their country a national holiday, of course, and only the faintest murmur of interest from a national media preoccupied with the day's gridiron. America's imminent appearance on sport's biggest stage found itself competing for space down the page with such events as the death of a journeyman NASCAR race driver. ESPN once again declined to show the match live, and their footage of Caligiuri's goal was immediately and unceremoniously followed by score flashes from the NFL. But for all who cared to notice, November 19, 1989 represented a defining moment in American soccer history, and not simply a tremendous relief to the USSF.

Performances in the friendlies leading up to Italy were erratic: a caning by the Soviet Union and defeats to Costa Rica, East Germany, Colombia and Hungary. Even the victories were far from satisfying. During an uninspiring 1-0 victory over Malta, one reporter confessed he had taken almost as much pleasure in watching the ground staff attempt to replace advertising hoardings blown down by a gust of wind as in the match itself. But crowds continued to build and the federation applied some of the unexpected ticket revenue towards bumping up player salaries, attempting to damp down some of the ill-will bred by its confrontational approach to contract negotiations. The USSF asserted its right to determine whether and for how much a player could be allowed to sign for a club, and to keep a portion of any transfer fee. Such parsimony led goalkeeper David Vanole to quit the team in protest but others, just months from fulfilling a lifetime's ambition, bit their lips.

The average age of the squad Gansler selected for Italy – college products to a man – was just 23. Three still played for university teams. The exiled Perez had only just recovered from a broken leg and was left at home, though without any chance to prove his fitness. For creative inspiration the team looked to the Uruguayan-born Tab Ramos, whose family had sneaked into the country when he was ten. Up front, another New Jersey product, Peter Vermes, playing in the Dutch first division with Volendam, was paired with Bruce Murray. A year earlier, the Hungarian-speaking Vermes had joined Raba ETO of Györ, playing in the same league where his father had ended his career three decades earlier. 'I know there is communism here, but it's not something I notice in my everyday activities,' he told one reporter. 'What I notice more is how much more culture and tradition there is ... everywhere you go to eat, there are violins playing.'

Sweeper Mike Windischmann, assigned to no club at all after parting company with the less urbane Albany Capitals, was captain. But perhaps the most prominent member of the team was its goalkeeper, Tony Meola, a multisport star at the University of Virginia who had made his full international debut only the year before. Torn between baseball and soccer, or even the possibility of kicking for the university gridiron team, Meola's performance in a friendly against Benfica had helped him make up his mind. 'This is it for baseball,' he announced after keeping a clean sheet against that year's European Cup finalists. 'I think it's time that I dedicate my life to soccer.' In four qualifying matches, including the Port-of-Spain clincher, Meola did not concede a goal, and soon became the latest soccer object of *Sports Illustrated*'s attention. ('Get ready, Europe. Here comes Tony Meola, the gifted goalie who promises to be the US's first world-class soccer star.')

Meola proved rather less frugal in the preparatory matches on European soil, where the team looked sluggish and disorganised – the 2-0 defeat to Hungary in March was America's first full international on that continent in nearly a decade. An unconvincing 4-1 win against Liechtenstein, who hadn't fielded a team in nearly six years, offered only slightly more encouragement. The final warm-up game, a 2-1 defeat by Switzerland in St Gallen, exposed the extent of Gansler's caution. The US took an early lead, then retreated into a defensive shell that eventually imploded. Beaten, but far from chastened, Gansler conceded only that his team had given away momentum, and stressed that he wouldn't hesitate to use similar tactics in Italy.

This was not a man short on self-belief. Critics maintained that Gansler, like his mentor Chyzowych, did not set much store by the advice of even the most respected foreign tacticians, perhaps because he considered himself their equal. He preferred to pick through footage of previous matches in search of chinks in the opposition's armour, in the obsessive manner of American gridiron coaches. 'From what we see on tape,' observed Windischmann after the draw, 'Austria and Czechoslovakia will have the same system. It's what you'd consider traditional European, with big target men and forwards who can turn pretty quickly. Italy has some of the same style, but they're so much better at it.'

Quite what the American style was, no one could say. 'Our formula is simple,' the manager claimed, '11 guys play offense, and 11 guys play defense. We're going to have to hope that is good enough in Italy.' Brian Glanville haughtily dismissed the unit as a 'galumphing side of corn-fed college boys'. Yet if their university experience and its emphasis on structured, disciplined team play did not lend itself to creative freedom and ball artistry, it had certainly built a competitive psyche and an indomitable spirit. 'I think the players will concur with me,' Gansler asserted, 'that our expectation is to get in the second round.'

Such optimism reached fever pitch in Florence on the night of June 10, the US's first World Cup appearance in 40 years. Gansler had decided to attack against Czechoslovakia, a team he realistically needed to defeat to advance. He inserted Eric Wynalda, a striker with limited defensive skills (and whose quick temperament led one magazine to claim his behaviour at San Diego State University had 'incited 34 letters to the athletic department'), as an attacking midfielder, a move which soon proved calamitous. For 15 minutes, as the Czechs felt their way into the match, the Americans nurtured hopes of a result; after that, they were overrun, 'humiliated to the point of embarrassment' in the words of the *New York Times*. Crushed by the aerial power of Tomas Skuhravy and flustered by the near-post corners whipped in by Jozef Chovanec, they gave away two penalties (although one was knocked straight at Meola) and found it almost impossible to contain the Czechs in midfield.

The 5-1 debacle left full-back Desmond Armstrong wide-eyed. 'The game was a lot harder than we expected,' he admitted. 'From a technical aspect, they were a lot better than we thought.' Meola sighed: 'I never gave up five goals at Kearny. Heck, in that town giving up one goal was bad enough. You'd hear about it for weeks. Give up two goals and they'd shoot the mayor.' The Czechs exposed Wynalda's temperament, baiting him into a needless shove on Chovanec which produced a red card. Caligiuri's adroit effort pulled the score back to 3-1, but it sparked no comeback, only further raids on the US goal. As Bruce Murray later confessed: 'They were lined up like airplanes on the runway, waiting to slam it home.'

It was clear that the lack of professional league experience and an endless string of exhibitions against half-interested opposition had left the Americans under-prepared. The furtive use of arms and elbows, stamping on toes, shirt-tugging and leg-clutching were not distinctive features of competitions like the Marlboro Cup or the World Series of Soccer with which the team had prepared. Withdrawn in the 85th minute, Murray raced on to the pitch after the final whistle to confront one Czech player he thought had kicked Ramos all evening.

'It's called paying your dues,' Gansler offered in sober reflection, but some had witnessed more than simply the subjugation of youthful inexperience. The London *Times* said the US 'were utterly exposed by such Bronze Age devices as an overlapping full-back'; **USA, What A Delusion** read the headline in Milan's *Corriere della Sera*. Perhaps the manager was referring to paying his own dues. Certainly, against the next opponents there would be little in the way of adventure.

There was no humiliating scoreline either, and instead of the ten-goal feast pessimists had anticipated Italy to dine on, the Americans nearly produced one of the shocks of the tournament. Gansler had little choice but to pack his defence and trust in his team's tenacity and luck, yet the score proved more flattering than even he could have hoped for. Almost on cue, the hosts scored after 11 minutes, but that was all they would get. Resolute defending, combined with Italian passivity, left the Roman crowd whistling with derision, particularly after Gianluca Vialli thumped a penalty against a post. Midway through the second half Walter Zenga failed to hold Murray's free-kick and watched Vermes's follow-up cleared off the line, the US's only threat of the match. 'The Americans proved they are an excellent team, nothing like the team that lost 5-1,' claimed Italy's besieged manager Azeglio Vicini, perhaps in self-defence. A relieved Gansler claimed that 'this is the US team I know', a statement which could scarcely be refuted in the light of its ultra-defensive performance.

The learning curve was steep, but the Americans were climbing it, thickening their collective skin and responding to the more physical demands of World Cup football. 'Guys came out to practice on Tuesday and really started banging into each other,' Vermes observed. 'Czechoslovakia pushed us around and we knew if we let the Italians push us around, we'd get buried again.'

There was plenty of pushing in the final match with Austria, a meaningless encounter for the Americans, though their opponents stood a slim chance of reaching the second round. In an ill-tempered, poorly-refereed anticlimax, the Austrians had Peter Artner sent off after only 33 minutes, but scored twice in the second half before Murray found the net in the dying minutes. The one-goal margin looked respectable enough, but the US had been soundly defeated, unable to capitalise on their hour-long advantage. To the surprise of very few – apart from themselves – they finished beaten, but not too bloodied. 'Even though we lost tonight, I think we ended on a high note,' Ramos claimed. Yet their World Cup represented only a faint improvement on what Canada, similarly bereft of a professional league, had produced in Mexico four years earlier: neither team had earned so much as a point, although the US had at least managed to score. Despite this, the experience had been one long *cadenza*. Playing in stadiums filled with real fans and cameras from around the world, attending huge multilingual press conferences, being recognised on the street – these were novelties for a squad unfamiliar with being treated as if soccer mattered.

It still didn't matter back home. Italian TV may have attracted record ratings for the match with the US, but America had tuned out. Ted Turner's TNT, the cable channel that had bought US rights to the tournament for $7.25 million, found its modest investment difficult to recoup: their telecast of the final failed to attract even 500,000 viewers. While this represented two per cent of the national audience, it compared unfavourably with edited highlights of a college volleyball match on a rival station (and, as one critic claimed, two per cent of the nation's TV audience 'would watch a man balance a pencil on the end of his nose'). TNT's coverage included five commercial breaks in each half, an array of pointless graphics and untold interruptions to promote the station's other programmes. During one of the semi-finals, viewers missed a goal because the director had been preoccupied with showing a picture of the trophy.

Watching the World Cup on TNT, one reviewer concluded, 'was like sitting behind a post at a baseball game'. Those who spoke Spanish, or just couldn't stand all the interruptions, had the alternative of the Spanish-language Univision network, which ran its commercials across the bottom of the screen. Their commentary team worked from a studio in California, but few seemed to mind. The station claimed it as 'the most successful program in the history of Spanish-language TV'.

The lack of interest from the mainstream audience was in some ways excusable. It was a dreadful tournament, notable for cynical, defensive play and inept officiating. Few could remember a less inspiring final. The noted sportswriter Frank Deford asked incredulously: 'They're going to bring this thing to the United States of America in 1994 and charge money for people to see it?' While Deford and his peers spent much of the month debating the merits of soccer and its biggest event, too often the game's supporters became sanctimonious and its critics narrow-minded. Rarely did such haranguing generate an honest assessment of the event itself.

Only those few sportswriters to whom the Cup was a familiar experience dared to point out what had been painfully obvious to the rest of the world: crippling levels of gamesmanship and overtly negative play were at fault, not the sport itself. FIFA at last began to address this malaise – about a decade too late for the NASL – by revising its laws.

Although it did not consciously draw on the American experience, the most radical changes of the early Nineties – clamping down on the tackle from behind and the 'denial of a goalscoring opportunity', tinkering with the offside rule and banning backpasses to the goalkeeper – would have warmed the heart of many an NASL owner keen to raise the entertainment level.

The amendments were slight compared with the rule changes American college soccer would soon consider in response to its own anxieties. Fewer than 4,000 attended the 1991 NCAA Division I final, the event's 14th consecutive year of four-digit gates. 'Our game is dying in almost every spot in the world,' claimed Cliff McCrath, a university coach and secretary of the NCAA's ever-industrious soccer rules committee. The means by which McCrath's committee took it upon itself to resuscitate the game were scarcely credible.

It proposed a battery of radical and horribly ill-conceived rule changes, including: restricting defensive walls to four players at free-kicks; no more than five players in the penalty area at corners; no offside once the ball passed a 35-yard line; and even a remedial NASL-style 'shoot-out' for any foul which thwarted a goalscoring opportunity. College soccer had already sanctioned a time-out in the middle of each half for matches with a television audience, and rescinded an earlier attempt to restrict substitutions. Now they threatened to create virtually a new sport. A flood of protest thwarted the most radical proposals – at which point the rules committee defended itself by claiming it was only playing devil's advocate.

It was hard to take college soccer seriously. The 1989 championship final sent the Universities of Virginia and Santa Clara of California to New Jersey in the middle of December. Under arctic conditions (a temperature of minus six degrees and a wind chill of minus 23) and only a day after each had won their semi-finals, the teams shivered to a 1-1 draw, then contested four additional 15-minute periods without further score. With the rules committee apparently oblivious to the fact that even staid FIFA now settled some of its matches on penalties, the result was declared a draw and the sides shared the championship. The entire gelid afternoon had been a complete waste of time.

While the college system continued to spawn many of the country's top players – Meola, among others, had played in the icy championship – their international pedigree was still in doubt. The prospect of several abbreviated seasons of college soccer compared unfavourably with learning the profession elsewhere. Meola left Virginia prematurely to try his luck overseas, while the most Ramos could say about his days at North Carolina State University was that 'maybe my workrate got better'.

The 1990 World Cup paved the way for many of the best performers on the national team to play in Europe. Ramos signed for UE Figueres of the Spanish second division. Midfielder John Harkes was sold to Sheffield Wednesday, full-back John Doyle played for Örgryte in Sweden, Caligiuri returned to Germany and Steve Trittschuh joined Sparta Prague, where he became the first American to play in the European Cup. Yet the young man for whom the greatest success had been predicted, Meola, soon ended up back home. Unable to attract the widely predicted interest of Italian clubs, he ended up with Watford and was released. 'All the signs I have received suggested he is not near the mark,' claimed manager Steve Perryman.

The trickle of American players moving overseas would have huge ramifications in the long-term, but the most immediately significant event that year took place at a hotel in Florida, two months after the team returned home from Italy. The USSF's lack of progress on the 1994 tournament – in particular, its inability to sell the event to corporate America and the dour, intransigent leadership of Werner Fricker – had infuriated FIFA to breaking point. In Orlando that August Fricker stood for re-election as president, and the world governing body took a sudden, unprecedented interest in the outcome.

Initially there was only one opposition candidate, Paul Stiehl, one of the engineers of the 1994 bid, a former friend of Fricker now turned bitter rival. Stiehl placed the blame for the lack of World Cup progress squarely on Fricker's shoulders, even going so far as to accuse him of financial improprieties (an odd claim, given that Stiehl was the federation treasurer). Ten days before the election, though, a third entrant announced his candidacy: Alan Rothenberg, the man responsible for the 1984 Olympic tournament which had so impressed FIFA, but a rank alien to the cliquish USSF. Claiming to possess a 'fresh perspective', Rothenberg made his election platform abundantly clear. The next World Cup was America's last chance to become a soccer nation, and it was being squandered. 'I have maintained my relationship with FIFA,' he declared, 'and they continually express their concern of the USSF leadership. It's just not up to the task.'

Predictably, the presence of a high-powered Los Angeles lawyer among the federation's old-country stalwarts and grass-roots enthusiasts attracted suspicion. Yet behind Rothenberg – whose association with soccer included vice-presidency of the short-lived Los Angeles Wolves and two seasons as part-owner of the LA Aztecs – stood a number of familiar and influential figures: the kingpin of the LA Olympics, Peter Ueberroth, folk hero Kyle Rote jnr and even Pelé. The biggest name of all emerged on the morning of the election when Stiehl, given the floor to address the delegates, revealed that he had received an early-morning phone call from a FIFA official asking him to stand down and back Rothenberg. Stiehl refused and, complaining of a 'hostile takeover' of the federation, made a last-minute plea to the voters not to 'surrender the castle'. A sympathiser expressed similar disdain. 'If the United Nations told us who to vote for in the presidential elections,' he thundered, 'American people would be very quick to tell them where to shove it.'

But Fricker had created too many adversaries. Perceived by many as aloof, and criticised for excessive loyalty to old friends (some could not believe he had not dismissed Gansler immediately after Italy), he had fallen out of favour with many of the state and regional associations who wielded considerable power, and who were warming to the idea of a house-cleaning. In the most pivotal election of the federation's 77-year history, the outsider was elected by a convincing margin. 'Together, we will take soccer in the United States closer to the goal we all share of worldwide pre-eminence,' Rothenberg proclaimed. An embittered Fricker was left only to conclude that a large majority of members were not interested in the sport. No one could accuse him of the same – nor, for that matter, of running an unsuccessful regime. He had begun his six-year reign by rescuing the federation from its latest flirtation with bankruptcy, and ended it watching the United States at the World Cup.

The humble USSF was going corporate. Rothenberg wasted little time in making sweeping changes to an organisation still heavily reliant on volunteers. Many were shown the door, replaced by salaried administrators with business acumen and experience in the burgeoning discipline of 'event marketing'. The new federation secretary, Hank Steinbrecher, had once coached at Boston University, but it was his most recent role, as marketing executive for a sports drink company, that secured his appointment. 'Our world is so incestuous,' he said, cocking an oblique snook at the old guard. 'Soccer needs new blood and new vigour.'

On a six-figure salary, rather more than any USSF administrator had ever drawn, Steinbrecher wasted little time in making his mark, declaring in the familiar argot of his profession: 'What we want is mom and dad, family income of $40,000 with a minivan and two kids who play on Saturday.' Inevitably, the federation fell prey to a 'rebranding' exercise and began referring to itself as 'US Soccer'. It discarded its 'old and busy' logo with one more akin to those of American sports teams, a soccer ball zooming skywards in front of a patriotic assembly of red stripes (a change Steinbrecher mysteriously hailed as 'a must if we were to convince people we were for real').

Of course the principal issues had little to do with names or insignia. Creating a viable professional league, for one, was a challenge no one seemed capable of meeting. By 1991 it was clear the American Professional Soccer League was anything but, with its merger of east and west coast teams sparking no renaissance. The 22 clubs who participated in 1990 had dwindled to just five by the end of 1991, with teams such as the Miami Freedom trying to survive on gates of a few hundred.

The change of guard that brought Steinbrecher and others to power also included the incomprehensible appointment of Earl Foreman to the federation's 'outdoor development committee', the group supposedly responsible for getting the new league off the ground. Foreman was still commissioner of the enterprise most responsible for distorting America's perception of 'soccer', one which had hideously rebranded itself as the Major Soccer League, and about which he had once boasted: 'We don't give two shits about outdoor soccer.' That he was now being asked to give at least one shit was attributed by some to a political favour owed to him by Rothenberg. Bizarrely, Foreman's eight ersatz-soccer franchises controlled one-third of the entire USSF vote, and they had cast their ballots en masse for the lawyer.

Yet by the summer of 1992 the MSL, with its Cleveland Crunch, Baltimore Blast and San Diego Sockers – whom Ron Newman had led to countless league championships – was bankrupt, ravished by rivals and the absence of meaningful television exposure. Foreman soon disappeared from the radar, but the damage had been done. Words such as 'technically infeasible' and 'impractical' kept cropping up whenever talk of a new outdoor league surfaced. Prospective owners were thin on the ground, many no doubt frightened by the collapse of Foreman's enterprise. If the all-American indoor game couldn't survive, there seemed little hope for any less synthetic alternative.

A year after his election, Rothenberg boasted of his regime: 'I really don't know how we could have accomplished more', and claimed US Soccer had 'totally dispelled the worldwide cynicism re our ability to stage the 1994 World Cup' (except for 'the British tabloids, who seem to want only scandalous, negative, cynical material'). Certainly, he had delivered the sort of high-flying leadership FIFA expected. He had also given short shrift to Chyzowych and Gansler, removing the former from his position of authority with the national team and accepting the latter's resignation a few months later. But the question most often asked by the soccer world had yet to be answered: could he make the American World Cup work?

8. Revenge of the Commie Pansies

The World Cup comes to America

I can foresee that the World Cup here will meet the conditions established by the Winter Olympics for pointlessness and trivia enhancement. It is well known in the media that the Winter Olympics are when you go to incredible inconvenience to cover a local competitor in an event you wouldn't normally cross the street to see. Biathlon. Luge. Soccer. Three of a kind.

Cleveland *Plain Dealer*

On July 21, 1991, a crowd of 31,871 came to Giants Stadium for a New York Cosmos reunion. Fifty-two players, representing every period of the club's roller-coaster 14-year history, laced up their boots and turned back the clock to a happier time for soccer in America. Franz Beckenbauer withdrew because of stomach trouble and Giorgio Chinaglia was ensconced in Italy, but Vladislav Bogicevic, Johan Neeskens, Carlos Alberto, Rick Davis and a host of others turned out – as did Pelé, who waved to the crowd but didn't play. Absence, it seemed, had made hearts grow fonder. In their final season seven years earlier, the Cosmos had not attracted a single gate of such a size.

Older fans might have looked back with wistful nostalgia, but most of the country had distanced itself from the Cosmos, the NASL and soccer's failed bid for 'sport of the Eighties'. A *Sports Illustrated* survey released that year asserted that only nine per cent of the public 'followed' soccer, a dismal figure that sent vested interests scurrying to the sport's defence. The Soccer Industry Council of America claimed its own research showed that more children under 12 played their game than gridiron, baseball or ice hockey, and that soccer was third behind basketball and volleyball among under-18s. Yet the council, like many before them, missed the point entirely: participation was one thing, 'following' quite another. It had become a standing joke that the reason so many Americans played soccer was that it enabled them to avoid watching it.

Eight months after Italia 90, just 6,261 showed up in Los Angeles for a North American Nations Cup tie with Mexico. Searching for a successor to Bob Gansler, the federation hankered after Franz Beckenbauer, but came to discover that the new manager of Marseille was, according to one source, 'willing to accept challenges, not fight lost causes'. Meanwhile the country's lone excuse for a professional league, the APSL, trundled down its anonymous path.

None of this deterred 27 cities from submitting their applications to stage 1994 World Cup matches, nor did it prevent Alan Rothenberg from predicting unprecedented success for the event. Bora Milutinovic, the Serb who had steered Mexico to the quarter-finals of the 1986 World Cup and Costa Rica to an improbable second-round berth four years later, was appointed as coach, some said on Beckenbauer's advice. Orphaned by the Second World War, Milutinovic had joined Partizan Belgrade at 17 but soon became a footballing vagabond, trying his luck with three French clubs and FC Winterthur in Switzerland before moving to Mexico and marrying there. He finished his playing career with UNAM Pumas, then guided them to the league championship in 1981.

More willing than his predecessor to look outside the colleges for talent – talent that didn't need to be a generation removed from the manager, as seemed the case with Gansler – Milutinovic scoured the country for an infusion of fresh blood, casting an eye over not just the cream of the college crop, but APSL stars, indoor league veterans and even a Polish émigré playing in an ethnic league in New England. But what differentiated him from his predecessor wasn't so much the players he chose as the way he coached them. 'Most coaches explain what they want,' said centre-half Marcelo Balboa. 'Bora shows you.' Doug Cress observed in *Soccer America*:

> He does it with little walks around the field with his players, his arm draped around their shoulders, the voice of reason in their ears. He does it in practices and just before games – not with every player, only a select few. And they have responded.

They responded, too, to his deceptively light-hearted approach to training sessions, where he usually played alongside them ('the best part of coaching', he confessed), and his insistence on keeping the game simple. The media responded sympathetically, referring to him as 'Bora' far more often than they had ever called Gansler 'Bob', and delighting in his disarmingly rudimentary command of English. It left the fraternity of clipboard-wielding American coaches bemused. 'Why does everybody ask me about my style?' Milutinovic cried. 'There are many books on soccer style – read those. If I wrote a book about my style, nobody would buy it.' Within a few months, this self-effacing approach inspired the

US to its first triumph in a senior tournament of any consequence: the Concacaf Gold Cup, a newly devised championship for the nations of North and Central America, staged in the summer of 1991.

The Gold Cup owed its existence largely to a momentous power shift within Concacaf. The previous year had seen the removal of Joaquín Soria Terrazas, the 80-year-old, nearly blind Mexican who had presided over the federation for as long as anyone could remember, and the installation of Trinidad's Jack Warner as his replacement. Warner wasted little time in making extensive changes, even moving the federation's headquarters from Guatemala City to Manhattan. But his election, and the appointment of other English-speaking officials to senior positions, alienated the Spanish-speaking bloc. With Mexico threatening to abandon Concacaf for South America, and the Central American countries keen to form a federation of their own, the Gold Cup was a tool to keep everyone within the fold as well as make money. The old Concacaf championship had certainly never done that. Since its demise in 1971, when the US did not even take part, the World Cup qualifiers had been deemed to provide the regional champions. The Gold Cup also marked another step in the US's march toward international respectability, receiving its baptism not in Mexico City, but in Southern California.

The Americans quickly took to the new competition, beating Honduras in the final on penalties to finish off a punishing fixture list of five matches in eight days, and producing the first fruits of Milutinovic's more attacking style. The US scored eight goals in their three group matches and beat Mexico 2-0 in the semi-final, the first meaningful victory over their southern nemesis since the 1934 World Cup and one which ushered in a new relationship between the two countries. The Mexico coach Manuel Lapuente, who resigned in the wake of the defeat, was reduced to a daunting, if face-saving, admission: 'We have to understand now that we are almost at the same level as the United States. Even though they don't have a professional league, they have established themselves.'

By the end of 1991 the absence of a pro league had prompted almost half the World Cup squad to pursue careers overseas, most with fairly meagre success and rarely with the opulence of home. Desmond Armstrong spent a few months living in a hotel room while playing for Santos; Steve Trittschuh found that life with Sparta Prague, the champions of Czechoslovakia, didn't entitle him to a familiar standard of living ('once the weather started getting cold, there wasn't a whole lot of food available'); and Paul Caligiuri ventured into East Germany to help Hansa Rostock to its first double in the final season before reunification, waiting ten weeks for the club to find him somewhere to live. 'It was furnished with 1960s furniture from Russia,' he recalled, 'and it was something my wife and I accepted to prove that we could live with their standards. We didn't want to be termed "rich Americans".'

John Harkes found life in Yorkshire somewhat less onerous. An injury to Roland Nilsson gave him an opportunity to break into Sheffield Wednesday's first team, albeit as a right-back instead of a midfielder, and it did not take long for the US sporting press to draw attention to their country's rare soccer export. *Sports Illustrated* noted that Harkes's new environs were rather more demanding than those of the USSF. The 'savagely intense practices supervised by [manager Ron] Atkinson', it observed, 'make the US team's pre-World Cup workouts look like rehearsals for an amateur production of *The Sound of Music*.'

Harkes's father was born in Scotland, which helped him secure a British passport and thereby alleviate the work permit restrictions that had thwarted other hopefuls. His ancestry had also instilled in him an unusual reverence for Wembley, and lent a special poignancy to Wednesday's presence in the League Cup final that season. Earlier in the competition, he had scored his first goal for the club, a sensational long-range strike against Derby County which, as the US press unfailingly pointed out, came at the expense of England's Peter Shilton. Against Manchester United on April 21, 1991, Harkes became the first American to appear in a Wembley final (Wednesday won 1-0), fulfilling an ambition few other New Jersey youngsters had harboured.

About 30 other young hopefuls had ended up in Europe, most in the middle echelons of the German pyramid, as progress on the domestic front stagnated. The 1992 target FIFA had set for a US professional league came and went, with the task of replacing the NASL frustrating even the new high-flyers at the federation. The principal issue, Alan Rothenberg insisted, was finding places to play. 'If we had 25,000-seat stadiums,' he declared, 'I'd launch a soccer league yesterday and prophesy 1000 per cent success.'

There were other hurdles, of course, but the prospect of big-league soccer playing to section after section of empty seats in some yawning gridiron cathedral hardly flooded potential investors with confidence. Even the satisfaction that dozens of cities wanted to stage World Cup matches was tempered by the knowledge that a number of showpiece stadiums did not comply with FIFA's demands – in particular, its insistence on grass pitches and a playing width of at least 68 metres.

Many of the proposed stadiums, such as the 101,701-seat facility on the campus of the University of Michigan, literally failed to measure up.

Most ominous was the absence of any bid from New York, whose only two major-league facilities were consigned to baseball over the summer and not really conducive to soccer anyway. Giants Stadium – in New Jersey, lest anyone forget – had been left off the shortlist because its pitch was a few metres too narrow and its proprietors did not wish to compromise its 'structural integrity'. The area's hopes seemed to rest on the Yale Bowl, 80 miles north-east of the city. FIFA put its foot down, insisting the organisers could do better than hold New York's matches in Connecticut. The response was almost laughable: enlarging 23,000-seat Rutgers Stadium in New Jersey or remodelling the Aqueduct race track in Queens. Giants Stadium, which in spite of the Cosmos' tenancy had not been built with soccer in mind, seemed the most sensible choice. But accommodating a wider pitch and covering it with real grass would not only cost millions of dollars but also inconvenience its most powerful tenants, the NFL's Giants, and the Jets, who had abandoned Shea Stadium in 1983.

When the organising committee came up with its definitive list of venues in April 1992, Giants Stadium magically appeared on it. Only eight other sites were to be used. FIFA claimed such a small number, the lowest since 1974, when the tournament involved only 16 teams, would provide 'better exposure to football', but less charitable sources pointed towards the cost savings. In truth, the decision had less to do with 'exposure' than an underwhelming level of support from corporate America. Werner Fricker claimed the original intention had been to stage the World Cup in the 12 cities most likely to be involved in a professional league. If that was true, it was difficult to justify the selection of Orlando, Florida, with a population of less than 200,000, or the exclusion of Philadelphia, the fifth-largest city in the country.

Chicago, Detroit, Boston (or at least Foxboro), Los Angeles (Pasadena), San Francisco (Palo Alto) and Washington DC joined Orlando and New Jersey in clearing the final hurdle. Completing the field was Dallas, home of American Airlines, a key USSF patron. Not all were tendering the country's finest stadiums. Crumbling venues such as Texas's Cotton Bowl would require something more than a new coat of paint, while the proprietors of Giants Stadium still balked at demands to expand the playing surface. FIFA threw the problem back at the organisers: 'If in the United States, the land of all possibilities, this is not overcome,' sniffed secretary Sepp Blatter, 'FIFA shall not bring the World Cup to New York.' The land of all possibilities duly produced its solution: a platform which would raise the pitch ten feet above the artificial surface and its constrictive retaining wall. Told the arrangement would set them back about $5 million, FIFA suddenly turned conciliatory and declared the conundrum to be 'haggling over a few centimetres' – though in fact there were more than three million square ones at stake. The undersized pitch was passed fit.

Attention also turned to the curious choice of the indoor facility in suburban Detroit – evidence, said Blatter, that at 'so-called conservative FIFA there are open-minded spirits' – whose problems with a similarly narrow pitch paled alongside the unprecedented challenge of staging matches indoors on a natural surface. A few years earlier its proprietors had experimented with growing grass indoors, but with little success ('It grew, but it was kind of a sickly green,' recalled one observer). A group of university scientists was engaged to round up all the horticultural expertise it could find.

The national team's progress, meanwhile, consisted largely of offering those players under contract as much international exposure as possible, a development which soon led to some fairly young heads accumulating staggering numbers of caps. It took Peter Shilton 15 years to make 70 international appearances, but Bruce Murray reached that mark in less than half the time, while he was only 25. The 72 caps Murray had collected by 1993 were more than twice the number with which Arnie Mausser had set a national record as recently as 1985. Half a dozen of Murray's Italia 90 team-mates, all under 30, closed in on 50-cap careers, paying for them in wearying denominations of air miles. In 1992 alone the US staged matches in North Carolina, Michigan, Texas, Florida, California, Illinois, New Jersey and Washington DC, and visited Ireland, Morocco, Costa Rica, El Salvador and Saudi Arabia. The 1993 schedule included 34 internationals from Texas to Tokyo, the most important of them squeezed into a two-month period when the US found itself entered in three competitions. To the outside world, the most significant of these were the South American championships in Ecuador, the Copa America, to which Concacaf teams had been invited. For the federation, it was more important to perform well at home in the US Cup, a competition the World Cup organising committee had first staged in 1992 as much to prepare itself for 1994 as the national team.

The 1992 event pitted the US against three European sides – Italy, Ireland and Portugal – who had failed to qualify for the European Championships that summer. Surprisingly, the Americans emerged with two victories and a draw to claim the trophy. Yet they returned to the competition the following year having won just one of their previous 14 internationals. Milutinovic expressed indifference to the results, insisting he was far more concerned with individual performances and longer-term aims. But for the men in the suits, a losing team was bad for business. 'Even with some players in Europe, we've got to do better than a tie at home against Iceland,' sighed one official.

The 1993 US Cup succeeded in landing crowd-pleasers Brazil as well as Germany and England, perhaps selected as much for the testing behaviour of their supporters as the appeal of their teams. The competition drew a total of 286,000 fans to a sort of dress rehearsal for the following summer. In Foxboro, an hour's ride from the site of the Boston Tea Party, England helpfully broke an American streak of five matches without a win by losing 2-0 in front of 37,000 startled fans. While the English press dismissed the result as yet another example of the failings of beleaguered manager Graham Taylor, to the home team it was a considerable accomplishment, a clean sheet against the motherland and the first victory over the English since Belo Horizonte.

'If this isn't on the front page of every paper tomorrow, I don't know what we have to do,' exclaimed Harkes – in vain, since the Montreal Canadiens won the Stanley Cup later that day and laid claim to the sport section. One USSF official, apparently unaware that the opposition were hardly the footballing giants of half a century earlier, gushed that the victory represented 'the highest point in American soccer since we beat England in the 1950 World Cup'. Though the Americans lost to Brazil and Germany, US Cup 93 – as seen on national TV – provided plenty of excitement, including a dramatic match that saw Germany retrieve a 3-0 half-time deficit against Brazil to draw 3-3 on a sweltering Washington afternoon.

But perhaps the most important occasion was the Germans' 2-1 win over England in front of more than 62,000. The debut of indoor grass at the Silverdome proved a success: 1,850 hexagonal trays, each weighing 1.5 tonnes thanks to a 15-centimetre base of loam, were wheeled inside and assembled for the contest, and the end result proved as playable as anything under the sky. The port-a-pitch was promptly taken apart, and would spend the next 12 months in an adjacent car park.

For Milutinovic, there was scarcely time to draw breath. Days later, an American team flew to Ecuador to play in the Copa America. The United States and Mexico, whose ambition had largely prompted the invitation, participated as guests, the first in the competition's history. But Milutinovic rested his Europe-based players, and the US capitulated, losing to the hosts and Uruguay and somehow contriving to throw away a 3-0 lead against feeble Venezuela. The third trophy to play for that summer was the Gold Cup the team had won two years earlier. Back came Harkes, now a minor celebrity in England, and Eric Wynalda, who had reached the German first division with Saarbrücken, though they were relegated that spring. Three other European players, none US-born, also returned. Earnie Stewart, the Dutch-born son of an American serviceman, had become a respectable goal-scorer in the Eredivisie with Willem II; he had lived in California between the ages of two and seven before moving to Holland with his mother. Roy Wegerle, a South African with a Scottish mother, German father and American wife (and a brother, Steve, who had spent eight seasons in the NASL), had the highest profile of the three, not only because of his seven seasons of English league experience but because of the variety of countries he was eligible to represent.

Perhaps the most curious arrival was Thomas Dooley, whose name alone had attracted the interest of USSF officials familiar with the progress of Kaiserslautern in the Bundesliga. Dooley had signed for the club in 1988 and helped them to a league championship in 1991, establishing himself as a first-rate midfielder. His father was an American serviceman, but he had abandoned the family shortly after his son's birth. In spite of his name, Dooley spoke no English and had never visited the US, yet he drove a Corvette, claimed to watch the Super Bowl and 'always considered the Americans among my friends'. Understandably, his ambition had always been to play for Germany, but after a series of injuries helped to deny him that opportunity, at 31 he pledged his international future to the US, rapidly developing a keen fascination for his adopted country. As Caligiuri later remarked: 'Everything with him's like a 33-year-old boy seeing Disneyland for the first time.'

Dooley and Wegerle turned in a number of impressive performances, and were ever-presents at the 1993 Gold Cup. Dooley scored the winner against Panama – a brutal match which produced fines for both sides – but his team played well only in spurts, while the meagre attendance in Dallas mocked the city's World Cup pretensions. Though the US finished top of its group, a total of only 43,500 had appeared at the three doubleheaders, a figure nearly eclipsed by the first match in the Mexico City group. The Americans' semi-final against Costa Rica, settled by Californian Cle Kooiman's extra-time goal, drew fewer than 15,000 to the Cotton Bowl. Kooiman played his club football with Cruz Azul, whose own Aztec Stadium staged the final.

Laden with World Cup qualifiers, the Mexicans had needed some persuasion to take the competition seriously, having made a better fist of the Copa America than their northern neighbours (to the extent of reaching the final, where they lost narrowly to Argentina). That success now steeled them with confidence for the Gold Cup final where, in front of 120,000 in the smoggy, thin air of the Estadio Azteca, the Mexicans turned in their customary forceful performance against the US, a 4-0 whitewash that left the Americans gasping for breath and desperate for a rest. 'We went to Bora's after the game, and when we thought about it, it was hard to take,' Kooiman said. 'But the tacos were great, the music was great, and the guys were thinking about vacations.'

But with the World Cup less than 12 months away, there was little respite for those hoping to make the final 22. The USSF arranged a battery of test matches: Iceland in Reykjavik; Ukraine in Bethlehem, Pennsylvania; Denmark in Hong Kong; Bolivia in Miami; Chile in Albuquerque, New Mexico; and dozens of others. Players walked a peculiar tightrope, needing to put in the effort that would earn them a place in the squad, yet desperate to avoid the sort of serious injury that had kept Marcelo Balboa out for most of 1993.

Milutinovic's axe surprisingly fell on several Italia 90 veterans: John Doyle, Desmond Armstrong, Peter Vermes and even Bruce Murray. He also shunned arguably his most experienced goalkeeper, Kasey Keller, whose performances for Millwall had attracted considerable acclaim. Keller's insistence that his time in the English First Division had provided him with more competition than the sum of his national team experience went unheeded. Meola, whose brief European sojourn had been damned with faint praise, seemed the certain first choice.

The inscrutable Serb offered little in the way of explanation for his decisions, relatively free from the sort of scrutiny they would have attracted in other countries. 'My job isn't hard,' he joked with reporters. 'You're the ones with the difficult job – trying to get me to tell you something.' Not that there weren't cogent criticisms to be made. The World Cup run-in was far from inspiring, with draws at home to Moldova and Saudi Arabia, a defeat by Iceland in San Diego and a narrow win over Armenia in Fullerton, California. Milutinovic persisted in shuffling his line-up and instigating a parade of substitutions which hinted more at panic than experimentation; for a while the team's top scorer was defender Frank Klopas. When he cared to, the manager defended his seemingly haphazard selections with references to his time with Costa Rica. The same approach, he claimed, had led to that team's success in Italy. In the end, he chose only eight who had gone to the 1990 World Cup, as well as five who had played for his college-based assistant, Sigi Schmid, at UCLA. Above all he wanted those with European experience: Harkes, Stewart, Dooley (now with Bayer Leverkusen), Wynalda (transferred to VfL Bochum), Tab Ramos (Real Betis) and Caligiuri (back in California).

In a confusing and largely predetermined draw, FIFA were exceedingly kind in naming the US as one of the six top seeds, if less kind in pulling much-fancied Colombia's name out of the hat to join them in Group A, along with Switzerland and a Romanian side at its peak, led by Gheorghe Hagi. There was little evidence that the Americans had been given the easy ride some had forecast. Not content with overtly orchestrating the draw for the greatest commercial potential (Ireland would get to play closest to Boston, Italy to New York, Germany in Chicago) FIFA banished from the glitzy Las Vegas ceremony the one person the country most readily associated with the game.

A feud with FIFA president João Havelange – over an affair that had nothing to do with the tournament – cost Pelé his place at the table, and even beseechings from Alan Rothenberg that 'the notion of having a draw in this country without Pelé is unthinkable' proved futile. Not for the last time, the unthinkable had happened. Havelange bristled: 'FIFA has the right to decide who will participate. The presence of one person is not that important.'

FIFA proved to be more open-minded when it came to the game itself. It decided to award three points instead of two for victories in group matches, and ordered referees to clamp down on rough tactics, especially the tackle from behind. Miscreants were to be severely discplined, and the offside law interpreted more generously for attackers. Blatter referred to the changes as 'an unequivocal sign that attacking spirit will be rewarded', and they did prove largely positive, but many questioned the wisdom of introducing them on the eve of the event. Some even claimed FIFA were responding not so much to the cynicism of the previous tournament as to the demands of a less accepting host audience.

But in the weeks leading up to kick-off, quizzical looks and contemptuous frowns largely gave way to broad smiles. Pointing to the astonishing fact that almost all tickets had been sold, the organisers proclaimed that USA 94 would be 'the best World Cup ever'. Whether it had captured the imagination of the local population was another matter, and an issue which seldom escaped the notice of the international media. Foreign journalists took endless delight in corralling the American-in-the-street and waiting for the inevitable response to their question: the World *what?* One pre-tournament poll claimed 71 per cent of Americans did not know the event was about to take place. The organisers were under no illusions. 'To 178 countries, it's the most important thing in the world,' one official acknowledged. 'We happen to be the 179th.'

That a World Cup could be considered the 'best ever' in spite of such widespread apathy seemed incongruous, but of course the definition of 'best' had never been made entirely clear. In *Soccer America*, Paul Gardner hinted at the most likely criterion:

> I've been an accredited journalist for the past four World Cups. Never, in the lead-up to any of those tournaments, did I receive a single piece of sales material. But this time, it's a rare day when I don't get in the mail some catalogue or expensively-printed brochure offering to sell me some official World Cup merchandise, or hotel rooms, or not-to-be-missed ticket deals. All, need I add, at alarmingly high 'special' prices. A lot of this uninvited, unwanted stuff comes direct from the World Cup people. Money has evidently become an obsession with them.

It was not difficult to find similar views from other journalists, whose employers were forced to hand over $500 to obtain a press pass or were relieved of $100 just to use their own telephones in the press box. George Kimball of the *Boston Herald* discovered that at the press car park at Giants Stadium: 'I could pay $10 at the gate, show my media badge and park alongside the poor sap who had paid FIFA $40 to put his car there.' Fans, naturally, were confronted with similar avarice. After discovering he could not buy tickets for one World Cup match at a time, a disillusioned fan wrote to the *New York Times* that organisers in California had told him the block purchase scheme guaranteed full stadiums, which was 'important for television' – and that touts represented the best chance for anyone unable to part with $200 or more for the standard three-match 'package'.

Such commercial opportunism was by no means limited to soccer, of course. Steep ticket prices and a surfeit of television money had helped basketball's NBA to a record $195 million profit in 1992-93, with sales of its licensed merchandise exceeding $12 billion. TV rights to the NFL now amounted to about $4.4 billion, even though ratings had marginally declined – networks simply ordered that play be stopped more frequently for commercial breaks. (The broadcast of a 60-minute gridiron contest, which takes about three hours, typically contains anywhere from 45 minutes to an hour's worth of advertising and trailers.) And though average NFL ticket prices had nearly doubled in ten years, attendances continued to rise.

This loyalty (some would say gullibility) was fanned by the sudden proliferation of sports broadcast media, and in particular ESPN, the all-sports cable channel whose modest beginnings in 1979 scarcely hinted at its future as the dominant voice of US sports culture. By 1994, ESPN was available in almost 70 per cent of American homes and had secured the rights to an impressive array of competitions. Gone were its low-budget presentations of professional slow-pitch softball and pre-packaged highlights of Australian Rules football; in came the NFL and major league baseball. In consolidating its output and focusing on events with the broadest appeal, ESPN in effect marginalised many sports, even those – soccer among them – it continued to indulge with air-time.

This was part of a broader trend. *Sports Illustrated*, which once imaginatively reported on pursuits as varied as fencing, judo and contract bridge, now restricted itself largely to the achingly familiar and popular. Hardly a month of the basketball season passed without Michael Jordan appearing on its cover. 'I'll be the first to admit,' allowed one *SI* editor, 'that I'm contributing to the narrowing of the interest of the American sports fan.' Thus, the World Cup put the American media in a quandary. Though anything with a reputation as the world's biggest sporting event could not help but demand their attention, the sport was still soccer, dreary and incomprehensible, and something few could comment on lucidly. It also interfered with the traditional summer rituals of baseball, the NBA play-offs, US Open golf and Wimbledon.

Until the dawn of the event, interest remained sporadic and sketchy, which was a source of considerable frustration to Alan Rothenberg, judging from a June 1993 issue of *Sports Illustrated*:

> Since January of last year, Rothenberg has sent several memos to his public relations staff bemoaning the Cup's low profile in the press and his own poor standing among the 100 most powerful people in sports, as ranked by the *Sporting News*. After dropping from No 86 in 1991 to No 95 last year, he wrote: 'I expect to be listed in the Top 25 as of January 1993, Top 10 as of January 1994, and No. 1 as of January 1995. Start working on it now.'

Some media outlets persisted in giving the World Cup short shrift (the *Sporting News* chose to ignore it altogether), but by June Rothenberg's efforts to promote himself and the lofty international status of his tournament had won most of them over. Though much of the reporting was facile – meaningless comparisons with the indigenous mega-events of the Super Bowl and World Series, frequent references to rioting fans and a concluding word or two on the slim chances of the US team – it still pushed soccer to the front of the sports pages. Furthermore, ABC and ESPN had agreed to show all 52 matches – remarkably, without commercial interruption – filling the airwaves with more live coverage in a month than the nation had seen from the previous 14 tournaments put together.[*]

Sportswriters were as fiercely divided about soccer as they had been in the days of Pelé's Cosmos or Dick Young's 'commie pansies' jibe. Though some approached the World Cup with an open mind and a handful even claimed to be devotees, others were steeped in far less charitable views. At times their antipathy amounted to little more than jingoism ('This may be the world's most-beloved sport, but the world has always been overrated,' sniffed a columnist on the *Orlando Sentinel*) or, in the case of *Sport* magazine's Scott Ostler, xenophobia:

> They keep going to games, thinking that with all that kicking going on, and with those big nets, a lot of goals will be scored and it will be terribly exciting and fun. When that doesn't happen, the fans express their disappointment by fighting, drinking, getting tattoos and rioting.

But not all the sceptics were so jaundiced. Some merely defended themselves from the rather shrill clarion call sounded by a growing band of soccer evangelists convinced that anyone professing dislike for their game was narrow-minded and worthy of scorn. If somewhat crude, the attitude of Tom Knotts in the *Washington Post* towards such lobbyists was not unreasonable. 'I'm getting tired of the soccer weenies lecturing me on what I'm missing,' he fumed. 'You love the game. Fine. Great. Go for it. Work yourself into a frenzy over corner kicks ... but spare me

---

[*] Ten summers later, ESPN produced a series of hour-long programmes reviewing its 25 years of existence. For 1994, pride of place was offered to the New York Rangers' first ice hockey championship in 54 years, the Olympic ice-skating fracas between Tonya Harding and Nancy Kerrigan, and hard-luck speed-skater Dan Jansen. The World Cup was not mentioned even in passing.

your condescending rhetoric. I don't think we're talking a cure for cancer or anything.'

The build-up did reveal a few supporters in unlikely quarters. In June, ABC-TV's news programme *Nightline* aired a feature on the World Cup, probably the first time a network news division had paid serious attention to the event. This, though, was not nearly as remarkable as the near-blasphemous confession of the show's erudite host, Ted Koppel, that he 'would choose to watch a good soccer match [rather than] baseball's All-Star game any day of the week'. Yet Koppel, who had played for Syracuse University in the late 1950s, found precious few kindred spirits. John McEnroe made sympathetic noises as a broadcaster at that summer's Wimbledon, but it only seemed to underline Koppel's apparent heresy.

The attitudes of Oprah Winfrey and Diana Ross towards the game were doubtless less enthusiastic, yet it didn't prevent them being hired to get World Cup 94 off to a celebrity-studded start in Chicago. The opening ceremony, rarely one of sport's prouder moments, produced a catalogue of embarrassments: master of ceremonies Winfrey fell over and sprained her knee; the B-52s provided a dire musical interlude; and, in the *pièce de résistance,* the giant inflatable goal into which Ross was meant to 'score' toppled over, after the pop star failed to hit the target.

False notes during the ensuing match, a dull 1-0 win for Germany over Bolivia in searing lakefront heat, were less evident, save for a cruelly officious red card for Marco Etcheverry. Returning from injury as a substitute, the Bolivian star's World Cup finals career came to an end after a four-minute appearance. But there were few unoccupied seats among the crowd of 63,117, and no sign of the German hooligans who some had anxiously expected to ruin the day. Colourful street banners and an abundance of 'welcome' signs had attempted to raise the interest of a public far more interested in the progress of its Cubs and White Sox, but most remained apathetic. A hotel doorman told one reporter he hadn't noticed much interest in the tournament but claimed 'there would be more if Americans were in it'. Another bystander, watching a group of German fans parading their tricolour through the streets, was overheard to enquire: 'Are you guys Republicans?' And any chance the occasion had of capitalising on a slow news day disappeared when the media event of the year unfolded across a Southern California highway within hours of kick-off: the infamous 'low-speed chase' instigated by gridiron superhero OJ Simpson. Simpson's eventual capture and arrest would create an unfortunate backdrop which the World Cup and all its sporting rivals found impossible to upstage.

Nevertheless, the full house at Soldier Field proved to be the first of many. Well before Simpson's freeway escapade, 3.5 million of the 3.65 million available tickets had been bought, two-thirds of them in the United States. Never before had a single event so effectively unified the disparate strands of the country's soccer community: immigrant fans, soccer moms and dads, wistful NASL devotees, college and high school coaches, and all those millions of youngsters. The World Cup had never seen such numbers. That more than 56,000 could nearly fill a Massachusetts stadium on a stifling Thursday afternoon to watch Bolivia play South Korea was little short of astounding.

Those more worried about whether the tournament would re-establish the attractive football so conspicuously absent in Italy four years earlier were also pleasantly surprised. In the group phase goalscoring increased by about 13 per cent on 1990, with only two of the 36 first-round matches ending 0-0 (Bolivia v South Korea unfortunately being one of them). It was almost as if the world had recognised the need to produce something more edifying for their sceptical hosts.

The other element vital to the tournament's success was, naturally, a competitive host team. Many predicted a soccer apocalypse were the Americans to repeat their three-and-out performance of 1990. In the final preparatory match, they had claimed a 1-0 victory over Mexico in front of 92,000 largely hostile fans in the Rose Bowl, but it was only their fourth win in 17 attempts. Milutinovic continued to shuffle his line-up. In 30 matches, he had never once named an unchanged side, offering ample international experience to youngsters in the squad while allowing his European contingent to mature overseas.

The Americans kicked off in the Pontiac Silverdome against Switzerland before a crowd of more than 73,000 which produced a partisan level of support the home team had rarely, if ever, encountered: flags waving, banners encircling the upper deck, and chants of *U-S-A!* filling the air. It wasn't enough to stop a free-kick from Georges Bregy giving the Swiss a 39th-minute lead, but the US soon equalised with a free-kick of their own, a spectacular effort from Eric Wynalda that cannoned in off the crossbar and created, according to *Soccer America*, a 'deafening roar, surely the loudest an American player on the field had ever heard for an American goal'. Struck by a mysterious attack of hives he later attributed to a sports drink, the ailing Wynalda lasted only 13 minutes of the second half before being substituted, but in the muggy 40-degree heat – the Silverdome was not equipped with air conditioning – both teams wilted and the match ended 1-1. Dooley, Stewart and Harkes were largely outduelled by Alain Sutter and Stéphane Chapuisat, but the result helped to put many of the four-year-old observations about American naivety to rest. For the first time since Belo Horizonte, the US had gained a point at the World Cup.

One of the strongest performances came from the team's most flamboyant member, centre-half Alexi Lalas. In high school, the gangly Lalas had led his ice hockey team to the Michigan state championship, and his prowess on the rink helped to fashion his physical, uncompromising presence on grass. Casual observers, though, knew rather less about the way Lalas played than they did about his bright red hair and dangling goatee (the *New York Times* called him a 'heavy-metal Ronald McDonald'), and his free-spirited and eloquent persona quickly established him as a media attraction. Against the Swiss, he played to his strengths, combining effectively with Balboa to keep the dangerous Chapuisat at bay and largely answering those critics who had drawn attention to his technical deficiencies.

Like the rest of his team-mates, Lalas had a profound self-belief which would help carry the team into the second round and, fleetingly, take some of the nation with it. Four days after the Silverdome sweat-fest the Americans produced one of the most sensational results of the competition, defeating a Colombia side many had earmarked as contenders. The afternoon's excitement, in front of 93,000 in the Rose Bowl, was sparked by an own goal from Andrés Escobar which separated the teams at half-time. When in the 52nd minute the fleet-footed Earnie Stewart latched on to a lofted pass from Tab Ramos and clipped it into the net, heads began to turn: the Colombians had already lost to Romania, and were now perilously close to a premature exit. Augmented by a strong performance from 37-year-old Fernando Clavijo, the central defensive barrier of Balboa and Lalas held firm. By the time Colombia finally scored, in the 90th minute, the match was over.

The 2-1 victory may have been attributable more to the sloppy play of jaded opponents who, in the words of their coach, 'came to the party, but didn't dance', but the US had taken advantage and all but secured a place in the second round. Grim memories of Florence and Rome suddenly drowned in a sea of flags. With some justification, the *New York Times* proclaimed: 'American soccer desperately needed a moment this exalted and galvanizing, something that would urgently lift the game from the back burner to the front of the country's sporting consciousness.'

While some players allowed that their victory had 'shocked the world', few expressed any surprise ('I'm uncomfortable with the word "upset",'

Wynalda maintained). Many in the media thought differently, claiming – or perhaps wanting desperately to believe – they had witnessed the kind of national sporting 'miracle' that occurred once in a generation, the latest incarnation of the 1980 Olympic 'miracle on ice'. Had this been a corresponding 'miracle on grass'? 'Hell no,' insisted Lalas. 'A miracle is a baby surviving a plane crash or something like that.'

Clive Toye, the one-time NASL architect now working as a USA 94 official, was left beaming. 'It was no fluke,' he insisted. 'Colombia had more possession of the ball, Colombia didn't play badly. It was just an absolutely bloody phenomenal game by the US players.' In the *Washington Post*, though, Britain's Rob Hughes, a guest columnist, saw things rather differently:

> Never before, in six World Cups, had I seen a team so obviously superior in quality, touch and control lie down and allow defeat to brush over them. The Colombians were a real dog, all four paws submissively in the air ... Milutinovic has made absolutely the most of [his team's] abilities by instructing them to squeeze the space of arguably craftier opponents in midfield. They do it well, but it becomes soldierly, stereotyped, and therefore when they meet a team with Colombia's skill, but with far more desire to match the American physical input, they will be undone.

Explanations for Colombia's sorry performance soon came to light. Before the tournament their colourful goalkeeper René Higuita had been jailed for illegally accepting money to help arrange the release of a kidnap victim, while death threats kept Gabriel Gómez from playing against the US. Yet it wasn't until the murder of Escobar two weeks later – a tragedy at which some of the more virulent soccer-bashers couldn't resist taking a morbid swipe – that everyone could sense the duress under which the Colombians had played.

Not since Uruguay 1930, though, had the American game scaled such giddy heights, and a surprisingly large audience witnessed the historic transformation. ESPN's telecast registered 2.7 million viewers, better than for any soccer match it had ever shown. The figure might have been risible compared with the 50 million American homes that tuned in to the deciding game of the NBA championship that same night, but international soccer had never come as close to attracting the interest of mainstream sports fans as it did in the days that followed.

Not only did photographs of jubilant, flag-draped American players reach the front page of many newspapers, but the phrase 'World Cup' passed the lips of millions of readers for the first time. Celebrities began seeking out tickets. ABC News made a trip to Kearny to document where Harkes, Ramos and Meola had grown up. Even sports radio phone-ins, usually home to the most dogmatic of fans, began accepting calls from excited US supporters. 'We're a trendy country,' noted Leigh Steinberg, an agent for the national team players who now found himself besieged with endorsement requests. 'All of a sudden, soccer is hot.'

Some of the euphoria faded four days later, when a disjointed American performance ended in defeat against Romania. Meola was beaten to the near post by an 18th-minute strike from Dan Petrescu and in the merciless heat of the Rose Bowl (the temperature at pitch level registered 46 degrees) the visitors' experience and tactical discipline proved insurmountable. Romania finished on top of Group A, leaving the US to qualify somewhat fortunately as one of the four best third-place finishers. They were rewarded with a Fourth of July date against Brazil.

Sixty-four years had passed since their first World Cup appearance, but in some respects American soccer had still not familiarised itself with the international game. Three-time champions though they were, the capacity of Brazil to inspire awe in their hosts was limited. 'To be honest with you,' Lalas confessed, 'I don't know any of the guys on their team. They're not my idols. People tell me they are great.' How great they were was still to be determined, but their defeat of the US, though only by 1-0, was certainly the most predictable result of the second round. Thoroughly outplayed, and unable to fashion so much as a shot on target, the US fought an incessant rearguard action to hold down the score, and as late as the 73rd minute their packed defence combined with a generous measure of good fortune to keep the match goalless. Shortly before half-time Ramos suffered a fractured skull after being elbowed in the face by Leonardo – for which the Brazilian was barred from the rest of the tournament – but his red card seemed largely to even things out. The elusive Romário, who supplied Bebeto with the winning goal, proved a constant menace, and Clavijo was dismissed near the end for pushing him off the ball.

Confident assertions from the American camp that 'we can play with anyone' now seemed hollow. And although an unprecedented audience witnessed the performance – the ABC network counted 28 million viewers – it soon emerged than many of them did not love the sport nearly as much as they loved a successful team. For some, like Steve Jacobson of *Newsday*, the narrow defeat merely underscored soccer's inherent lack of appeal:

> The US team played its stripes out Monday and managed to hold the great Brazil team to a 1-0 victory. Hooray for our side, except that the US never put a shot on goal. The Brazil coach called it 'supremacy'. If 1-0 can reveal supremacy, what kind of a game is it?

Other novices among the millions may have formed similar views, but those who cared to look harder found their reward. The noted baseball writer Thomas Boswell had turned cheerleader after seeing a group match in Washington. He wrote in the *Washington Post*:

> Belgium plays Saudi Arabia at RFK Stadium this afternoon at 12.25pm. Take a tip from a friend. Find a way to go. As anybody who was at RFK yesterday for the 1-1 tie between Mexico and Italy will tell you, this World Cup is truly special. And it's probably not coming back to America in any of our lifetimes. Sometimes, the thing itself proves to be as good as the hype. That's true of the World Cup. Its appeal isn't just the high quality of the soccer. Or the intensity and variety of the international fans. Or the transformation of RFK from an aging eyesore into a gorgeous, world-class venue. It's all of it.

Those heeding Boswell's exhortations – nearly 53,000 of them – were treated to one of the best goals of the tournament, a mesmerising solo run from Saeed Owairan that helped send the Saudis unexpectedly through to the second round. Memorable occasions were proving plentiful. Apart from the banishment of Diego Maradona for failing a drug test, there was plenty that was positive to say about Ireland's victory over Italy at a packed Giants Stadium, the elimination of Germany by a surprisingly resourceful Bulgaria, and Romania's thrilling second-round victory over Argentina, probably the best match of the competition. Goals continued to flow: 40 in the second round and quarter-finals, 60 per cent more than in the same stages four years previously.

It was a particular shame, then, that the United States of all hosts was burdened with the first goalless World Cup final, even if the match itself represented a merciful improvement on the equivalent in Rome four years earlier. What had begun with a botched effort from Diana Ross ended with a more catastrophic miss by Roberto Baggio, leaving soccer-bashers to have the last laugh. 'The two greatest teams on the globe can't score one stinking goal,' sneered Woody Paige in the *Denver Post*. 'And finally, they have a shootout, soccer kicks at 12 paces, to decide the champion. That's not boring; that's dumb. Why not flip a coin, just as they did before the game?'

Many could see his point. More than one observer likened the manner of Brazil's victory to a basketball championship being settled by free-throws, or a field-goal competition deciding the Super Bowl. Far from being thrilled by the prospect of the ball entering the net several times, many newcomers felt let down. Even the American television commentators, describing events for 10 million households, provided a strangely low-key account of the shoot-out – for which they were roundly criticised. 'If soccer is 90 per cent emotion,' wondered the *San Francisco Chronicle*, 'why call it like the Greater Greensboro Open?'

World Cup 94 may not have been the 'greatest ever', but it was a remarkable success, devoid of crowd disturbances, empty stadiums or embarrassing performances from the host nation. Indeed, perhaps the greatest humiliation the American team suffered was its ghastly Adidas playing strip, dismissed by *Soccer America* as 'like a T-shirt your maiden aunt gave you, that you wore a couple of times just to be nice. Then you washed it, it faded badly and then you threw it to the back of your closet.' For the rest of the world, the event offered hope. Top-class international football had not succumbed to even more dispiriting levels of caution, cynicism and fear. Most agreed the goalless final had been more an example of defensive prowess and exhaustion than a lack of attacking will. The proud sentiments of the *Boston Globe's* Bob Ryan were hard to argue with:

> They have loaned us their treasure and we have enhanced it. We turned out not to be heathens at all, but respectful curators instead ... it turns out we were the perfect country to host the World Cup. Name the ethnic group, and it's here on our shores, somewhere. No team went unsupported or unloved.

Far from being punctuated with an exclamation mark, though, the 1994 World Cup ended, inevitably, with another question: where would American soccer go from here?

9. Clash and Burn

MLS: back to square one

The media will give soccer a fair shake. But it will have to be presented well. It can't screw up.

Steven Goff, *The Washington Post*

In the 1990s, sporting entrepreneurs looking for a way on to America's major league map were faced with a bewildering array of investment opportunities. In 1995, a professional cycling league made its inauspicious debut in the parking lot of New York's Shea Stadium, its promoters vowing to produce 'more of a contact sport'. CBS television, which had lost its NFL rights to Rupert Murdoch's Fox network, mulled over an ominous new gridiron proposal in which teams were to be backed by corporations instead of private investors. Before the end of the decade, two women's basketball leagues came to fruition, one with the blessing and financial support of the NBA. Even the television series *Gladiators* looked set to turn professional.

Into this fiercely contested scrap for the leisure dollar stepped Alan Rothenberg, president of the USSF, chairman of the 'greatest World Cup ever' and now the driving force behind another bold new offering: the soccer league pledged to FIFA as part of USA 94's legacy. It had taken nearly eight years to set up, with progress drip-fed to an often sceptical public. No one, it seemed, had realised just how difficult honouring the promise would be.

The proposal which emerged, and which was christened Major League Soccer, marked a sweeping departure not just from the NASL but from American professional leagues in general. MLS was as much a reflection of the way sport had changed as Rothenberg's own indubitable savvy. That it came about at all – after a few near-collapses – reinforced beliefs that the gold Porsche-driving, unsinkably optimistic Californian had become the most significant figure in the game's history, despite a less-than-intimate knowledge of the sport. 'I don't think you have to play the game, coach the game, line fields to know the game,' he once said. 'It might be better if you haven't.'

As a former NBA and NASL owner, Rothenberg spoke the language of a big-league operator. He recognised that MLS's pretensions would be abruptly dismissed without regular exposure on national television and residency in the country's top stadiums. For the right price these ambitions could be realised. An increasingly fragmented market, brought on by the growth in cable and satellite channels, had made even network TV far more attainable than it had been for the NASL, while even the busiest of stadiums still lay dormant for much of the year.

But gate-crashing the American sports psyche – if that was what was required – took more than just a hefty wallet. It meant producing super-stars, not just familiar faces but the sort of luminary icons who could command the attention of the ordinary fan and force their way into the privileged domain of *Sports Illustrated* and ESPN's *SportsCenter*. This, too, would cost money, far more than Rothenberg thought wise.

Pro sports owners had paid a steep price for their lack of financial self-control since the advent of player free agency in the 1970s. Major league baseball salaries had risen from an annual average of $29,000 in 1970 to $1.2 million by 1994, by which time the average NBA player was making close to $2 million a season. MLS was not in a position to compete with such fairytale sums, or the paranoia of cut-throat owners which largely fuelled them. Though it soon found television 'partners', it had to pay for the privilege, buying airtime from ABC.

Even with a more lucrative network deal, the success of MLS would scarcely have been guaranteed. Television and its parade of commercial advertising had helped to subsidise professional sport's salary explosion, but did nothing to control it. Increasingly, owners desperate to shore up their diminishing returns turned to local politicians and taxpayers, who offered them new or improved stadiums, or even lured them away from their traditional homes. The NFL and its legions of devoted fans could withstand such noxious developments (they had done so for decades), but an emerging pro soccer league would not – as the wild city-hopping sanctioned by the NASL illustrated.

It was largely for these reasons that Rothenberg hit upon the idea of a 'single-entity' league. Rather than being offered the opportunity to make money through ownership of a club, investors would buy into MLS as a whole, splitting profits (and sharing losses) with their rivals. This would limit the owners' autonomy, but it would also curb their avarice and smooth the disparities between markets. There would be no New York Cosmos; equally, there would be no Rochester Lancers.

For someone like Rothenberg with the free market to thank for his wealth, it was a decidedly socialist approach. It was also very alluring, allowing club payrolls to be kept in check and all but eradicating the negotiating power of the players. For each 18-man squad, MLS would impose a frugal salary cap of $1.3 million – roughly what the major leagues paid a single baseballer – resulting in an average wage of about $72,000 a year. Of course, if international talent were to be obtained and US World Cup stars tempted back from Europe, the journeyman players would be paid rather less: as little as $25,000, the earnings of a librarian or a sheet-metal worker.

Rocketing salary costs had hastened the NASL's demise, and Rothenberg had first-hand experience of this, having paid Johan Cruyff $750,000 a year to play for his Los Angeles Aztecs before off-loading him to Washington. Yet sagging attendances had been a more visible enemy. Initial MLS projections were modest: average gates of about 11,000, hardly an imposing figure when sprinkled across the cavernous stadiums it sought to hire. To mitigate what officials termed the 'rattle factor', stadium capacities were to be 'downsized', with expanses of empty seats and vacant upper tiers cloaked in brightly-coloured canvas. In time, such compromises were to give way to more intimate new venues which, at around $30 million a throw, would finally demonstrate the long-term commitment pro soccer had found so hard to make.

The desire to start a new professional league from scratch was not confined to the federation. A Chicago businessman named Jim Paglia put forward an interesting, if ambitious, single-entity concept called League One America, which hinged on the construction of a series of multipurpose venues. 'We intend to buy land and build stadiums, as private real-estate developers,' he asserted. 'If Chicago wanted a stadium for soccer, we'll build it.' But his thinking seemed light-years distant from the actual state of the game. The American Professional Soccer League, named more out of hope than achievement, had by 1992 been whittled down to five clubs, surviving only through the absorption of teams from the failed Canadian Soccer League. Though the APSL insisted it represented the sensible future of the professional game, the USSF disagreed. In 1991 it classified the APSL as a 'Division II' league, helping to clear a path for something bigger. The divisional nomenclature may seem esoteric – and misleading to anyone assuming promotion and relegation would take place between 'divisions' – but it was important, since the USSF would sanction only one Division I league. The APSL, perhaps naively, sought an upgrade from the federation, believing this would transform its dwindling fortunes.

Another league worthy of mention, a sprawling entity known latterly as the United States Interregional Soccer League, had been classified as Division III. Lacking the pretensions of the APSL, the USISL had perhaps become more successful because of it. Launched in 1986 as a five-team indoor circuit, by 1993 it encompassed 38 outdoor teams in 16 states. Few anticipated it at the time, but this was a sturdy foundation on which more ambitious plans could be built.

In December 1993 the three proposals to fill the Division I vacancy – League One America, the APSL and MLS – were placed in front of the USSF's national board of directors. Not surprisingly, MLS, with its chief proponent doubling as president of the federation, emerged the clear winner. Rothenberg insisted that everything was beyond reproach, that votes had been cast without undue influence from him, even if he had appointed many of the board members (though the APSL could also claim friends in high places). He now called on the rival bidders to join forces with him, but the APSL declared its aversion to single-entity soccer and vowed to fight on. So too did League One America, which had received no votes at all. But Jim Paglia soon disappeared from view, his threats to counter MLS with a 'soccer' using multi-coloured pitches, eight match officials and players dressed in unitards mercifully failing to surface.

With the APSL to placate, investors to court and a World Cup to produce, 1994 was perhaps as taxing a year as any a federation president had faced – though not taxing enough for Rothenberg to give up his legal practice, from which he continued to draw a salary. But this was a man whose tigerish zeal and commitment had earned him the nickname Rothenweiler, and whose hopes for MLS were couched in the confident prose of USA 94. 'I think the time is right for pro soccer to be successful in this country,' he said, vowing MLS would soon become the elusive 'fifth major league of American sports'.

Still, the World Cup came and went without the chance for prospective fans to buy MLS tickets or T-shirts, or even identify their nearest team. Even as Brazil were being crowned world champions in Pasadena, only seven of the intended 12 franchises had been earmarked and Rothenberg found himself with just one committed patron, a New York investment banker. Yet he still insisted he would raise the $50 to $75 million needed to kick off the following April.

Tempting the super-rich with soccer was not an easy proposition, not even for a man who had been awarded $7 million from the World Cup's estimated $50 million 'surplus' by an organising committee he had largely appointed. Rothenberg was soon forced to compromise over MLS, halving his entry fee to $5 million and designating a new category of 'investor-operator', individuals who would be permitted to control a club while still adhering to the single-entity framework. Yet hopes for a 1995 kick-off faded. By November Rothenberg, unable to produce a full list of teams, was forced to admit defeat, though he remained confident enough to begin handing out contracts. Tab Ramos had signed the first 11 months earlier, but was now left to reflect: 'It seems like soccer has disappeared again.'

By the time the full MLS line-up was revealed, most of the World Cup momentum was lost. Even Rothenberg, who had presided over the most prosperous years the USSF had ever known, only narrowly avoided a re-election defeat, an outcome which almost certainly would have strangled his fledgling league. But the year's delay served its purpose. Ownership capital ultimately reached $75 million, spearheaded by the doggedly optimistic, soccer-friendly oilman Lamar Hunt.

Finally, the focus could shift toward the teams, and in particular which of America's World Cup stars would return from exile. Alexi Lalas, who after the 2-0 defeat of England in Foxboro had famously begged of visiting journalists 'Somebody find me a job! Anywhere!' had been loaned to Padova of Italy, discovering the fishbowl existence of a Serie A footballer ('It's like being in the zoo'). Californian winger Cobi Jones, whose dread-locks ran Lalas a close second among national team coiffures, joined Coventry City. Thomas Dooley returned to the Bundesliga with Bayer Leverkusen after a year of full-time commitment to the World Cup squad. VfL Bochum made Eric Wynalda their record signing, but the million dollars it cost to bring him to the Ruhr failed to produce a single goal – Wynalda broke his ankle and missed most of the season. Tony Meola, on the other hand, placed his faith in a new career as a kicking specialist for the NFL's New York Jets. When that failed, he took his soccer indoors with a team called the Buffalo Blizzard.

Milutinovic disappeared too: the federation said he had resigned, but he claimed to have been dismissed. Much of the confusion stemmed from federation secretary Hank Steinbrecher's master plan of 'vertical integration', widening the role of the national manager to include devel-oping other coaches, an obligation Milutinovic had never warmed to. The federation eyed the former Portugal manager Carlos Queiroz, but failed to sway him from Sporting Lisbon. Approaches to World Cup-winning manager Carlos Alberto Parreira were also rebuffed.

As the hunt continued, responsibility for the national team fell on the unlikely shoulders of 38-year-old Steve Sampson, one of four assistants the USSF had made available to Milutinovic. The tenure of the Utah-born

Sampson was expected to be brief. He had last been in charge of a team five years earlier at Santa Clara University, where he claimed a share of the national championship in the icy 1989 stalemate with Virginia. But the interim choice soon muddied the selection waters by stringing together a series of attention-grabbing victories. At the 1995 US Cup the Americans romped to a record 4-0 victory over Mexico, the product of a more attack-minded philosophy.

His shining moment came in Uruguay at the Copa America a few weeks later. For the second time the US had been invited as a guest, but unlike in 1993 the event now received their undivided attention. Using primarily World Cup players, Sampson orchestrated a surprising 2-1 defeat of Chile. An even more eyecatching 3-0 victory over Argentina in Paysandú sent his team into the quarter-finals, and his stock into orbit. Detractors called attention to Argentina's rather arrogant decision to rest nine members of their first team, but the result was still creditable, and a beaming Sampson seemed at ease in his new role, capably fielding press conference questions in Spanish and English.

After dispatching Mexico on penalties, the Americans proved no match for the world champions. Even without Romário or Bebeto, Brazil made short work of the semi-final, though the 1-0 scoreline was one of few similarities to the same fixture at USA 94. Sampson asserted that his team had gone down with guns blazing, refusing to merely guard the net as Milutinovic had done the year before. His players agreed. 'We played 50 times better,' Lalas claimed. 'For example, we actually touched the ball this time.'

None of the TV networks bothered with the Copa. ABC had handed the federation $1 million for the rights to ten national team matches, but neither it nor ESPN, which affixed its name to 52 other games, seemed able to separate relatively meaningless, home-grown competitions like the US Cup from events with more international gravity. Fans, though, were beginning to do so. Like the American player, they were reaching maturity. The World Cup had left a legacy of enthusiasts who spoke a more cosmopolitan language, supporters who were no longer prepared to accept half-hearted interest from the media or its frequent lapses into derision and antipathy. One of the most infamous moments of ESPN's coverage of the World Cup had occurred when a commentator, struggling to wrap his tongue around the name of Italy's goalkeeper, Gianluca Pagliuca, blurted out: 'I hate soccer!' Too many journalists continued to pass judgement on the game instead of providing insight, while some newspaper editors remained happy to ignore it altogether.

But fans were taking matters into their own hands. Two men from Buffalo, New York, added to the international roll-call of fanzines with *Bookable Offense*, whose pages teemed with the home-brewed mixture of passion, irreverence and indignation more commonly found overseas. By the time of the 1995 US Cup their efforts had helped to produce a band of red-shirted fans calling themselves (Uncle) Sam's Army and offering the kind of noisy, passionate support which in America had traditionally been confined to visiting teams. Another influence, and one too readily overlooked, was the internet, which allowed American soccer's relatively affluent fan base to create networks and information channels that effectively bypassed the mainstream.

The *Hartford Courant* sportswriter Jerry Trecker hinted at this sea-change in the wake of America's performance in Uruguay:

> A few years ago you couldn't find a soccer score in an American newspaper or expect a highlight on ESPN's *SportsCenter*. Copa America turned into proof that there is a demand for soccer information. The fans obviously let the media know that and the media responded.

After Uruguay, few could deny that Sampson had earned his chance at managing the team for good. Yet the USSF offered him the job only begrudgingly, its president perhaps disappointed not to have his ego stroked by a more famous name. 'As I told Steve, "Suppose the best thing happens and you do phenomenally well. You'll still have all of a ten-game international career",' Rothenberg confided before the Copa. 'Do we think that is enough to put an awfully huge responsibility on him when there are people who have hundreds of games of international experience?' His players seemed to think it was, and they helped end the intercontinental talent-hunt.

In August 1995 Sampson became the national team's first native-born, full-time manager. His route to the top had been unconventional, to say the least. He had never coached or played for a professional club (he had torn up his knee in college) and had been an administrator at the 1984 Olympics and 1994 World Cup. When a reorganisation, induced by FIFA, stripped him of a job – but not a contract – he was hastily assigned to Milutinovic's staff. Reservations over his appointment as national coach were understandable. The largely self-contained milieu of college soccer in which he had flourished, while producing swarms of coaches with impressive win-loss records and offices festooned with awards and certificates, had not made an especially welcome contribution to the sport. Its season was still ridiculously short, and the decision of the NCAA to ban all instances of 'outside ball' – playing for club teams, even in the close-season – bordered on the shameful. College soccer still tended to produce dreary, combative teams that prized workrate above all else.

One pleasant exception was the University of Virginia, which by the mid-1990s had become not only the most successful college team in the country, but also one of the most attractive. The typical diagram-plotting American coach would have been unnerved to hear a Virginia player declare, as one did on the eve of the national championship game of 1994: 'I can't say we don't have any tactics, but basically we just go out and play.'

The source of this inspiration, coach Bruce Arena, was an unlikely muse. Much of his career had been divided between keeping goal for Cornell University and playing lacrosse for them, in which he earned national honours. Drafted by the Cosmos in 1973, the Brooklyn-born Arena never played in the NASL and instead joined a professional league in his other sport. When that collapsed he returned to soccer, hooking up with an ASL team in Tacoma, Washington, and coaching at a nearby university. Appointed to head the Virginia programme in 1978, Arena soon moulded the Cavaliers into a stylish soccer power. Future national team mainstays such as John Harkes and Jeff Agoos were kitted out in the school's orange, which seemed an appropriate reflection of their manager's philosophy. 'If we're playing well and confidently,' Arena claimed, 'we don't have positions.'

In preparing for the 1998 World Cup, Sampson pinned much of his hopes on a recent Virginia product, New Jersey-born Claudio Reyna, a midfielder gifted enough to have been courted by Barcelona. Widely touted as the creative force around which a US team could be built, Reyna's post-college career began frustratingly. He earned a place in the 1994 World Cup squad but was kept out by a hamstring injury, then signed for Bayer Leverkusen and never appeared in the first team. His perform-ances in a US jersey were plagued by inconsistency – attributable, some claimed, to the shortcomings of even the best college programmes.

Reyna's departure did not stop Arena leading the Cavaliers to a fourth consecutive national championship in 1994. But to some fellow coaches his candour and self-assuredness bordered on arrogance. 'I'm not the most popular figure at the cocktail parties, and they're a major feature of the soccer scene in this country,' he maintained. 'Too much happens behind the scenes at social and political gatherings rather than on the field. Everyone's constantly working on protecting their turf. Maybe that's why I'm an asshole, why a lot of people feel threatened by me.'

If the USSF had ever felt threatened by Arena – and its own coaching ranks were no less incestuous – by the winter of 1995 it had summoned enough courage to appoint him coach of the Olympic team. By then he had also become a target of Major League Soccer, which finally settled on its complement of clubs less than a year before kick-off.

The line-up featured only ten clubs, not 12, and the investment target had been reached only through a last-minute phone call from Colorado billionaire Philip Anschutz. A grateful league agreed to place a team in Denver, near his base, even though both the city's NASL franchises had swiftly crashed. MLS also decided to stick its neck out in Kansas City, where Phil Woosnam's league had last trodden in 1970. The selection of New York and Los Angeles was more conventional, but the next five largest cities in the country (Chicago, Houston, Philadelphia, San Diego and Detroit) were passed over in favour of smaller, if more familiar, markets such as Tampa and San Jose, as well as the virgin professional territory of Columbus, Ohio, whose supporters had pledged to buy more than 10,000 season tickets. The established big-league markets of New England, Dallas and Washington DC completed the line-up, leaving the one-time NASL stronghold of the Pacific northwest conspicuously without representation.

To have unearthed $75 million worth of interest in professional soccer was no small achievement, but ten clubs did not really constitute a major league, and as the investors began writing cheques, an air of fallibility lingered over their project. Few seemed prepared to gamble millions of dollars on soccer in an era when America's appetite for exhibitionism and spectacle had given rise to wildly successful sport-entertainment hybrids such as the X-Games and the World Wrestling Federation, whose 'shows' were much more likely to attract the neutral's attention than anything which might end 0-0.

Not surprisingly, MLS sought FIFA's permission to spice up the rules, an appeal which drew a far more sympathetic response from Zurich than anything the NASL had ever garnered. Gamely, the humble USISL agreed to serve as a guinea pig, piloting such distinctively American innovations as stopping the clock each time the ball went out of play and offering a shootout-style chance at goal after a team had committed a certain number of fouls. In some of its regions goals were made larger, traditional corner kicks were replaced by shorter ones and free-kicks were defended from 15 instead of ten yards.

Purists, of which America has its share, pointed out in horror that the best-attended matches in US history had been those played under conventional rules: World Cup and Olympic tournaments, replete with draws, time-wasting, feigning injury and the other unsavoury elements of the game as it stood. That MLS should risk losing the interest of a committed audience in search of a more transient, thrill-seeking fan seemed a dubious strategy, one which also hinted at an alarming inability to learn from the mistakes of the NASL. But the threat was mitigated by an important factor: for once, a pro league and the USSF were essentially on the same side, both effectively answerable to Alan Rothenberg. This demanded that owners show a healthy respect for the game's wider world and recognise the value of a symbiotic relationship with governing bodies and the national team. Indeed, the latter had produced MLS's most marketable commodity, Alexi Lalas, whose return from Serie A was heralded by the league as one of its most significant acquisitions.

In the end, deviations from what one official termed 'the classic rules' were few, though MLS was far less restrained when it came to its principal obsession: marketability. This was never more apparent than at the official unveiling of team names, logos and strips in October 1995. A generation earlier, such relatively trivial disclosures would have been met with overwhelming indifference, but a sports merchandising tidal wave had subsumed North America and millions of dollars now rode on a choice of name, colours and jerseys. A year earlier, the owner of the NBA's expansion team in Toronto confessed the decision to use the nickname Raptors – a dinosaur, of all creatures – had been driven by a desire for 'an aggressive, intimidating image and a logo that would sell merchandise'. An unprecedented $20 million worth of Raptors gear disappeared in the first month alone.

As other NBA clubs furiously 'repackaged' themselves, MLS sensed the opportunity to appeal to the fan as a consumer. In fact 'MLS Unveiled', as the event was christened, struck many as an outright capitulation to the creative excesses of designers, with no one on the soccer side brave enough to channel their creative juices. The league's franchise in San Jose appeared to be named after a pop group, the Clash (one of their songs wailed from the loudspeakers as it was revealed), with what might have been a lobster – or was it a scorpion? – on its badge. Dallas's entry was called the Burn, whatever that was, its logo a fire-breathing horse. If there was an association between the word 'burn' and a horse, or 'clash' and a crustacean, nobody seemed prepared to make it. Nike, responsible for both creations, had apparently moved on from such quaint notions.

Equally strange was Tampa's entry, the Mutiny, its logo featuring a sort of bat; and the scatological connotations of Kansas City's nickname, the Wiz – surely not an oblique reference to *The Wizard of Oz*, since the club's home was Kansas City, Missouri, not Dorothy's Kansas. 'We expected to receive some chiding from the name,' a club official admitted, before drawing attention to the 'great creative springboard' the three letters provided: 'Our youth programme will be known as the WizKidz, our mascot could be the Wizard and one of our premium giveaway nights may be Wizbees.'

The mind boggled at premium giveaway night opportunities for New England's team, the Revolution (Molotov cocktails?), or the creative springboard offered by the first syllable of the Los Angeles nickname, Galaxy (cheerleaders called the Gal-Gals?). Denver chose to call themselves the Colorado Rapids, more of a geographical feature than a team name, while fans in the league's biggest market would be saddled with something called the New York/New Jersey MetroStars, perhaps the most ungainly sobriquet in the history of American sport (soon thankfully shortened to MetroStars). Washington settled on the distinctly un-American designation of DC United, a choice which had finished second to 'Force' in a fan poll even though it hadn't even appeared on the ballot. Some sportswriters insisted on referring to the team as 'the United'. The Columbus Crew's shadowy logo featured three men in hard-hats, arms menacingly folded, an image which seemed rooted more in *A Clockwork Orange* – or, more charitably, the Village People – than professional sport.[*] Mutiny, Revolution, Clash and Burn – family entertainment, or subliminal apocalypse? Meanwhile, the nickname with perhaps the greatest brand leverage of all, Cosmos, was left undisturbed.

The creative people were also permitted to run amok with the playing strips, described by *Soccer America* as having been 'stolen from the most deranged of designers of skateboarding attire' and fashionably heavy on black, the worst colour to wear in the heat of summer. Even colour schemes reeked of self-indulgence: Tampa Bay's were listed as 'chlorophyll green, midnight navy, chrome yellow and tropical blue', San Jose's a nightmarish 'celery green, forest green, red, light teal and black'.

Though the league had resisted the temptation to tamper too much

---

[*] The Crew's appearance in Columbus soon marked the end of the minor-league Columbus Xoggz, whose bewildering nickname was apparently devised precisely because it didn't mean anything.

with the rules, it proved more impressionable when confronted by the fact that soccer matches often end in a draw – and in particular the chilling possibility that a television commentator might utter a final score of 0-0. Wedded to the conviction that contests in America should never end level, it dusted off the NASL's Shootout. To fit matches into a precise, network-friendly timeslot, it also opted to dispense with extra time, so that everything might finish inside two hours. Traditionalists shook their fists, but further nods to the old league were few: there would be no bonus points for goals, no smaller offside zone, no extra substitution and no Mini-Game.

Nor would there be artificial pitches, a condition the league adhered to with surprising rigidity. While America's fetish for simulated grass had diminished significantly since the NASL's heyday (though a new generation of synthetic surfaces was about to make its mark), a number of cities still swathed every desirable venue in some variant of Astroturf, effectively keeping them off the MLS shortlist. One exception – or part-exception – was Giants Stadium, which in spite of its plastic remained the logical home of any soccer team from the area with major league ambitions. The MetroStars announced they would wheel in expensive Silverdome-like trays of genuine turf, which they could use until the Jets and Giants began their NFL exertions. This meant finishing the season on a different surface to the one they had started with, and one no other team possessed.

Though most had expected Rothenberg to elevate himself to the position of league commissioner, as kick-off loomed it emerged that the $7 million man had ruled himself out of contention, a decision which sent many a corporate sponsor and much of the American soccer public into a mild state of panic. Rothenberg, though, had never demonstrated much appetite for the detail required of such a role, and in FIFA and Concacaf there were other rainbows to chase. Yet suspicions also festered that, having brought the USSF into the corporate milieu and American soccer onto the sports pages, he could only lose with MLS, and that his ego would not tolerate such embarrassment.

The man chosen to head the league was Doug Logan, a 52-year-old marketing executive who had made his name in sports and event promotion and was apparently sensitive to soccer's working-class appeal. Born in New Jersey, Logan had been raised in Cuba, where his grandfather owned a baseball team and delighted in rubbing shoulders with his patrons, displaying a common touch that would leave a strong impression on his grandson ('The biggest piece of garbage in American sports is the luxury box, with its couches faced away from the field, facing a huge colour television set with everybody eating sushi'). The bilingual Logan had spent two years working in Mexico – credentials ideally suited to a league openly courting Latino fans – and owned a minor-league basketball team in San Diego. As a promoter, he had flogged tickets for everything from rock concerts to ballet.

Logan's ability to generate large sums of money was naturally his most desirable skill but, with parallels to the ill-fated pro ventures of three decades earlier, his negligible soccer pedigree was dismissed by his employers as an irrelevance. As in 1967, MLS seemed ominously dependent more on a belief in the power of marketing than any passion for the game. As well as Anschutz, Rothenberg had recruited John Kluge, one of the wealthiest men in the country (*Forbes* magazine estimated his worth at $5 billion) and the Kraft family, owners of the NFL's New England Patriots and about to build them a new $325 million home. None of them could really be described as 'soccer people'. When the Krafts' elder statesman, Robert, declared, 'What my family really likes about soccer is that it's a game played by young boys and girls, and is coached by fathers and mothers,' one was left to wonder what it was about a professional venture that attracted their interest.

The one executive with a firm grounding in the sport was a Columbia professor of economics named Sunil Gulati, a USSF executive who was appointed as Logan's deputy. Born in India, Gulati's appreciation of the international game and his prodigious intellect – he had worked at the World Bank and for a time was the national economist of Moldova – served him well at the federation. He emerged as the most powerful man in MLS, responsible for populating the rosters of all ten clubs. Balancing the league's aspiration to recruit talent worthy of its name with single-entity pragmatism was a difficult tightrope to walk, but by the time MLS kicked off in April 1996, Gulati boasted that the league's entire playing roster had cost him just $15 million, about three-quarters of what Newcastle United paid to acquire Alan Shearer from Blackburn Rovers that summer.

Inevitably, the deputy commissioner became reviled, not just among clubs frustrated by a lack of control over their playing squads (Gulati assigned all the designated 'marquee' players himself), but also among the players, who bridled at his take-it-or-leave-it approach to salary negotiation. Of course, home-grown players – many unable or unwilling to obtain an overseas work permit – had little choice but to sign up, even if the $25,000 minimum was rather less than what the typical NBA bench-warmer might spend on his wardrobe. Gulati succeeded in wooing most of the national team stalwarts: Harkes, Caligiuri, Klopas, Wynalda, Jones (who had 50 caps before signing for his first professional team) and Balboa (who had reached 100 without ever appearing in a first division). Heading the list was Lalas, the man referred to by at least one excitable investor-operator as 'our Michael Jordan – no one else comes close'.

An NASL-style haven for journeyman Brits it was not. Arrivals from anywhere in Europe proved exceedingly few. Milan's Roberto Donadoni, who had helped Italy reach the World Cup final two years earlier, was the most celebrated, and while British internationals such as Chris Woods and Maurice Johnston surfaced during the season, only one bona fide Englishman, Norwich City's Ian Butterworth, appeared on an opening-day roster. Gulati stressed that his league's desire to produce 'attacking, entertaining soccer' meant focusing recruitment efforts on Latin America, whose talent also happened to come more cheaply than most of Europe's. Even better value, of course, were the products of the US's own melange of leagues – indoor, outdoor, college, semi-professional, ethnic – which would represent 75 per cent of each squad. Clubs were limited to four non-citizens, a regulation which offered an unprecedented opportunity for hopeful native talent.

For the most part Gulati chose his imports wisely, recruiting several he deemed as the biggest stars in their respective countries. Doctor Khumalo of South Africa and Mauricio Cienfuegos of El Salvador might not have been familiar to World Cup fans, but Carlos Valderrama of Colombia, Marco Etcheverry of Bolivia and Mexico's Jorge Campos all were. Some had passed their peak. A struggling Etcheverry was plucked from the Chilean league and the 35-year-old Valderrama became one of MLS's oldest recruits, though he was not quite as seasoned as 37-year-old Hugo Sánchez, the former Mexico international who had spent seven seasons with Real Madrid as well as two in the NASL.

If the sprinkling of foreign signings carried some weight, the most significant of them had been made with an eye on marketability: the hugely popular Campos, with his self-designed jerseys and daredevil forays out of the penalty area; the bushy-haired Valderrama, who had inspired the sale of a thousand look-a-like wigs at USA 94; and Etcheverry, whose nickname of *El Diablo* was familiar from the World Cup even if his appearance had been fleeting. Gulati carefully allocated them to the clubs where they were likely to sell the most tickets. There was never any doubt that Campos would end up in Los Angeles, where his fan club was enormous, or Donadoni in Italian-laden New York. But MLS pinned its hopes primarily on the image of hip young American talent, much of it conspicuously coiffed: Lalas and his red goatee; Jones and his dreadlocks; Meola and his black ponytail.

For all that, and the tedious commercial detritus of modern sport ('MLS announces that All Sport Body Quencher is the 12th commercial affiliate to join the new league'), soccer's return to something approaching a big stage was worth celebrating. That it existed at all, that for the first time in more than a decade the best Americans could earn a living playing in their own country, was of considerable credit to Rothenberg and his associates, as was the fact that the fans finally had something to follow apart from indoor chicanery or minor league ephemera.

Perhaps the greatest cause for rejoicing was the new, strangely joined-up world of American soccer that now emerged. It led the top professional clubs back into the Open Cup, a competition the NASL had steadfastly ignored, and eventually forced the APSL, its talent largely siphoned off by MLS, to accept its fate as a feeder league, a welcome semi-professional underpinning. Rechristened the A-League, the APSL merged with the USISL in 1997, producing an even stronger pyramid, which extended to a Division III semi-professional league and even a fourth-level development league. Teams this far down the ladder came and went – the Maryland Mania, the Lehigh Valley Steam, the Myrtle Beach Boyz – but some took root, and a few even drew the odd crowd.

Such encouraging developments were overshadowed for the time being by the success of MLS's inaugural season, which saw more fans passing through turnstiles than anyone had expected. The season kicked off in San Jose, with dancers, fireworks, a mini-concert and an overflow crowd of 31,683 at Spartan Stadium. Predictably, the match was sloppy and scrappy, and it remained 0-0 until three minutes from the end, when Eric Wynalda produced the historic first goal. Big-time soccer was back, and it was pleasing enough to leave the *Boston Globe* exclaiming: 'If this game was a test, MLS passed.' Others were less charitable. *Sports Illustrated*, which largely ignored the league that season, headlined its brief report **Goal-Poor**, the first paragraph of which displayed a shocking ignorance of both the league's struggles and the sport itself:

> Starting a professional soccer league from scratch turned out to be the easy part. The truly Herculean labor at the inaugural game of Major League Soccer was getting someone to propel one of the colourful new MLS balls into the back of one of the virgin MLS nets.

Not every assessment was as facile, and in fact scoring proved relatively frequent. The Shootout was summoned to resolve just five goalless draws from 160 regular-season games. While a fertile goal average of 3.4 was partly attributable to mediocre defending, it was only to be expected with teams that had been built in a matter of months, and it was probably just as well, for far fewer journalists were prepared to pounce on shoddy play than a dearth of goals.

Familiar names occupied most of the league's managerial positions. Kansas City had landed the veteran Ron Newman, frequently heralded as 'the winningest coach in American soccer' even if the majority of his victories had come in a version of the game few outside the country recognised. ('I get frustrated by outdoor people who run down the indoor game,' he protested. 'To me, it's un-American.') Other veterans of the NASL – Timo Liekoski, Laurie Abrahams and Tom Rongen – took charge at Columbus, San Jose and Tampa respectively. Most nostalgically of all, the MetroStars reacquainted Eddie Firmani with Giants Stadium. The former Cosmos boss had spent the past few years with clubs in the Middle East, where he had been taken captive during the 1990 Iraqi invasion of Kuwait.

The 62-year-old Firmani survived less than two months at what proved to be the revolving door of the league, plagued by early-season defeats and the prima-donna peevishness of its three American stars, Meola, Ramos and Peter Vermes. His replacement, Carlos Queiroz, helped the club climb out of an early-season hole, but he quit at the end of the season. Any hopes the league held about the MetroStars inheriting the Cosmos mantle disappeared amid a sea of inconsistency. Not even the manifest talents of Donadoni could retrieve their fortunes.

Progress was more encouraging on the other coast, where former national manager-cum-waiter Lothar Osiander led the Los Angeles Galaxy to a 12-match unbeaten start. Two years earlier Osiander had guided the San Francisco Greek-Americans to Open Cup success, then turned his attentions to a team called the Atlanta Ruckus, leading them to within a Shootout of the A-League championship. In LA Osiander found himself in charge of what turned out to be the best-supported club in the country, with a fan base leaning unapologetically towards Latin America. The Galaxy's home average of nearly 29,000 easily doubled anything the NASL had ever produced in the city, and more than 69,000 turned up for the club's home debut, quickly establishing Campos as one of MLS's principal attractions. A few months later, 92,616 saw him perform the surely unprecedented feat of playing in a league match and a full international in the same afternoon, keeping goal for Mexico in a US Cup tie against the Americans, then turning out for the Galaxy against Tampa Bay, even finishing the last 17 minutes as centre-forward.

No other club could boast a player with Campos's appeal, and not everyone was captivated by his eccentricities, but in openly courting the Latino fan MLS was rewarded both off the pitch (it gauged that nearly 40 per cent of its fans were Latin Americans) and on. Tampa Bay's Valderrama was named the Most Valuable Player, though his Colombian team-mate Leonel Alvarez, the chief weapon of the Dallas Burn, might have been more deserving. Even the greying Hugo Sánchez finished second on the Burn's goal-scoring chart. In New England, Alberto Naveda from Argentina was one of the few heroes of a dismal Revolution side, and Uruguay international Adrian Paz, acquired from Ipswich Town, became a striking presence for the Columbus Crew. Playing alongside Campos and Cienfuegos for the Galaxy was Ecuador's powerful Eduardo Hurtado, scorer of 21 goals.

Americans made their presence felt – their sheer numbers meant it was almost impossible for them not to – though the names weren't always those the marketers had counted on. In particular, Lalas failed to emerge as a league icon, falling out with New England manager Frank Stapleton and only rarely displaying the fruits of his World Cup experience. Cynics joked, perhaps unfairly, that his best performance of the season had been reserved for the league's championship final, where he was invited to sing the national anthem.

League performances were rendered almost meaningless by a ridiculously forgiving post-season format in which eight of the ten teams, split into two 'conferences', made the play-offs. The Valderrama-inspired Mutiny finished with the league's best record, but they were eliminated in the semi-finals by DC United, a team they had finished comfortably ahead of in the Eastern Conference.

Having wrested Bruce Arena away from the University of Virginia, United reached the single-game, winner-take-all final after starting the year with six defeats in seven. Etcheverry recovered spectacularly from an indifferent start to become the team's creative inspiration, while 23 goals from Salvadoran Raúl Díaz Arce was the second-best haul in the league. Alongside them, Arena included many of his Virginia proteges, including John Harkes, Jeff Agoos and midfielder Richie Williams.

United defeated the Galaxy 3-2 to claim the first MLS Cup – no Soccer Bowls for this generation – on an afternoon almost as memorable for the weather as the event. Temperatures hovered precariously above freezing, with torrents of rain driven sideways by a howling wind. But for the presence of ABC television, the pitch, laced with standing water, would surely have been declared unplayable. Yet fewer than 8,000 of the 42,000 ticket-holders stayed away, and those who braved the storm were treated to an improbably captivating contest, settled by a United goal five minutes from what surely would have been the most farcical Shootout of the season. 'That soccer could be played at all on that field is remarkable enough, but that it should be so enthralling, so skilful, and so dramatic is downright astounding,' claimed *Soccer America*. 'Words can't do this game justice,' gushed a sodden commissioner.

Less than a fortnight later, United claimed a rare professional double, winning the Open Cup to restore some badly needed prestige to what had once been the showpiece of the American game. To all but the most dedicated fan, the Open Cup hadn't mattered for more than half a century, and the sudden inclusion of professional clubs would not shatter that indifference. Only 7,234 saw DC's 3-0 victory, and few newspapers paid any attention to the impressive run of their A-League opponents, the Rochester Raging Rhinos. The Rhinos, who had come into existence only a few months earlier, were the real success story of the year, eliminating two MLS clubs on their way to the final and averaging almost 10,000 fans for their league games, a figure nearly as high as some in MLS. In Rochester, at least, the NASL had left a fertile legacy.

A proud Doug Logan was left to reflect on a banner first year, one he deemed to have exceeded expectations by 80 per cent at the turnstiles. MLS crowds averaged more than 17,000, with even bottom club Colorado's 10,300 figure welcomingly close to the original target. But television ratings were modest, and Logan lamented the infrequent appearance of highlights on ESPN's *SportsCenter*, whose rare forays into soccer territory often elicited little more than sarcasm from the show's notoriously irreverent presenters ('2-1! A veritable goal-fest!'). Even the biggest MLS stars failed to register on the scales that measured the sporting heroes of the year: Olympic sprinter Michael Johnson, boxing's Evander Holyfield, Tiger Woods and the omnipresent Michael Jordan.

Six of MLS's top 15 goal-scorers were American-born, suggesting the arrival of a home-grown superstar might not be far off. On top of the pile with 27 goals was Roy Lassiter, a former college star acquired by the Mutiny. Playing for North Carolina State University, Lassiter had been implicated in a series of burglaries and ended up in Costa Rica, where he played for three years. When an observant police detective read in a newspaper that Lassiter had scored the winning goal for the US in a friendly against Benfica at the Meadowlands, the striker was given a ten-year suspended prison term.

Yet the penitent North Carolinian – who served 30 days in jail – kept his place in Steve Sampson's squad, and his intimate familiarity with the Costa Rican league proved useful to the national team over its strenuous World Cup qualifying course, which took in 16 matches spread across little more than a year. The unprecedented number of fixtures was tempered by the expansion of the final tournament to 32 teams, making the Americans' path considerably easier.

The run-up to qualification had been anything but ideal: a poor showing at the 1996 US Cup followed a few months later by a player walkout over bonus money, leaving Sampson to field a 'replacement' team for a friendly in Peru just two weeks before the opening game. The dispute dragged on for months, but the players came back in time to win their first three qualifiers and all but reserve a place in the final group of six, from which three would go to France. Lassiter scored the goal against Costa Rica in California that put them there, by which time some began to suspect that Mexico were no longer Concacaf's top dogs.

Though the asterisk next to his job title had been removed, Sampson was still under pressure to prove himself at each game. His contract was renewable on a year-to-year basis, and faint praise from Rothenberg ('of course I want Steve to do well; he's my baby') did little to bolster his confidence. In fact, the federation refused to rule out bringing in a new manager even if the team qualified. While only a display of resounding ineptitude was likely to keep the US from reaching France, ineptitude was no stranger to American World Cup campaigns. After three draws in their first four games of the final round, they stood only a point clear of last place, and the twitching of federation officials grew more pronounced.

Financially there was little to worry about, since Nike was setting off on its conquest of international football, poised to tattoo its swoosh on the USSF for $120 million. The federation agreed to stage a crucial game against Costa Rica near the corporation's headquarters in Oregon, installing a temporary $100,000 grass surface in the former home of the Portland Timbers. In turn, the corporate leviathan equipped fans with missile-shaped noisemakers and ordered everyone to turn up for the game in a white shirt. If the resultant atmosphere was 'impressive', as *Soccer America* claimed, it was also surreal. The teams skidded across the mysteriously slippery pitch to little effect until Ramos drove home the winning goal with 11 minutes to spare.

Sampson was almost home and dry, but in Washington DC Jamaica put another dent in his credibility, outplaying his team again in an embarrassing 1-1 draw. Then it was down to Mexico, where the US had never done anything except lose: in 17 qualifying fixtures spread over 58 years, they had fallen every time. With the match barely half an hour old, Jeff Agoos was sent off, but Sampson moved Harkes into defence and emerged with a 0-0 draw before nearly 115,000 in the Aztec Stadium. The result was decisive enough for Mexico's jaded fans to turn on their own team and coach, the returning Milutinovic. It was also achieved with a team drawn entirely from Major League Soccer.

Ostensibly, Sampson's precarious footing should have been shored up a week later, in the less animated surroundings of a Vancouver suburb where the Americans beat Canada 3-0 to earn their place in France. Rothenberg doled out cigars while a relieved manager stood proudly in his corner. For all his lack of experience, Sampson had suffered just two qualification defeats, both in the hellish atmosphere of Costa Rica's Estadio Ricardo Saprissa, the 'Monster's Cave'. Yet it was another month before ambiguous pronouncements from Rothenberg ('He's the coach until he's not the coach') dried up and the incumbent manager was assured of leading his team into the finals.

Perhaps the most remarkable victory of Sampson's tenure came a few months later at the Gold Cup in California, an event Concacaf organised as a preamble to France 98. The victims were Brazil, albeit a Brazil somewhat removed from the incumbent world champions. Fewer than 13,000 were on hand in the LA Coliseum to see it, and the late kick-off kept the news out of many of the next morning's papers, but for a nation which hadn't so much as scored against the South Americans since 1930, the 1-0 semi-final victory deserved a wider audience. It came through a sensational goal from a naturalised striker, Belgrade-born Predrag (Preki) Radosavljevic – one of the few players to have graduated from an American indoor circuit to England's top division, with Everton – but the hero of the evening was another Premiership representative, Leicester City goalkeeper Kasey Keller. The afterglow faded quickly: the Americans lost the final to Mexico in a Coliseum jam-packed with hostile fans, a sight many hoped World Cup 94 had consigned to history.

By now, the coach who had trusted his players and nourished their team spirit considered his apprenticeship over. Sampson had spent much of the previous year fighting for his job, and in the process settled into the more autocratic demeanour of the typical American coach, tinkering with line-ups and formations, placing a premium on video analysis and tactics and identifying players who could 'do a job'. Some in the squad found little fault with this – most were used to it from their college days – but others took umbrage. Deploying John Harkes at left-back instead of central midfield in an effort to make room for Reyna, Sampson found fault with the player's unenthusiastic response and, after Harkes had committed a series of minor disciplinary indiscretions, removed his captain from the final list of 22. Castigated for unspecified 'leadership concerns' and a lack of enthusiasm for playing at the back, Harkes was left hoping for a change of heart which never came. Though some suspected Harkes's ego had spun out of control, the bombshell seemed to complete a transformation in Sampson's character, one Harkes later recounted in his autobiography, *Captain For Life and Other Temporary Assignments*:

> In meetings, he would stop the videotape and examine every little play. He was constantly stopping our training sessions to tell a player he needed to be five more yards this way or that, overanalysing every move. He wouldn't let us play. He had gone 180 degrees from where he was two years earlier. He would tell Eric Wynalda how to hit a free-kick, Joe-Max Moore how to hit a corner, or Preki how to swerve a ball. You've heard of micromanaging? Well Steve was microcoaching.

Sampson had other shocks in store. Balboa, Lalas and Wynalda were all missing from the final warm-up games, while starting roles were given to peripheral figures such as Chad Deering, a striker from Texas who had played sporadically for Bundesliga debutants Wolfsburg, German-born David Wagner, once of Schalke 04, and the Columbus Crew's Brian Maisonneuve.[*] They joined Reyna and North Carolina-born Eddie Pope, both under 25, and Frankie Hejduk, a quicksilver 23-year-old Californian who had represented his country as a surfer. When that team produced an emphatic 3-0 win in a warm-up game against Austria, Sampson was left to conclude that fresh blood – and the 3-6-1 formation he had devised for the occasion – would serve him well in France.

The coach also exploited a loophole in American immigration policy

---

[*] Wagner's presence in the American team had led the Canadian Soccer Association to protest against the US's 3-0 victory in the qualifier in California. The Canadians claimed Wagner was ineligible as he'd appeared for the country of his birth at a youth level, but this turned out to be a different David Wagner. When the US travelled to Canada for the return fixture eight months later, members of Sam's Army took a snipe at the Canadian association by wearing 'Hello my name is' badges and writing in 'Wagner'.

to land Bundesliga centre-half David Regis, a native of Martinique who had an American wife but spoke almost no English. Regis was named in the squad at almost the last hour, after his wife agreed to work for a travel agency, in effect fast-tracking her husband through a citizenship procedure that ordinarily might have taken years. Agoos, whose position was most under threat from the newcomer, was even told by Sampson to help him pass his citizenship test. Regis did – and appeared in every US match in France. Agoos didn't play a single minute.

Fourteen days after his team kicked its first ball of World Cup 98 Sampson resigned, his plan in tatters and his squad close to meltdown. He had been given a difficult draw: Germany in the first fixture and Yugoslavia in the last, with a politically-charged confrontation with Iran in the middle. But his team came bottom of the unofficial 32-nation table and many of his most experienced players left no doubt as to who they believed was at fault. Tab Ramos, whose participation in France the manager limited to 78 minutes, was among the most scathing. 'From the beginning, this whole World Cup has been a mess,' he complained. 'I blame the coaches for the losses.'

It took Germany's Andy Möller only eight minutes to unpick the American defence at the Parc des Princes, with the US offering serious resistance for little more than a quarter of an hour. The 2-0 scoreline might have been less emphatic than the 5-1 pasting Czechoslovakia had handed Bob Gansler's youngsters in Italy eight years earlier, but in some ways it reeked of the same naivety, the belief that slavish devotion to the whiteboard could triumph over international nous. Seven of Germany's starting line-up had been in Franz Beckenbauer's World Cup-winning squad of 1990; seven of the US team had never played in the finals before. Sampson had chosen to build his team around one of them, Reyna, whose first-minute slugging from Jens Jeremies seemed to leave a match-long impression. The curious 3-6-1 formation was successful only in isolating Eric Wynalda up front.

Unfortunately, the veterans who were called upon had largely let the side down. Thomas Dooley was badly beaten on both the German goals, 73-cap Mike Burns was given the run-around by Jörg Heinrich and the performance of Earnie Stewart was almost imperceptible. Down, but not out. 'We lost to the Germans. So what? Everybody loses to the Germans. Let's forget about it and think about Iran,' Ramos implored.

American politicians and commentators had been thinking about Iran ever since the draw had been made. The occasion was widely perceived as a diplomatic ice-breaker that might begin to restore relations severed in the wake of Iran's Islamic Revolution two decades earlier. Parallels were drawn with the 'ping-pong diplomacy' of 1971, when the US table-tennis team toured communist China, paving the way for President Nixon's visit the following year. Bill Clinton did not turn up in Lyon – the highest-ranking US government official at the tournament was the head of the Environmental Protection Agency, Carol Browner, a self-confessed soccer mom – but the match went some way towards softening national prejudices.

With his team in the unusual role of favourites, Sampson produced still more changes. He removed Deering, whose performance against Germany had been better than most, and introduced striker Joe-Max Moore as a defensive midfielder. Wynalda, Stewart and Burns were benched. Deploying a 3-5-2 formation with a line-up which to one *New York Times* correspondent 'looked like a mixer on the first night of a cruise', Sampson nearly managed to produce the result expected of him. But his team botched their chances and conceded a late first-half goal to encourage the largely pro-Iranian crowd. On four occasions the US struck the frame of the goal, and by the time Columbus's Brian McBride connected with an 87th-minute effort, Iran had doubled their lead and buried any notions that they were the poor relations of Group F.

Away from the pitch the atmosphere was rather more hopeful. The hostilities anticipated by international journalists unfamiliar with the largely middle-class, liberal sensibilities of the typical American soccer fan never surfaced. *Soccer America* observed with some incredulity:

> Anyone who'd read or heard about or remembered the simmering tensions sparked by the Islamic Revolution and subsequent imprisonment of 52 American hostages in 1979 could not have believed the sights and sounds in the streets outside the stadium: chants of 'U-S-A!' and 'Iran!' ringing out from groups joined at the hip trying to out-shout the other: fans wearing Iran caps festooned with American flags; and on some faces, the colour of one nation painted on the left cheek and the other nation daubed on the right.

The result, though, left some to prepare for less encouraging reactions back home. Creating interest in a World Cup was challenging enough, but a World Cup in which the US team didn't win was nearly impossible. The American media had chronicled events in France in unprecedented depth, producing much less of the condescending and often banal prose of 1994. Incendiary events such as Sampson's cold-shouldering of Harkes, which traditionally merited just a sentence or two, no longer passed without serious comment. Sampson had even announced his final squad live on *SportsCenter* and ESPN aired the manager's behind-the-scenes diary two days before the Germany match.

Encouraged by the size of its audience in 1994, television prepared for even greater things from France. ABC rescheduled its popular daytime soap opera *General Hospital* to accommodate the United States' first game, but wound up taking a ratings nosedive squarely on the chin. Not only did the defeat by Germany attract fewer viewers than the fictional goings-on in Port Charles, it also fared considerably worse than any of their American fixtures four years earlier.

Only diehards bothered with the final, meaningless match with Yugoslavia, another fixture rife with political overtones given America's role in the Balkans conflict. What had once been anticipated as the group's most crucial game turned out to be a backdrop to the animosity and bitterness festering in the American camp. Preki, incensed at not being named in the starting line-up against his former compatriots, complained bitterly ('I've been overlooked every day'), while Lalas warmed up the reporters ('everybody's ready to explode'). One report even suggested Lalas, Wynalda, Stewart and Balboa had been close to being sent home.

Despite all that, the US produced their most competent performance of the three, but were again suckered by an early goal and crippled by poor finishing. The 1-0 defeat left them to swim out of the competition with the other minnows. Once more Sampson had made wholesale changes, punctuating the second half with substitutions, but in replacing the shifty Hejduk he withdrew what many considered had been his most potent weapon.

'They stunk. And they hated their coach,' was the pithy summary of one Associated Press writer, and as the players packed their bags their hatred seemed to intensify. 'We were naive to think an inexperienced coach would see the value of experienced players,' concluded Wynalda, who only once appeared in the starting line-up. 'We should never let this happen again.' Ramos insisted he had played his last match for the team with Sampson in charge. His assessment of the manager's competence – 'as he became more of a coach, we became less of a team' – drew the threat of a fine from the USSF. Agoos, a player volatile enough to have burned his training gear upon learning he had not been selected for the 1994 World Cup, also declared himself through with the national team, as did Lalas, who took aim at Sampson's integrity. 'We all have a scrapbook, and I would have liked to at least have a picture of myself on the field,' he reflected, having spent every minute of every match on the bench. 'The most important thing is having the respect of the people you associate with yourself ... Steve is going to have to settle for a scrapbook, and that's all.'

Though bruised, the coach remained unapologetic. He had no regrets about leaving Harkes at home or keeping veterans on the bench. But it was his contention that few Americans were yet capable of playing at a World Cup level that jarred the most. It was a surprisingly harsh indictment of MLS, well into its third season and the home of all but four of the US's outfield players. The comments and the team's performance seemed to add weight to the view that the league was more of a proving ground for aspiring talent than a showcase for the nation's elite.

As the unbowed manager stood down and Alan Rothenberg began his search for a replacement, MLS played out its third season hoping to rebound from what its commissioner had termed the 'terrible twos' of its second year. Far from climbing towards Doug Logan's bold target of 20,000 a game, gates had fallen by more than 16 per cent in 1997. Imaginatively, Logan excused the drop with a reference to President Clinton's welfare reform bill. 'Not only was the Government going to take away health benefits and food stamps from poor people,' he contended, 'but on Spanish radio everybody was talking about *la Migra, la Migra* – as if [US] Immigration was going to scoop them all up at mass events like a soccer game ... I blame the government, totally.'

MLS's surveys indicated the Latino element of its fan base had fallen significantly, but the size of the decline could not be explained by mere paranoia. Television ratings also foundered, with coverage – at least in English – often lamentably poor (one director even failed in the moderately simple task of capturing a penalty kick). Meanwhile, not a spade had been lifted in pursuit of a soccer-specific stadium. Voters in Columbus comprehensively rejected a proposal to fund a new facility from a sales tax increase, leaving the Crew stranded in the mammoth home of the Ohio State University gridiron team.

Playing standards might have improved, but ageing imports such as Thomas Dooley, whose Bundesliga career had ended, could still quickly establish themselves among the league's elite, while more youthful, world-class talent remained out of Sunil Gulati's price range. The easiest way to sell tickets, it seemed, was to put on a fireworks display. LA's Fourth of July match with New England drew 51,700 to the Coliseum.

Rather than splashing out on better talent, MLS was resigned to making the most of what it had. Its marketing arm went so far as to devise nicknames for star players (John 'the Juggler' Harkes; Cobi 'the Missile' Jones, Roy 'Lights Out' Lassiter), which mercifully failed to catch on. Other gimmicks succeeded only in alienating committed fans. Not everyone wanted to clap along to piped-in music or gorge themselves on pyrotechnic displays, yet many clubs persisted in taking a patronising approach to match day. The assessment of *Soccer America's* Ridge Mahoney was unequivocal:

> Ambience consisting entirely of roaring rock music, beach balls bouncing in the stands, and dance programs is rubbish ... you can put all the icing you want on a plain cake donut, and it's still a donut. And fans in some MLS cities aren't even being sold the donut. They're being sold the hole.

Being much more doughnut than hole, DC United repeated their championship victory in 1997, defeating the Colorado Rapids in the final. Similarities between the second MLS Cup and the first were almost uncanny: a rain-drenched field, a surprisingly healthy throng of hardy fans thumbing their nose at the elements (all 57,431 tickets were sold) and another close-run victory for United, this time by 2-1 on their own pitch.

If the second season ended with noticeably less optimism than the first, it was to the league's credit that all its teams remained right where they had started, and that close-season gossip never drifted into the more familiar pro soccer territory of guessing which clubs might be moving where. The only change of any note was Kansas City's gratifying decision to rename themselves the Wizards, allegedly because of the threat of legal action from a similarly-named electronics retailer. 'Flushing the Wiz', though, had long been a temptation of mischievous headline-writers.

Yet ten teams still represented only about half a professional league, a hindrance that was partly remedied by the addition of franchises in Miami and Chicago in 1998. The latter, nicknamed the Fire (suggesting a limitless appetite for naming teams after catastrophes), claimed the MLS Cup at their first attempt. Coached by former DC United assistant Bob Bradley, they rarely displayed the kind of open, attacking soccer league officials had pursued, but an infusion of Polish talent, headed by midfielder Peter Nowak, proved a hit in a city home to thousands of eastern European immigrants. More than 36,000 turned up for the Fire's home debut, with the club's average of nearly 18,000 easily outstripping anything the NASL had achieved with the Sting or the Mustangs.

The story was rather different for the new Miami Fusion, who had opted to play down the coast in Fort Lauderdale after failing to find a stadium anywhere closer to their nominal home town. Owners who had spent more than $20 million to land the team sank another $5 million into converting the former residence of the Fort Lauderdale Strikers into something beyond a high school football stadium. With an intimate capacity of 21,000 and an international-size pitch, the Fusion possessed one of the most soccer-friendly venues in the league, but they were unable to match even the modest crowds the Strikers had once attracted. Even the arrival of Carlos Valderrama from Tampa Bay failed to galvanise Latino fans, and he lasted only one turbulent season.

The match-up of the Fire and United at the 1998 MLS Cup drew more than 51,000 to a Rose Bowl blissfully free of rain, with Chicago's stingy defence and two goals from Nowak bringing Bradley's 'blue collar' team the title. The Fire then took the Open Cup as well to complete a remarkable first-year double. United had opted out of the latter competition partly to focus on Concacaf's Champions Cup, a decision that proved far-sighted: in defeating Toluca of Mexico in front of 12,000 at RFK Stadium, they became the first American winners of the competition. To Bruce Arena, the achievement pointed to MLS's impressive pedigree. 'I take offence to any comment that this is not a good league,' he declared.

Perhaps it was a good league, if not a great one, but after three years its survival was still in doubt. Crowds had dipped further, if only slightly, and TV ratings were the worst yet. Even Univision found the audience for its Spanish-language broadcasts slipping away, confirming the league's own suspicions about its fading popularity amongst Latinos. Painful numbers of Americans were still unable to identify any native soccer player, and the national team's anonymous performance in France hadn't offered them many clues. Spurious correlations continued to be drawn between wanting to play the game and wanting to watch it, though it was now 30 years since the birth of the NASL and several generations of eager young kickers had grown up without ever clamouring for season tickets.

But the owners stood their ground. Anschutz had spent another $5 million putting the Fire in Chicago, and the Kraft family briefly added the San Jose Clash to their holdings. The financial losses may have looked daunting, but they were still a pittance compared with those being suffered by the likes of the NHL's Pittsburgh Penguins, the 1991 and 1992 Stanley Cup champions, who filed for bankruptcy claiming two-year debts of $37 million (they were rescued by a former player at a cost of $99 million).

Even ESPN seemed happy to bring soccer into what seemed an intolerably small number of households. Its advertisers might not have been thrilled by the size of the audience, but they certainly liked its demographics: young, malleable consumers whose 'brand loyalties' were not yet 'entrenched'. Eager to accommodate them, Nike stepped forward with another $380-million USSF marketing deal, increasing its financial obligations to an extraordinary $500 million spread over 12 years.

By and large, though, the nation showed little sign of wavering from its fascination with the usual sporting agenda. Though one survey had found that 50 million Americans considered themselves soccer-literate, another determined that only 52 per cent of the nation could even identify the World Cup as a soccer competition. The game had not touched the heart of the American sports fan, and some now began to wonder if it ever would.

10. Momentary Insanity
In and out of love with the women's game

Americans like winners, in tiddlywinks or in soccer.

Bruce Arena

In the eyes of most fans, it remains the country's proudest soccer moment, witnessed by more than 90,000 in person and another 40 million on television, and settled by the nail-biting vagaries of a penalty shootout. It came on a sunny July afternoon in California, one which put America finally on top of the football world, its players feted by an adoring public and a sympathetic national press.

Outside the United States, the women's World Cup final of 1999 is not treated particularly seriously. The competition suffers from the same kind of indifference and deprecation the game as a whole receives from the typical American. In Associated Press's worldwide poll of the ten most important sports stories that year – a soccer-sympathetic list topped by the clutch of trophies accumulated by Manchester United – the event was nowhere to be found. Yet in its domestic poll, and countless other equivalents, it finished first. *Sports Illustrated* hailed the American team as its sporting personalities of the year.

The foreign fan who unwarily refuses to equate the talents of Mia Hamm or Michelle Akers with those of Ronaldo or Maradona can expect a stern reprimand – not to mention accusations of snobbery and sexism – from his counterparts in America, where the top female players are generally held in greater reverence than their male equivalents. As far back as 1993, when the draw was made for the men's 1994 World Cup finals, the American organisers placed Akers, who three years earlier had led her team to victory in the first women's equivalent, on the same stage as Franz Beckenbauer. Some non-Americans winced: to them it was sacrilege, a deplorable level of posturing from a nation manifestly unable to appreciate the gravity of the occasion. Football, especially at its highest level, was still a man's game. But America disagreed, and by the 1990s it disagreed strongly enough to have unwittingly yielded another epithet for its soccer-loving males to dodge. While for decades the game had been ridiculed as the domain of 'commie pansies' and other undesirables, in the 1990s soccer also became a 'girls' sport'.

For this they could thank, among others, Richard Nixon. In 1972 he signed into law Title IX of the Education Amendments Act, prohibiting gender discrimination in any educational programme or activity receiving federal aid. Sporting equality was hardly the focal point of the legislation, but its effects proved far-reaching. When universities – private and public alike, since both received government assistance – learned that spending on their sports teams had to be in proportion to the ratio of male and female athletes, what seemed a commonsense edict developed into perhaps the most contentious issue in the history of college sport.

Guidelines issued in 1993 further inflamed the controversy, requiring the male-female ratio of participants to mirror that of the university's total enrolment, not just those who played in teams. Though the intent of the legislation had been to expand opportunities for women, compliance could often be more easily achieved by reducing the options open to men. Of course, male-dominated athletic departments would not allow such developments to encroach on their most visible programmes, chiefly gridiron and basketball, which they sought to preserve in their bloated, quasi-professional guise. But lower-profile men's sports were not always as fortunate. Even the national pastime found itself under threat at institutions the size of the University of Wisconsin (undergraduate enrolment: nearly 30,000), which terminated its baseball programme in 1991.

Periodic legal challenges limited Title IX implementation for decades, yet between 1981 and 1999 the number of women engaged in intercollegiate sport grew by 81 per cent to 163,000, while the number of men increased just 5 per cent to 232,000. By 1999 there were more female teams than male ones – nearly 9,500 across the country – and the sport that benefited most was soccer, spreading from 80 schools in 1981 to 926 by 1999. The University of North Carolina soon emerged as the game's towering force and its manager, Anson Dorrance, a sort of coaching paragon. Born in Bombay, the son of an oil executive, Dorrance spent his childhood in a number of soccer-friendly countries, yet it was his experiences as a player at North Carolina in the early 1970s ('I had the touch of a goat and the creativity of a table') that converted him. In 1977 he took charge of the men's programme, a position he held for 12 seasons, but it was with the women's team that he became indelibly associated. Within two years of becoming the first head coach of the Lady Tar Heels[*]

* North Carolina was once famous for producing tar and the 'tar heel' nickname is said to derive from an obscure incident in the Civil War. Many women's teams rather clumsily follow the practice of adding the prefix 'Lady' to the school nickname.

in 1979, he steered them to the first of 18 national championships in 23 years.

With much of the best talent in the country playing for him at UNC, Dorrance's appointment as part-time manager of the national team in 1986 came as no surprise. As far back as 1983 the US had put out a women's team of sorts, its players sewing jersey numbers onto hand-me-down shirts and competing in rank anonymity, but their rise to international prominence came far more quickly than the men. FIFA organised the first women's World Cup in 1991, just as Title IX was beginning to leave its legacy. In their first qualifying match, the American women scored more goals against Mexico, 12, than the men had accumulated against the same country over 31 years.

Nearly half that team had played for Dorrance in college, including Mia Hamm, yet to turn 20, and captain April Heinrichs, who at the end of the decade would become the team's first female manager. Embarrassingly lopsided victories over Martinique (12-0), Trinidad & Tobago (10-0) and Haiti (10-0) underlined the yawning disparities of an emerging international competition.

The squad Dorrance took to China for the finals was anonymous to all but the keenest fan. Yet from the start Akers and her compatriots put the US on equal footing with the best in the world, however modest that world was. A 2-1 win over Norway in the final, in front of 65,000 in Guangzhou, earned them the trophy, but little else. The country was not yet ready to embrace a world championship-winning team in what was still a decidedly un-American and unfeminine pastime. The *New York Times* was one of the few newspapers to herald the team's accomplishments, observing that on the coach trip from the stadium 'team members passed around the FIFA trophy to the theme music from the movie *Working Girl*, a story about a talented secretary who rises in the male-dominated business world'.

Dorrance stepped aside, to be replaced by a former ASL goalkeeper, Tony DiCicco, but few tears were shed at home when the Americans were beaten by Norway in the semi-final in Sweden four years later. The transformation of the women's game required a showcase event in their own country. In 1996 the Olympic Games came to Atlanta and, after fierce lobbying from the Americans, women's soccer made a hasty debut (with no time for a qualification phase, organisers merely drafted in the eight teams that had reached the previous summer's World Cup finals). Few eligibility restrictions were placed on the participants, meaning the US Olympic squad looked very similar to its World Cup equivalent.

As with the men, national duties were largely unencumbered by obligations to club teams, providing almost limitless opportunities for international call-ups. Midfielder Kristine Lilly received her 100th cap before she was 25. By the time of the Atlanta Games three others had reached the milestone as well, including the blossoming Hamm. Yet the player most likely to have surpassed them all, Akers – who had been among the first American women to play overseas, joining a club in Sweden – found herself struggling with a debilitating chronic fatigue virus. With the drugs that might have helped proscribed as performance-enhancing, she was pressed into a defensive midfield role, confining her game to short, energetic bursts ('It was an awful feeling, knowing before a game started that I'd be sick for the next two days'). In Atlanta Akers appeared in all five games, though her need for post-match intravenous feeding nearly caused her to miss the medal ceremony.

Uncertain how many tickets women's Olympic soccer was capable of selling – stadiums for the Sweden World Cup had often been embarrassingly empty – organisers decided to schedule many of the early-round matches as curtain-raisers to the men's tournament, making it difficult to judge the level of interest in each event. But by the time of the semi-finals there was little doubt the women had established a substantial following. At the University of Georgia's gridiron stadium, its hallowed hedges pruned to accommodate more seats, the US tamed their semi-final nemesis of the previous summer, Norway, in front of more than 64,000. A few hours later at the same venue, 54,000 saw China beat Brazil in arguably the most dramatic match of the competition.

As with Los Angeles in 1984, television – NBC this time – ignored a momentous Olympic soccer story, preferring less alien disciplines which could more readily accommodate commercial breaks. Even the prospect of 76,481 filling a gridiron mecca for the gold medal match between the US and China – a crowd deemed by organisers to be the largest ever for a women's match – was shunned in favour of the latest incarnation of basketball's 'dream team' easing its way to a meaningless victory over Australia. Network executives made it clear they had no intention of letting soccer creep into their schedules, and so presented only the last minute of the match and the celebrations of the home team. 'Has NBC secretly discovered that women draw the line at their gender playing sweaty team sports that were once male preserves?' wondered the *New York Times*, noting that the network had also shunned the gold medal-winning performance of the women's softball team.

There were many, though, who had taken notice of women's soccer, and a few who even began to rally around it. By 1997 an amateur circuit called the W-League, formed after the 1994 men's World Cup, had expanded to 32 teams, and plans for a professional league, to be known as the National Soccer Association, were submitted to the USSF. Title IX seemed to be bearing fruit – two women's professional basketball leagues had formed a year earlier – but the federation was still nursing its infant MLS, whose own survival was far from certain, and had little appetite for what it regarded as an even more speculative venture. 'People are not going to invest as a statement for women; in the end they want to make money,' noted the chairman of the committee examining the proposal.

The NSA never got off the ground, but America was due to host the next big women's tournament, and its legacy would prove more spectacular. The 1999 World Cup attracted unprecedented interest and even turned a modest profit. Just as 1984 had opened FIFA's eyes to the drawing power of soccer in the US, 1999 convinced American entrepreneurs that the women's game carried commercial potential. One could sympathise with that point of view. The team might not have been household names like Venus and Serena Williams, but many were familiar faces, particularly the 27-year-old Hamm, playing in her third World Cup and extolled as the most prolific goalscorer American soccer had produced. The daughter of an air force colonel, Hamm was born in Selma, Alabama, but lived the nomadic childhood of an armed forces family in California, Italy, Virginia and Texas – all before she turned six. As a 17-year-old undergraduate at North Carolina she was entrusted to Anson Dorrance, who was made her legal guardian while her parents were stationed in Florence. In 1998 the USSF named Hamm its female player of the year for a fifth consecutive time. The commercial appeal of a white, middle-class, graciously humble Olympic heroine was not lost on corporate America: Nike claimed her as a client and even named one of its office blocks after her.

By the time of the World Cup Hamm had appeared in Nike's ubiquitous television commercials with Michael Jordan, written a book (subtitled *A Champion's Guide to Winning in Soccer and Life*) and may have been profiled in more of the nation's media than any soccer player of either gender. Not since Billie Jean King had a woman so personified her sport. Yet she was uneasy in the role, a reluctant superstar whose team-first ethos jarred with the look-at-me *zeitgeist*. *Salon* magazine said of her:

> Hers is not the forced modesty of a media-savvy star. It is rooted
> in a relentless will to win coupled with an understanding that,

at its heart, soccer is a team sport. On the field, she is a vocal and dominant competitor. Off the field, you get the sense that she would prefer to fade into the woodwork of the US squad, to just be an athlete.

Yet Hamm was inspiring millions of young players of both sexes, and her unpretentious demeanour was reassuring to a Middle America weary of the blustering pronouncements of sport's male brigade of millionaire egoists. National team matches thronged with pony-tailed young fans draped in 'Hamm 9' jerseys, desperate for autographs and a goal or two from their heroine. Hamm obliged with smiles and remarkable patience. In the countless features written about her before USA 99, it was virtually impossible to find a word against her, either as a footballer or a human being.

The irony of the media's Mia-obsession was that American success had far more to do with team dynamics than individual brilliance. Some of the names might have seemed more appropriate for romance novels than shin-guards – Tiffeny Milbrett, Brandi Chastain, Lorrie Fair – but they were anything but a collection of lovelorn damsels, and their desire to play as hard for each other as they did for themselves had instilled an impressive chemistry and an egalitarian team spirit.

The summer of 1999 proved even more memorable than the one five years earlier, and the country's appetite for hosting top-class soccer was again dramatically underestimated. Officials had targeted an aggregate attendance of 312,000 but sold half a million tickets a week before a ball had been kicked. Nearly 194,000 saw the three group matches in which the US outscored Denmark, Nigeria and North Korea 13-1 on aggregate, with eight different players registering goals.

A winning American team playing on its own soil to enormous crowds was too intoxicating a combination to pass unnoticed. The media's response was relentlessly favourable, typified by Christine Brennan, a *USA Today* columnist who admitted to not especially liking soccer:

> The US women, the ones I had begun noticing in those ingenious TV commercials, took no time at all to grow on me. They looked so wholesome and all-American, they almost didn't seem real. I had heard that they were all college-educated. None, I believe, has a police record. In the sports-weary Nineties, could this really be possible? ... What was not to like about this team?

Millions were similarly captivated. In the quarter-final against Germany, played in front of nearly 55,000 in the home of the NFL's Washington Redskins, the US twice came from behind to win 3-2. Their semi-final victory over Brazil drew more than 73,000 to Stanford Stadium, where the American men had been knocked out by the same country in 1994. For the final against China – a repeat of the gold medal contest in Atlanta – the Rose Bowl was nearly as full as it had been for the men's equivalent five years earlier.

It, too, was decided on penalties, and suffered from a similar lack of open play and scoring opportunities. Indeed, the tournament as a whole was plagued with growing pains – particularly a rash of brutal tackles scarcely kept in check by referees seemingly overwhelmed by the intensity of play. In a 7-1 pasting of Nigeria, the US were awarded 29 free-kicks to their opponents' three, and Hamm was substituted shortly after half-time, to a chorus of boos from a Chicago crowd unaware that their heroine was being hacked to pieces.

In the final, despite the flag-waving exhortations of a shrieking crowd, the Chinese came closest to scoring, with Kristine Lilly needing to head an extra-time effort off the line. Across the nation, nerves jangled; for the first time, millions of Americans found themselves completely absorbed by a soccer match that did not produce a goal, though it did offer a few surprises. In open play the outstanding US performer was not Hamm, who was kept quiet by tenacious Chinese marking, but Akers, who somehow kept her imposing medical condition at bay until she had to be taken off in extra time.

But her heroics were largely forgotten amid the drama of penalties. The US coolly converted each of theirs, all five takers – including a reluctant Hamm – veterans of the World Cup-winning team of eight years earlier. With goalkeeper Briana Scurry having pushed aside a Chinese kick, the chance to win the match fell to the feet of Brandi Chastain, the 30-year-old California full-back nicknamed 'Hollywood' because of her taste for melodrama.

Much, probably too much, has been made about the scenes that followed her left-footed strike: Chastain removing her shirt to reveal a black sports bra, then sinking to her knees in triumph. Some accused Chastain of indulging the exhibitionist traits that had earlier led her to be photographed for a men's magazine crouching behind a soccer ball, wearing nothing but her boots and a layer of body oil. Others sensed she had bowed to commercial opportunism. The bra happened to be a Nike prototype, and multinational behemoths looking for 'product placement' had moved on from the days of Soccer Bowl 77, when, after scoring for the Cosmos, Steve Hunt removed his Pony brand boot and held it aloft (an image which appeared in several papers the following morning). As one *New York Times* columnist hypothesised, somewhat tongue-in-cheek:

> Nike stood to gain millions if viewers detected the teensy black-on-black swoosh on Chastain's bra and made the obvious trek to Nike Town. And Chastain is a Nike endorser, as are five other teammates, including Hamm. All the pieces were in place that day for an ingenious Nike executive to leverage the power Nike already held by outfitting the team, to require all 20 players to wear its sports bra, mandate the shooting order of the United States penalty kickers, with Chastain last, figuring that anyone who would essentially pose nude for *Gear* magazine would act as if throwing off her shirt were a naturally exultant reaction to winning the World Cup.

Both player and outfitter denied any conspiracy, Chastain defending herself with a celebrated plea of 'momentary insanity'. But this was far from the only cloud hanging over what should have been a proud moment. Some African-American commentators castigated ABC for what they perceived as yet another example of white America turning to its own kind whenever the skin of the real hero happened to be the wrong colour. Why, they asked, had the cameras not focused on Scurry, the black Minnesotan whose save moments earlier was the turning point of the shoot-out?

Television's fixation with sexual imagery may have been a more likely rationale. Chastain's actions quickly provoked excited sociological discussion about stereotypes of the female athlete as sex object. Many women may have cringed to hear the bubbly co-captain Julie Foudy refer to her team as 'booters with hooters', but in an age when racy and often vulgar self-promotion – of men as well as women – was largely perceived as a justifiable means of selling tickets, such epithets seemed relatively tame. Chastain ('For us, it doesn't matter what motivates them to come to the stadium, as long as they come') and Foudy seemed merely products of their time. The latter had posed with her husband for *Sports Illustrated*'s swimsuit annual, yet her interest in 'gender issues' soon propelled her to the presidency of the Women's Sports Foundation. 'If we can make sure we're successful on the field,' she insisted, 'I think people will come for the product, rather than what the product looks like.'

The 'product' had in this case prompted a national celebration, and the inevitable trappings of celebrity followed: TV appearances and product endorsements, Disneyland parades and pro-am golf tournaments, even a White House audience with President Clinton (who, unlike in 1994, had attended the final). Chastain's sports-bra moment reached the cover of *Sports Illustrated* and *Newsweek* and the match made the front of *Time* and *People*.

Any remaining doubts that the 'Babes of Summer' had become the sporting sensation of the season disappeared once ABC revealed the size of its audience for the final: 40 million, a figure far in excess of any other soccer contest shown on American TV and nearly twice that of the 1994 men's World Cup final. Media analysts were stunned. 'These are NFL-type numbers,' exclaimed one. 'It's phenomenal.'

Inevitably, the frenzy of crystal-ball gazing that accompanied every significant American soccer match was revived. 'I think we're on the cutting edge of one of the most significant cultural revolutions in the world,' boasted a delirious USSF official. 'It states that in team sports, women are full partners of men, not subordinates.' Not everyone was so certain. 'Some of the white-heat attraction, undoubtedly, stems from America's fascination with the Big Event that comes around once in a lifetime,' wrote the *Boston Globe*. 'Some comes from the recent explosion of interest in female spectator sports, from figure skating to gymnastics to basketball to tennis to soccer. And some because the home team (unlike the US males in 1994) is supposed to win.'

What seemed clear enough was that, at last, the nation had come to terms with the game itself. Little was made of the fact that the final had ended goalless or that, for all its suspense, it had produced few thrills over the 120 minutes of normal play. One account claimed that the 'biggest reaction of regulation time was when the crowd booed as Clinton was shown on the scoreboard'. Even fidgety children seemed to have been riveted. 'It was never boring,' one nine-year-old told a reporter. 'We didn't score for a while, but the end was very, very exciting.'

While television had worked wonders for the women, it seemed to be conspiring against Major League Soccer. The Premiership and Champions League were encroaching into American homes through cable TV, captivating many fans for whom the empty stadiums and inferior talent of MLS, its matches plagued with artifices like the Shootout, represented strictly Minor League Soccer. Curiously, in Britain, the NFL was struggling with a similar phenomenon in reverse, even after relaunching its foundering World League of American Football in 1995 as NFL Europe. Trudging off to see the London Monarchs remained a poor substitute for an armchair viewing of the latest big game from America. The Monarchs, and others, soon disappeared.

For the fourth straight year average MLS attendances fell, though almost imperceptibly (only about 30 fans a game) and neither ABC nor ESPN claimed any upsurge of interest as a result of the women's World Cup. The league had attracted a modest share of fans, but signs of growth were limited. 'We had this infant baby sitting in a cradle,' Doug Logan reflected. 'Everyone had taken great delight in the birth. As with newborn babies, nothing goes wrong. Everything is terrific. Everyone overlooks even the soiled diapers.'

By 1999 the mood had turned less charitable. Salary cap restrictions, league expansion and management decisions combined to ensure that many of the most recognisable names didn't stay in one place for long. John Harkes, Alexi Lalas, Tony Meola, Carlos Valderrama, Eric Wynalda, Leonel Alvarez and Roy Lassiter had all changed clubs. Raúl Díaz Arce moved three times. 'Competitive balance' further clouded the issue. MLS still assigned arriving 'marquee' players to their 'markets', a practice that produced countless allegations of favouritism and rule-bending. Yet for all its even-handed intentions, the league was still left with weak teams: in particular, San Jose, New England and its problem child, the MetroStars, who had never progressed past the first round of the play-offs and were anything but the big-city flagship franchise the league craved.

The RotMasters, as *Soccer America's* Paul Gardner termed them, appointed their fifth manager, the ever-available Bora Milutinovic, only to plummet to a new low, winning just seven of 32 matches. With gates dropping below 15,000 and the club having run through 76 players during its brief existence, Giants Stadium was now playing host to a club about as far removed from the Cosmos as it was possible to be. The acquisition of Lalas in 1998, expected to shore up both the club's defence and its fan appeal, did neither. Dismissed by one writer as 'one of the worst defenders ever to play in MLS', Lalas's celebrity value was all but exhausted. He stayed at the Meadowlands only a year and a season later announced his retirement ('I'm going to drive across the country'), though he would resurface with a vengeance in 2001.

Lalas spent the 1999 season with the Kansas City Wizards, arriving with another MetroStars cast-off, Tony Meola. But neither of the two World Cup heroes made much of an impact at the gate. The club's pitiful average of around 8,000 was for the third straight year the worst in the league, looking all the more tiny in 79,000-seat Arrowhead Stadium. An early-season losing streak brought Ron Newman's 31-year career as manager of various indoor, outdoor, professional and semi-professional teams to an unceremonious end.

His dismissal left only one manager where he had started in 1996, David Dir of the Dallas Burn, a team whose regular-season proficiency was habitually betrayed by the poor play-off form that eventually cost him his job. The Burn, like the Tampa Bay Mutiny, remained without an investor-operator and continued to be run by the league, with the anticipated ethnic support largely failing to materialise. Dallas's most impressive player was not some prized Latin import, but a Nebraska-born college product named Jason Kreis, the league's leading scorer in 1999. In Los Angeles crowds were down by nearly 25 per cent even though the Galaxy won their division for the second year in a row, while in Miami support for the expansion Fusion plummeted almost as badly.

In Columbus, though, gates were up by more than 5,000 a game, and with good reason. The Crew had made American soccer history with what MLS insisted was the country's first big-time stadium designed for the sport (the league has repeatedly dismissed the claims of the stadium Sam Mark built for Fall River in the 1920s on the grounds that neither the ASL nor the capacity of Mark's Stadium amounted to 'major league'). Unable to convince the city's taxpayers to assist, Lamar Hunt funded most of it himself. It went up in just nine months, at the modest cost of $28.5 million (the Cleveland Browns' new gridiron home would come in at ten times that amount) and with an intimate capacity of 22,500. For the self-styled 'hardest-working team in America', the stripped-down design of laudably unsponsored Columbus Crew Stadium – no roof, no enclosed concourses and only 30 glass-fronted 'club loges' – seemed appropriate. More importantly, front-row fans were now just eight feet from the touchline, no longer separated from it by the athletics track of Ohio Stadium. An overflow crowd of 24,741 saw the Crew's first match in its new home, a 2-0 win over New England. Hunt, who gave passes to 850 construction workers who had put in extra hours to ensure it would be ready in time, reflected: 'One stadium in one city and one sold-out game don't make a success, but this stadium will be here for 50 years, even if I won't be.'

The 1999 MLS Cup turned out to be a repeat of the first, with DC defeating Los Angeles in Foxboro. Two crass mistakes from a normally frugal Galaxy defence settled the outcome, but for some the selection of Foxboro Stadium, its pitch narrowed for the gridiron season, was a bigger blunder than any committed during the match. The league had declined to reconfigure the stadium to accommodate a wider pitch (saving itself $30,000) and the unyielding, furrowed surface – chewed up by an NFL battle less than a week earlier – featured a wide swathe of bare earth almost the length of the pitch. 'The ball was bouncing around like bunnies,' observed Marco Etcheverry, who once again emerged as United's play-off saviour. Harsher critics looked beyond the sorry turf. 'The incongruous image of teenage diva Christina Aguilera prancing about a stage at half-time, lip-synching her selections, personifies what MLS has been passing off as marketing,' lamented *Soccer America*, 'and many fans believe its product on the field is just as ersatz as Aguilera.'

The architect of the league's leading club begged to differ. 'I've seen a lot of teams in Europe that DC United could beat, teams that are playing in the Bundesliga and the Premiership,' Bruce Arena maintained. 'I'm not ready to tell people to get on the boat and go to Europe if you want to learn something about soccer. We know what we're doing here.'

Now Arena had the chance to prove his assertion on the biggest stage, filling the national team vacancy left by Steve Sampson. His domestic record may have been outstanding, but his international experience was confined to a mediocre showing at the 1996 Olympics, when the US went out at the group stage. With the luxury of a four-year, $2 million contract – the likes of which had never been offered to his predecessor – Arena also found himself with nearly two years to prepare his team for its first qualifying match of the 2002 World Cup.

Arena made no drastic changes in personnel, though MLS proved capable of drawing new talent to his attention. Where MLS was getting its talent from, though, became a source of grave concern. The college season remained derisively brief and continued to blunt the most promising careers, as the former college boss Arena realised: 'No one is questioning the ability of college coaches, but is the college system the right environment to develop international players? The answer is no.' While basketball and football seemed to bend over backwards for the pro leagues, college soccer disowned all obligations to MLS and profession-alism, insisting its only responsibilities were to itself and the education of its 'student-athletes'.

So began what came to be termed Project-40, a joint effort between MLS and the USSF to identify the nation's top 17- to 22-year-olds and in effect pay them not to play college soccer, offering instead a 'develop-mental' MLS contract which engaged them year-round while providing funds for further education. The bold scheme caught the universities off guard, leaving many to complain they hadn't been properly consulted. But their insular stance had scarcely merited much co-operation.

One the earliest aims of Project-40 was to produce an Under-23 team capable of success at the 2000 Olympics, yet the US unexpectedly crashed in qualifying (beaten at the final hurdle by Guatemala) and never reached Australia. A few years would pass before players such as Josh Wolff, who lasted three years at the University of South Carolina, and DaMarcus Beasley, an Indiana high school student who signed his first MLS contract two months shy of his 17th birthday, established themselves as national team mainstays. But by November 2000 the 46 players acquired by Project-40 included just 13 who had never played at a university level, suggesting the college game had little to fear. Some prodigies did slip through the programme's fingers, most notably the captain of the US Under-17 team, Landon Donovan, who ended up with Bayer Leverkusen. Though he eventually returned to MLS without playing a minute in the Bundesliga, one could hardly blame the Californian midfielder for looking overseas, since the salaries offered to Project-40 recruits were as frugal as the league's pay-scale on the whole.

Yet Europe sometimes proved as frustrating as four years of university. In 1992, Manchester United signed another Californian high schooler, Jovan Kirovski, and gave him an extensive run in their reserve team. Difficulties in securing a work permit resulted in his transfer to Borussia Dortmund, where he played only sporadically. Kirovski then wandered from club to club (Fortuna Cologne, Sporting Lisbon, Crystal Palace, Birmingham City) before somewhat unceremoniously joining MLS at the age of 28.

One source of talent remained largely untouched by Project-40 or the college system: America's enormous base of Latinos, many of whom played outside the sanctioned boundaries of 'organised' US soccer. Though about 13 per cent of the US population was Latin American, the proportion playing in MLS had never come close to that level. The USSF admitted it lacked an appropriate system for identifying and targeting Latino talent, while colleges focused their recruitment efforts on suburban high schools. More strenuous efforts had been made to attract Latino supporters, but the results were almost as disappointing. Those with backgrounds in the smaller Central American countries had a relatively sympathetic view of the league, but the more numerous Mexican-Americans saw little reason to be swayed from the *Primera División Nacional*, broadcasts of which were readily available on Spanish-language television. An MLS team largely stocked with *gringos* and playing in an unsympathetic style was hardly enticing. When the Los Angeles Galaxy sent Jorge Campos to the Chicago Fire in 1998, league officials hoped his transfer would galvanise support from Mexican-Americans there, but Campos fell out of favour with manager Bob Bradley and played just eight times before leaving the league.

While MLS struggled to pull together the disparate strands of its fan base, its clubs proved more successful at integrating with the international fraternity. DC United nearly won a second Concacaf championship in 1999, losing in the semi-finals along with the Fire in a double-header curiously staged in Las Vegas. The following season the Galaxy defeated CD Olimpia of Honduras to become only the second American club to claim the zonal crown. Though organisers continued to tinker with the format of the competition – and never finished the 2001 tournament – MLS steadfastly offered its support in spite of generally meagre rewards. The Galaxy's victory took place in front of just 8,500 in the LA Coliseum.

A similar lack of interest plagued the Open Cup, which celebrated its 85th anniversary in 1999 to typically scant attention. Its largest crowd, for any tie, was still the 21,583 who had seen the 1929 final between the Hakoah All-stars and Madison Kennel Club of St Louis. Though most MLS clubs patronised the competition – and dominated it – their fans were much less enthusiastic. As few as 1,200 saw the 1997 semi-final between the MetroStars and Burn, inexpensively staged on the campus of Columbia University in Manhattan.

Only fans of the Rochester Raging Rhinos took to the cup in a big way. But the A-League side's elimination of four MLS clubs in 1999 helped to illustrate the difficulties the USSF faced in soliciting interest in its showcase competition. Victories over Chicago and Dallas, both in front of more than 10,000 at home, put the Rhinos into the semi-finals, which the federation had consented to stage far from the grounds of any of the four participants – Colorado, Columbus, Rochester and an A-League entry from South Carolina called the Charleston Battery – at a modest new soccer-specific facility in Virginia. A tropical storm held the attendance down to less than 2,500, by which time the decision to play the final in the Crew's new stadium had already been taken. When Columbus twice failed to hold on to a lead against the Rhinos and dramatically conceded a long-range match-winning goal in injury time, hopes of a large gate for the final evaporated.

Though Rochester stood on the brink of a small piece of soccer history, the premature decision to play in what was now a neutral and largely uninterested city meant a potentially rousing final – shown live on national television for the first time – became a pitiful anticlimax. A scant 4,500 saw the Rhinos beat the Rapids 2-0 despite the absence of three regulars. 'If you can't join them, beat them' read the T-shirts of their band of rapturous fans, most of them convinced that Rochester's cup exploits (in four seasons, they had won six of nine ties against MLS opposition), together with appearances in the two most recent A-League championship games, merited 'promotion' to the higher league. What held the Rhinos back may not have been pedigree so much as facilities – their home had been built three years earlier for a minor league baseball team and held only 13,000. The club's owners promised to build a new arena, realising that for MLS soccer-specific stadiums were now *de rigueur*.

With certain exceptions. There was, for example, little chance that the Kansas City Wizards would ever leave Arrowhead Stadium, not with Lamar Hunt's family owning both. The single-entity structure in effect subsidised the rent charged to the club by the stadium corporation while allowing the Hunts to keep the car parking and concessions revenue. For similar reasons, one could see why the Kraft family did not wish to move the New England Revolution out of their NFL home in Foxboro. But where investor-operators were merely tenants, the craving for 'ancillary revenue' had grown acute. As Columbus's new facility took in money from gridiron exhibitions, pop concerts and even a lacrosse championship, the owners of the MetroStars found themselves parting with about $1 million each season for the use of Giants Stadium, while DC United insisted that the proprietors of their ground pocketed more from an MLS match there than they did. The MetroStars, Fire, Burn and Galaxy all vowed to follow Columbus in leaving their gridiron quarters, but in the search for homes of their own suffered from the vagaries of local politicians and property owners.

Having pronounced 1999 the 'year of no excuses', MLS's disappointing progress left Doug Logan in a precarious position, and he resigned before the play-offs. The man who had boldly targeted 20,000 fans a game in the happy aftermath of a promising debut season had instead presided over four straight years of gradually declining crowds and flat television ratings, a hand further weakened by his hasty pre-season dismissal of Sunil Gulati. The Krafts promptly hired Gulati to preside over their MLS interests and soon their preferred choice as Logan's successor, Don Garber, was handed the commissioner's reins.

The 42-year-old Garber was popular with the Hunts as well as the

Krafts, largely because he had spent the past 15 years working for the NFL, most recently as the successful managing director of its international division. Like Logan, he had no background in soccer (he numbered among his five immediate priorities 'developing a working knowledge of the game') but after mingling in the stands with his new customers wasted little time in endearing himself to the most traditional of them.

Within three months of his arrival, and to the cheers of purists, Garber abolished the Shootout ('We want to align our game with the rest of the world ... We do not want a contrived device to end our games'). In its place came two five-minute golden-goal periods, meaning that although America's vaunted thirst for winners would not be completely ignored, for the first time in a quarter of a century a big-league American professional soccer match could end in a draw – even a goalless one. 'We have to go back and shore up our existence with the core soccer fan,' Garber insisted. 'We do know in our research that there are approximately 60 million people in this country that consider themselves soccer fans. We don't have 60 million people going to our games.'

The league also eliminated the Americanised practice of counting down the official time on a scoreboard clock, and even toned down its garish playing strips. Garber spoke enthusiastically of expansion, including the possibility of placing a second team in the New York area to compete with the flaccid MetroStars. 'Not since the Cosmos rocked New York with one blockbuster signing after another in the mid-1970s has so much change shaken American soccer so quickly,' claimed an excited *Soccer America*.

Soon MLS revealed a blockbuster signing even the Cosmos would have been proud of, and one which the MetroStars hoped would transform their fortunes in 2000: Lothar Matthäus, Germany's veteran midfielder, who at 38 had been released by Bayern Munich yet continued to turn out for the national team as he closed in on a record 144 caps. Matthäus would earn around $1 million in salary and endorsement deals, yet the league expected to make money from his acquisition, largely through a deal with German television. To veteran reporters such as Alex Yannis of the *New York Times*, the arrival of an international superstar at Giants Stadium offered a throwback to the glamour days of the NASL:

> His introduction resembled the fanfare generated by Pelé and
> Franz Beckenbauer of the Cosmos two decades ago. Television
> cameramen and still photographers jostled for position, a crush
> of reporters asked questions in several languages and even the

food was up to Cosmos' vintage ... The thing he liked the most, Matthäus said, was that he went around asking people if they knew the name Lothar Matthäus and they said no.

Unfortunately, for most of the season Matthäus's performances were equally anonymous, the ebbing of his skills leaving behind only a towering ego. In a match against Kansas City, incensed that a foul had not been given in his favour, he spent an age remonstrating with the referee's assistant, then removed his captain's armband and threw it at him. When the assistant tossed it back, Matthäus lingered on the touchline as play continued, then took up an argument with Kansas City's manager.

The MetroStars claimed their first division crown, though they generally performed better without the 1990 European Footballer of the Year than with him. Matthäus featured in only half the club's 32 regular-season matches, partly because of his ill-fated appearance at the European Championships that summer, and partly because he had been hampered by a back injury. Told to find somewhere warm to recuperate, he was photographed with his girlfriend on the beach at St Tropez – an incident that nearly prompted his dismissal – but such high-profile antics proved irresistibly valuable to an attention-seeking league (Garber confessed that he liked how the German superstar kept MLS 'in the news'). *Soccer America* reported that Matthäus, unhappy with the rented furnishings in his New York apartment, for which MLS was paying $10,000 a month, had sent out his girlfriend to stock it with items more to his taste. His 'thirst for tufted chairs could have been tolerated,' it claimed, 'had he not played with the immobility of a leather ottoman for most of the season.'

Rather more vision and guile came from another European Footballer of the Year, Hristo Stoichkov, who broke off an eight-month retirement to join the Chicago Fire. His appearances, too, were limited by injuries and temper, but he helped the Fire to a division championship and knocked the MetroStars out of the play-offs, scoring a superb goal in the deciding match. 'I don't miss Europe at all,' he claimed. 'Life here is calm.' (Though not always. In a pre-season friendly against a university team, Stoichkov was sent off for a high tackle that broke the leg of a first-year college player in two places and forced the abandonment of the match.)

Perhaps the best import of the lot was the Tampa Bay striker Mamadou Diallo, a journeyman Malian international whose professional career had accommodated stays in Morocco, Switzerland, Turkey and Norway. Benefiting from the midfield wizardry of Carlos Valderrama, who at 36 continued to torment defences, Diallo became the league's leading scorer with 26 goals. Yet his reputation was tarnished by a collision with the MetroStars goalkeeper Mike Amman – in a one-on-one situation where it appeared he had time to avoid contact – that left Amman with a punctured lung, three broken ribs and facial bruising. The injuries helped to end Amman's career, which had included two seasons with Charlton Athletic, and effectively put Diallo out of the running for the year's Most Valuable Player award.

That honour went to Tony Meola, a name many had written off but who had been reunited with his former national team boss Bob Gansler in Kansas City. Appointed the season before, Gansler quickly turned the Wizards around with a team built, predictably enough, on a cautious defence. Meola kept 16 clean sheets during the regular season – a significant statistic to a league which insisted on assigning win-loss records to goalkeepers – and helped the Wizards to their first championship. In the MLS Cup against Chicago, he made a series of crucial saves in the final ten minutes to be named man of the match in a 1-0 win.

The Washington crowd of 39,000 had been largely starved of entertainment, but few begrudged Lamar Hunt his first soccer championship since the Dallas Tornado's invisible NASL triumph of 1971. The USSF even took the unusual decision to rename the Open Cup in honour of soccer's most benevolent sugar daddy. The 'Lamar Hunt US Open Cup (for the Dewar Trophy)' hardly tripped off the tongue, but few millionaires had stood by the game for as long as the impassive 68-year-old, still as confident about the game's future as ever. 'I believe the league will be a successful financial entity within five years,' he predicted, adding – not for the first time in his life – 'I seriously think soccer will become a major spectator sport in this country.'

Evidence to support such optimism was flimsy, with another small decline at the gate in 2000. ABC trimmed its broadcasts to just two matches, leaving the bulk of coverage on ESPN's fledgling second channel. Only about a million households watched the Wizards' title-clinching victory, but Garber remained outwardly cheerful. 'Right now it's vogue to bash MLS,' he claimed. 'I think it would have been much easier if we said initially we were expecting only 5,000 fans a game. We said 10,000 and nearly doubled that. Then we set our goal at 20,000, so 15,000 is seen as a failure.'

Arguably the most impressive area of growth had been in the labyrinth of rules, quotas and definitions the league had imposed on itself in pursuit of 'competitive balance'. The limit of four foreign players per club excluded 'youth internationals', 'transitional players' and 'youth discovery players', though only the latter two counted against the league's 19-man roster. For 2000, the selection of college, Project-40 and other hopefuls had been funnelled into what the league termed a Superdraft, a development which may have been precipitated by exasperated comments from coaches such as David Dir, who said he didn't have any problems following the rules, but 'could never find out what the rules were'.

Just how tortuous player personnel matters had become is painfully evident in this extract from a wire-service report detailing the arrival of the Mexican striker Luis Hernández:

> Under MLS' single-entity structure, all players sign contracts with the league. Players of Hernández's stature are then assigned to teams. Because the Galaxy were not due to be allocated a player, they agreed to make midfielder Clint Mathis and defender Joe Franchino available to all 11 other MLS teams for a special draft. The New York/New Jersey MetroStars had the first choice in the draft based on it having the fewest points in the league over the past 32 matches and selected Mathis. The New England Revolution then chose Franchino. The Galaxy will also have to relinquish one of their four other foreign players to stay under MLS' salary cap and foreign-player limitations. Costa Rican midfielder Roy Myers is expected to be that player, likely returning to the MetroStars, which traded him to the Galaxy last season.

With his long blond hair and eye for goal, Hernández was widely expected to rejuvenate flagging interest in the Galaxy, and 40,000 turned up in the Rose Bowl for his home debut. But he ended the day in hospital with a sprained shoulder and his MLS career proved short and woefully undistinguished.

Garber began a second full year with his debt-ridden league still bent on expansion, but most of the soccer talk in 2001 centred on the new professional circuit that had been created to capitalise on the apparent surge of interest in the women's game. Underwritten by $40 million from cable television companies – and after intense consultation with MLS, which was contemplating a league of its own – the Women's United Soccer Association received the blessing of the USSF and kicked off an inaugural 21-game season in April.

Big-time sports leagues for women were not entirely new – the Women's National Basketball Association had been around since 1996 – but they were rare, and the WUSA seemed to stem from emotion as much as solid business principles. Hardly a famous name in the American team could resist making references to dreams having come true, even if the modest salaries amounted to rather less than a college graduate might expect to earn in other professions. But money seemed to weigh less heavily on some players' minds then posterity. 'Have you ever planted a seed yourself, and it actually grows after you've watered it for months and months, and then it blossoms?' wondered Brandi Chastain. 'That's how I feel about this league.'

'The women's World Cup players have demonstrated enormous drawing power,' asserted John Hendricks, a cable TV executive who emerged as the WUSA's main benefactor. Like most American soccer entrepreneurs, Hendricks hadn't grown up with the game, but he had taken his soccer-playing children to the Atlanta Olympics, where he was overwhelmed by 'the deep connection made by most of the kids in the audience' towards the American team. 'I just knew in the stands that night that the missing ingredient was television,' he insisted, 'that if television was added, it would be overwhelming for the country.'

In fact the nation was far from overwhelmed by the eight-team, single-entity league, and television failed to nurture an audience large enough to please its advertisers. Things started brightly enough, with 34,148 in RFK Stadium watching Mia Hamm and the Washington Freedom take on a team from San Jose bewilderingly named the Bay Area CyberRays (no one, it seemed, could explain what a CyberRay was).[*] Though the WUSA would never again produce such a gate, business remained sufficiently brisk. The league had originally set itself a target of 6,500 fans a game but ended up averaging above 8,000.

Part of this could be attributed to a level of player recognition and empathy strong enough to make MLS jealous. Before a ball had been kicked, fans from coast to coast lined up behind their World Cup heroines: Hamm of the Freedom, Chastain of the CyberRays, Foudy of the San Diego Spirit, Kristine Lilly of the Boston Breakers, Carla Overbeck of the Carolina Courage, Tiffeny Milbrett of the New York Power. From the first day, as one official related to USA Today, affections ran high:

---

[*] League officials had directed WUSA teams to avoid use the of plural nicknames, presumably in the hope of creating more fashionable 'identities'. The Bay Area team ignored this advice and settled on the CyberRays, evidently in homage to the San Francisco Bay area's links with Silicon Valley and a local marine hazard, the Pacific electric ray (*Torpedo californica*). Officials had also considered calling the team the CyberLynx, but abandoned the idea after discovering a pornographic website with that name.

> At our inaugural game, Julie Foudy was on the field at halftime
> ... and Hyundai had donated a car. So Julie announces who
> won and the woman is just crying and Julie is like, 'I know, it's
> so exciting.' And the woman says, 'I don't care about the car.
> Can I have a picture of you?' The fact that she was face to face
> with this heroine for her, that's what we're about.

This was not necessarily unique to the league, or to women's soccer.
The president of the WNBA, Val Ackerman, claimed her fans had 'a very
emotional connection to the league' and supported it 'for reasons that
go beyond basketball'. Indeed, the essence of WUSA's appeal may have
had little to do with the sport itself, as John Powers of the *Boston Globe*
suggested:

> The WUSA understands that what will make the league thrive
> is not so much what the players do on the field as what they
> do off it. What made Kristine Lilly and her US teammates
> special was not so much their gold-medal soccer skills as their
> gold-medal people skills. They understood what their fans
> wanted – a smile, a handshake, an autograph, an arm-around-
> the-shoulders photo. Just a moment's intimacy that would be
> remembered for a lifetime.

More than 21,000 attended the inaugural championship game in
Foxboro, won by the CyberRays on penalties over Atlanta after an
engaging 3-3 draw. The winners took possession of a trophy which had
been named the Founders' Cup in honour of the 20 marquee players the
league had first signed – and who happened to be financial stakeholders
themselves.

Having budgeted $40 million to see it through the first five years, the
league claimed to have exhausted that amount after just one season, but
the turnstile success and overwhelmingly favourable media coverage kept
officials pointing towards prosperity. Yet many of the changes instigated
for the second season proved disastrous – particularly new television
arrangements with a less conspicuous cable network. Gates fell by 15 per
cent and the championship match, won by the Carolina Courage, was
attended by less than 16,000. Players were asked to take pay cuts of up
to 25 per cent, rosters were trimmed from 18 to 16 and league officials
searched for corporate sponsorship with increasing desperation.

As fans sobered up from their lingering 1999 hangover, a number of awkward truths came clearly into focus. It appeared that men were far more likely to be sports fans than women, and that the sports they preferred to follow were those in which males took part. Research compiled by a Los Angeles university classified 20 per cent of men as 'devoted' sports fans, compared with about 5 per cent of women, and found that broadcasts of big sporting events typically attracted twice as many males as females. Even for women's tennis or women's basketball, the majority of viewers were of the opposite sex. At least one television media buyer had asserted before the WUSA's first season that 'the biggest thing that makes soccer an attraction is nationalism' and 'nobody in this country will care about city against city'. Some, undeniably, had cared; but not enough of them, and as the league limped into its third season the women found themselves facing the same sombre realities as the men – namely, that waving the flag for a team of winners was as much as mainstream America wanted to do with soccer. A heady concoction of patriotism, proficiency and pride had turned both male and female World Cup stars into heroes and heroines; its absence relegated them back to dreary soccer players.

Marketing analysts attacked the league's strategy. Young girls, whom the WUSA had regarded as its target audience, became 'somewhat embarrassed' to identify themselves as fans once confronted with adolescence, and in any event mothers were less likely to take their kids to a sporting event than fathers. 'I was intoxicated by what I witnessed in 1999,' Hendricks confessed, 'and mistakenly assumed it would flow over.' Though some of it had, what patently had not was an appetite from well-heeled sponsors. Over three years, the league claimed it had lost close to $100 million.

When the SARS epidemic forced China to withdraw from hosting the 2003 World Cup, FIFA, flushed with happy memories of 1999, hastily reassigned the tournament to the US. Optimists expected new corporate backers to come to the WUSA's rescue, but less than a week before the start of the tournament the league announced it was folding – for the time being, it insisted. In the build-up to what should have been the highlight of the year, players and fans were left reconciling mixed emotions.

With just four months to organise the Cup, American officials were under no illusions that they would replicate the startling accomplishments of 1999. Of course, the success of USA 03 hinged largely on the performance of the American team, for whom nothing less than another world title would do. They began by destroying their Group A opposition – Sweden, North Korea and Nigeria – by a combined score of 11-1 in front

313

of healthy, if not spectacular, gates: more than 34,000 at RFK Stadium for the first victory, and a capacity 23,000 in Columbus for their third.

Under April Heinrichs, who had replaced Tony DiCicco as the team's manager shortly after the 1999 title, the team had adopted a rather less flowing and more physical style of play, exemplified by the intimidating presence of six-foot, 11½ stone Abby Wambach up front. Wambach scored the winner in a relatively easy 1-0 quarter-final victory over Norway and fans began unfurling their flags in anticipation of another championship. But a strangely subdued performance against Germany, before a full house of nearly 28,000 in Portland, Oregon, denied them the opportunity. Though the 3-0 scoreline flattered the victors, with two goals coming in stoppage time, the Germans' confident, fluid play merited a place in the final. And this time the 40 million Americans had been watching the NFL.

The stars of the American team were ageing, and many announced they would end their careers with the 2004 Olympic tournament in Greece. Attention focused particularly on the hopes of five who had appeared in the first World Cup 13 years earlier – Hamm, Foudy, Lilly, Chastain and Joy Fawcett – who together were reckoned to have made more than 1,200 appearances for their country. The 2-1 extra-time victory over a largely superior Brazil for the gold medal – witnessed by fewer than 11,000 in Athens, but carried live and without commercial interruption on American TV – represented all the closure fans could have wished for. Jim Litke of Associated Press reflected:

> It was not going to be about selling their game, the way the gold medal in Atlanta or the silver in Sydney was. Or about proving to TV, corporate sponsors and the other half of America that women athletes can draw an audience and keep it. It wasn't going to be about their coach or their sport or even their country. It was payback for all the sacrifices those five made for each other, for the long stretches away from home, for postponing marriages, careers and school.

Now there was no WUSA to tide over the devoted fans until World Cup 2007. But even after 100 years the men's game still struggled for acceptance and recognition. The women could hardly expect an easier ride.

11. Take Me Out to the Soccer-specific Facility

The 2002 World Cup and beyond

It's no coincidence that only two things happen in Italy on Sunday: church and soccer. Soccer there is not a show. It is not entertainment. And that's part of the problem for the game here. Soccer in America is never, ever going to be the same experience it is overseas. It will always be uniquely American – and that's not necessarily a bad thing.

Alexi Lalas

Just how much of a soccer nation has the United States become? It's a tricky question. Certainly the game has not managed to permeate popular culture – office conversations, school playgrounds, radio phone-ins and so forth – the way the major sports do, and it seems a long way from doing so. It has not left much of a historical imprint, either. Though catalogues of the country's greatest sporting moments are certain to include all manner of World Series and Super Bowl victories, basketball triumphs, gold-medal-winning Olympic performances and highlights from golf and tennis, they are almost as certain to exclude soccer achievements of any description. In their 2001 book *Offside: Soccer and American Exceptionalism*, Andrei Markovits and Steven Hellerman go so far as to assert that 'there is no soccer in the United States', on the basis that the vast majority of its citizens are not 'emotionally attached' to the game in the way other nations are, or as Americans are to pastimes of their own.

Others, with eyes fixed firmly on the millions of young people playing the game, are more generous. They point to how soccer has supplanted Little League baseball in many communities, and how at some high schools coaches have been forced to take rejects from the soccer team to bump up the numbers for gridiron. Young women are playing the sport in record numbers, to the extent that more female collegiates are engaged in soccer than any other competitive sport.

Perhaps an argument can be made that the US has become a soccer-playing nation. A study by the Sporting Goods Manufacturers of America claimed that almost 18 million Americans played the game at least once in 2002 – an impressive figure, though whether picnic kickabouts and parents cajoled into a few minutes' practice with a son or daughter are the activities of 'soccer players' is questionable. On a more formal level, the USSF's youth division claims three million registered participants between the ages of five and 19, with the adult division adding another 250,000. More than 20,000 high schools field interscholastic teams, turning out some 700,000 players; 2,000 colleges contribute another 40,000. And none of these figures includes the unaffiliated clubs operating under the radar.

The numbers of spectators are far less encouraging. The proportion of Americans who regularly watch the game – particularly those who do so of their own free will rather than out of family obligations, and are willing to pay an admission charge – can be charitably described as modest. MLS's average gates of around 15,000 may be the highest any American soccer league has known, but alongside the NFL's 2004 average of more than 67,000 and the 30,000 for Major League Baseball, they are not very impressive. At college level, where gridiron teams at the universities of Michigan, Tennessee and elsewhere consistently play to crowds in excess of 100,000, the disparity is even more glaring: soccer's best average in 2004 was a mere 2,385 at the University of Indiana.

Advertisers and film-makers have displayed an occasional interest in the game, but soccer's most significant contribution to American culture may have been political, in a peculiar sort of way. Many analysts claimed the election of Bill Clinton in 1992 and 1996, and possibly that of George Bush jnr in 2000, hinged on the vote of the Soccer Mom, the archetypal busy suburban mother who bundled her children into the minivan or SUV and ferried them to and from their various extracurricular activities, a woman whose political concerns were assumed to encompass everything from the quality of the local schools to the lyrical content of popular music.

None of this really suggests that the game has entered the American mainstream. A quarter of a million soccer-playing adults – less than half the number registered with the English FA – represents about 0.1 per cent of the US population. The inroads made into high schools may be impressive, but gridiron participation still surpasses boys' soccer by nearly three to one, and by about 10,000 to one in terms of public interest. Even dear old Soccer Mom has become an outmoded political demographic, supplanted by the likes of Security Mom and NASCAR Dad.

But if the measure of a soccer country is how well it has performed in international competition, and how well its best players measure up to the international elite, then the United States' progress towards nationhood looks more promising. No longer are Americans treated as a curiosities at foreign clubs, and victories over the established footballing nations of Europe and South America have become unexceptional. Many tired, decades-old questions – 'When will our country start producing international stars?', 'When will the rest of world take the US team seriously?' – have been laid to rest. There will be no more Belo Horizontes.

All this has happened with a certain inevitability. In the four decades since the start of the American participation boom, the game never lost its grip on the young. Improvements to coaching, facilities and the level of competition eventually came to yield a thin but steady stream of professional exports, just as the NASL was subsiding and attitudes in other countries towards the use of overseas players were changing (it's easy to forget that as late as 1978 foreign professionals were not allowed in the Football League). Much the same has happened to other nations with modest football histories – most conspicuously Australia, but also Canada, South Korea, Japan and, most recently, China. As American soccer entered the 21st century, all it seemed to be missing on the pitch were a few finishing touches, and in the summer of 2002, Bruce Arena provided the first of them. Unencumbered by administrative meddling or lack of confidence from the USSF, the new national manager also benefited from a hefty dose of World Cup luck.

As early as Arena's third match in charge, the wounds suffered at France 98 began to heal. In February 1999 the US beat Germany 3-0 in a friendly in Jacksonville, Florida, a surprising result magnified by the fact that all three goals were scored by German-based players. The scoreline may have reduced visiting reporters to fits of despair ('When did a German team ever get beat so badly?' lamented one) but six months later, at the Confederations Cup in Mexico, Arena beat the Germans again with almost a reserve squad. By then he had also engineered victories over Argentina and Chile.

To reach the 2002 finals meant wending a two-phase, 16-match course, but with three places again reserved for Concacaf even a middling performance was likely to suffice. Breezing through qualification rounds, though, had always been anathema to American World Cup entries, and even with the benefit of four MLS seasons and more enlightened fixture arrangement from the USSF, Arena still managed to turn what seemed fairly routine work into a disappointing struggle, in which the US almost contrived to be eliminated at the first group stage.

By now the trickle of American internationals leaving MLS for Europe had become a stream. DC United lost right-back Tony Sanneh to Hertha Berlin of the Bundesliga ('It's a better league than Major League Soccer, but I didn't necessarily play for a better team'), while Joe-Max Moore left the New England Revolution for Everton. Loaned to Preston North End, Columbus's Brian McBride received a rough welcome to the Football League: 'It was five minutes into my first game. It was a 75-25 ball I knew I wasn't going to get, but I wanted to make sure the fans and team-mates knew I wasn't afraid to get involved in a little collision.' Complications from the blood clot he suffered kept him out for five months. Another member of the Crew, Brad Friedel, famously signed for Liverpool in 1997, though the move came to little. By 2000 Graeme Souness had taken him to Blackburn Rovers, where his star shone much more brightly.

Through to the final qualifying phase, the USSF at last succeeded in weaning itself away from the money-spinning tradition of staging home fixtures with Mexico in Los Angeles. They opted instead for chilly Columbus, where Latino support was far more limited. The federation's bold thinking reaped the reward of a full stadium virtually devoid of Mexican support, and a 2-0 victory. There was even greater satisfaction after an unexpected win in Honduras. Though far from emphatic (the deciding goal came in the 86th minute), a 2-1 victory put them in pole position for Japan and South Korea, even if Arena still insisted: 'I think this is going to get crazy.'

It did. After the traditional defeat in Mexico City – 1-0 this time, with Claudio Reyna suspended and Ajax's John O'Brien absent after the club threatened to bench him for the rest of the season if he went – and a 3-2 home loss to Honduras, the Americans' three-point advantage disappeared. The Honduras match, forced by ESPN to kick off at 10am because of college gridiron commitments, was the first qualifier lost at home since Costa Rica had knocked the US out of the 1986 World Cup. 'Give our guys credit, they never quit,' Arena reflected. 'They were running around like a bunch of idiots, but they didn't quit ... idiots with a heart.'

The more easily outraged supporters began to throw stones at the manager, with suspicions festering that Arena had succumbed to the college coach's preoccupation with tactics and formations. When Costa Rica claimed an emphatic 2-0 home win in one of the US's bogey grounds, the 'Monster's Cave' of Estadio Saprissa, detractors scornfully pointed to what they construed as a seven-man defence. A month later, an 81st-minute penalty from Moore gave the US a vital 2-1 win against Jamaica in Foxboro. But the best news was yet to come: the Mexico-Costa Rica match had ended goalless and Trinidad & Tobago had inconceivably won in Honduras. The unlikely combination of results – so improbable no one had thought to bring along any champagne – meant the Americans qualified with a game to spare.

A few months later, with nerves soothed, the US claimed their first Gold Cup since the inaugural event 11 years earlier, with a performance far more persuasive than their qualifying form had suggested. By now Arena had largely made up his mind about who would be going to Korea, and few eyebrows were raised at his final selection: 11 from MLS, six from the English leagues and six from elsewhere in Europe. Their average age, close to 29, was greater than that of the team's oldest player at Italia 90, yet it still included 20-year-old Landon Donovan, whom Leverkusen had loaned to San Jose for the summer, and 19-year-old DaMarcus Beasley, the ten-stone prodigy of the Chicago Fire.

But the man who drew more of the media attention was, inevitably, nearer to New York: Clint Mathis, the 25-year-old MetroStars striker whose clinical finishing had turned heads during the team's run-in. *Sports Illustrated* chose the Georgia-born Mathis for the front of their World Cup preview issue, name-dropping Bayern Munich as a potential suitor while focusing on his desire to play in the Premiership ('he already knows his way around a proper English breakfast, since it resembles the traditional Southern breakfast his mother cooks for him'). 'My life could change drastically after two months,' Mathis observed hopefully.

When the draw for Korea-Japan was made, odds-makers rated the US as the usual hundreds-to-one outsiders, well aware that the Yanks had not won a World Cup match on foreign soil since 1950. 'We're not going to win [the Cup] because we're not a good enough team,' Arena freely conceded. 'I don't think anyone is going to be damaged by us saying that. I mean, how many countries have ever won it?' Yet he was not about to dismiss his chances of reaching the second round. 'If we can get a point in the first game, it will put the whole group in chaos.' Few imagined the chaos that would follow.

At a press conference shortly before the opening match against Portugal, Arena bet journalists that none of them could name the 11 players he would start with. An injured Reyna gave way to 25-year-old Pablo Mastroeni of the Colorado Rapids, with only a handful of caps to his name, while Mathis was left out, ostensibly over fitness concerns. Most surprising of all, both Beasley and Donovan were in. It was a calculated risk, and a combination of players the manager had never used before.

Four minutes into the match, O'Brien provided an early pay-off.

Hurrying and harassing Portugal's 'golden generation' over the next half-hour, the Americans turned his goal into a 3-0 advantage, a scoreline tinged with fantasy. 'After the first goal, I didn't really celebrate, I just jogged back,' Mastroeni recalled. 'The second goal, same thing. But after the third goal, it was like, "This is for real".'

Not since 1930 had a US team scored three times in the World Cup, but a quick response from Beto Severo and a 70th-minute own-goal from the luckless Jeff Agoos ('one of the finest ever to grace the World Cup', according to one account) left them hanging on for 20 minutes. Emerging with a victory few could have imagined, the US suddenly found themselves on course for the second round. 'The whole world thought we were going to lose,' claimed Friedel, who had narrowly wrenched the goalkeeping position away from Tottenham's Kasey Keller. 'But we thought we were going to win.'

South Korea's defeat of Poland threw the group wide open. Now the two underdogs met in Taegu in front of 60,000 excitable fans, all seemingly dressed in Korean red, with a place in the second round waiting for the winners. Mastroeni and Stewart made way for Reyna and Mathis, and once again Arena's changes reaped a generous reward. In a new haircut which a *New York Times* correspondent compared to 'David Beckham circa 2001 or Travis Bickel, the Robert de Niro character in *Taxi Driver*', Mathis scored the lone American goal. But the team leaned heavily on Friedel, who blocked a first-half penalty and twice denied Seol Ki-Hyeon with breathtaking saves. Only a second-half header from Ahn Jung-Hwan beat him, a goal celebrated with the famous speed-skating routine that referred to a controversial incident at the Salt Lake City Winter Olympics earlier in the year. Even though the Americans had played poorly, Arena's stock was rising. One Italian journalist described his team as 'beautifully organised – like a European power, like Real Madrid'. Not everyone gushed so effusively, but now even the haughtiest British journalist could not reject out of hand the former lacrosse coach's desire to manage in the Premiership.

But two goals in the first five minutes from already-eliminated Poland sent his team perilously close to going out as well. Decisively beaten, 3-1, only a breathtaking volley from Park Ji-Sung in Korea's match against Portugal kept them in the tournament. American World Cup campaigns had produced some odd twists and turns, but here was perhaps the strangest of all – one which, Arena joked, had sent him to the shops the next morning in search of thank-you gifts. Few sniped at the manager now. Supporters had frequently defended him by pointing to his 'winning percentage' which, as far as these things went, was the best in national team history. But, with a helping of good fortune, he had also proved himself when it mattered most.

Paired against Mexico for a place in the quarter-finals, the US came up with an inspiring performance against their bitterest rivals: a 2-0 victory in Chonju, fashioned by an early goal from McBride and a second-half header from the impressive Donovan. In between, the Mexicans had controlled much of the possession and might have had a penalty – and probably a man advantage – after O'Brien appeared to punch a shot clear with his hand. Strewn with ten yellow cards and one red, the match did not yield much vintage football, but few agreed with Javier Aguirre's claim that his Mexico side had simply been unlucky.

Four years earlier, the tactics of Steve Sampson in France had been condemned as the product of a college manager who believed internationals could be won with radical formations and team changes. Arena tinkered even more compulsively – he had already used 18 of his 19 fit outfield players – but for him virtually every change seemed to click. Against Mexico he gave a World Cup debut to defender Gregg Berhalter of Crystal Palace, playing him alongside Eddie Pope, a former college team-mate, to great effect. Eddie Lewis, whose appearances for Fulham had been largely confined to the reserves, was also in from the start for the first time, and his cross produced the clinching goal. Donovan, one of the few ever-presents, had been asked to play in a different position in every match, but seemed to thrive in each of them. Even the agonising decision to leave out Keller was vindicated, since in Friedel the Americans possessed perhaps the best goalkeeper in the tournament.

Had the manager's uncanny acumen suddenly thrust the US into the higher echelons of world football? 'Not even close,' he insisted. 'We're not pretending to be at the same level as the established teams, but the gap has closed considerably.' In the quarter-final against Germany in Ulsan, the narrowness of the gap was there for all to see. The *Washington Post* maintained the US 'had out-run, out-shot and out-played the Germans on nearly every count but the final score'; the *Boston Globe* said they 'played the three-time champions off their feet for most of the evening'. Others claimed the victors had merely sat back, absorbed the pressure and waited for the right moment: a 39th-minute free-kick headed into the net by Michael Ballack. But a different referee might have given the US a penalty when Berhalter's volley struck Torsten Frings on the arm, and on another day Sanneh's 87th minute header would have levelled the score instead of sailing inches wide. The Americans had stood toe-to-toe with their more celebrated opponents and found themselves separated largely by the amazing performance of Oliver Kahn in goal.

Arena accepted the Frings incident with a poise not normally associated with losing World Cup managers. Perhaps coming from a country which had largely been asleep – literally – throughout the tournament, it was easier to accept defeat graciously. 'It's nice to hear all the praise that we played well and we should have won, could have won, this call, that call', he added. 'But the bottom line is we should have won.'

Not many American sportswriters put in an appearance in Korea. Only 15 newspapers bothered to send reporters, far fewer than had travelled to France four years earlier. But for the handful of veterans on hand in Ulsan that night, among them George Vecsey of the *New York Times*, the rewards were unexpected:

> Three German sportswriters packed up their laptops and stopped by our little American cluster. 'You guys outplayed us,' one of them said. 'You should have won.' 'One-nothing,' I said. 'Germany won.' I know these guys – good colleagues, always willing to explain the sport to bumpkins from the New World, like me. But there is no code of effusive sportsmanship in a soccer press room, only pragmatic judgements of who played well and who did not. From Old Europe came the rather startling possibility that the United States is now a player.

Nearly four million American households had stirred themselves early that morning to watch the live transmission, with commentary piped in from a studio in Connecticut. It may not have matched the 40 million who three years earlier had spent a Sunday afternoon watching the US women edge China in Pasadena, but it was more than had ever seen a soccer match on ESPN before, and it eclipsed all the station's big-league baseball telecasts that summer. Once again, though, interest peaked with the performance of the American team. More than a million fewer households bothered with ABC's broadcast of the final.

For as long as anyone could remember, it had been customary for any significant development in American soccer to be detailed not just for its own sake, but in terms of its impact on the future of the game. This was as true as ever in the summer of 2002. The World Cup performance was not merely to be celebrated, it had to mean something for soccer's march on the national conscience. Eight years earlier, in the run-up to USA 94, Ann Killion of the *San Jose Mercury News* had lamented sagely that 'we won't be allowed to simply enjoy the event ... every TV rating, opinion poll and ticket sale will be sliced and diced and analysed ...' Not much had changed since then: a large crowd, a budding star or a World Cup victory was still as much a means to an end as an end in itself.

Many, then, busily plotted their lines from Korea towards the ultimate 'goal', which seemed to be MLS muscling up to the level of the 'big three' professional leagues, or at least reaching the less dizzy heights of the NHL. World Cup success didn't send the MLS turnstiles spinning, but Don Garber's preoccupation with the 'core fan', together with a decision to reduce the number of midweek fixtures, had already reaped modest rewards. In 2001 the league managed to celebrate its first increase in average attendance, and gates went up again the following year. Yet there were some puzzling anomalies. The 2001 champions were San Jose – no longer the Clash but the more nostalgic Earthquakes – whose gates dropped by nearly a quarter that season to become the lowest of any club: 9,600. And the league still carried more than a whiff of gimmickry. The highlight of the season, some claimed, was a farcical All-Star game that ended 6-6 and saw Donovan and Miami's Jim Rooney remove their shirts after scoring to reveal Brandi Chastain-style sports bras.

Those in MLS who still regarded the march toward sporting prominence as mostly a matter of marketing bluster were made to think twice that year. The latest pro gridiron venture, the XFL, launched by wrestling tycoon Vince McMahon, lasted all of one season before collapsing. With McMahon's name, a prime-time network TV contract and a surfeit of soft-porn cheerleaders, many expected the likes of the Los Angeles Xtreme and Memphis Maniax to titillate the same American public that had responded so fanatically to the spectacle of McMahon's wrestling events. But the XFL's combination of showmanship and skin proved a surprising failure. In much the same way MLS was looked down upon by those enamoured of the big European soccer leagues, the XFL drew unfavourable comparisons with its more established rival.

Garber insisted his league was not only staying put, but going places. Yet after the 2001 season it opted to contract, removing itself from an area of the country once considered crucial. Despite enjoying its best season on the pitch and at the gate, the Miami Fusion had lost too much money – $50 million – for its investor-operator, telecommunications magnate Ken Horowitz. Across the peninsula, the Tampa franchise was also disbanded, the league-run Mutiny having set a new MLS low by winning just four matches that season. Combined with the departure of Carlos Valderrama to Colorado and a scandal involving the embezzlement of

$100,000, it made for a wretched year. Overtures failed towards Malcolm Glazer, whose NFL team played in the same new $169 million Raymond James Stadium as the Mutiny. Glazer had cast a predatory eye across the Atlantic towards the altogether more tempting proposition of Manchester United, and by May 2005 he would controversially acquire a controlling interest in the club.

Down to its original size of ten teams, MLS seemed to be back where it started. 'I know many out there think this is the end of Major League Soccer, and that couldn't be further from the truth,' Garber insisted. 'It's something we feel is a new, strong beginning.' After the Los Angeles Galaxy had clinched the 2002 MLS Cup in front of a record crowd for the fixture, 61,316, it was tempting to sympathise with that view. For the first time, all the clubs in an American soccer league had averaged more than 10,000 fans, and most had exceeded 15,000. Part of this could be attributed to a remarkable level of parity (just 19 points separated the best and worst teams). Beneath the veneer, though, lay a familiar bedrock of transience. The size of the MLS Cup crowd, for instance, was due almost entirely to the presence of the home-town New England Revolution, and the *Boston Globe* for one noted that 'two months ago most of the people in Gillette Stadium couldn't have named three players on the [team], but yesterday they were claiming them as their own, and feeling their pain.'

Two of the Galaxy's most visible players helped to keep the trophy in California: Guatemalan international Carlos Ruiz, whose 24 goals made him the league's leading scorer, and a rejuvenated Alexi Lalas, *sans* goatee. It was an overdue achievement for a club finally claiming the title after losing in three previous finals, and which now replaced the slumping DC United as the league's most formidable side.

Further east, the multi-billionaire Philip Anschutz, a staunch conservative with close ties to Vice-President Dick Cheney, increased his holding to five clubs, buying the MetroStars and DC United to leave him in charge of half the league. Quite how a man once described by *Fortune* magazine as 'the nation's greediest executive' had come to place his faith in a sport few had made money from was difficult to fathom. Some pointed to a track record of extracting profit from opportunities rivals failed to identify – 'he has made his career out of proving others wrong,' Garber boasted – but as the cost of propping up teams playing in oversized stadiums with hefty rental fees began to bite, Anschutz soon reduced his portfolio.

With progress on soccer-specific grounds largely confined to drawing boards, other clubs felt the same sort of pinch. The MetroStars combed

Harrison, New Jersey, in search of a refuge from pricey Giants Stadium, while the Dallas Burn thought they would be moving into a new home in nearby McKinney, Texas, only for local officials to change their mind about helping them build it. The Burn spent a disastrous 2003 season playing in a 13,000-seat high school facility, which curbed their attendance by nearly 40 per cent. The Chicago Fire looked as though they might have no home at all after Soldier Field was earmarked for a refurbishment to pacify the NFL Bears. Sent away for nearly two seasons, the Fire had to make do with a small college facility in suburban Naperville and a tiny artificial pitch.

The lone breakthrough was one Anschutz helped to broker on the west coast. In the industrial suburb of Carson, 30 miles south of the enormous Rose Bowl – a stadium so large even its famous college gridiron tenant rarely filled it – the Los Angeles Galaxy took possession of a new purpose-built stadium in 2003. Part of a $150 million complex that also included a velodrome, an athletics track and a tennis arena, the inevitable 'naming rights' were sold to a DIY chain with no obvious link to sport. Yet the appeal of the Home Depot Center was hard for most fans to resist: a cosy 27,000-seat rectangular stadium decidedly upmarket from the facility in Columbus, boasting 42 luxury suites, a further 1,500 'club seats' and a restaurant overlooking the pitch. Its appeal was such that the organisers of the 2003 Women's World Cup had forsaken larger grounds to stage the final there. 'If the Los Angeles Galaxy don't make money this season, then maybe there's just none to be made in professional soccer in the United States,' concluded one writer. They did, just, but manager Sigi Schmid was among those who appreciated a longer-term significance. 'It means we are putting down roots, that we're not a temporary situation,' he declared. 'You don't build a stadium like this and in two years hang it up.' The new surroundings failed to stop Schmid's team from slumping to the worst record of their eight-year existence, yet average regular-season gates of nearly 22,000 – the highest figure anyone had managed since the league's first season – kept their new home pleasantly full.

Such enthusiasm remained elusive in San Jose, whose own stadium had been built in 1933. Even though the Earthquakes claimed a second MLS Cup in 2003, their gates continued to hover around 10,000. Local fans were strangely ambivalent towards a team far more successful than its NASL namesake, their frame of mind all the more puzzling since in Landon Donovan they possessed one of the most marketable players in the league. Having become only the second manager to win the championship more than once, San Jose's Frank Yallop emulated Bruce Arena by becoming manager of a national team, though in trying to get Canada to the 2006 World Cup the one-time Ipswich Town defender could not duplicate Arena's international success. The Canadians were eliminated after finishing bottom of their second-round qualifying group.

For most of America, soccer in 2003 didn't mean MLS so as much as it meant Freddy Adu, the precocious Ghanaian teenager who had moved to the US after his family won an immigration lottery and who burst on to the US sports scene in a blaze of publicity. After signing him for $500,000 (half the amount Nike had already paid for his services), DC United issued 315 press passes for their first match of the season, in which the centre of attention, two months short of his 15th birthday, obligingly came on as a substitute to give the league a welcome publicity coup. Not since 1887 had someone so young played for an American professional team.

Apparently more significant for MLS's credibility was Tim Howard's move from the MetroStars to Manchester United. While Keller, Friedel and Reyna had all become established Premiership material, none had struck gold with the country's most prominent club. Still looking for an heir to Peter Schmeichel, United had been impressed by Howard on a close-season tour, and for $3.6 million in the summer of 2003 they helped to break down one of the last frontiers of American soccer: a home-grown, MLS-bred product with no links to the mother country and no previous European experience had been hunted down by one of the biggest teams in the world. But after a spectacular first season in which he displaced Fabien Barthez and became the first American to secure an FA Cup winner's medal, the New Jerseyan's form slumped and he soon found himself in the reserves.

Howard was far from the league's first sizeable export – Friedel had left after its first season and the Trinidadian striker Stern John moved from Columbus to Nottingham Forest in 1999 – but his departure came at a time when MLS was redoubling its efforts to nurture and retain younger talent. There were exceptions, the most infamous being DC United's flirtation with Paul Gascoigne in 2002. 'It's the promise of magic ... you may be reaching into the fire, but it may be worth it,' a club official admitted. (It wasn't.) And there was still a liberal helping of veterans such as the evergreen Preki Radosavljevic of Kansas City, who defied his 40 years to claim the league's Most Valuable Player award in 2003. But by and large MLS had grown younger as it grew older. At the end of the 2003 season, more than two dozen players with at least 100 appearances left the league, dropping the average age below 26 for the first time.

Worryingly, some on their way out were established internationals. Hanover 96 signed Clint Mathis, DaMarcus Beasley headed for PSV Eindhoven and Landon Donovan returned to Bayer Leverkusen, a move again fated to end in disappointment. These players should have represented the future of the league, but investor-operators were loath to compete in the global market. Shep Messing, the nonconformist-goalkeeper-turned-agent, was all too familiar with the wage disparity. 'I have a lot of clients in Europe who would love to play in MLS,' he claimed. 'But after I explain what MLS pays, they say, "OK, I'll visit there on vacation."'

DC United claimed their fourth MLS Cup in 2004 with the league's youngest championship team. Two goals from 22-year-old striker Alecko Eskandarian, son of the famous Cosmos defender, led them to victory over Bob Gansler's Kansas City Wizards. Another former US coach, Steve Sampson, had joined Los Angeles after two years in charge of Costa Rica. Chastened by his experiences in France ('I was not as seasoned as I needed to be … at the time, I felt I had all the tools'), Sampson took the Galaxy to within 90 minutes of the championship game.

In other seasons, he might have been more fortunate. The league made the curious decision to reduce the 2004 semi-finals to the same one-off, winner-take-all match as the final, while keeping the quarter-final round two-legged. The aggregate system (though not quite the one practised elsewhere; away goals didn't count double) had produced a memorable semi-final the year before – a 5-4 aggregate win by San Jose over the Galaxy after trailing 4-0 from the first leg, one of the most memorable contests in league history – but for some this had represented just another reason to loathe soccer. 'Imagine a world in which you could lose the final game of your postseason series – and advance,' bellowed one soccer-phobic columnist. 'That's the world of MLS. In any postseason in any sport anywhere, all that matters is that you win; in MLS, all that matters is how much you win by. This isn't just un-American, it's downright inhuman.'

Of course, the league had embraced other more American practices which seemed even less rational – most notably, deciding its champions through a play-off system, a concept so deeply embedded in American sport few could contemplate anything different. And in allowing eight of the ten teams to participate, it continued to render six months of regular-season matches almost meaningless, with 30 games resolving the fate of only two teams. Persisting with play-offs seemed to run counter to the league's policy of targeting the hard-core soccer fans who, among other

things, preferred 0-0 draws to Shootouts (in 2004, MLS boldly eliminated extra time from regular season play altogether).

The play-off system alone may not have been enough to turn away
prospective fans, yet soccer snobs remained aloof and even hostile to a
league they regarded as second-rate. Looking down one's nose at MLS,
caustically referring to it as Minor League Stupidity or even Mostly Like
Shit, had become a popular pastime for those enamoured of the televised
glamour of the European leagues. To elitists swathed in imported replica
jerseys, the performance of Manchester United, Juventus or Barcelona,
religiously tracked via the internet and cable TV, was of far greater consequence than anything they could buy a ticket for.

Millions of Americans with only a passing interest in soccer were now
familiar with David Beckham, who had never so much as kicked a ball
in the US, and the red jersey of his principal employers. United were, as
American reports unfailingly termed them, 'the New York Yankees of
soccer', a connection cemented in 2001 when the two clubs reached a
marketing and merchandising agreement. In 2003 Manchester United
arrived in the US for a series of midsummer friendlies, christened
ChampionsWorld, between some of the most recognisable club 'brands'.
The football significance of these contests was virtually nil, but their
turnstile appeal was almost without precedent.

Despite charging as much as $125 a ticket for essentially meaningless
games, the four US fixtures the Premiership champions appeared in
that summer attracted more fans than nine of the ten MLS clubs could
manage across their entire season. Though Beckham had been sold to
Real Madrid and missed the trip, nearly 67,000 flocked to Seattle's new
$300 million stadium for United's first match, a 4-0 win over Celtic. 'Fans
savored the spectacle', noted one report, observing how they 'turned the
stadium into a giant bowl of twinkling flashbulbs every time a player
fired a free kick'. Plenty more twinkling followed. More than 57,000
turned up at the LA Coliseum for United's exhibition with Mexico's
Club America; a duel with Juventus drew 79,000 to Giants Stadium; and
68,396 saw them baptise Philadelphia's new $512 million stadium with
a victory against Barcelona.

Was this a boost for US soccer, or a kick in the teeth? In some ways,
things had changed little since the original ASL had sputtered to a halt
during the Great Depression. The American fan was still attracted to
foreign clubs playing under summer skies, not the season-long grind
of workaday teams with largely unknown players. The intensity of the
promotion may have changed, but watching an exhibition between

Barcelona and AC Milan – as 45,864 did in Washington that summer – still sold tickets in a way bona fide competition did not.

In the 1980s, the NASL had staged a Trans-Atlantic Challenge Cup between two of its top clubs and two from overseas, and crowds of 30,000 or more showed up in Giants Stadium to watch the likes of Roma and Fluminense play the Cosmos, at a time when the league's gates were falling. MLS failed to devise an equivalent – one which, aside from the obvious financial considerations, might have helped to establish its credibility in the eyes of the more disparaging fan. But the ChampionsWorld clubs and impresarios, which included Giorgio Chinaglia, saw little to be gained from playing American teams, and they returned in 2004 to continue their spectacular plunder.

In deciding where and how to expand its humble footprint, MLS pinned its hopes not on star-studded exhibitions or high-profile acquisitions but on finding permanent homes for its members. 'I would much rather invest in brick and mortar that will be around for 50 years,' maintained Don Garber, 'than have what people perceive as the fix in terms of players.' But the expansion of the league by two clubs for 2005 involved building only one new facility. The other entrant would share a stadium, and take the league in a new and contentious direction.

In August 2004 Jorge Vergara, the owner of Mexican League club Deportivo Guadalajara (known as Chivas), was granted an MLS franchise aimed overtly at enticing the elusive Mexican-American fan. Funding a team for MLS, which borrowed the Chivas nickname, sent a comforting message to league officials about the viability of their operation. Yet what was initially expected to be a victory for the city of Houston (teeming with Latinos and with a disproportionately high audience for MLS telecasts) or San Diego (close to the Mexican border), evolved into a novel proposition for Carson, California. Not since the ill-fated year of 1967 had two professional soccer teams used the same ballpark, but the Galaxy would now share their home with Chivas USA, sparing the league the expense of hiring one elsewhere.

That decision, combined with Chivas's Latino-conscious marketing strategy (slogan: 'Goodbye soccer, hello futbol'), appeared to push the Galaxy down a more Anglocentric path. But it soon emerged that loyalties did not necessarily follow ethnic lines. Many Latinos, especially those who weren't Mexican-Americans, saw no need to shift loyalties. Criticised in some quarters for fielding what appeared to be a reserve Mexican League team, Chivas finished bottom of their division and well out of the play-off race. Though their average gate of 17,000 was reasonably healthy, it was distorted by a crowd of 88,816 in the Coliseum for a 'Night of the Super Clasicos', a double-header that included a friendly between Vergara's Guadalajara and the immensely popular Club America of Mexico City.

The other newcomer, operating out of a market no larger than Columbus, was just as much of a surprise: Salt Lake City, Utah. For a $1 million deposit and the promise to build a soccer-specific facility, a consortium of investors headed by Dave Checketts, a former pro basketball executive, trumped several more likely candidates (among them Cleveland, which dropped out after its likely owner died during the preparation of a bid). Oddly, the franchise was christened Real Salt Lake, apparently an appeal to the international grounding of the core fan, and one which could scarcely have been more different to the Rowdies, Roughnecks and Rogues of the NASL.

With the emergence of Real Salt Lake – spelled ReAl on the logo as a pronunciation aid – it seemed the professional game was coming full circle. The days of clubs unashamedly named Eintracht and Hispano had eventually given way to more self-conscious entries purporting to be Americans or Nationals, with the professional renaissance of 1967 attempting to drive the sport further into the mainstream. Now things had swung in the other direction, but in an odd sort of way. 'ReAl Salt Lake' had no connections to royalty or any Spanish heritage (Utah's Spanish-speaking population is well below the national average). Its name was just as much a fabrication as the two Zs of the city's minor-league entry, the Utah Blitzz.

Foreignness, it seems, is now hip. For 2005, the Burn ditched MLS's silliest remaining nickname and rebranded itself simply FC Dallas, replacing its fire-breathing horse with a Texas steer. An imminent move to a $65 million, soccer-specific facility in the suburbs – lamentably christened Pizza Hut Park – convinced Lamar Hunt, the team's new investor-operator, that it was 'the ideal time to unveil a team name that is more synonymous with the sport', even if one wire service report still saw the need to mention that 'FC is short for Football Club'.

Of course, expansion is no indication of prosperity, and the league cannot necessarily bank on the unwavering support of its two most committed patrons, Anschutz and Hunt. When taxpayers in Kansas City voted in a referendum against paying for improvements to Arrowhead Stadium, Hunt put the Wizards up for sale, diplomatically claiming that he 'did not fully recognise [soccer-specific facilities] as a primary need when the league started'. By then Anschutz had divested himself of the Rapids (sold to a billionaire property developer with NBA, NFL and NHL interests), and announced DC United and San Jose were available as well. Just about every other big city in the country, as well as some in Canada, has been spoken of as a potential MLS market, meaning the possibility of an NASL-style franchise merry-go-round – something the league has commendably avoided thus far – still exists. So does another purge of less promising teams.

The rechristened Dallas reached the Open Cup final, where they lost away to the Galaxy, but played host to the 2005 MLS Cup, and Pizza Hut Park filled to its modest 21,000 capacity for a match between teams with contrasting regular-season form. New England, managed by ex-Liverpool defender Steve Nicol, had accrued the most points in its history, while Los Angeles, limping into the play-offs with the fewest of the eight qualifying teams, had spent much of the summer contemplating the future of Steve Sampson.

Yet on the back of a few play-off victories – including an upset of San Jose, who had finished 19 points in front of them in the Western Conference – and a narrow extra-time win over the Revolution in the final, the Galaxy claimed an improbable double, boosted by the arrival of Donovan from Leverkusen (he made it a condition of his return that MLS assign him to Los Angeles). The Most Valuable Player award went to St Louis-born Taylor Twellman of the Revolution, whose 17 goals made him the league's leading scorer. He, too, had spent a joyless time in the Bundesliga – in two seasons he never appeared in Munich 1860's first team – and cited the September 11 terrorist attacks as a determining factor in his return home ('I suggested the players wear black armbands ... the coach said I must be nuts').

'If we didn't have a professional league in the United States, I don't know where we'd be today,' remarked Bruce Arena as the league completed its tenth season. But the grim years following the collapse of the NASL offer a pretty good clue. Aspiring to create 'the fifth major league sport in America' is still regarded by many as a pipe dream, if not an outright impossibility. Yet depending on how 'major league' is defined, this may already have happened. Surviving for a decade is in itself some kind of success. The number of teams is growing, as is the number of top-quality American players and maybe even fans who will sit through a 0-0 draw of their own free will. A survey conducted by *USA Today* in early 2004 indicated that less than five per cent of the country was 'very interested' in MLS (more than 74 per cent said they were 'not at all interested'), but five per cent amounts to about 15 million people, close to the population of the Netherlands.

The league still faces a long, uphill road, but most of its steps seem to have been in the right direction, and rarely has it cast its gaze too high into the heavens. No doubt it has learned from the NASL not to make Phil Woosnam-style pronouncements about overtaking the NFL or turning the US into the centre of the football world. Rival leagues may not currently be in the rudest of health – a players' strike cancelled the entire 2004-05 pro ice hockey season – but all are such integral parts of the sporting landscape it is hard to imagine any of them losing their grip. Thus, while disappointing ratings prompted ABC-TV to end its 36-year association with the NFL's *Monday Night Football* in 2005, ESPN quickly stepped in with $8.8 billion for an eight-season helping of its own. It is likely to be a very long time before MLS is offered that kind of money – or appears on network TV during peak viewing hours.

Generating a large TV audience remains the league's biggest challenge. It's one compounded by the attitude of US broadcasters, whose indifference and ineptitude quickly becomes apparent to anyone switching over to Spanish-language coverage of the Mexican League. Almost 40 years after CBS first brought it into the country's living rooms, television still hasn't figured the sport out. Soccer continues to be presented as if it were gridiron, despite the fact that its near-continuous play does not lend itself to the interruptions of the padded game (pre-recorded interviews, recaps of earlier highlights, diagrams of 'plays' on screen), nor to such frivolous baggage as the 'field reporter', whose generally desperate attempts to contribute something useful from the touchlines serve mainly to disrupt the flow of play. Commentary remains woefully rudimentary, even amateurish. Though many 'play-by-play' men have become adept at shouting very loudly into the microphone during goal-scoring opportunities – presumably in an effort to convey 'passion' for the game, like their Spanish-speaking counterparts – they often fail in the more essential tasks of correctly identifying players, the reason for a foul or even the direction a free-kick has been given. The reason soccer ratings remain pitifully low may not be entirely down to the sport itself.

MLS has pursued the construction and ownership of soccer-specific stadiums as its holy grail, and over the next few seasons the majority of teams are likely to find themselves in homes of their own. This may be the most honest evidence of a long-term commitment to the sport, and it's certainly one of the most positive developments American soccer has known. But whether owning one's own turf makes a significant difference to the bottom line is yet to be seen. Six years on from the first match in Columbus Crew Stadium, the league is still losing an awful lot of money and there is no empirical evidence that fabulous riches await the billionaire willing to underwrite the construction of a modest stadium or two.

The best hope for MLS may be in developing itself as a niche professional league, one that grows without attempting to compete with its more celebrated rivals. Markovits and Hellerman suggest in *Offside* that precedent has been set by other recent developments in American consumerism:

> Certain aspects of American culture have become uniform across this vast continent as never before. Yet, an equally impressive array of identity-forming experiences have undergone processes of fragmentation and segmentation that are new ... Bagels, café latte and microbrewed beers have not replaced doughnuts, Maxwell House instant coffee, and Budweiser beer in contemporary America; rather, these products and their cultures have found a relatively comfortable way of coexisting in America's consumption space. However, this space either got larger or much more diverse – or most likely both – in the course of the last two decades of the twentieth century. The world of sports mirrors both these processes.

Some have argued that the league's modest existence could even be turned into a selling point, that the huge amounts of money and avarice swirling around big-time American sport have alienated large numbers of fans. The biggest stars of MLS are more approachable than those in other sports and figure much more rarely in arrests, 'substance abuse' and other foibles. But the idea that hordes of disillusioned baseball fans would warm to soccer primarily out of despair seems no less fanciful than thousands of jaded British football fans suddenly discovering basketball. Others maintain that until MLS begins to compete on a global scale for top international talent, well-behaved or otherwise, interest will remain scant. This, though, is an attitude not far removed from the one that brought the New York Cosmos to prominence 30 years ago, one that certainly helped to popularise the game but also sowed the seeds of the NASL's extinction.

Of course, soccer in America has moved on considerably since then, and perhaps nowhere have the past 30 years brought about greater change than with the national team. The US qualified for the 2006 World Cup with two games to spare, having lost only one of their 16 matches (away to Mexico, of course) and won every meaningful contest at home. They scored in every game, claimed victory by two or more goals eight times, and never showed any sign of losing their way. Only with qualification assured were Bruce Arena's team required to enter the Monster's Cave – they lost, 3-0, but with a weakened team. 'You'll look back on it and say it's real easy and it's a breeze,' Arena reflected. 'But it's not a breeze. It's very difficult.'

Not nearly as difficult, though, as it once had been. Even a fourth-place finish in the final group of six now earned a play-off berth with an Asian representative, and few doubted that the most half-hearted American performance was capable of that. The question was never really whether the US would make it to Germany for 2006, it was what they would do once they got there. Never, in six decades of qualifying, had presumption reached such giddy levels.

Of the slew of hopeful newcomers, one in particular made a breath-taking impact. Dallas's Eddie Johnson scored five times in his first three internationals, including a 17-minute hat-trick against Panama, enthusiastically celebrated by US fans as a world record. Far from the suburban stereotype, Johnson grew up in an inner-city neigh-bourhood in Florida, where friends introduced him to the sport, and headed the list of goalscorers at the 2003 World Youth Cup, the first American to do so. Benfica soon weighed in with a $5 million offer, one bravely turned down by an MLS still looking for stars.

While in recent years African-Americans have become a common sight in the national team (though less so behind the scenes), inner-city and working-class minorities still find it hard to break into the largely middle-class, suburban world of American soccer. In particular, Latino players who have ascended from MLS or anywhere else to national team stardom are thin on the ground. The league has made some progress – Mexican-American Herculez Gomez was one of the brightest stars of the Galaxy's 2005 championship-winning team – but, as Hector Tobar asserted in the *Los Angeles Times,* the issues run deeper than the profes-sional game:

> Some [Latino] youngsters are willing, even, to turn their back
> on that Holy Grail of American youth soccer, the college schol-
> arship. In a sense, two cultures are competing for these young
> men. One sees sports as a path to college and assimilation into
> the American dream. The other believes that soccer can be an

end in itself ... More and more Latino youngsters are choosing overseas soccer, rejecting not only college but the United States' own burgeoning soccer system. This speaks volumes about what critics say is a gaping ethnic divide in the sport here. Hundreds of the best players in the United States are funneled each year into the 'Olympic Development Program' ... The players nurtured by this system are, almost exclusively, products of suburban leagues.

While it is tempting to think that Latino interest in the domestic game might blossom with (for example) a Mexican-American rising to prominence with the US national team, the situation with African-Americans is rather different, especially in less privileged areas, where few are likely to have heard of Eddie Johnson, or even to have watched much soccer (Johnson himself had never heard of the World Cup until after he took up the sport). Basketball remains the inner-city obsession, which fuels young dreams as football does in other parts of the world. Though soccer has made efforts in this direction – a not-for-profit initiative called 'Soccer In the Streets' claims to have 'positively changed the lives of over 100,000 urban kids in 75 cities' since its founding in 1989 – alongside the millions of youngsters determined to become the next Michael Jordan its impact is small.

There is certainly nothing wrong with putting together programmes for the uninitiated or vulnerable, yet organisation as a whole is probably something soccer in America has too much of for its own good, a curse disguised as a blessing. Americans kids do not learn the game from their peers as they might with other sports – impromptu kickabouts are almost as rare as makeshift games of pelota. Soccer has no equivalent to the cultural language of basketball: shirts and skins duking it out in the schoolyard, the familiar off-shoots of 'Horse' and 'Around the World', the youngster diligently perfecting his or her jump-shot in the family drive. It is, invariably, arranged – regulated, administered, governed, measured, documented and otherwise controlled by adults, an activity requiring flashy boots, laundered uniforms, shiny balls, goals with nets and licensed referees and coaches. Some believe this doesn't matter, and in terms of national team progress and the development of elite players, that may be true. But if playing for the sheer joy of the game, rather than the rewards it produces, is an important attribute of a soccer nation, then the assertion that 'there is no soccer in the United States' may not be altogether unfair.

Yet if America's embrace of soccer is still half-hearted, there is no doubt that soccer has become a lot more American. Seventeen years after the NASL was threatened with expulsion from the international governing body for (among other things) daring to permit a third substitution, FIFA moved to three for the World Cup. Fourteen years after the National Professional Soccer League announced a new points system to encourage attacking football, the Football League introduced an extra point for a win for much the same reason, and FIFA followed suit for USA 94. And the American proclivity for 'sudden death' tiebreakers – stretching as far back as 1955 with the NFL and the 1967 NPSL final in soccer – preceded the international 'golden goal' by almost half a century.

The same can be said of the influence of American sports marketing, something which the Tampa Bay Rowdies and their ilk took to new levels in the late 1970s. Though happily there have been no further incarnations of Fannies, today hardly any top British professional clubs do not employ, or at least consult, 'creative' people who speak in terms of 'match-day experiences' and 'wow factors'. Britain's 'product', for better or worse, is far less alien to the US sports fan than it was a generation or two ago, and much of what the British once sniffily dismissed as 'American-style razzmatazz' has become standard practice: surnames across the backs of shirts, celebratory anthems after home goals, cheer-leading public address announcers, even giant video screens. Sadly, less gaudy manifestations of American promotional fervour – group ticket discounts, for example – do not seem to have been seized on with nearly the same enthusiasm. And it is certainly worth remembering that no NASL jersey, however lurid, was ever defaced with the name of a corporate sponsor.

It is with the women's game that America may have left its greatest impression, helping to elevate the World Cup to a competition of genuine significance, while according national team stars levels of respect and adulation only men had received elsewhere. The chance for a woman to pursue a career as a professional footballer in the United States was even cursorily addressed by the British film director Gurinder Chadha, who portrayed the WUSA in aspirational terms for her 2002 comedy *Bend It Like Beckham*, which found its way into American cinemas the following year.

Such dreams seem to have died with the WUSA's passing, and the women's game as a whole has suffered since the gold-medal run in Athens. Only a handful of US internationals were staged in 2005 – all to meagre crowds – and without the chance to play professionally in the US, many players have been left to think twice about holding on for

the 2007 World Cup. Yet the effects of Title IX have been incredibly far-reaching. The women's World Cup has been transformed into something approaching an international media event, while America's interest in its own team has set a worldwide precedent. The day of female footballers in other countries being celebrated with the same fervour as their male equivalents may still be some way off, but it surely won't be long before fans of the men's game at least begin to recognise their names.

The US men may not have won a World Cup, but some telling milestones are within sight. No American has yet been carried from the domestic coaching ranks into a prominent managerial position overseas, but steps have been taken in that direction. Just as his time at Bournemouth and Crewe helped pave the way for American players in Europe 20 years ago, Brent Goulet's appointment in 2005 as manager of Elversberg in Germany's third division has set a helpful precedent.

Shortly before the 1998 World Cup, the USSF unveiled its blueprint for international success: 'Project 2010', a strategy aimed at providing the most realistic chance of winning the World Cup by that year. Heavily subsidised by Nike, the $50 million programme was strangely redolent of the single-mindedness of communist regimes in their quest for Olympic medals. But in a country where nothing less than being 'champions of the world' – however large or small that 'world' may be – defines success, the development was hardly surprising. Narrowly losing a World Cup quarter-final to Germany does not translate well into American sporting parlance, as Bruce Arena has pointed out:

> I would think a majority of people in the United States probably think we failed at the last World Cup because we're all about winning. That's all they understand ... We win in all the other sports. We are the world champions at American football because nobody else plays it and our NBA champions are the world champions at basketball. That's the way it is in the United States – you have to be a world champion.

While only hardened sceptics could perceive Project 2010 as a flight of fancy, if anything is certain about the future of soccer in America it is that no watershed moment will suddenly thrust it onto the sporting consciousness of the nation. Even winning the World Cup would not transform MLS into a money-making juggernaut. Too much of the country continues to regard soccer as foreign, effeminate or just plain dull, and too many in the media berate the game because they fear it.

Much of this is attributable to familiarity and tradition – something built up over more than a century, from Tom Cahill to the Carolina Courage – and not to any innate shortcoming of some un-American activity.

For all that, one thing is certain: there has never been a better time for soccer in a football world. The game is as successful and well-run as it has ever been, and far from the domain of the eccentric, the marginalised and the un-American it used to be. Most of the country may still struggle with it, but there is now a fair proportion that doesn't. To soccer fans who spent many decades searching for hopeful signs among crushing defeats, that may be the biggest moral victory yet.

Index